PLAYS OF THE YEAR
Volume 36
1968-1969

'I do not claim that they are the best plays of their period. I submit merely that all are good of their kind, and that they share qualities for which a true playgoer looks.'

Preface to *Plays of the Year*, Volume One, 1949

PLAYS OF THE YEAR

EDITED BY
J. C. TREWIN

THE PRINCE OF HOMBURG
Heinrich von Kleist, translated by
Jonathan Griffin

THE UNKNOWN SOLDIER AND HIS
WIFE
Peter Ustinov

THE SECRETARY BIRD
William Douglas Home

THE SERVANT OF TWO MASTERS
Carlo Goldoni, adapted by David Turner

VOLUME 36
1968-1969

FREDERICK UNGAR PUBLISHING
COMPANY
NEW YORK

THE PRINCE OF HOMBURG
Translation © by Jonathan Griffin

THE UNKNOWN SOLDIER AND HIS WIFE
© Peter Ustinov

THE SECRETARY BIRD
© William Douglas Home

THE SERVANT OF TWO MASTERS
adaptation © by David Turner

Printed in Great Britain

FOR WENDY
Who Interprets

CONTENTS

INTRODUCTION

This is our thirty-sixth half-yearly volume. It moves between the eighteenth century and our own day, taking in work by the Venetian dramatist, Carlo Goldoni (1707-1793), in an English text by David Turner; the German Heinrich von Kleist (1777-1811), represented here in a translation by Jonathan Griffin; Peter Ustinov (1921————), whose play, The Unknown Soldier and His Wife, *in effect swings back our starting-point to the world of Imperial Rome; and William Douglas Home (1912————), who has shown in* The Secretary Bird *that polished English comedy (a mirror 'meant to glass the opulent', as Hardy said in another context), can survive all theatrical alarums.*

Jonathan Griffin has written about the famous play, Heinrich von Kleist's *Der Prinz von Homburg, that he has now translated. Let me speak of Mr Griffin himself, one of the most expert British translators. as well as dramatist and poet in his own right. I think in particular of* The Hidden King. *There has been no more moving and ambitious production in the record of the Edinburgh Festival: one remembers from the summer of 1957 the splendour of this poet's drama: Robert Eddison and Robert Speaight, Pauline Jameson and Michéal MacLiammóir, Ernest Thesiger, Sebastian Shaw, playing on the transformed stage of the Assembly Hall in Leslie Hurry's setting and a production by Christopher West. The 'hidden king' of the title*

7

is Dom Sebastian, *King of Portugal, thought to have been killed in 1578 at Alcazar during the sanguinary battle with the Moors. Twenty years have passed, and there is an enigmatic Stranger in Venice. Has he indeed been 'fording a river twenty years wide'? We are told of him that now and then he 'says noble things, as if he had the right to say them'. Jonathan Griffin can say many noble things.* The Hidden King, *glowing under the sunset of the Renaissance, that angry, colour-rifted sky, needs to be seen again in its full elaboration. One recalls so much from it, in particular the Sicilian interlude and the description of the Venetian Bridal of the Sea.*

More recently, Mr Griffin's versions of Montherlant have been prizes for the fastidious playgoer. Donald Wolfit appeared in two of them. The Master of Santiago *and* Malatesta. The Cardinal of Spain, *which Laurier Lister directed at the Yvonne Arnaud, Guildford, in the spring of 1969, with Max Adrian and Sian Phillips, will certainly find other stages. Meanwhile, I commend to you the text of Heinrich von Kleist's play which Mr Griffin now restores so richly to the theatre.*

Peter Ustinov, I said twenty years ago, would be a major dramatist. It was the most facile of prophecies. I need not speak here of Ustinov's range, expressed in The Love of Four Colonels, The Moment of Truth, Romanoff and Juliet, Photo Finish, *and* The Unknown Soldier and His Wife. *Always he has written from an overflowing, independent mind: he is actor, director, story-teller, wit. At Chichester, besides playing the Archbishop—a variety of Archbishops—in* The Unknown Soldier and His Wife, *he also directed: the most authoritative person to govern such a piece as this, one that slides back to the Romans, lunges forward across*

8

the centuries, and looks to the future. It puts into Ustinov's own terms the ancient cry, 'Would ye be wise, ye cities, fly from war'. The same men, it says, and the same forces (only the names vary) have been responsible for war: General, priest, inventor—and the ranker whom Ustinov studies in a way best discovered from the text.

The play is 'two acts of war separated by a truce'. One of the earliest directions is typical: 'The setting and the costuming are left to the discretion of the director throughout, the only admonition of the author being that the action should be as fluid and theatrical as possible. Any excess of the imagination is an error on the right side.'

William Douglas Home, another dramatist of uncommon range—remember Now Barabbas, The Thistle and the Rose,* *and* The Reluctant Debutante—*has written in* The Secretary Bird *a piece that might once have been called Lonsdale-type: a country-house, husband-wife-and-lover comedy more human than any invention of Lonsdale's. Home's liveliest work since* The Reluctant Debutante, *it is unlikely to please partisans of the Theatres of Protest, Panic, and Cruelty. Kenneth More, at the Savoy, knew exactly how to deal with a husband, resolutely understanding, who has his own method of squelching an affair between his wife and a dull dog of a thrice-divorced philanderer.*

Finally Carlo Goldoni, whose statue, gently smiling, stands in Venice in the Campo San Bartolomeo: the dramatist in whose work lovers and fathers and servants and innkeepers recur like

* The Thistle and the Rose *appeared in Volume 5 of* Plays of the Year, *and* The Queen's Highland Servant *in Volume 35.*

dancing decimals: the dramatist of whom Browning wrote:

> *Goldoni—good, gay, sunniest of souls—*
> *Glassing half Venice in that voice of thine . . .*
> *There throng the people: how they come and go,*
> *Lisp the soft language, flaunt the bright garb—*
>   *see—*
> *On Piazza, Calle, under Portico,*
> *And over Bridge! Dear King of Comedy.*

The central scene of The Servant of Two Masters, *among the plays Goldoni developed and shaped from the* commedia dell'arte, *is a prolonged show-piece during which the man serves two meals simultaneously to a pair of masters, each hidden from the other, one in a room to the left of the stage, the other to the right. All we hear and see is the servant's frenzy as he grapples with an endless chain of dishes, with tureens, hams, fowls, puddings, fruit, piled plates, quivering jellies. He darts to and fro like a desperate juggler keeping half-a-dozen walking-sticks in the air with last-minute grabs and saves. At the Queen's (Christmas, 1968) where David Turner, himself a distinguished dramatist—*Semi-Detached, *for example—had adapted into supple and colloquial English a literal translation by Paul Lapworth never unwisely starched, the Truffaldino was Tommy Steele, and the period was brought forward to the early nineteenth century.*

J. C. TREWIN

Hampstead,
June 1969

My warm gratitude, as ever, to Miss Judith Farmer for her invaluable help and patience in preparing this volume.

MILES MALLESON

Miles Malleson, who died in March, 1969, aged 80, was a firm friend of Plays of the Year. *His version of Molière's* The Miser *appeared in our first volume during 1949, and we published six more of his Molière texts, all prepared with his own inspired comedian's feeling for stage effect and without doing any injustice to his dramatist.*

Malleson was author, director, and an extra-ordinary actor. I remember him as Jourdain in Le Bourgeois Gentilhomme *(which he called* The Prodigious Snob*), a part in which he resembled a happy cod with blood-pressure—resolved, more-over, to use only the best parts of the ocean. As Quince in the Haymarket* Midsummer Night's Dream *of 1945 he was one of the elder statesmen of his parish; we knew that he would be heard often debating matters of high policy. I suppose Malleson was never more remarkable than as the reverend mouse, Nathaniel the curate, in the Old Vic* Love's Labour's Lost *of 1949 at the New: he had only nineteen speeches, but for some of us it remains the most fully satisfying piece of Shakespearean comedy in recollection.*

During his last months when, tragically, his sight had failed, he was preparing to dictate his auto-biography. It would have been a book of detailed value. Even so, we do not need it to remember an actor whom, in his own sphere and without ex-aggeration, we can call great.

J.C.T.

THE
PRINCE
OF
HOMBURG

a play
by
HEINRICH VON KLEIST

Translation and Introduction
by
Jonathan Griffin

INTRODUCTION

'He was,' wrote Thomas Mann in an essay (1954)
that is among his last'* 'one of the greatest, boldest,
most aspiring poets of the German language, a
dramatist without parallel.' A few pages later,
Mann pays tribute to Goethe and Schiller as
dramatists, but adds : 'Kleist is the only one from
whose work, with its rejection of all beauty of
measure' (*schönen Mass*) '—and I am thinking
especially of the work which defeated him, the
Guiskard fragment—there emanates the power, the
primal dramatic shock, the mythic shudder, the
holy terror of ancient tragedy.' Kleist's last play,
Friedrich Prinz von Homburg, was a new beginning : the naked tragic power is still present, but
now combined with some of the 'beauty of
measure'. This must (I remember thinking after
reading it for the first time) be the finest of all the
German poetic plays. There are plays by Goethe,
also by Schiller, that carry a bigger load of high
poetry, that handle important questions eloquently
and fully; but Kleist's integration of poetry into
a masterpiece of dramatic construction generates a
power that is unique— a terrific immediate impact
as well as ramifying after-effects. In *Homburg*
Kleist fuses poetry and stagecraft together, so that
they constantly enhance each other : he never sacrifices action or character to extended poetry, yet
poetry is always forthcoming when required—and of

* Preface to an American edition of Kleist's stories.
German original in the *Nachlese* of Thomas Mann (S.
Fischer Verlag, Frankfurt-am-Main, 1956.)

the kind required. Searching, burning issues in astounding number are discussed, and others implied, yet they never hold up the action or twist any character out of true. One's breath is taken away by the narrative virtuosity,—the sheer quantity of events packed in without overcrowding, in the most effective order, each told at the right length, with suspense and surprise forming a continuous, controlled succession. And the result? A play that is itself a poetic image, a new myth, which hauls one's mind back to it again and again. Being unlike any other play, it is the nearest thing in German to one of Shakespeare's.

How did this masterpiece come into the world? Bernd Heinrich Wilhelm von Kleist lived his mature years in the shadow of the Napoleonic Wars. He was born on October 18, 1777, at Frankfurt-on-the-Oder, in the kingdom of Brandenburg—Prussia. The family, noble but not very wealthy, had produced a physicist and a poet, but most of its men had been army officers (sixteen of them generals and two fieldmarshals) : it has been well said* that 'he inherited all the obligations of his class without the wealth that would have enabled him to break away'. He was put into a Prussian regiment when he was fifteen, saw two years of active service against France, and then returned to garrison duty at Potsdam. What he described as 'seven wasted years' ended in April 1799 : he had applied for and was granted, release from the army. A letter he wrote at the time shows his state of mind clearly :

'The greatest marvels of military discipline, which to every expert were the object of

* By Mr Michael Hamburger, in *Reason and Energy* (Routledge, London, 1957); p. 111.

astonished admiration, became the object of my most heartfelt contempt; I regarded the officers as so many drill sergeants, the men as so many slaves, and when the whole regiment was performing its tricks it seemed to me a living monument to tyranny. What was more, I began to feel keenly the bad effect my situation was having on my character. I was often compelled to punish where I would have liked to pardon, or else I pardoned where I should have punished; and in both cases I saw myself as deserving punishment. At such moments there arose in me, naturally, the wish to leave an occupation in which I was bound to be incessantly bludgeoned by two opposed principles and was always in doubt whether I ought to act as a human being or as an officer; for to unite the duties of both seemed to me impossible, with armies as they are.'

Yet the ideals and reactions of an army officer remained a part of Kleist. And, near the end of his life, that early tormenting experience of dividedness rose to the surface when he needed it for his *Prince of Homburg*. Emotion recollected—in tranquillity? scarcely; but shaped in him during eleven years, until just controllable. Of the conflict in this play, which reaches tragedy force, Kleist had lived both sides.

Leaving the army was a grave step, it risked the King's displeasure. Kleist took it in order to devote himself to study : philosophy, mathematics, physics. But within two years a reading of the works of Kant had thrown him into the first of his many crises of extreme despair : from Kant's demonstration that the thing-in-itself is inaccessible, that space

17

and time are properties of the mind, that truth in most fields is elusive, Kleist leapt to the conclusion that all pursuit of knowledge is futile. He announced this in agonized letters to his fiancée, Wilhelmine von Stenge, and to Ulrike von Kleist, his half-sister :

> 'We cannot decide whether what we call truth really is truth, or only seems so to us. If the latter, then the truth which we here collect *is*, after death, no more . . . My only, my highest aim is sunk, and I now have none left . . . If I stayed at home I could only lay my hands in my lap and think; so I prefer to move about, and think.'

With Ulrike he set out for Paris and then Switzerland, the first of many wanderings. From place to place and project to project he blundered into his true vocation.

Of middle height and sturdy build, with a childish face and a slight stammer, he was difficult to draw out, and talked, when he did talk, with a disconcerting harshness; but people were sometimes startled by the good smile in his eyes; a trifle would throw him back into stuttering and blushing; he was apt, also, at a chance word, to switch off from the conversation and begin mouthing phrases from some work in progress. His first play, *Die Familie Schroffenstein*, a bad one with very fine things in it (one scene especially), he seems to have written very quickly, at the beginning of 1802; almost at once he started work on *Robert Guiskard*. Interrupted by an illness and much besides, this was far from complete when, in the 1802/3 winter, the poet Wieland coaxed him into declaiming a bit of it. Wieland was bowled over : 'If the spirits of Aeschylus, Sophocles and Shakespeare were to unite to create a tragedy,' he wrote, later, to a friend, 'it would be like Kleist's Death of Guiscard the Norman', so far as the whole measures up to what he then let me hear,' and he added that Kleist seemed to him destined to fill a gap which even Goethe and Schiller had left. And Wieland persisted, taking the trouble to write to him in July, 1803 :

'You must finish your Guiskard, even were the whole of the Caucasus and Atlas pressing down on you.'

In vain. Three months later Kleist wrote to Ulrike :

'I have now spent half a thousand consecutive days, the nights of most of them included, on the effort to add one more wreath of glory to the many already won by our family : now our holy tutelary Goddess calls out to me that it is enough ... It would, at least, be mad of *me* to apply my powers any longer to a work which, as I must at last recognize, is too difficult for me ... Hell gave me my half-talents, Heaven gives men a whole one, or none at all.'

Three weeks later :

'In Paris I read through, condemned and burned my work, so far as it had got. Heaven refuses me fame, the greatest of earthly possessions; I throw after it, like a stubborn child, all the others ... I am rushing into death.'

She was not to worry—it would be the beautiful death, death in battle : he had gone to the north coast of France, to join the French forces—those with which Napoleon hoped to invade England.

Coldly received when he returned to Prussia, Kleist was given after many months a routine job in the Ministry of Finance. While doing it (mainly at Königsberg), he finished his masterly comedy, *Der Zerbrochene Krug*, and the first two of his eight wonderful prose stories; he also began *Amphitryon*, his transformation of the Molière. He must have known by now that Heaven *had* given him a whole talent. But illness and breakdown followed, with Ulrike to the rescue as usual : he obtained leave from his job, and did not go back to it. On his way to Dresden in January 1807 (four months after Prussia's defeat at Jena) the French arrested him as a spy : the charge was unfounded, but he spent five months in French prisons.

When at last he reached Dresden in August 1807, he found himself the talk of the town, the new literary star, and for a short time tasted real success. He finished *Penthesilea*, a savage tragedy full of swingeing poetry, which responds to—but requires—strong direction and a great actress in the name part. More of the prose stories were soon ready. He began another play, *Das Kätchen von Heilbronn*, a faulty but ravishing Gothick piece, which he described (autumn 1807) as the 'reverse side' to *Penthesilea*, its heroine being the Amazon's 'opposite pole, a creature as powerful through total submission as the other is through action'.* He even started to write *Robert Guiskard* again—what survives of it, the 524-line opening, dates from this time (1807/8). And with his friend Adam Müller he founded a review.

This review, *Phöbus*, made a brilliant start, but was soon in financial trouble. And Goethe's hoped-

---

* Kleist's view of *Das Kätchen von Heilbronn*, by the summer of 1811, was that he had spoilt a 'quite splendid inspiration' by making concessions to the taste of the theatre-going public. It has a long record of success in German theatres.

for contribution never came. The first number, which contained a part of *Penthesilea*, had been sent to Goethe by Kleist, with a covering letter in which extreme humility and extreme pride coexist unresolved; and Goethe in his reply, after saying that it would take him time to get into a thing so 'foreign' as *Penthesilea*, added :

It always troubles and grieves me when I see young men of wit and talent who are waiting for a theatre that has still to come. A Jew waiting for the Messiah, a Christ for the New Jerusalem, a Portuguese for Don Sebastian, produce in me no greater discomfort.'

Goethe did, shortly afterwards, stage *Der Zerbrochene Krug*, at Weimar. But not as it was written : he thought he knew better, adapted it, chopping it into three acts, and so ensured a resounding failure for a play which—too late for Kleist—became and has remained one of the sure-fire favourites in the German theatre. Kleist even challenged Goethe to a duel—a typical folly, but the failure had been a humiliating and crippling blow.

After five issues *Phöbus* collapsed. Kleist was again in a sad state : out of work, in debt, humiliated, thrashing about from project to project —Ulrike had helped with money so often that she had now to be cautious. And this was the time— after another breakdown—when Kleist, who (remember) had left the army because of the claims of the human and had, at various stages, embraced liberal ideals with fervour, moved over to rabid nationalism. His short poems of this period include at least one hymn of hate against the French that makes one feel sick; and his next play, *Die*

Hermannsschlacht, glorifies a hero to whom all means—ingenious treachery, the scorched earth policy, whipping up hatred by lies, massacring prisoners ('the good ones are the worst')—are justified if they will free Germany from an invader. One would have to be either a neo-Nazi or very obtuse to read this play of Kleist's, for all its beauty, without sadness and fear. Yet it is wrong to judge him without remembering that Kleist in post-Jena Prussia was in much the same situation as a Frenchman in Vichy France in 1941. We in Great Britain or the United States were glad enough then to have on our side, in the countries occupied by Hitler, patriots of the Kleist kind.

Early in 1810—another of Kleist's amazing recoveries—*The Prince of Homburg* was complete, presenting (among so much else) a very different vision of German patriotism.* And in October of that year he started the first German daily paper, the *Berliner Abendblätter.* For a time the appeal of its defiant nationalism and the brilliance of many contributions (Kleist's and others') made it a success. Then, inevitably, there came diplomatic protests : censorship was applied, making the paper seem dull, and circulation dropped. The last numbers appeared in March, 1811.

Once again he was desperate : loaded with debts, out of work and widely suspect. *The Prince of Homburg* had not helped : in his fantastic lack of judgment Kleist had expected to be welcomed as a patriotic service : it was, of course, found

---

* The Elector's famous soliloquy (beginning : 'Odd. Now suppose I were the Dey of Tunis . . .') drew this comment, in 1817, from a friend to whom Tieck had lent the manuscript : 'That is something altogether different from the hollow grandiloquence and crude heartiness sold to us as patriotism.'

22

deeply shocking (especially one scene in the third act), and was not published, let alone staged. Friends worked hard for him but when, in September 1811, the King offered him a commission in the army, Kleist had not the money to fit himself out. His family—who had suffered much from him—now scorched him with reproaches. After describing this in a letter (October 1811) to his devoted cousin Marie von Kleist, he added: 'the alliance which the King is now concluding with the French is also not calculated to make me willing to stay alive.' The same letter contains the terrible sentence:

'My soul is so sore that—I can almost say—when I stick my nose out of the window, the daylight that shines on it hurts.'

Marie von Kleist had been his close friend for some years; she cared for his work, and her opinion of it mattered to him; they were perhaps in love. Being in favour at Court, she could and did often help him—it was she who sent *The Prince of Homburg* to the Princess Amalie von Hessen-Homburg, in the fair copy (with dedication to the Princess) through which the work survived. But now he met Henriette Vogel, a young married woman who had cancer. Deeply moved, he said he would do anything to help her. She answered by proposing a suicide pact. The effect on Kleist—he had proposed just that to Marie, who had refused—was decisive. On November 20, 1811, he went with Henriette Vogel to a small inn by the Wannsee (not far from Berlin), where they spent the night and wrote letters of farewell. (Kleist's own are eerily serene, and phrases in them—such as: 'In this hour when our souls are lifting above the world like two ships of the air'—remind one of Homburg's last soliloquy.) Next morning, after breakfast, he paid, and the two went off, hand in hand and evidently light-hearted, for a walk along the lakeside. Two shots were heard. Kleist had killed her and then himself. His age : thirty-five years, one month and three days.

'A year before his death,' wrote Thomas Mann, 'he produces his . . . (for all the perturbing elements it too contains) serenest, most relaxed, most felicitously shaped play, *The Prince of Homburg*. Then he breaks off his painful life. It is completed. A life does not need to last eighty years to be, in its own way, fully established and victoriously completed.' Sentimentality, rhetoric of the bad kind,—to be excused only as a reaction against the complacency with which his suicide was (and sometimes still is) condemned. His life completed? If Kleist had held on for about two years longer, he would have seen his King's appeasement of Napoleon changed into victory : Leipzig and, in another couple of years, Waterloo. Fresh hope might have given him the strength to complete *Robert Guiskard* at last,—and what else? To create works fulfilling the promise of *The Prince of Homburg*,—in which achievement is so perfect that one easily forgets the promise in it.* No, Kleist's life was not completed, and his death was a loss—it is as well we do not know how great. But Thomas Mann does point out that, very much as the fainting-fits at the key points of so many of Kleist's plays and stories were 'recover-

*"The crowning irony of Kleist's career is that his last play and his last story point to a resolution of the metaphysical, moral and emotional dilemma to which all his personal failures were due. His literary works were always well ahead of his personal development . . . Kleist did not live to catch up with *Friedrich Prinz von Homburg* and *Der Zweikampf.*' Michael Hamburger (*Reason and Energy*, 1957); p. 139.

24

ies by deep entry into the subconscious, to the springs of life', so Kleist emerged from despair and illness to a new bout of creative exertion, time after time, in a way that puts most healthy men to shame. Knowing this, who can help grieving that he did not do it just once more?—but also, who dares cast a stone at him for his suicide? Who can reproach him for not having made yet another almost superhuman effort of recovery, when exhausted by so many? It is more decent to be grateful that the last he did make gave us *Homburg*.

Kleist never saw any of his plays performed†— which means that his stagecraft is the product of an unaided self-discipline that may be unique. *The Prince of Homburg* was first published in 1821, by Tieck, who also managed in the same year to get it performed in Vienna, where the authorities quickly suppressed it. It was not produced in Berlin till 1828—and then it was withdrawn, by royal command, after three performances. A long time passed before it became, what it now is, one of the classics of the German stage. It can also, given strong casting and devoted direction, be transplanted : this was shown when a French version, put on by the Théâtre National Populaire with Gérard Philippe in the name part, proved to be one of the unforgotten triumphs of the Paris theatre after the second world war.

This introduction must not spoil anyone's pleasure in a first reading, so I must avoid making comments that would give away the plot. But I may be able to increase that pleasure by quoting

† Authority: Helmut Sembdner, in the *Nachwort* to his edition of the complete works of Kleist.

from Kleist's sources. These, it appears, were two : the memoirs of Frederick the Second of Prussia; and *Mein Vaterland unter den Hohenzollerischen Regenten* by K. H. Krause. Here is part of K. H. Krause's account of the Battle of Fehrbellin :

'The Prince of Hessenhomburg was sent out at daybreak, with orders to observe the enemy, but to hold off and not attack them. He ran up against the Swedish outposts; from youthful ardour and the desire to distinguish himself, he attacked them, and drove them as far as the main army. But this now counter-attacked, and the Elector was forced to join battle before he wished.'

Fortunately the Elector 'had already placed a battery on a sandy eminence', and it kept the enemy under continuous fire; but when he led his own left wing to the attack, the Prussians in turn came under heavy fire : the Elector himself was for a long time in extreme danger. At length 'he put the enemy's left wing to flight, the right soon followed, and the victory was soon decided'. But it was incomplete : The Elector had, according to Frederick the Second, 'no infantry to hand', and so 'could neither take the Fehrbellin bridges nor pursue the enemy'. After the battle (again according to Krause),

'Prince Friedrich von Hessenhomburg, conscious of his failure in obedience, stood some way off and dared not raise his eyes to the face of the sternly just Sovereign. The Elector signed to him, in a friendly way, to come forward. "Were I disposed," he said to him, "to deal with you according to the rigour of military

26

law, you would have deserved death. But God forbid that I should stain my hands with the blood of a man who was an outstanding instrument of my victory." With these words, and a fatherly warning to be more prudent in future, he embraced him and assured him of his full esteem and friendship.'

Compare this with what Kleist made of it in the play—one is more and more astonished and fascinated by his boldness. The measure of greatness in a so-called historical play is: how far it moves away from history (having also in some way really arrived there). A basis in history is one means—one of the best—of taking a play into a field where men and women face decisions of huge consequence, and of giving it the solid political and social reality that will suspend disbelief in the parts of it that explore hidden things; but these are the main points of the play. What most distinguishes Schiller's *Maria Stuart* is the meeting of Queen Mary and Queen Elizabeth: there was no such meeting. In *The Prince of Homburg* the distance between what Kleist wrote and what he had read is one of the great leaps of imagination.

What made Kleist deeply disturbing in his own day has made him a growing influence in ours. Not only the Prussian ruling class found his content and style shocking. Goethe did: not just in the savage *Penthesilea* but in the limpidly profound *Amphitryon*, Goethe saw what he called '*Verwirrung der Gefühle*', a turning upside down, a tangling, a derangement of the feelings—one thinks of Rimbaud's '*dérèglement des sens*'. Years later, speaking of Kleist's work as a whole (so far as

he knew it—he may not have known *Homburg*),
Goethe still used strong and agitated language:

> 'Despite the most honest effort on my part to
> be fair and understanding, this poet always
> aroused in me shuddering and abhorrence, like
> some body beautifully designed by Nature but
> stricken by incurable disease.'

It may be said—Mann says it—that, having himself written *Werther* and *Tasso*, Goethe ought to
have had less antipathy towards sickness and the
abnormal; I think Goethe feared and hated Kleist
with the fervour of a convert just because he had
been a bit like him. He had renounced—surely at
great cost—the *Sturm und Drang* of his early
work, in order to set the example of a wide-ranging
wisdom and the beauty of measure; and here, un-
hampered by that self-denial, came a young man
flaunting heresy. Goethe's sanity made him at times
a prophet: he was led to a foresight of Bismarckism
—perhaps even to fore-glimpses of Hitlerism—
along with an insight into the way certain tendencies in German literature might, if they took
hold, favour what he dreaded and detested:
unscrupulous nationalism, deification of the
State.

Was Goethe right? Some people in our time
have thought so: Kleist is now more controver-
sial than ever. At one point Thomas Mann,
discussing Goethe's rejection of Kleist, says: 'How
I understand it, how I *share* it!' And a living
British writer, Mr Ronald Gray, in an impressive
book,* treats Kleist almost as the Devil. 'It was in
Hitler's time that Kleist's reputation reached a

* *The German Tradition in Literature 1871-1945*;
(Cambridge University Press, 1965.)

climax,' he writes, and clearly means that that was
no accident. The Germans, he contends, gave
Hitler power partly because the main tradition
of their literature had softened them up. The tradition dictated that, if a man wanted to win accept-
ance, or even to regard himself, as an important
German writer, he must preach a Weltanschauung
of his own; he was therefore under strong temptation to fabricate one. You did this by taking pairs
of opposites ('Justice' and 'mercy', 'the Dionysian'
and 'the Apollonian', etc.), intensifying them to
their extremes and then finding, or imagining you
had found, a synthesis, which you must treat as a
higher unity superseding them. Hegel and Marx
were the arch-dogmatists of this process,—which
led, in both their cases, to making a God of the
State. Other, reinforcing tendencies converged :
these included (though surely one of the least
system-bound of writers) Kleist, and of course
Nietzsche; but also several usually considered as
innocent, like Rilke and Thomas Mann when
(though not without horror) they supported World
War One because it was reality. It became natural
for many highly civilized Germans to feel that
Hitler was right because he was there. The guilty
tradition is, for want of searching criticism, still
active. To Mr Gray 'it is an oppressive thing to
hear, for instance, that one of the most popular
authors among sixth-formers in German schools
today is Kleist'.

To judge a writer by his influence is a shaky
business. The Devil can quote Scripture—Hitler
exploited Goethe as well as Kleist; and just how
far does one blame Karl Marx for the Stalin
labour camps? We can choose our words, but not
all their contexts : no writer is safe from the

textually correct misquotation : every serious writer longs to be heard also when dead, but he has precious little say in what he will then be made to say.* A responsible critic judges an artist by the quality of his work as well as his by-products, by his best work along with his aberrations. The fact remains, Mr Gray has amassed formidable evidence of an insidious danger,—that dedicated writers, striving to show the world as it is and yet to give it a meaning for those who must live in it, may help to make a climate for tyranny. Then who shall 'scape whipping? If poor Kleist is to be con- nected with the rise of Hitlerism and with the danger of its reviving, what are some of us prepar- ing? German writers especially, but not only they —all of us should try to know what we are doing : we should ask ourselves what our words are laying up for those poor devils, posterity.

In accusing Kleist Mr Gray—though too serious and fair to base his charge solely on by-products or aberrations—does, I think, misinterpret the two major works he chooses to cite as evidence. One of these is *The Prince of Homburg.* 'There could be no clearer instance than this,' he says, 'Of the coming together of opposites, the individual and the State, condemnation and pardon, justice and mercy, self-denial and self-assertion, total un- worthiness and supreme worthiness. Moreover, both sides have been driven to extremes . . .' The dénouement of the play 'is very close to the repent- ance of the sinner, especially as it has been regarded in the Lutheran Church,' whose teaching is 'that a man must know himself damned before he is saved.' But, he adds, 'there is this important difference,'

* Even if his own words are used. We know now that many of the Nietzsche passages which the Nazis found most useful are forgeries.

that both the Prince's last action and, 'so far as one can see', the Elector's include

'no element of love. What takes place is rather a secularisation of the religious concepts, in which the repentance of the sinner becomes the self-abnegation of the military subordinate or the subject of the State, and where a loving embrace becomes the self-alignment of the individual with the State in which he exists. What is at stake is never love or redemption.'

No element of love? Readers of the play will judge for themselves. To me it does not feel like that at all. There are surely scores of touches suggesting that the Elector loves his wife, his nephew, Natalie and Kottwitz, and that his love persists while he is carrying through a piece of sustained statesmanship which is, perhaps, the most remarkable thing of the kind ever put into a play. As for the Prince and Natalie, Kleist makes me feel, strongly and definitely, that after the crisis of acts three and four there is between them a new love, of a lasting kind.

Not that they say much (they have not the time). Kleist conveys it by what I would call *poetic stagecraft*, by the effect of what they do coming after what they have said. It is a kind of art in which Kleist is unsurpassed. The antenna precision of it may well have been one of the reasons why Kleist has had a particularly deep influence on writers whom no-one would accuse of having aided the Nazis,—for instance, of Kafka. That Kleist meant a great deal to Kafka is shown, touchingly, by this entry in his diary, dated November 23, 1911:

'On the 21st, the hundredth anniversary of Kleist's death, the Kleist family had a wreath placed on his grave with the epitaph : "To the best of their house." '*

Kleist's works, as Mr Hamburger has said brilliantly, 'are like the products of the successful collaboration between a maniac and a mathematician', which is why

'Kafka could learn from Kleist to illuminate nightmare with a day-time lucidity; not to explain his paradoxes, but to render them; and, however outrageous his visions, to maintain that outward assurance of a somnambulist.'†

Not only in method but in message—the two inseparable—Kleist was one of us. The shock he received from Kant pitched him—Prussian officer upbringing and all—forwards into touch with our time and predicament. What Kant laid bare, the progress of the sciences has verified, bringing us up against relativity and the uncertainty principle : we know we are in a world where truth is elusive, and still we must seek it. Kleist lived here before us, a pioneer of our frontier; after his first despair he went on seeking truth, through his art, in new ways. He enlarged the subject-matter to something like its present range. With his sleep-walkers, dreams and descents into the subliminal through fainting, he was about the first since Shakespeare to present on the stage the subconscious at work, in true proportion to the rest. There was absolutely nothing about which he would not be honest.

Lastly, his handling of the language. In the prose stories a personal Kleistian style leaps at you off the pages. In the dramas, especially *Homburg*,

* The Diaries of Franz Kafka, 1910-23, edited by Max Brod; (Penguin, London); p. 125.
† *Reason and Energy*; p 142.

it does not, or far less, and for the best of reasons. What sets Kleist, as dramatic poet, in a class above Goethe or Schiller, is the almost unique degree to which his dialogue is sensitive to character: in this, truly, Kleist is Shakespearian. Often, with him, a character's words seem to be bringing to the surface a thought he was unable to think until he spoke. There is an essay by Kleist *On the Gradual Creation of Thought in Speech*; he says there:

'If you want to know something and cannot come at it by meditation, I advise you . . . to talk about it with the first acquaintance you happen to meet . . . For someone who is talking, there is a special source of inspiration in a human face opposite; and a look, which tells us that a half-expressed thought is already understood, often bestows on us the complete expression of the other half.'

He illustrates this from experiences of his own, from certain historical events and from *viva voce* examinations; and his plays, especially *Homburg*, are full of it. Dialogue that feels like speech, not writing; speech that is half creating what it expresses: with this at his command Kleist can give all-dimensional reality to Homburg, the Elector, Natalie and Kottwitz (four acting parts of the first magnitude), can catch every stage in Homburg's complex metamorphosis, can make Natalie (to me a heroine comparable with Imogen) grow up before our eyes. Readers will themselves spot the beautiful details, but I may be forgiven for pointing out one that is perhaps easy to miss: it concerns a less prominent character, the Electress. She is a conventional woman—not just because her position requires it of her: she is so, one feels, in herself.

A moment comes when she has heard a rumour of disaster : she faints, she recovers, the messenger is brought in to report. What does she do or say? She puts on the act she knows is expected of her, addresses him in conventional high rhetoric, even calls him 'herald of terror'. And yet Kleist contrives that one never seriously doubts that her feelings are simple and sincere. It takes rare courage in a playwright to be truthful in that way.

This version is meant both to be acted and to be read. It is a translation, not an adaptation. A farce cannot be translated, must be adapted; an ornate masterpiece like *Cyrano de Bergerac*, translated without freedom, would emerge lifeless and useless. But *The Prince of Homburg*, where every touch of the interacting poetry and stagecraft is essential and rightly placed, would be falsified and weakened by adaptation; and so there is nothing for it but to attempt what is hardest, a close translation that will live on stage and on the page. I have tried to catch the tone in an English that is, in Mr Robert Lowell's phrase, 'idiomatic and ageless'. And a kind of verse had to be found that would make rather the same noise as Kleist's with its strong beat, yet have a little more freedom. The use of that slight extra freedom? to enable me—while not missing Kleist's subtle changes of tone and ambivalences of sense—to keep the English down to the same length as the original (a necessity in the theatre) and to make it always speakable on a stage. Not, at every point, easy to speak—any more than the best music is always easy to play : one should not worry too much if a talented actor, conditioned by work in films and television, complains that a passage gives him trouble. Difficulties, though, must never be pointless; they must be only of the kind that an actor with a Shakespearian training alive somewhere in him will take as a worthwhile challenge. This play, if I have managed not to spoil it, is a superb vehicle for a first-class Shakespearian company.

Warm thanks are due to Mr George Hill for having read and discussed this translation. He is not responsible for the faults it may still have.

CHARACTERS

FRIEDRICH WILHELM, *Elector of Brandenburg*

THE ELECTRESS

PRINCESS NATALIE OF ORANGE, *his niece,
Colonel of a regiment of dragoons*

FIELD-MARSHAL DÖRFLING

PRINCE FRIEDRICH ARTHUR OF HOM-
BURG, *General commanding the Cavalry*

COLONEL KOTTWITZ, *of the Princess of
Orange's regiment*

HENNINGS

COUNT TRUCHSS

} *Infantry colonels*

COUNT HOHENZOLLERN, *of the Elector's staff*

BARON VON DER GOLZ, *a cavalry officer*

COUNT GEORG VON SPARREN

STRANZ

SIEGFRIED VON MÖRNER

COUNT REUSS

} *cavalry captain*

A SERGEANT-MAJOR

Officers; corporals and cavalrymen; equerries and
courtiers

Ladies-in-waiting

Pages; Heyducks; other servants

Town and country people, of various ages and both
sexes.

*The action takes place in June, 1675: at and near
Fehrbellin (Brandenburg), and in Berlin.*

ACT ONE

Scene 1

*Fehrbellin. A garden in the classical French style.
In the background a palace, from which a stairway descends. It is night.*

The Prince of Homburg, bare-headed and with his shirt-neck open, is sitting, half-awake and half-asleep, under an oak-tree, and plaiting a wreath for his head.

*The Elector and his wife, with the Princess Natalie,
Count Hohenzollern, Rittmeister Golz and others
steal out from the palace and look down at
him from the balustrade of the stairway. Pages
with torches.*

HOHENZOLLERN : The Prince of Homburg, our
    brave cousin, who
for three days, at the head of the cavalry,
has gallantly pursued the routed Swedes
and only today—quite winded—
rejoined Headquarters here at Fehrbellin :
did you not order him to stay here three
hours at most—the time to fodder the horses—
then at once to set out afresh and sweep
right on to the Hackel Heights, opposite Wrangel
who has been trying to entrench along the Rhyn*?
THE ELECTOR : That is so.
HOHENZOLLERN : Well, he gave the formal orders,
according to the plan, to the leaders of all
    squadrons
for the march out, tonight, at stroke of ten;
and then, exhausted, panting like a boar-hound,

*Pronounced 'Rewn'; a tributary of the Havel.

37

pitched down on some straw, to give his worn-
out
limbs a little rest before the battle
which faces us tomorrow with the dawn-ray.

THE ELECTOR : So I hear. Well?

HOHENZOLLERN : The hour strikes, it is ten,
and all the cavalry is in the saddle,
the horses stamping the ground before the Gate,
and one man missing. Who? The Prince of
Homburg,
their leader. So with torches and with lanterns
the hero's searched for—and discovered. Where?
(*He takes a torch from the hand of a page.*)
Like some night wanderer—look, there—on that
seat,
to which the moonlight, though you
disbelieve me
has led him in his sleep, there he sits, busy
plaiting, like one of his own posterity,
the glorious crown of Fame—in a dream.

THE ELECTOR : What?

HOHENZOLLERN : Fact. From here you can see:
there he sits! (*From the stairway he casts the
light on the Prince.*)

THE ELECTOR : Sunk in sleep? Impossible!

HOHENZOLLERN : Fast asleep.
Call him by name and he would topple over.

[*Pause.*]

THE ELECTRESS : As I live, the young man must be
ill.

PRINCESS NATALIE : A doctor—!

THE ELECTRESS : We ought to help him, it seems
to me,
not spend the precious time making game of him.

38

HOHENZOLLERN (*giving back the torch*) :
You ladies waste your sympathy : I swear
he's no more sick than I am! as the Swedes
tomorrow, on the battlefield, will find !
This, take my word for it, is nothing more
than a plain aberration of his spirit.
THE ELECTOR : Well! I thought it an old wives'
    tale.—Here, friends,
follow me down, let's take a closer look.

[*They move down the steps.*]

AN EQUERRY (*to the Pages*) : Back with the torches.
HOHENZOLLERN : No, friends, let them be !
The whole place might go up in flames, and he
no more aware of it than is the diamond
he wears upon his finger.

[*They gather round the Prince and Pages bring
the torches.*]

THE ELECTOR : What leaves are those he is twining?
    Willow leaves?
HOHENZOLLERN : Willow leaves, my Lord?—That
    is the laurel,
as he has seen it in the heroes' portraits
hanging in the Armoury at Berlin.
THE ELECTOR : Where did he find it, in my sandy
    Marches?
HOHENZOLLERN : The just Gods *may* know!
THE EQUERRY : Possibly in the garden
behind the palace. The gardener has a fancy
for raising plants not native here.
THE ELECTOR : By God, it's
strange ! And yet I'd wager I know what
passion it is, at work on the young fool's heart.

HOHENZOLLERN : O—that! Why, sir, tomorrow's
  battle! He's
a stargazer, and already, I'll wager, sees
weaving for him a victory crown of suns.

[*The Prince holds up the wreath and gazes at it.*]

THE EQUERRY : He's finished it!
HOHENZOLLERN : A shame, an eternal shame
that there's no mirror in the neighbourhood!
He'd mince up to it, with a girl's vanity,
and try the crown on, this way and then that,
like a gauzy hat.
THE ELECTOR : God! I must stay and see how far
  he'll take it.

[*The Elector takes the wreath from the Prince's
hand. The Prince blushes and gazes at him. The
Elector places the jewelled chain from his own neck
over the wreath and hands this to the Princess.
The Prince leaps up. The Elector moves back,
drawing with him the Princess, who holds the
wreath up high. The Prince follows, with his arms
outstretched.*]

THE PRINCE OF HOMBURG (*in a whisper*) : Natalie!
  My bride-to-be!
THE ELECTOR : Quick, away!
HOHENZOLLERN : What is the fool saying?
THE EQUERRY : What did he say?

[*They all move up the stairway.*]

THE PRINCE OF HOMBURG : Friedrich! My Prince!
  My father!
HOHENZOLLERN : Hell and devils!

THE ELECTOR (*as he retreats*): Someone open the
   door for me!

THE PRINCE OF HOMBURG: O my mother!

HOHENZOLLERN: He's raving! He's—

THE ELECTRESS: Whom does he mean by that?

THE PRINCE OF HOMBURG (*groping for the wreath*):
   O dearest! Why are you leaving me? Natalie!
   (*He snatches a glove from the Princess's hand.*)

HOHENZOLLERN: Heavens and earth! What did he
   take?

THE EQUERRY: The wreath?

PRINCESS NATALIE: No, no!

HOHENZOLLERN (*opening the door*): In here, Sir,
   quick! Make

the whole vision vanish from him again.

THE ELECTOR: Back with you into nothing, Lord
   Prince of Homburg,

to nothing, to nothing! We'll meet again,

if you will, upon the field of battle.

Such things as these are not won in a dream!

[*They all go in. The door rattles to in the Prince's
face.*

A pause.

*The Prince remains for a moment standing, with
an air of amazement, before the door; then lost
in thought, holding the hand with the glove before
his forehead, he walks down the steps. As soon as
he is down he turns, and gazes up again at the
door.*

*The Count of Hohenzollern comes in below,
through a garden door. A Page comes after him.—
The Prince of Homburg has remained.*]

41

THE PAGE (*softly*): My Lord Count, listen, please!
   My gracious Lord!
HOHENZOLLERN (*reluctantly*): Sh! little cricket!—
   Well? what is it?
THE PAGE: I am sent—
HOHENZOLLERN: Just take care not to wake him
   with your chirping!
—Right! What is it?
THE PAGE: I am sent by the Elector.
His orders are, when the Prince wakes,
you should not breathe a word about the sport
he indulged in, just now, at his expense.
HOHENZOLLERN (*softly*): Ay! run along, tumble
   into the cornfield
and have your sleep! I knew that! Off with you!

[*The Page goes.*

*The Count takes up a position at some distance
behind the Prince, who is still, exactly as before,
gazing up the stairway.*]

Arthur!

[*The Prince falls to the ground.*]

There he lies; a bullet could not do better! (*He
   comes up close.*)
Now all my curiosity is: What tale
will he invent for my ears, to explain
why he lay down to sleep here? (*He bends over
   him.*)
Arthur! Heh!
Are you possessed? What are you doing here?
Why have you come by night here, of all places?

THE PRINCE OF HOMBURG : It's you, friend.

HOHENZOLLERN : There! Well, I had better tell
  you :
the Cavalry, of which you are commander,
is on the march, has been for the last hour,
and you—here you lie in the garden, sleeping.

THE PRINCE OF HOMBURG : What cavalry?

HOHENZOLLERN : The Mamelukes, of course.—
Sure as I live and breathe, he has forgotten
he's in command of the Cavalry of the
Marches!

THE PRINCE OF HOMBURG (*standing up*) : Quick!
  my helmet! weapons!

HOHENZOLLERN : Yes, where are they?

THE PRINCE OF HOMBURG : On your right, Heinz,
  on your right; on the stool!

HOHENZOLLERN : Where? On the stool?

THE PRINCE OF HOMBURG : Yes, I put them on it,
did I not?

HOHENZOLLERN (*staring at him*) : Pick them up,
  then, off the stool.

THE PRINCE OF HOMBURG : What glove is this?

HOHENZOLLERN : How should I know?
(*To himself.*) Damnation!
So that is what, in the confusion up there,
he snatched from the arm of the Elector's niece!
(*Abruptly.*) Well, hurry! What are you waiting
for? On your way!

THE PRINCE OF HOMBURG (*throwing the glove
  away*) : Yes, yes—
Where's Franz? the rascal—he was supposed to
call me!

HOHENZOLLERN (*looking him up and down*) : He
  is quite raving mad!

THE PRINCE OF HOMBURG : By all that's sacred,
I do not know, dear Heinrich, where I am.

HOHENZOLLERN : At Fehrbellin, poor tangle-witted
  dreamer,
on a path in the garden
that spreads out its broad calm behind the palace.
THE PRINCE OF HOMBURG (*to himself*) : If night
  would swallow me! Without my knowing,
I have again gone wandering in the moonlight.
(*He pulls himself together.*)
Forgive me, I see now. As you know, that heat
made lying indoors hardly to be endured.
Utterly weary, I slipped out to this garden
and when night put such gentle arms about me,
with her fair hair, all dropping with sweet odours
—ah! as a Persian bride entwines her bride-
  groom!—,
I yielded, and lay down here, in her lap.
—What is the time now?
HOHENZOLLERN : The half-hour before twelve.
THE PRINCE OF HOMBURG : The squadrons have, you
  said, moved off?
HOHENZOLLERN : Of course!
at stroke of ten; according to the plan.
The Princess of Orange Regiment of Dragoons
has, at their head, without a doubt
already reached the Heights of Hackelwitz,
there to stand cover to our Army's
silent march tomorrow against Wrangel.
THE PRINCE OF HOMBURG : No matter! they've old
Kottwitz leading them,
and he knows fully the purpose of this march.
Besides,
I would have had to ride back to Headquarters
by two in the morning, for our further briefing :
better, therefore, now stay where I am.
Let's go. The Elector knows nothing of this?
HOHENZOLLERN : O, he—Long since in bed, asleep.

[*They move to go. The Prince suddenly stops, turns back and picks up the glove.*]

THE PRINCE OF HOMBURG : What a rare wonder of
    a dream I've dreamt!—
It was as though, gleaming with gold and silver,
a regal palace all of a sudden opened,
and down to me, down its tall marble stairway
came, like the company of a solemn dance,
the whole company of the beings my heart loves :
the Elector, the Electress and the—third,
—What *is* her name?
HOHENZOLLERN : Who?
THE PRINCE OF HOMBURG : Hers. The one I mean.
A man born dumb would have *her* name on his
    tongue!
HOHENZOLLERN : The Platen girl?
THE PRINCE OF HOMBURG : No, not her.
HOHENZOLLERN : The Ramin?
THE PRINCE OF HOMBURG : Not her, either.
HOHENZOLLERN : The Bork? The Winterfeld?
THE PRINCE OF HOMBURG : No, no, my dear man,
    please! You seem unable to
see the pearl for the ring that is its setting.
HOHENZOLLERN : Dammit, tell me! Is this a guess-
    ing game?
—Which lady do you—?
THE PRINCE OF HOMBURG : No matter, no matter!
The name, since I awoke, has fled from me,—
and to the understanding of my dream
it is no matter.
HOHENZOLLERN : Good! Then go on!
THE PRINCE OF HOMBURG : But do not interrupt
    me!
And he, the Elector with the brow of Zeus,
was holding in his hand a wreath of laurel :

45

he came and stood close up before my face,
and flung about the wreath—setting my soul
    ablaze—
the jewelled chain he wears around his neck,
and handed it, that she might crown me with it,
to—O my friend!

HOHENZOLLERN: To whom?

THE PRINCE OF HOMBURG: Dear friend!

HOHENZOLLERN: Well? Whom?

THE PRINCE OF HOMBURG:—It must have been the
    Platen, after all.

HOHENZOLLERN: The Platen? What?—She is in
    Prussia now.

THE PRINCE OF HOMBURG: The Platen. Certainly.
    Or the Ramin.

HOHENZOLLERN: Ah, the Ramin! What? her, with
    the red hair?—
The Platen, with those roguish violet eyes,
—she, we know, pleases you.

THE PRINCE OF HOMBURG: She pleases me.

HOHENZOLLERN: Well, and she, you were saying,
    gave you the wreath?

THE PRINCE OF HOMBURG: She raises—like a Genius
    of Fame she
raises the wreath, with the chain dangling from it,
up high, as though about to crown a hero.
I stretch, in inexpressible emotion
I stretch out both hands to take hold of it,—
and meanwhile long to sink down at her feet.
But, as the fragrance floating over valleys
scatters before the sharp breath of a breeze,
that company sweeps away from me up the stair-
    way.
The stairway, as I set foot on it, extends,
endless, up to the very gate of Heaven:
I clutch to right, I clutch to left, in anguish

trying to hold back one of those dear beings.
In vain! The palace door suddenly opens;
a brightness, flashing from within, like lightning,
swallows them all; and the door clatters to.
Only, roughly, in the pursuit, I wrench
from the arm of the sweet dream-form a glove:
and—
    almighty God! when I awaken,
a glove
      I am holding
          in my hand!

HOHENZOLLERN: By all that's sacred—So you think
the glove is hers?

THE PRINCE OF HOMBURG: Whose?

HOHENZOLLERN: Why, the Platen's!

THE PRINCE OF HOMBURG: The Platen's. Certainly.
Or the Ramin's.

HOHENZOLLERN (*with a laugh*): Rogue that you
are, with these visions of yours!
I wonder from what hour of love-sport
—wide-awake, flesh-and-blood—the glove was
carried
here, where it has stayed clasped in your hand?

THE PRINCE OF HOMBURG: I do that? By my love!—

HOHENZOLLERN: There now! Damn it,
for all I care it was the Countess Platen,
or the Ramin!—The post to Prussia goes
on Sunday: you can soon find out
whether your exquisite lady has missed this glove.
—Come! It is twelve. Why do we stand here,
talking?

THE PRINCE OF HOMBURG (*staring in front of him*):
There you are right. We had best go to bed.
But there was this, my friend, I meant to say:
Is the Electress still here,—and her niece

the sweet Princess of Orange, who has just
    arrived at our encampment?
HOHENZOLLERN : Why?—I do believe the fool is—?
THE PRINCE OF HOMBURG : Why?—
You know I was to detail thirty horse
to escort her back, out of range of the battle.
I had to see Ramin, give him this mission.
HOHENZOLLERN : There! They left long ago. Or
    will leave soon.
Ramin has been at the palace gate all night,
ready to start.
But, come! it's midnight, and before this battle
I, for one, would like a little more rest.

They both go.

Scene 2

*Fehrbellin. A hall in the palace. Sound of distant
firing.*

*The Electress and Princess Natalie, dressed for a
journey, come in led by an equerry, and attended
by ladies-in-waiting. They move to one side and
sit down.*

*Enter, now, the Elector, Field-marshal Dörfling,
The Prince of Homburg (wearing the glove thrust
into his riding-jacket), the Count of Hohenzollern,
Count Truchss, Colonel Hennings, Captain von
der Golz and more generals, colonels and other
officers.*

THE ELECTOR : What is that firing?—Is it Götz?

FIELD-MARSHAL DÖRFLING : Yes, sir, Your High-
    ness, it is Colonel Götz,
who went ahead, yesterday, with the vanguard.
He has already sent an officer
to reassure you. A Swedish post, one thousand
strong, pushed forward up to the Hackel Heights.
Nonetheless Götz will answer for those heights
and sends to tell me : you can proceed as if
already his vanguard holds them and will hold.
THE ELECTOR (*to the officers*) : Gentlemen,
the Marshal is familiar with the order
of battle : take your pencils, please, and note it.

[*The officers gather, on the other side, about the
Field-marshal, and bring out their notebooks.*]

(*Turning to the equerry.*)
Ramin has had the carriage brought round?
THE EQUERRY : Sir,
this moment. They are putting the horses in.
THE ELECTOR (*sitting down in a chair behind the
Electress and the Princess*) :
Ramin will now escort my dear Elisa,
with thirty sturdy troopers riding behind him.
You're going to my Chancellor Kalkhunn's castle
at Havelberg,—beyond the River Havel,
where no Swede any more dares show his face.
THE ELECTRESS : The ferry is repaired?
THE ELECTOR : At Havelberg?
That is in hand.
Besides, it will be day before you reach it.

[*A pause.*]

Natalie is so quiet, my sweet girl
—What ails the child?

PRINCESS NATALIE : I am afraid, dear Uncle.
THE ELECTOR : And yet my little daughter is so safe—
never was more so in her mother's lap.

[*A pause.*]

THE ELECTRESS : When, do you think, shall we see each other again?
THE ELECTOR : If God grants me the victory, and of that
I have no doubt, perhaps in a few days.

[*Pages come and serve a light breakfast to the ladies.—Field-marshal Dörfling dictates.—The Prince of Homburg, pencil and notebook in hand, gazes at the ladies.*]

THE FIELD-MARSHAL : Gentlemen, the plan for the coming battle
devised by 's Highness the Commander-in-Chief
has this aim :
to smash the Swedes' retreating army, having
cut them off from the bridgehead on the Rhyn
by which their rear is covered. Colonel Hennings!—
COLONEL HENNINGS : Here ! (*He begins to write.*)
THE FIELD-MARSHAL :—who, the Chief has decided, has today
command of the right wing,
will, through the Hackel Thickets, with all stealth
endeavour to work round the enemy's left,
and throw himself boldly in between him
and the three bridges; then, in liaison with
Count Truchss—Count Truchss !
COUNT TRUCHSS : Here ! (*He writes.*)

THE FIELD-MARSHAL :—in liaison with Count
Truchss—(*He pauses.*)
—who meanwhile has established his artillery
in positions on the heights opposite Wrangel—
COUNT TRUCHSS (*writing*) : Heights opposite
Wrangel.
THE FIELD-MARSHAL : You have that? (*Continuing*).
—will seek to hunt the Swedes into the swamp
which lies behind their right wing.

[*Enter a Heyduck*.*]

THE HEYDUCK : Gracious Lady,
the carriage is at the door.

[*The ladies rise to their feet.*]

THE FIELD-MARSHAL : The Prince of Homburg—
THE ELECTOR (*also rising*) : Is Ramin in readiness?
THE HEYDUCK : Yes, Sir. Mounted already. By the
gateway.

[*Leave-taking among the Elector's family.*]

COUNT TRUCHSS (*writing*) : Which lies behind their
right wing.

THE FIELD-MARSHAL : The Prince of Homburg—
Where is the Prince of Homburg?
HOHENZOLLERN (*discreetly*) : Arthur!
THE PRINCE OF HOMBURG (*with a start*) : Here!

---

*Heyducks, originally, were brigands; then a particular
kind of footsoldiers in Hungary. The term came to be
applied to liveried attendants at the courts of Eastern
Europe.

51

HOHENZOLLERN : Are you mad?

THE PRINCE OF HOMBURG : Marshal, I am at your service. (*He blushes, takes up pencil and parchment, and writes.*)

THE FIELD-MARSHAL :—to whom His Highness has once more entrusted

the command, rendered lustrous at Rathenow

already, of all the cavalry of the Marches—(*He pauses.*)

—but without prejudice to Colonel Kottwitz,

who will accompany him with his wise counsel—

(*In a mutter to Captain Golz.*) Is Kottwitz here?

CAPTAIN VON DER GOLZ : No, General, as you see, he has deputed me

to hear the battle orders from your mouth.

[*The Prince is again gazing at the Ladies.*]

THE FIELD-MARSHAL (*continuing*) :—takes up position on the plain outside the village

of Hackelwitz, facing the enemy's right,

well out of cannon-range.

CAPTAIN VON DER GOLZ (*as he writes*) : Well out of cannon-range.

[*The Electress arranges a scarf round the Princess's neck. The Princess makes to put on her gloves, then looks about her, as if seeking something.*]

THE ELECTOR (*approaching her*) : Little daughter, what is it?

THE ELECTRESS : Have you lost something?

PRINCESS NATALIE : I am not sure, dear Aunt, my glove—

[*They all look about.*]

THE ELECTOR (*to the ladies-in-waiting*): Fair ladies, would you mind making a search?

THE ELECTRESS (*to the Princess*): You have it, child.

PRINCESS NATALIE: The right glove; but the left?

THE ELECTOR: Perhaps still in her bedroom?

PRINCESS NATALIE: O Bork, dear!

THE ELECTRESS (*to the young lady-in-waiting*): Quick, quick!

PRINCESS NATALIE: Look on the chimney-piece!

[*The young lady-in-waiting is gone.*]

THE PRINCE OF HOMBURG (*to himself*): God of my life, did I hear right? (*He takes the glove from his jacket.*)

THE FIELD-MARSHAL (*looking down at the paper in his hand*): Well out of cannon-range. (*He finds his place and reads on.*) His Highness the Prince will—

THE PRINCE OF HOMBURG: She has missed the glove! (*He looks at the glove, then at the Princess.*)

THE FIELD-MARSHAL:—according to our Chief's express command—

CAPTAIN VON DER GOLZ (*writing*): According to our Chief's express command.

THE FIELD-MARSHAL:—no matter how the battle may develop,

not move from the position assigned to him.

THE PRINCE OF HOMBURG: Quick, let me prove whether this is the one! (*He lets the glove fall, together with his handkerchief. He picks up the handkerchief and leaves the glove lying where all may see it.*)

THE FIELD-MARSHAL (*showing surprise*): What is the Prince's Highness doing?

HOHENZOLLERN (*discreetly*) : Arthur!

THE PRINCE OF HOMBURG : Here!

HOHENZOLLERN : Are you possessed, man?

THE PRINCE OF HOMBURG : Marshal, at your service.

[*He takes up pencil and notebook again. The Field-marshal looks at him inquiringly for a moment.—pause.*]

CAPTAIN VON DER GOLZ (*having finished writing*) : Not move from the position assigned to him.

THE FIELD-MARSHAL (*continuing*) :—until, pressed back by Hennings and by Truchss—

THE PRINCE OF HOMBURG (*in a whisper to von Golz, at the same time looking down at his notebook*) Who? my dear Golz! What? I?

CAPTAIN VON DER GOLZ : Yes, you! Who else?

THE PRINCE OF HOMBURG : Am not to move—?

CAPTAIN VON DER GOLZ : Of course not.

THE FIELD-MARSHAL : Well? You have that?

THE PRINCE OF HOMBURG (*aloud*) : Not to move from the position assigned to me—(*He writes.*)

THE FIELD-MARSHAL :—until, pressed back by Hennings and by Truchss—(*He waits, then.*) —the enemy's left is prised loose and flung back against his right, and all his fighting units press in confusion towards the meadowlands, among whose marches, with their maze of ditches, the purpose of this plan is to destroy him.

THE ELECTOR : Pages, the lights here!—Your arm, my beloved!

[*He moves off with the Electress and the Princess.*]

THE FIELD-MARSHAL : Then he will order the fan-fare to be sounded.

THE ELECTRESS (*as some of the officers bow to her*) :
Till we meet again, gentlemen!—Let us not
disturb you.

[*The Field-marshal also bows to them.*]

THE ELECTOR (*suddenly stooping*) : Look! the young
lady's glove! Quick! there it is!

A COURTIER : Where?

THE ELECTOR : There, at the feet of the Prince
our Cousin!

THE PRINCE OF HOMBURG (*chivalrously*) : At my—?
What? does that glove belong to you? (*He picks
it up and carries it to the Princess.*)

PRINCESS NATALIE : I thank you, noble Prince.

THE PRINCE OF HOMBURG (*wildly*) : Is the glove
yours?

PRINCESS NATALIE : It is my glove; the one that I
had lost. (*She takes it and puts it on.*)

THE ELECTRESS (*to the Prince, as she is going*) :
Good-bye! Good–bye! Fortune, health, blessings
with you!
And may we meet again soon and in gladness!

[*The Elector goes out with the Electress and the
Princess; ladies-in-waiting, courtiers and pages
follow. The Prince of Homburg stands for a
moment, as though thunderstruck; then he turns,
and strides back triumphantly to the circle of
officers.*]

THE PRINCE OF HOMBURG : Then he will order the
fanfare to be sounded! (*He pretends to be writing.*)

THE FIELD-MARSHAL (*looking down at the paper*) :
Then he will order the fanfare to be sounded.—
But
His Highness the Elector, to make sure

The blow fall not too soon, through some misunderstanding—(*He waits.*)

CAPTAIN VON DER GOLZ (*writing*): The blow fall not too soon, through some misunderstanding—

THE PRINCE OF HOMBURG (*in a whisper to the Count of Hohenzollern, with deep emotion*): O Heinrich!

HOHENZOLLERN (*angrily*): Well, what is it? What's the matter?

THE PRINCE OF HOMBURG: What? You saw nothing?

HOHENZOLLERN: No! Be quiet, damn it!

THE FIELD-MARSHAL (*continuing*):—will send to him an officer of his staff,

who will convey to him—mark this—expressly the order to attack the enemy.

Till then he is not to have the fanfare sounded.

[*The Prince stands in a dream, staring in front of him.*]

You have that, noted down?

CAPTAIN VON DER GOLZ (*writing*): Till then he is not to have the fanfare sounded.

THE FIELD-MARSHAL (*raising his voice*): You, Prince, Your Highness! Have you that?

THE PRINCE OF HOMBURG: Yes, Marshal?

THE FIELD-MARSHAL: Have you that, written down?

THE PRINCE OF HOMBURG:—About the fanfare?

HOHENZOLLERN (*whispers angrily, with emphasis*): The fanfare! Devil take you! Not until he—

CAPTAIN VON DER GOLZ (*likewise*): Not until he himself—

THE PRINCE OF HOMBURG (*interrupting*): Of course! not till—

But then, then he will have the fanfare sounded. (*He writes.*)

56

[*A silence.*]

THE FIELD-MARSHAL : With Colonel Kottwitz—
  listen, Baron Golz—
I wish, if he can make it possible,
before the action starts, to speak in person.
CAPTAIN VON DER GOLZ (*significantly*) : I will take
  care of that. Rely on me.

[*A silence.*]

THE ELECTOR (*returning*) : Well, my Generals and
  Colonels, here's
the day-star in the dawn-grey. You have your
  notes?
THE FIELD-MARSHAL : Your Highness, that is done :
  your plan of battle
point by point conveyed to your field commanders !
THE ELECTOR (*picking up hat and gloves*) : Lord
  Prince of Homburg, to you I commend calm !
Lately, remember, on the banks of the Rhine
you cost me two victories. Govern yourself,
and do not make me, today, miss the third—
on which my throne and realm, no less, will
  hang.
(*To the Officers.*) Follow me !—Franz

[*A Groom, appearing.*]

GROOM : Sir.
THE ELECTOR : Quick ! my horse—the white !
—I mean to race the sun to the battlefield !

[*He strides off; the generals, colonels and other
officers follow. The Prince of Homburg comes
forward.*]

THE PRINCE OF HOMBURG : So now, riding upon your
   globe, wild Goddess
whose veil, for this new day, the breath of the wind
is filling like a sail,—roll here to me !
Already, Fortune, you have stroked my hair,
thrown—as you flew by—smiling—down to me
out of your cornucopia a token.
Today, Child of the Gods, I shall pursue you,
Fugitive ! and shall snatch at you on the field
and spill out all your blessings round my feet,—
and would, if you were bound fast—sevenfold,
by iron chains—to the Swedish victory chariot !

He goes off.

ACT TWO

Scene 1

Field of battle, outside Fehrbellin.

Colonel Kottwitz, Count Hohenzollern, Captain von der Golz and other officers, entering, at the head of the cavalry.

COLONEL KOTTWITZ (*off stage*): Halt the Cavalry here, let 'em dismount!

GOLZ
HOHENZOLLERN } (*coming into view*): Halt!— Halt!

COLONEL KOTTWITZ (*off stage*): Which of you friends will help me from my horse?

GOLZ
HOHENZOLLERN } : Coming, old fellow, coming!

[*They disappear again.*]

COLONEL KOTTWITZ (*off stage*): Thanks!—Uff!
Plague take me!—For that kind service
may God give each of you a noble son,
to do the same for you when you are crumbling!

[*He comes on; Hohenzollern, Golz and others follow.*]

Yes, on horseback I feel full of youth;
but, once dismounted, a shindy starts, as if
body and soul were fighting to part company! (*He looks about.*)

Where's His Highness the Prince, our Commander?

HOHENZOLLERN: The Prince will soon come back
to you.

COLONEL KOTTWITZ: Where is he?

HOHENZOLLERN: He rode into the village—the one
you passed,
hidden among thickets. He will join us soon.

AN OFFICER: Is it true that, while it was still dark,
he had a fall?

HOHENZOLLERN: I think so, yes.

COLONEL KOTTWITZ: He fell?

HOHENZOLLERN (*turning to him*): Nothing serious!
His horse shied at the mill-wheel,
but he slid off, well to one side, and was not
hurt in the least. Not worth a second's worry.

COLONEL KOTTWITZ (*climbing a small eminence*):
A lovely day, as sure as I'm alive!
A day that God, the high Lord of the world,
created for a sweeter thing than killing!
The sun shimmers ruddily through the clouds,
and all one's feelings flutter with the lark
up to serene sweet-smelling fields of Heaven.

GOLZ: Did you succeed in finding Marshal
Dörfling?

COLONEL KOTTWITZ (*coming down and forward
again*): Damn it, no! What's His Excellency
think I am?
Am I a bird, an arrow, or a thought,
that he should dodge me all over the field of battle?
I've been to the vanguard, up on Hackel Heights,
and right down Hackel Gulley to the rearguard:
the one man I did *not* find was the Marshal!
So turned about to find my cavalry again.

GOLZ: That will upset him. He had, if I'm not
mistaken,
something of consequence for your own ear.

AN OFFICER : Here comes His Highness the Prince,
  our Commander!

[*Enter the Prince of Homburg, with a black
bandage about his left hand.—The others as
before.*]

COLONEL KOTTWITZ : My greetings to you, my
  young, noble Prince!
Look how, while you were down there at the village,
I've placed the cavalry along the valley track :
I think you'll be content with what I've done.
THE PRINCE OF HOMBURG : Good morning, Kott-
  witz!—Good morning, friends!
—You know I praise everything that you do.
HOHENZOLLERN : What were you up to, Arthur, in
  the village?
—You look so grave!
THE PRINCE OF HOMBURG : I—I was in the chapel
that gleamed from the quiet thicket round the
  village.
The bell was ringing, just as we rode past,
calling to worship : it compelled me in
to kneel down too, before the altar, and pray.
COLONEL KOTTWITZ : A devout young Lord, that I
  must say!
The work, believe me, that begins with prayer
will crown itself with health, glory and victory!
THE PRINCE OF HOMBURG : Heinrich, there's some-
  thing that I meant to ask you. (*He leads the
  Count forward a little.*)
What was it Dörfling said, that concerned me,
at Battle Orders?
HOHENZOLLERN : You were absent–minded.
That I could see, plainly.
THE PRINCE OF HOMBURG : Absent-minded—

all in pieces; I don't know what was wrong with me.
Writing to dictation makes me confused.—
HOHENZOLLERN : This time, luckily, nothing much
   for you.
Truchss and Hennings, commanding the foot-
   sloggers,
are to lead off the attack on the enemy;
your part is, to stay put here in the valley,
poised to strike with the cavalry, until
the order to attack is sent to you.

[*A silence, while the Prince stands gazing in front
of him in a dream.*]

THE PRINCE OF HOMBURG :—The strangeness of the
   thing.
HOHENZOLLERN : What, my dear fellow? (*He stares
   at him.*)

[*The boom of a cannon.*]

COLONEL KOTTWITZ : Holla, my Lords, holla!—
   Mount, mount!—
That's Hennings, and the battle is beginning.

[*They all move up on to an eminence.*]

THE PRINCE OF HOMBURG : Who is that, there?
HOHENZOLLERN : That's Colonel Hennings, Arthur.
He's crept up to the rear of Wrangel's forces!
Come over—yes, there you can see it all.
GOLZ (*from the top*) : Look now, how formidably
   he's deploying
along the Rhyn!
THE PRINCE OF HOMBURG (*holding his hand up to
   shield his eyes*) : Hennings, on our right wing?

FIRST OFFICER : Yes, Your Highness.
THE PRINCE OF HOMBURG : Well, upon my soul!
His place, yesterday, was upon the left.

[*Cannon-fire in the distance.*]

COLONEL KOTTWITZ : Thunder and lightning!
  Look, twelve mouths of flame
at once, let loose by Wrangel against Hennings!
FIRST OFFICER : Some bulwarks I call those, the
  Swedish ones!
SECOND OFFICER : God, yes! piled up as high as the
  church-tower
of the village there beyond, behind their rear.

[*Shots, near by.*]

GOLZ : That will be Truchss!
THE PRINCE OF HOMBURG : Truchss?
COLONEL KOTTWITZ : Yes, that is Truchss,
turning aside to come to the aid of Hennings.
THE PRINCE OF HOMBURG : How is it, Truchss today
  is in the centre?

[*Violent cannonade.*]

GOLZ : Heavens, look! I think the village has
  caught fire!
THIRD OFFICER : It's burning, as I live!
FIRST OFFICER : It's burning! burning!
The flames already shooting up the tower!
GOLZ : Whee! Swedish messengers running, right
  and left!
SECOND OFFICER : They're moving forward!
COLONEL KOTTWITZ : Where?
FIRST OFFICER : On the right flank!—

THIRD OFFICER : So they are. In column! Three
    regiments!
Their aim seems to be to support their left.
SECOND OFFICER : By God, yes! And some cavalry
    riding forward
to give their right wing cover as it marches!
HOHENZOLLERN (*with a laugh*): Ha! they'd soon
    leave the field empty again
if they could see us, hidden here in the valley!

[*Musket fire.*]

COLONEL KOTTWITZ : Look! Brothers, look!
SECOND OFFICER : Listen!
FIRST OFFICER : Musketry fire!
THIRD OFFICER : They are engaged, now, close to
    the bulwarks!
GOLZ : By God! I never heard in all my life
such a brute thunder of artillery!
HOHENZOLLERN : Shoot! Shoot!—till you split the
    Earth's belly open!
The gap you make shall serve as grave for their
    corpses.

[*A silence. A victory shout in the distance.*]

FIRST OFFICER : O Lord on high, giver of victory!
Wrangel's withdrawing already!
HOHENZOLLERN : No! Are you certain?
GOLZ : By Heaven, friends, he is! On the left
    flank!
With his field guns, he's abandoning the bulwarks.
ALL : Victory! Victory! Victory! The battle's
    ours!
THE PRINCE OF HOMBURG (*coming down*): Up,
    Kottwitz, follow me!

COLONEL KOTTWITZ : Calm, calm, my lads!

THE PRINCE OF HOMBURG : Up! Have the fanfares
sounded! Follow me!

COLONEL KOTTWITZ : I say : keep calm now.

THE PRINCE OF HOMBURG (*wildly*) : Heaven, Earth
and Hell!

COLONEL KOTTWITZ : Our Sovereign and Chief, at
the before-dawn briefing,

instructed us : we are to wait for orders.

Golz, read aloud the record of the briefing.

THE PRINCE OF HOMBURG : For orders!

Kottwitz! man! are you such a sluggish trooper?

Have you still not received them from your heart?

COLONEL KOTTWITZ : Orders?

HOHENZOLLERN : Please! Please!

COLONEL KOTTWITZ : From my heart?

HOHENZOLLERN : Hear the instructions, Arthur!

GOLZ : Do listen, Colonel.

COLONEL KOTTWITZ (*humiliated*) : Oho! Would you
round upon *me* like that,

my young Lord?—when you know, at a pinch, I'd
tie

your winded jade to the tail of mine and tow him!

March, march, all of you! Trumpeter, the fanfare!

To battle! Into battle! Kottwitz is with you!

GOLZ (*to Kottwitz*) : Colonel, sir, no! Never that!
Never that!

SECOND OFFICER : Hennings has not yet reached the
bank of the Rhyn!

FIRST OFFICER : Quick, take his sword from him!

THE PRINCE OF HOMBURG : My sword from me?
Ah-ye! insolent boy, who have still not learned
(*He knocks him backwards.*)

the ten commandments of a soldier of the Marches!

Here is your sword, together with the scabbard!
(*He tears off the Officer's sword and belt together.*)

FIRST OFFICER (*reeling*) : Prince, such an act, by
    God—!

THE PRINCE OF HOMBURG (*advancing on him*) : Your
    mouth still not shut?

HOHENZOLLERN (*to the Officer*) : Be quiet! Are you
    quite mad?

THE PRINCE OF HOMBURG : Orderlies. (*He hands the
    sword to one of them.*)
Take him prisoner, lead him to Headquarters.
(*To Kottwitz and the rest of the officers.*)
And now your briefing, gentlemen! he's a scoundrel
who does not follow his General into battle!
—Which of you will hang back?

COLONEL KOTTWITZ : You heard. Objections?

HOHENZOLLERN (*appeasingly*) : It was advice,
    simply, being offered you.

COLONEL KOTTWITZ (*to the Prince*) : Upon your
    shoulders take this. I will follow.

THE PRINCE OF HOMBURG (*serene again*) : I take it
    on my shoulders. Follow me, brothers!

They all go.

Scene 2

A room in a village.

*A peasant and his wife are sitting at a table, work-
ing. Enter a courtier, booted and spurred.*

THE COURTIER : God bless you, worthy people!
    Have you room,
in your house, to give shelter to some guests?

THE PEASANT : O yes ! With all our hearts.

HIS WIFE : May we know who—?

THE COURTIER : The noble Mother of our land ! No
less !
At the gate to the village, an axle snapped;
and since we hear the victory has been won,
there's no need for this journey any more.

BOTH (*rising to their feet*) : The victory won?—
Heavens !

THE COURTIER : You did not know?
The Swedish army is utterly defeated :
if not for ever, still for a good year
the Marches are secure from their sword and fire !
—But look ! Here the Electress comes, already.

[*Enter the Electress, pale and distraught, followed
by the Princess Natalie and several ladies-in-waiting. The courtier and the two peasants remain.*]

THE ELECTRESS (*on the threshold*) :
Bork ! Winterfeld ! Come; give me, each, an arm !

NATALIE (*hurrying to her*) : O Mother !

THE LADIES-IN-WAITING : God ! She's turning pale !
She's fainting !

[*They support her.*]

THE ELECTRESS : Lead me to a chair, let me sit
down.
—Dead, did he say? dead?

NATALIE : O dear Mother !

THE ELECTRESS : I will speak, myself, with the
messenger of disaster.

[*Captain von Mörner enters, wounded, with two
cavalrymen helping him.*]

What are you bringing me, herald of terror?

MÖRNER : What, alas, dear Lady, these eyes of mine
saw for themselves, to my eternal sorrow.

THE ELECTRESS : So! Tell!

MÖRNER : The Elector is no more!

NATALIE : O Heaven!
is it Your Will this monstrous blow should strike
us? (*She covers her face.*)

THE ELECTRESS : Report to me the manner of his
falling!
—And as the lightning, that strikes down the
traveller,
shows him the world lit, purple, one last time,
so let your word be : once you have spoken, may
the Dark clap together over my head.

[*Mörner, aided by the two cavalrymen, moves till
he is standing before her.*]

MÖRNER : The Prince of Homburg had—soon as the
enemy,
hard pressed by Truchss, wavered from their positions—
launched an attack on Wrangel in the plain.
Two lines he had, with his cavalry, already
broken and cut to pieces as they fled,
when he came up against a field redoubt.
Here such a rain of iron, so murderous,
lashed him, that his body of cavalry
bent and bowed, like a field of wheat being reaped :
halt he had to, between thickets and hills,
for his dispersed cavalry to re-form.

NATALIE (*to the Electress*) : Beloved! Courage!

THE ELECTRESS : Dearest, let me be!

MÖRNER : But now—torn clear of the dust cloud—
we see

68

the Chief, close to the colours of Truchss's corps,
riding out against the enemy :
there he sits, superb, on a white horse
in a shaft of sunshine, lighting the way to
victory.
All of us, at this sight, rush to re-form
on the slope of a hill, in deep anxiety
at seeing him there in the thick of the fire,—
when suddenly the Elector—horse and rider—
sinks
    down
        in dust before our eyes;
two standard-bearers fell across him,—they
covered his body over with their colours.
NATALIE : O my dear Mother !
FIRST LADY-IN-WAITING : Heaven !
THE ELECTRESS : Go on ! Go on !
MÖRNER : At once, at this vision of horror, pain
beyond all measure grips the Prince's heart;
and like a bear goaded by rage to vengeance
he bursts out, with us all, straight at the entrench-
    ment,—
in the charge both the ditch and the earthworks
are over-run; the men who held 'em hurled
right out, scattered, pursued and cut to pieces;
artillery and colours, drums and standards
and the whole baggage-train of the Swedes
    captured :
and had not then the bridgehead on the Rhyn
choked us back, not one Swede would return
to the hearth of his fathers and there say :
'At Fehrbellin I saw the Hero fall.'
THE ELECTRESS : A victory bought too dear ! No
joy to me.
Give me again the price which it has cost. (*She
faints.*)

FIRST LADY-IN-WAITING : Help, God in Heaven!
  She has fainted away.

[*Natalie weeps.*

Enter the Prince of Homburg.]

THE PRINCE OF HOMBURG : O my Natalie, my
  dearest one! (*Deeply moved, he lays her hand
  against his heart.*)
NATALIE : So it is true?
THE PRINCE OF HOMBURG : Oh! If I *could* say : no!
If, with blood out of this loyal heart,
I could call back his own heart into being!
NATALIE (*wiping away her tears*) : Have they, then,
  already found the body?
THE PRINCE OF HOMBURG : Ah! till this moment my
  concern has been
vengeance on Wrangel, nothing else; how could I
turn to that task till now? But I have sent
some of my men to search the field of death :
before night, without doubt, he will come in.
NATALIE : Who, in the fearful war that lies before
  us,
will now hold the Swedes down? Who is there now
to shield us from the world of enemies
earned for us by his fortune, by his glory?
THE PRINCE OF HOMBURG (*taking her hand*) : I,
  sweetest lady, take your cause on me!
Let me, an angel with the sword of flame,
stand on those orphaned steps below your throne!
The Elector wished, before the year is out,
to see the Marches set free; well, then! I shall
be the executor of that last will!
NATALIE : My dear, beloved Cousin! (*She draws
  her hand away.*)

THE PRINCE OF HOMBURG : O Natalie! (*He hesitates for a moment.*)

How do you look on your own future now?

NATALIE : Yes. Where—now that this lightning-stroke has blasted

the ground from under me—am I to turn?

My Father is at rest, and my dear Mother,

at Amsterdam in the tomb; rubble and ashes

are what is left of Dordrecht, my inheritance;

and, hard pressed by the Spanish tyrant's armies,

Maurice, my princely cousin of Orange, scarcely

knows where to look for his own children's

safety.

And now there sinks from beneath me the last prop

that still held the vine of my fortune up.

Today, the second time, I am an orphan!

THE PRINCE OF HOMBURG (*putting his arm about her*) : O dear friend! Were it not that this hour is

sacred to mourning, I would wish to say :

Twine your branches here, about this breast,

this breast that, growing all alone, for years

has longed for the sweet fragrance of your blossoms!

NATALIE : My dear and generous Cousin!

THE PRINCE OF HOMBURG : Will you? Will you?

NATALIE : If I might grow into its inmost marrow? (*She leans upon his breast.*)

THE PRINCE OF HOMBURG : What? You said—what?

NATALIE : No, leave me!

THE PRINCE OF HOMBURG (*holding her*) : To its core!

To the heart's core of it, Natalie! (*He kisses her; she breaks away from him.*)

O God, if only he, whom we are mourning,

were here, to see this troth! If only we

could stammer to him : 'Father, give your blessing!'
(*He covers his face with his hands.*)

[*Natalie turns again to the Electress.*

A sergeant rushes in.]

SERGEANT : My Lord Prince, by the living God I
  scarcely
dare to tell you the rumour that's now spreading!
—The Elector's living!
THE PRINCE OF HOMBURG : Living!
SERGEANT : Yes, by high Heaven!
Count Sparren is himself here with the news.
NATALIE : Lord of my life! Mother, did you hear
  that? (*She falls on her knees before the Electress
  and puts her arms about her.*)
THE PRINCE OF HOMBURG : No, say again—!
  Who—?
SEARGEANT : Count Georg von Sparren,
who with his own eyes saw him, safe and sound,
over in Hackelwitz with Truchss's corps!
THE PRINCE OF HOMBURG : Quick! Run, old fellow!
  bring him in to me!

[*The Sergeant goes out.*]

THE ELECTRESS : O do not twice strike me down
  to the abyss!
NATALIE : No, no, dear Mother!
THE ELECTRESS : Friedrich is alive?
NATALIE (*holding her, with both hands, from
  falling*) : The crest of life is again drawing you
  up!

[*Re-enter the Sergeant, with Count Sparren.*]

THE SERGEANT : Here is the officer!

THE PRINCE OF HOMBURG : My Lord Count of
  Sparren!

His Highness the Elector, fresh and active,

with Truchss's corps, in Hackelwitz,—you saw
  him?

COUNT SPARREN : Yes, my Lord Prince, in the courtyard of the priest's house,

issuing orders, with his staff around him,

for the burial of the dead of both the armies!

THE LADIES-IN-WAITING : O God! Upon Thy
  bosom—

[*They embrace one another.*]

THE ELECTRESS : O my daughter!

NATALIE : No—this happiness—almost too great!
  (*She presses her face into the Electress's lap.*)

THE PRINCE OF HOMBURG : Did I not, as I led my
  cavalry,

see, from afar, him and his white horse fall,

shattered by cannon-shot, into the dust?

COUNT SPARREN : The white horse, yes, did fall;
  with him, his rider;

but the man riding him was not the Chief.

THE PRINCE OF HOMBURG : Not? Not the Chief?

NATALIE : O joy! (*She rises to her feet, and stands
  beside the Electress.*)

THE PRINCE OF HOMBURG : Man! the whole story!

Your word sinks heavy as gold into my breast!

COUNT SPARREN : O let me now recount to you the
  most moving

action that human ears ever yet caught!

Our Sovereign, who again, deaf to all warnings,

was riding the white horse, the gleaming white one

that Froben lately found for him in England,

73

was again—as before, every time—
the target for the enemy cannon-fire.
Those of his personal train could hardly come
within a circle of a hundred paces;
cannon-balls, grape-shot and grenades were rolling
down on him like a broad river of death,
and all things living there edged to the bank :
he only, the bold swimmer, did not flinch,
kept beckoning his friends on, and still steered
gaily towards the heights, where the source
welled.

THE PRINCE OF HOMBURG : By Heaven, yes ! It made
us shudder to see it.

COUNT SPARREN : Froben, Master of the Horse,
who of his train
followed him closest, shouted out to me :
'Cursed, today, be the bright coat of that horse
bought by me in London for heavy gold !
Gladly now I'd give fifty ducats, could I
cover it all over with mouse grey.'
Desperate, he caught up with the chief and said :
'Highness, your horse is shying,—better let me
take him back to the school for further training !'
With that he jumped down from his chestnut, seized
the white horse by the bridle and held it still.
The chief got down, smiling calmly, and answered :
'The art that you, old fellow, have a mind
to teach him, he'll not learn by this day's light.
Take him, please, well away,—behind those hil-
locks,
where no enemy eyes may see his failing !'
He leapt into the saddle of Froben's chestnut
and headed back to where his duties called him.
But Froben barely had swung himself astride
the white when, from the field redoubt,
a mortal shot tore horse and rider down :

to dust he sinks, victim of his devotion,
and not another sound was heard from him.

[*A brief silence.*]

THE PRINCE OF HOMBURG : He is rewarded!—if I
   myself had ten lives,
I could not put them to a better use!
NATALIE : Valiant Froben!
THE ELECTRESS : There are few like him!
NATALIE : A less good man would still deserve our
   tears.

[*They weep.*]

THE PRINCE OF HOMBURG : Enough! To action.
   Where is the Elector?
Are his headquarters now in Hackelwitz?
COUNT SPARREN : Excuse me, but the Chief left for
   Berlin,
and all commanders are to join him there.
THE PRINCE OF HOMBURG : What? To Berlin!—Is
   the campaign, then, ended?
COUNT SPARREN : Certainly,—I am amazed you
   have heard nothing!
Count Horn, the Swedish general, came across :
instantly, through the camp, 'Cease fire' was
   ordered.
If I have understood Field-marshal Dörfling,
negotiations have been joined, and it is
likely, even, the outcome will be peace.
THE ELECTRESS : O God, how wonderfully it is
   clearing! (*She stands up.*)
THE PRINCE OF HOMBURG : Come, let's follow him
   to Berlin at once!
—Would you, to get me there more quickly, grant
   me,

of your great kindness, a place in your own
    carriage?
—One moment only, while I write a line
to Kottwitz, then I'll go with you at once. (*He sits
    down and writes.*)
THE ELECTRESS : With all my heart!

[*The Prince of Homburg folds the note and hands
it to the sergeant; then, returning to the Electress
and gently putting his arm round Natalie's waist.*]

THE PRINCE OF HOMBURG : I have a wish, which I
    am
still shy of disclosing,—of which I will
unburden myself to you during the journey.
NATALIE (*breaking away from him*): Bork! Quick!
    My scarf, please!
THE ELECTRESS : You? A wish, of me?
FIRST LADY-IN-WAITING : Princess, you have the
    scarf about your neck!
THE PRINCE OF HOMBURG (*to the Electress*): What?
    Have you not guessed anything?
THE ELECTRESS : No, nothing.
THE PRINCE OF HOMBURG : What? Not one syllable?
THE ELECTRESS (*cutting him short*): It does not
    matter!
—Today to no petitioner on Earth,
whatever he might ask, do I answer : no.
Not, above all, to you, the battle's victor.
—Let's go!
THE PRINCE OF HOMBURG : O Mother! What have
    you just said?
Am I to take it as I long to do?
THE ELECTRESS : Let's go, I say! More of this in
    the carriage!
Come, give me your arm!

THE PRINCE OF HOMBURG : O divine Caesar!
I am setting up the ladder to your star!

He leads the ladies away; the rest follow.

Scene 3

Berlin. Garden in front of the old palace. In the background the Schlosskirche, with steps leading up to it. The bells are ringing; the interior of the church is brightly lit; the body of Froben is seen, being carried past and placed on a magnificent catafalque.

Enter the Elector, Field-marshal Dörfling, Colonel Hennings, Count Truchss and several more colonels and other officers. One or two officers with despatches hover near the Elector.—Both in the church and in the square, there are bystanders of both sexes and all ages.

THE ELECTOR : Whoever it was who led the cavalry
on the day of the battle, and, before Colonel
    Hennings
had the time to destroy the enemy's bridges,
took it upon himself to attack, so putting
the enemy to flight before I ordered,—
that man, I now declare, has deserved death,
and I shall have him tried by a Court Martial.
—The Prince of Homburg was not leading them?
COUNT TRUCHSS : No, Your Highness, Sir!
THE ELECTOR : On what evidence?
COUNT TRUCHSS : The fact can be confirmed to you
    by troopers

who brought the news to me before the battle :
the Prince, Sir, was thrown from his horse
and, with severe wounds on head and thigh,
was seen in a village church being bandaged.
THE ELECTOR : No matter. Today's victory is
    brilliant—
at the altar steps tomorrow I thank God.
But were it ten times greater, still it does not
absolve the man through whom chance gave it me;
I shall have further battles yet to fight,
and mean to see obedience to the Law.
Whoever it was, led them into the fight,
has forfeited his head,—this I repeat
and before a Court Martial herewith cite him.
—Follow me, my friends, up to the church.

[*Enter the Prince of Homburg, carrying three
Swedish colours; Colonel Kottwitz with two more;
Count Hohenzollern, Captain Golz and Count
Reuss with one each; and several other officers,
corporals and troopers bearing colours, drums and
standards.*]

FIELD-MARSHAL DÖRFLING (*as soon as he sees the
    Prince*) : The Prince of Homburg!—Truchss!
    What has possessed you?
THE ELECTOR (*with a start*) : Where have you come
    from, Prince?
THE PRINCE OF HOMBURG (*stepping forward a few
    paces*) : From Fehrbellin,
    my Sovereign, bringing you these victory
    trophies.

[*He lays the three colours on the ground before
him. The officers, corporals and troopers do the
same with theirs.*]

THE ELECTOR (*bewildered*): You are, I am told, wounded, and dangerously?
—Count Truchss?

THE PRINCE OF HOMBURG (*serenely*): Forgive me!

COUNT TRUCHSS: By heaven, I am astounded!

THE PRINCE OF HOMBURG: My bay horse fell, before the battle started;

this hand, which a field surgeon dressed for me, does not deserve that you should christen it 'wounded'.

THE ELECTOR: Does this mean that you led the cavalry?

THE PRINCE OF HOMBURG (*staring at him*): I? But of course! Is it for me to tell you?

—I have just laid the evidence at your feet.

THE ELECTOR: Take away his sword. He is prisoner.

FIELD-MARSHAL DÖRFLING (*shocked*): Whose?

THE ELECTOR (*stepping among the colours*): Kottwitz! Hearty greetings!

COUNT TRUCHSS (*to himself*): O damnation!

COLONEL KOTTWITZ: By God, Sir, I am deeply—

THE ELECTOR (*looking hard at him*): What are you saying?—

Look, what a harvest here, reaped for our glory!
—This is the Swedish Guard's own colours!
Surely?

(*He picks up one of the flags, unfurls it and contemplates it.*)

COLONEL KOTTWITZ: What, my Lord Chief?

FIELD-MARSHAL DÖRFLING: Excuse me, Sir?

THE ELECTOR: Of course, yes!

Dates from the days of their King Gustav Adolph!—
What's the inscription?

COLONEL KOTTWITZ: I think—

FIELD-MARSHAL DÖRFLING: *Per aspera ad astra.*

THE ELECTOR : 'Through struggles to the stars'.
They did not hold to that at Fehrbellin.

[*A silence.*]

COLONEL KOTTWITZ (*timidly*): My Lord Prince,
  Sir,
allow me one word—
THE ELECTOR : What can I do for you?—
Take up these—colours, drums, standards, all—
and hang them on the columns of the church;
I need them at tomorrow's victory service! (*He
  turns to the courtiers and takes from them the
  despatches, which he begins to open and read.*)
COLONEL KOTTWITZ : That, by the living God, for
  me goes too far!

[*The Colonel, after some hesitation, picks up his
two flags; the other officers and troopers follow his
example. In the end, when the three flags brought
by the Prince are left lying there, Kottwitz picks
up these too, so that he now has five.*]

AN OFFICER (*stepping up to the Prince*): Prince,
  Sir, your sword, please.
HOHENZOLLERN (*with his flag, coming to the
  Prince's side*): Friend, keep calm!
THE PRINCE OF HOMBURG : Am I
dreaming? waking? living? in my senses?
CAPTAIN GOLZ : Prince, I advise you, give up your
  sword, keep silence!
THE PRINCE OF HOMBURG : I, a prisoner?
HOHENZOLLERN : That is so.
CAPTAIN GOLZ : You heard.
THE PRINCE OF HOMBURG : May one be told the
  reason?

HOHENZOLLERN (*forcibly*) : Not just now !

—You pressed too soon, we warned you at the
    time,

into the fight; the order was,

not to move from our place without being
    summoned.

THE PRINCE OF HOMBURG : Help, friends, help ! I
    have gone mad !

CAPTAIN GOLZ (*cutting him short*) : Silence !
    Silence !

THE PRINCE OF HOMBURG : Were the troops of the
    Marches then defeated ?

HOHENZOLLERN (*stamping*) : No matter ! Orders
    have to be obeyed.

THE PRINCE OF HOMBURG (*bitterly*) : So !—So, so !

HOHENZOLLERN (*moving away*) : It will *not* cost
    you your neck.

CAPTAIN GOLZ (*likewise*) : You may tomorrow, even,
    be free again.

[*The Elector gathers the despatches together and
returns to the group of officers.—The Prince of
Homburg unbuckles his sword, and stands holding
it.*]

THE PRINCE OF HOMBURGH My Cousin Friedrich
    fancies the part of Brutus*

and sees himself already immortalized

on canvas, seated in the Curule Chair : †

foreground, the Swedish colours; on the desk

the Articles of War of the Army of the Marches.

---

* Lucius Junius Brutus, according to legend the founder
of the Roman Republic, allowed his sons to be condemned because they had taken part in a conspiracy
against the Republic.

† The chair occupied by the highest officers of the
Roman State.

By God, in me he does not find that son
who, under the axe of the hangman, will admire
   him.
A German heart, one of the old stamp,
I am used to magnanimity and love;
and if he comes to meet me, at this moment,
in all the stiffness of Antiquity,
he gives me pain, and I must pity him. (*He hands
   his sword to the officer, and goes.*)
THE ELECTOR: Take him to Fehrbellin, yes, to
   Headquarters,
and there set up the Court Martial, to judge him.

*He moves off, into the church. The captured
colours follow him, and while he and his staff kneel
and pray by Froben's coffin, are hung up upon
the pillars. Funeral music.*

ACT THREE

Scene 1

Fehrbellin. A prison.

The Prince of Homburg.—In the background two cavalry troopers on duty as guards.

Enter the Count of Hohenzollern.

THE PRINCE OF HOMBURG : Look who it is! Friend
    Heinrich! You are welcome!
—So, it is true, and I am again free?
HOHENZOLLERN (*astonished*): Praise be to God on
    high!
THE PRINCE OF HOMBURG : What'd you say?
HOHENZOLLERN : Free?
Has the Elector sent you back your sword?
THE PRINCE OF HOMBURG : Me? No.
HOHENZOLLERN : No?
THE PRINCE OF HOMBURG : No!
HOHENZOLLERN : Then how could you be free?
THE PRINCE OF HOMBURG (*after a pause*): I thought
    . . . that you were bringing it.—No matter!
HOHENZOLLERN : I know nothing.
THE PRINCE OF HOMBURG : No matter, I said; no
    matter
He's sending someone else with the announcement.
    (*He turns, and fetches chairs.*)
Sit down. Well, and now tell me, what's the news?
The Elector has arrived back from Berlin?
HOHENZOLLERN (*absently*): Yesterday evening.
THE PRINCE OF HOMBURG : And there the victory
was celebrated, was it not? Of course!
—Was the Elector present in the church?

HOHENZOLLERN : He and the Electress and
   Natalie.—
The church was lit—a ceremony of light;
from Palace Square salvoes offered the sound
of their grave pomp to the thanksgiving service;
the Swedish flags and banners hung as trophies,
trailing their captive glory down the high pillars;
and from the pulpit, by the Sovereign's
express command, you were named as the victor.
THE PRINCE OF HOMBURG : I heard so.—Well, what
   else? What news do you bring?—
Your face—or am I wrong, friend?—is not cheerful.
HOHENZOLLERN : Have you yet spoken with anyone?
THE PRINCE OF HOMBURG : Yes; Golz;
up at the Palace,—where, as you know, I went
to the Court Martial.

[*Pause.*]

HOHENZOLLERN (*looking at him in perplexity*) :
What, in that case, Arthur, do you think
of your situation, now so strangely altered?
THE PRINCE OF HOMBURG : I? Why, as you and Golz
   do—and the judges!
The Elector has obeyed the claims of duty
and now will turn and listen to his heart.
'You did wrong', he will gravely say to me,
adding perhaps a word on death and prison,
'but I am giving back to you your freedom'—
and round the sword that won him victory
there may, also, be twined some jewel of grace;
—if not, still good; for I have not deserved it.
HOHENZOLLERN : O Arthur ! (*He hesitates.*)
THE PRINCE OF HOMBURG : Well?

HOHENZOLLERN : Are you so sure of that?

THE PRINCE OF HOMBURG : I should think so ! I am
   dear to him, I know,
dear as a son; his heart has given me,
since early childhood, countless proofs of that.
What can it be, this doubt that troubles you?
Did he not, at the growth of my young fame,
seem to feel almost more joy than my own?
Am I not everything I am through him?
And is he—he?—to trample lovelessly
—jealously—into the dust the plant
that he himself tended, simply because
it rushed a trifle wantonly into bloom?
This I would not believe from his worst enemy,—
still less, coming from you, who know and love
him.

HOHENZOLLERN (*earnestly*) : You stood your trial,
   Arthur, by Court Martial,
and still hold your belief?

THE PRINCE OF HOMBURG : Because I stood it !—
Nobody, by the living God, will go
so far, who's not determined to grant pardon !
It was there, there, before the bar of justice,
there it was, that my confidence came back.
For—look !—was it a crime, deserving death,
to have laid the might of Sweden in the dust
a couple of instants earlier than ordered?
What other outrage weighs upon my breast?
How could he, nonetheless, cite me before
that bench of heartless judges who, like owls,
keep singing at me a dirge of death by bullets,
unless he meant, with a calm master sentence,
to step into their circle like a god?
No, friend, he's gathering this night of clouds
about my head merely that, through its dark
siege, he may rise radiant like the Sun :

and this delight, truly, I cannot grudge him!

HOHENZOLLERN : But the Court Martial has, they
    say, passed sentence.

THE PRINCE OF HOMBURG : So I hear; yes; of death.

HOHENZOLLERN (*in amazement*) : You know
already?

THE PRINCE OF HOMBURG : Golz, who was there
    when the Court pronounced sentence,
gave me a full account.

HOHENZOLLERN : Well then, by God!
—this circumstance does not disturb you?

THE PRINCE OF HOMBURG : Me?
Not in the slightest.

HOHENZOLLERN : You are raving mad!
And what, pray, is your certainty founded on?

THE PRINCE OF HOMBURG : On what I feel he is.
    (*He stands up.*) Please, leave me! Why
must I torment myself with baseless doubts?
(*He has second thoughts, and sits down again—
A pause.*)
The Court was bound to pass sentence of death :
the law, by which it judges, lays that down.
But he,
before ever allowing such a judgment
to be enforced, and giving over to
the bullets, at the dropped handkerchief's sign,
this heart of mine which loves him loyally,—
he, before that, will open his own breast
and spatter his own blood about the dust.

HOHENZOLLERN : Well, Arthur, I assure you—

THE PRINCE OF HOMBURG (*refusing to listen*) : O my
    dear fellow!

HOHENZOLLERN : The Marshal—

THE PRINCE OF HOMBURG (*as before*) : Leave me,
    friend!

HOHENZOLLERN : Two words more! Listen!

If they too leave you untouched, I'll keep silence.
THE PRINCE OF HOMBURG (*turning to him again*):
You have heard, I know all.—Well, then? What
is it?
HOHENZOLLERN: The Marshal—it is most unusual
—at once
brought the death sentence to him at the Palace;
and he, instead of, as he is free to do
by law, granting you pardon,—he commanded
it should come up to him for signature.
THE PRINCE OF HOMBURG: No matter. You hear
what I say.
HOHENZOLLERN: No matter?
THE PRINCE OF HOMBURG: For signature?
HOHENZOLLERN: My oath on it. I assure you.
THE PRINCE OF HOMBURG: The sentence?—No! the
verdict—?
HOHENZOLLERN: The death sentence.
THE PRINCE OF HOMBURG:—Who told you this?
HOHENZOLLERN: He did; himself, the Marshal.
THE PRINCE OF HOMBURG: When?
HOHENZOLLERN: Just now.
THE PRINCE OF HOMBURG: As he came back from
the Chief?
HOHENZOLLERN: As he walked down the stairs
from the Chief's presence.—
He added, when he saw me taken aback,
that it was not yet hopeless, and tomorrow
is still a day on which to pardon you;
the pallor of his lips, though, gave the lie
to his own words, and said: 'But I fear, no!'
THE PRINCE OF HOMBURG (*rising to his feet*): He—
no!—he, in that heart of his, could be
revolving such unnatural decisions?
What? for a flaw the glass could hardly catch
within the diamond he has just accepted,

trample the giver into dust? A deed
that burns the Dey* of Algiers white, with wings
like the wings of the Cherubim, glittering silver,—
that graces Sardanapalus, and hurls up
to the right hand of God all Ancient Rome's
dynasty of tyrants, now made innocent
as babes who die upon their mothers' breasts?

HOHENZOLLERN (*who has also stood up*) : You must,
my friend, admit that it is true.

THE PRINCE OF HOMBURG : And the Field-marshal
kept silence, said nothing?

HOHENZOLLERN : What should he say?

THE PRINCE OF HOMBURG : O heaven! All my
hopes!

HOHENZOLLERN : Have you ever, knowingly or un-
awares,
done anything that went too near his pride?

THE PRINCE OF HOMBURG : Never!

HOHENZOLLERN : Think, recollect.

THE PRINCE OF HOMBURG : Never, by Heaven!
To me the shadow of his head was sacred.

HOHENZOLLERN : Arthur, do not be angry if I have
doubts.
Count Horn, the Ambassador of Sweden, came,
and it is said the object of his visit
had to do with the Princess of Orange.
A word, too, spoken by her aunt the Electress
in the Chief's ear disturbed him visibly;
rumour has it, the girl has chosen already.
Are you concerned in no way in this thing?

THE PRINCE OF HOMBURG : O God! What are you
saying?

HOHENZOLLERN : Are you? Are you?

* 'The titular appellation of the commanding officer
of the Janissaries of Algiers, who in 1710 deposed the
pasha, and became sole ruler'—O.E.D.

THE PRINCE OF HOMBURG : I am, friend; now it all
  comes clear to me;
the treaty it is, bearing me to destruction;
that it is not signed is my fault, because
the Princess has betrothed herself to me.

HOHENZOLLERN : You thoughtless fool! What have
  you done? How often
my loyal frankness warned you against this!

THE PRINCE OF HOMBURG : O friend! Help, save me,
  save me! I am lost.

HOHENZOLLERN : Yes, what way out is there from
  such a pass?—
Will you perhaps speak with her aunt the Electress?

THE PRINCE OF HOMBURG (*turning*) : Heh, guards
  there!

A CAVALRY TROOPER (*in the background*) : Here,
  Sir!

THE PRINCE OF HOMBURG : Call your Officer!—
  (*In haste he takes down a cloak from the wall,
  and puts on a plumed hat which is lying on the
  table.*)

HOHENZOLLERN (*helping him*) : The step, taken with
  skill, may bring you through.
—If only the Elector can conclude
peace with King Charles at the determined price,
his heart, you'll see, will soften towards you
and then, in a few hours, you will be free.

[*Enter the officer.*]

THE PRINCE OF HOMBURG : Stranz, I am subject to
  you as my guard!
Give me leave, on a matter that's most urgent,
to absent myself for an hour from this place.

STRANZ : Your Highness, you are not subject to
  me.

The orders that were issued to me say :
to let you freely go wherever you will.

THE PRINCE OF HOMBURG : Strange !—Does that mean I am not prisoner?

STRANZ : Forgive me, Sir !—Your word, too, is a fetter.

THE PRINCE OF HOMBURG (*moving to go*): Good ! it comes to the same !—So then, good-bye !

HOHENZOLLERN : The fetter follows the Prince, on his foot !

THE PRINCE OF HOMBURG : I am going to the palace, to my Aunt,
no further. Before long I shall be back.

All go.

Scene 2

The Electress's room.

Enter the Electress and Natalie.

THE ELECTRESS : Come now, my daughter; now ! Your hour is striking !
Count Gustav Horn, Swedish ambassador,
with his attendants, has just left the Palace;
there, in your Uncle's study, I see a light.
Put on your shawl, quick, slip across to him
at once, and see if you can save your friend.

[*They are about to go. Enter a lady-in-waiting.*]

THE LADY-IN-WAITING : Prince Homburg, gracious lady, is at the door !

Truly I hardly know—did I see right?

THE ELECTRESS (*in amazement*) : O God !

NATALIE : Himself?

THE ELECTRESS : Is he not, then, under arrest?

THE LADY-IN-WAITING : He's standing, in plumed hat and cloak, outside,

desperately, urgently beseeching audience.

THE ELECTRESS (*signifying refusal*) : The reckless rashness of it ! To break his word !

NATALIE : Who knows, under what pressure?

THE ELECTRESS : Let him enter. (*She sits down in a chair.*)

[*Enter the Prince of Homburg.*]

THE PRINCE OF HOMBURG : O my Mother ! (*He sinks down on his knees before her.*)

THE ELECTRESS : Prince ! What has brought you here?

THE PRINCE OF HOMBURG : O let me put my arms about your knees,

Mother !

THE ELECTRESS (*with suppressed emotion*) : Prince, you are prisoner, and come here !

Why do you heap new guilt upon the old?

THE PRINCE OF HOMBURG : Do you know what has happened to me?

THE ELECTRESS : I know all !

But what can I—powerless—do for you?

THE PRINCE OF HOMBURG : O Mother, you would not speak in that way

if Death were breaking round you, as now round me !

To me you appear gifted with strength from Heaven,

saviours !—you, this girl, your ladies—people

on all sides; I could cling about the neck
of the humblest ostler busied with your horses
and clutch him tight and beg him : 'Rescue me!'
I, alone of all on God's wide Earth,
am helpless—an outcast—and can do nothing!
THE ELECTRESS : You are beside yourself, changed!
    What has happened?
THE PRINCE OF HOMBURG : Ah! On the way that
    led me here to you
I saw the grave, lit by the torches, open,
which is tomorrow to receive my bones.
Look at these eyes now gazing at you—they are
to be shut in with night, this chest of mine
to be drilled through and through by murderous
    bullets.
Bespoke already, the windows on the market
with the view down upon the desolate drama;
and he, who today still, from the peak of life,
surveys the future as a wonder kingdom,
lies tomorrow in a stench between two close
boards, and of him a stone tells you : 'He was!'

[*The Princess, who till now has been standing some
way off, leaning on the shoulder of the lady-in-
waiting, at these words collapses over a table, and
weeps.*]

THE ELECTRESS : My son! If that is Heaven's will,
    then you
will arm yourself with courage and composure!
THE PRINCE OF HOMBURG : O Mother! God's world
    is so beautiful!
Do not, I beseech you, let me go down,
before the hour strikes, to those black shadows!
Suppose I *have* done wrong, and he insists
on punishment, why must it be the bullets?

Let him even strip me of my offices,
flatly cashier me—if that is the law—,
cut me off from the Army: God in Heaven!
since I have seen my grave, I simply want to live,
no longer asking whether it be with glory.
THE ELECTRESS: Stand up, my son; stand up!
    What have you said?
You should not be so shaken. Control yourself!
THE PRINCE OF HOMBURG: No, Aunt, not until you
    have pledged to me
that, with that footfall which may keep me living,
you'll go into his sovereign presence, begging.
Hedwig, your childhood friend, as she lay dying,
entrusted me to you at Homburg, saying:
'You be his mother, when I am no more.'
And kneeling at her bedside, deeply moved,
you bent over her hand and answered: 'He
shall be to me as if myself had borne him.'
Now—now I remind you of that promise!
Go, as if you yourself had borne me, and say:
'Mercy, I implore you, mercy! Set him free!'—
Ah! and come back to me and say: 'You are!'
THE ELECTRESS (*weeping*): My dear son, that—
    that is already done!
But all my supplications were in vain!
THE PRINCE OF HOMBURG: I give up every claim to
    happiness.
Natalie—do not forget to tell him
this—I no more aspire to; in my heart
all tenderness for her has been put out.
Free she is, like deer on the moors, once more:
free, as if I had never been, to give
herself with hand and mouth,—if to Charles
    Gustav,
King of the Swedes, she has my praise for this.
I shall go to my lands beside the Rhine:

there I shall build things up and pull things down
till the sweat pours from me, shall sow, shall reap
as though for wife and child, but live alone,
and after having reaped, yet again sow,
and chase life in a circle round and round
until at evening it sinks down and dies.

THE ELECTRESS : So! Only go back to your prison,
  now!—
that is the first requirement of my favour.

[*The Prince rises to his feet.*]

THE PRINCE OF HOMBURG (*turning to the Princess*) :
  You, poor sweet maiden, weeping! Today's sun
lights all your hopes the way into the grave!
Your young first feeling made its choice for me,
and, true as gold, your face tells me you never
will dedicate yourself to another man.
If I could comfort you—yes, but what comfort
have I, the poorest of the poor, to give?
Advice? Go to the Main Valley, that convent
and your Thurn cousin—and there, in the hills,
seek out some man-child, with fair hair like mine,
pay gold and silver for him, to your breast
press him close, and teach him to stammer 'Mother'
and when he has grown bigger, teach him then
the proper way to close dying men's eyes.—
That is the only happiness lies before you!

[*Natalie stands up and lays her hand on his.*]

NATALIE (*courageously and communicating
  courage*) : Go now, young hero, back into your
  prison
and, on your way, look once again, serenely
at the grave they are opening for you!

94

It is no darker, not a whit more gaping
than what you faced a thousand times in battle.
I, meanwhile, faithful to you till death,
will brave our Uncle with a plea for you :
it may be given me to touch his heart
and from all heaviness to set you free.

[*A silence. The Prince stands lost in gazing at her,
with his hands folded over his breast.*]

THE PRINCE OF HOMBURG : Had you two wings,
    maiden, upon your shoulders,
truly I would believe you were an angel !—
O God, have I heard right? You speak for me?
—Where, then, in you, has the quiver of speech lain
at rest, dear child, till today, that you dare
to face the Sovereign in such a cause?—
O light of hope, suddenly quickening me !
NATALIE : God will hand me the arrows that strike
    home !—
But if the Elector cannot—cannot—alter
the sentence of the law, then, well ! then you will
bravely submit yourself to him, the brave :
one who in life has gained a thousand victories
will rise to be a victor even in death !
THE ELECTRESS : Go ! The favouring time is
    slipping by.
THE PRINCE OF HOMBURG : Now—O may all the
    Saints be there to shield you !
Farewell ! Farewell ! And, whatever it be,
send me, in your mercy, some sign of the outcome.

They all go.

ACT FOUR

Scene 1

The Elector's room.

The Elector stands, holding some papers, by a desk on which there are candles.

Natalie enters by the middle door, and falls on her knees at some distance from him.

NATALIE (*kneeling*): My noble Uncle, Friedrich of the Marches!

THE ELECTOR (*putting the papers from him*): Natalie! (*He moves to raise her up.*)

NATALIE: No, no!

THE ELECTOR: What is your wish, love?

NATALIE: Down in the dust at your feet, as is right,
to beg of you mercy for Cousin Homburg!
I do not ask that he be kept for me—
my heart longs for him and to you avows it;
I do not ask that he be kept for me—
whom he chooses let her be his wife;
Dear Uncle, I ask only, that he be there,
his own, upstanding, free and independent,
—there, like some flower whose mere life makes me glad:
this I do implore you, my lord and friend,—
and know that, when I plead so, you will listen.

THE ELECTOR (*raising her up*): My little daughter! What is this you have uttered?
—Are you aware of the crime Cousin Homburg has just committed?

NATALIE: O dear Uncle!

THE ELECTOR : Well?
Did he commit no crime?
NATALIE : O, but that stumble—fair-haired with
 blue eyes—
which, before he had time to stammer 'Please—!'
forgiveness should have raised up from the ground,
you will not, surely, kick out of your path!
Him you took to your heart for his Mother's sake,
exclaiming : 'Come, don't cry! You are as dear
to me—as dear as loyalty itself!'
What was it, as the armies clashed, if not
zeal for your name's honour, that tempted him
to break through the constrictions of the Law?
and, having like a youth broken it, ah!
how like a man he went straight at the dragon!
First, as victor, to crown him, then behead him
—that is not what History expects of you :
that, dear Uncle, would be so sublime
as to be easily called almost inhuman—
and God has made nothing gentler than you.
THE ELECTOR : My sweet child! Look, suppose I
 were a tyrant,
your words, I feel sharply, would have already
melted the heart behind the iron ribs.
But now I ask you what I ask myself :
to over-ride the Court's sentence have I
the right? What would the consequences be?
NATALIE : For whom? For you?
THE ELECTOR : For me; no!—What? For me!
Do you know nothing, girl, higher than me?
Have you no knowledge of a holy thing
whose name, in the field, is The Fatherland?
NATALIE : O Sir! But what endangers it? This
 Fatherland
will not go under, splintered into fragments
at one blow by this move of mercy in you.

Rather, what you, brought up in the field, call
disorder—I mean, in this case by authority
to tear up the act and sentence of the judges—
to me appears plainly as the fairest order.
Military law—this I well know—must reign,
but so, beside it, must the gracious feelings.
The Fatherland, founded for us by you,
stands as a safe stronghold, my noble Uncle:
it will endure more and quite other storms,
for sure, than this unbidden victory;
superbly it will build on, through the future
spread wide, in your descendants' hands gain
    beauty
—a faëry wealth of battlements and pinnacles—
to its friends' wonder and the terror of all foes:
it does not need this mortar—cold and dead,
made of a friend's blood—to survive beyond
my Uncle's autumn, glorious with peace.

THE ELECTOR: Does Cousin Homburg share this
    view?

NATALIE: Cousin Homburg?

THE ELECTOR: Does *he* think it is all one to the
    Fatherland
whether despotic power or the law reigns?

NATALIE: Ah, that poor boy!

THE ELECTOR: Well?

NATALIE: Ah, my dear dear Uncle!
To that I have no answer, except tears.

THE ELECTOR (*surprised*): But why, my little
    daughter? What has happened?

NATALIE (*shuddering*): He thinks of nothing, now,
    but the one thing: Rescue!
The gun-barrels raised to the guards' shoulders
to him appear so hideous—surprised, stunned,
every wish except simply to live
is silent in him: the whole realm of the Marches

could sink in lightning and thunder before his eyes,
and he would not ask: 'What is happening?'
—Ah, what a hero's heart you have slashed down!
  (*She turns away and weeps.*)
THE ELECTOR (*in extreme amazement*): Dearest
  Natalie, no! That is surely
quite impossible?!—He, begging for mercy?
NATALIE: Ah, if only you had never, never condemned him!
THE ELECTOR: No, tell me: he begs for mercy?—
  God in Heaven,
what's happened, my dear child? Why are you
  crying?
You spoke with him? Tell me all! You've spoken
  with him?
NATALIE (*leaning on his breast*): Just now—up in
  my Aunt's apartments,
to which, in cloak and plumed hat, he has stolen
—imagine!—under cover of the twilight;
timid, subdued, furtive—no dignity—
an unsavoury, lamentable sight!
Of those whom History glorifies as its heroes
none, I thought, could ever have sunk so low.
I—look—am a woman and would shrink
back from a worm that came too near my heel;
and yet death in the shape of a fell lion
would not find me so crushed, so stripped of all
dignity, demeaned, utterly unheroic!
—Ah! what is human greatness, human glory!
THE ELECTOR (*taken aback*): Well, by the God of
  Heaven and of Earth,
take courage, child; in that case he is free!
NATALIE: What, my Lord, Your Highness?
THE ELECTOR: He is pardoned!—
I will at once write to him what he needs.
NATALIE: O dearest! Is it really true?

THE ELECTOR : You heard!

NATALIE : He is to be forgiven? not now to die?

THE ELECTOR : You have my oath! I swear it! On
what shall I
take stand against the view of such a soldier?
In my inmost heart, as I am sure you know,
I set the highest value on what he feels;
if he can think the sentence unjust, I
cashier the Regulations : he is free!—(*He fetches a
chair for her.*)
Will you, please, for a moment, sit you down? (*He
goes to the desk, sits down and writes.*)

[*A silence.*]

NATALIE (*to herself*) : Ah, heart, why do you knock
so at your house?

THE ELECTOR (*as he writes*) : The Prince is in the
palace still?

NATALIE : Forgive me!
I should have said : he went back to his prison.

[*The Elector finishes the letter, seals it, and comes
over with it to the Princess again.*]

THE ELECTOR : My little daughter, my little niece,
was weeping!
And I, who am entrusted with her happiness,
must needs cloud the heaven of her sweet eyes! (*He
puts his arm about her.*)
Would you like to carry the letter to him
yourself?

NATALIE : What? To the City Hall?

THE ELECTOR (*pressing the letter into her hand*) :
Why not?—
Heh! Heyducks there!

[Several heyducks appear.]

Have the carriage brought!
   The Princess
has business with General the Prince of Homburg!

[The heyducks go.]

So, at once, he can thank you for his life. (*He embraces her.*)
My dear child, am I back in favour with you?
NATALIE (*after a pause*): What has aroused your graciousness so suddenly,
my Lord, I do not know and do not ask.
But one thing, look, I feel in my heart: you
will not ignobly make a mock of me.
Whatever be the content of the letter,
I believe it will save him—and I thank you! (*She kisses his hand.*)
THE ELECTOR: Of course, my little daughter, of course! Just as
surely as that is Cousin Homburg's wish.

They go.

Scene 2

The Princess's room.

Enter Princess Natalie.—She is followed by two Ladies-in-Waiting, then by Count Reuss.

NATALIE (*in haste*): What brings you here, Count?
   —From my Regiment?

Is the thing urgent? Can I hear it tomorrow?
COUNT REUSS (*holding out to her a document*):
This is from Colonel Kottwitz, gracious Lady.
NATALIE: Quick! Give it me! What's in it? (*She
opens it.*)
COUNT REUSS: A petition
—bold, as you see, but full of deep respect—
addressed to his Serene Highness the Sovereign
in favour of our Chief the Prince of Homburg.
NATALIE (*reading*): 'Address of Humble Supplica-
tion. From
the Regiment of the Princess of Orange.'

[*A pause.*]

By whose hand is it drawn up, this petition?
COUNT REUSS: By—as the faltering of the handwriting
shows at a glance—Colonel Kottwitz himself.—
Besides, his noble name stands at the head.
NATALIE: Whose are the thirty signatures that
follow?
COUNT REUSS: All the officers, by rank and section.
NATALIE: And I—this document now comes to
me—?
COUNT REUSS: Most humbly, Ma'am, to ask if you
are willing
to fill the first place, which has been left open,
with your name, as the Colonel of the Regiment.

[*A pause.*]

NATALIE: The Prince, I hear—My noble Cousin
has,
it seems, been pardoned by the Sovereign
unasked; and if so, such a step is needless.

COUNT REUSS (*delighted*): What? Truly?

NATALIE: Nonetheless, I will not hold
back from a document which, used with wisdom,
may weigh in the balance of our Sovereign's judgment—
will perhaps, for presenting the decision,
be welcome to him; and, as you wish, herewith
I place myself, with my name, at your head. (*She
goes and sits down to write.*)

COUNT REUSS: You will have earned our eager
gratitude.

NATALIE (*turning again to him*): I find only *my*
Regiment here, Count Reuss!—
Why do I not see Bomsdorf's Cuirassiers
and the Dragoons of Götz and Anhalt-Pless?

COUNT REUSS: Not, as perhaps you fear, because
their hearts
beat for him more sluggishly than our own!—
It falls unluckily for our petition
that Kottwitz is encamped at Arnstein, some
distance away, cut off from all these other
regiments quartered here close by this town.
The document was not free to deploy
its strength easily and safely in all directions.

NATALIE: Does not that, all the same, make it
weigh light?—
Count, are you sure that, if you had the chance
and spoke to all the gentlemen gathered here,
they also would subscribe to the petition?

COUNT REUSS: Here in the town, my Lady?—to a
man!
All the Cavalry—every man would pledge
himself by name; and by God, I believe
we could collect signatures, and not fail,
through the whole of the Army of the
Marches.

NATALIE (*after a pause*) : Why do you not send out your officers

to do precisely that, here, in the camp?

COUNT REUSS : Forgive me, but—the Colonel has said no :

he was unwilling, he said, to do anything

that might seem to deserve an ugly name.

NATALIE : What a strange man ! now bold, now hesitant !—

Luckily—I was forgetting !—the Elector,

hard pressed by other business, has deputed

me to transmit to Kottwitz, whose quarters

there are cramped, the order forthwith to march here.

I'll sit down now at once and write it out. (*She sits down again, and writes.*)

COUNT REUSS : By Heaven, Ma'am, a stroke of fortune ! Nothing

could be more favourable for our petition !

NATALIE (*still writing*) : Use it, my Lord Count Reuss, as best you can. (*She finishes, applies her seal and again stands up.*)

But first . . . this order—understand !—will stay

in your portfolio : you are not to go

to Arnstein with it, not hand it to Kottwitz,

till I have given you more precise instructions. (*She hands him the order.*)

[*Enter a heyduck.*]

THE HEYDUCK : The carriage, Ma'am, by the Sovereign's command,

stands ready in the courtyard, waiting for you.

NATALIE : Have it brought to the door. I am coming down.

[*The heyduck goes out. A pause, during which, deep in thought, she goes to the table and picks up her gloves.*]

Would you, Count, be willing to accompany me
to the Prince of Homburg, with whom I have to
    speak?
COUNT REUSS : My lady, truly, this is a great
    honour! (*Offers her his arm.*)
NATALIE (*to the ladies-in-waiting*) : Follow us,
    friends.—Perhaps when I am there
I shall decide finally about the order.

All go.

Scene 3

The Prince's prison quarters.

The Prince hangs his hat up on the wall, and sinks down listlessly on a cushion that is lying on the floor.

THE PRINCE OF HOMBURG : The Dervishes say life
    is a journey,
and a short one. They are right! From six feet
above the earth to six feet underneath it.
I for a moment will sink down half-way!
He who today has his head still on his shoulders
tomorrow dangles it, swaying, from his trunk,
and next day it lies level with his heels.
They do say that out there also a sun

shines, and on yet more glowing fields than here :
I believe that; a pity, only, that the eye,
which should be gazing on that glory, rots.

[*Enter Princess Natalie, on the arm of Count Reuss.
The ladies-in-waiting follow. They are preceded by
a runner with a torch.*]

THE RUNNER : My Lord, her Highness the Princess
    of Orange !
THE PRINCE OF HOMBURG (*rising*) : Natalie !
THE RUNNER : She is here, herself, already.
NATALIE (*bowing to the Count*) : Leave us, please,
    for a few moments, alone.

[*Count Reuss and the runner go.*]

THE PRINCE OF HOMBURG : My dear sweet Lady !
NATALIE : Good, beloved Cousin !
THE PRINCE OF HOMBURG (*leading her forward*) :
    Well, tell me ! What news? Speak ! How do I
    stand?
NATALIE : Well. All's well. As I said to you just
    now,
you are pardoned, you are free; here is a letter
written by his own hand, confirming it.
THE PRINCE OF HOMBURG : It is not possible ! No !
    It is a dream !
NATALIE : Read ! Read the letter ! Then you'll see
    the truth.
THE PRINCE OF HOMBURG (*reading*) : 'My Prince of
    Homburg,—When I set you in prison
because of your attack, delivered too soon,
I believed I was doing nothing but
my duty; I counted on your own approval.
If you think an injustice has been done you,

I beg you, now tell me so in two words—
and I at once will send you back your sword.'

[*The Princess turns pale. A pause.—The Prince
looks at her, questioningly.*]

NATALIE (*expressing sudden joy*) : Well now, there
    it stands ! Just two words needed—!
O sweet, beloved friend ! (*She presses his hand.*)
THE PRINCE OF HOMBURG : My dear, sweet girl !
NATALIE : O what a happy hour has risen for me !—
Here, take this, here's the pen ; take it, and
write !
THE PRINCE OF HOMBURG : And here, the signature?
NATALIE : The F ; his sign !—
O Bork ! you too, rejoice with me ! O, his kindness
is infinite, I knew it, like the sea.
Bring a chair, quickly, he must write at once.
THE PRINCE OF HOMBURG : He says, if I, if in my
    view—
NATALIE (*interrupting*) : Of course !
Be quick ! Sit down ! I will dictate your answer.
(*She makes him sit down on a chair.*)
THE PRINCE OF HOMBURG : I wish to read the letter
    through again.
NATALIE (*seizing the letter out of his hand*) : Why?
    —Did you not see
already in the precincts of the Minster
the grave with open jaws gaping at you?—
Time is pressing. Sit down now, and write !
THE PRINCE OF HOMBURG (*with a smile*) : But, really,
    you describe it as though it were
a panther, ready to spring and claw me down.
(*He sits down again, and picks up a pen.*)
NATALIE (*turning away, in tears*) : Write, if you do
    not mean to make me angry !

[*The Prince rings for a servant; the servant appears.*]

THE PRINCE OF HOMBURG : Bring us paper and ink, wax and the seal!

[*The servant fetches these things, and goes. The Prince writes. A silence. The Prince tears up the letter he has begun and throws it under the table.*]

A stupid opening. (*He takes another sheet of paper.*)
NATALIE (*picking up the letter*) : Why? What did you say?—
My God, but that is good; it's excellent!
THE PRINCE OF HOMBURG (*muttering*) : Pah!—
Style of a cringer, not a prince.—
I must think out a different turn of phrase.

[*Silence. He reaches for the Elector's letter, which the Princess has in her hand.*]

What does he say, exactly, in the letter?
NATALIE (*withholding it*) : Nothing, nothing at all!
THE PRINCE OF HOMBURG : Give it to me!
NATALIE : You've read it all!
THE PRINCE OF HOMBURG (*seizing it*) : And if I have?—I only
want to see what tone I ought to take. (*He unfolds it and reads it.*)
NATALIE (*to herself*) : O God, Lord of the world! Now he is doomed!
THE PRINCE OF HOMBURG (*disturbed*) : Look at this! As I live, strange—very strange!
You read the passage properly?
NATALIE : No—Which?

THE PRINCE OF HOMBURG : He calls on me myself
for the decision !

NATALIE : Of course !

THE PRINCE OF HOMBURG : Truly brave that is !
truly fine !
truly the way a great heart must behave.

NATALIE : O friend, his magnanimity has no limits !
—But now you, too, do what you have to do
and write as he desires; you see, the pretext,
the outward form only, is what is needed :
soon as he has your two words in his hands,
in a flash the whole strife is over !

THE PRINCE OF HOMBURG (*laying the letter down*) :
No, love !
I shall defer this thing until tomorrow.

NATALIE : Incomprehensible man ! What is this
change?
Why? To what end?

THE PRINCE OF HOMBURG (*jumping to his feet*) : I
beg you, do not ask !
You have not caught the meaning of the letter.
That he has wronged me,—as I am here required,
I cannot write that to him; if you force me
to send to him an answer of that temper,
by God ! then I shall put : 'You are just to me.'
(*He sits down again at the table, with folded arms,
and stares at the letter.*)

NATALIE (*pale*) : You madman ! What is this that
you have said? (*Deeply moved, she bends over
him.*)

THE PRINCE OF HOMBURG (*pressing her hand*) :
Quiet, one moment ! I think—

NATALIE : What did you say?

THE PRINCE OF HOMBURG : I shall soon know how I
must write.

NATALIE (*desperately*) : Homburg !

THE PRINCE OF HOMBURG : I'm listening. What is
it?

NATALIE : Dearest friend!
I praise the impulse which has gripped your heart;
but this I swear to you : they have their orders—
the regiment that tomorrow, when you are sunk,
will fire, above your mound, the last salute.
If you, noble as you are, cannot oppose
the Court's judgment—will not, to have it lifted,
do what he, in this letter, asks of you—,
I tell you, as things stand, he will then act with
sublime severity and let the sentence
be executed, pitilessly, tomorrow!

THE PRINCE OF HOMBURG (*who is now writing*) : No
matter!

NATALIE : No matter?

THE PRINCE OF HOMBURG : Let *him* act as he may;
it becomes *me* to proceed as I ought!

NATALIE (*frightened, moving close to him*) : Cruel
man, I believe, you have been writing?

THE PRINCE OF HOMBURG (*finishing*) : 'Homburg;
given at Fehrbellin; the 12th—'
There, done already.—Franz! (*He puts the letter
in an envelope and seals it.*)

NATALIE : O God in Heaven!

THE PRINCE OF HOMBURG : Take this letter to the
Palace, to my Sovereign!

[*The servant goes.*]

When he so nobly stands before me, I
will not, as one ignoble, stand against him!
Guilt, and it is grave guilt, weighs on my breast,
as I now see; if he cannot pardon me
unless I will dispute that guilt with him,
I prefer to know nothing of his mercy.

NATALIE (*kissing him*) : Receive this kiss!—And if,
    after this, twelve
bullets drilled you to dust, I could not hold from
exulting, weeping, crying aloud 'I love you'.
—But meanwhile, if you follow your own heart,
I have the right, surely, to follow mine.
—Count Reuss.

[*The runner throws open the door; the Count
enters.*]

COUNT REUSS : Here!
NATALIE : Rush now with your letter
to Arnstein, take it straight to Colonel Kottwitz!
The Regiment will strike camp, at the Sovereign's
command; by midnight I expect it here!

All (except the Prince) go.

ACT FIVE

Scene 1

A room in the Palace.

The Elector enters, half-undressed, from the next room; he is followed by Count Truchss, Count Hohenzollern and Captain von der Golz. Pages, with lights.

THE ELECTOR : Kottwitz? With the Princess's Own Dragoons?
Here in the town?
COUNT TRUCHSS (*opening a window*): Yes, Your Highness, Sir!
Marched in, and drawn up before the Palace .
THE ELECTOR : Well?—Will you gentlemen solve me this riddle?
—Who sent for him?
HOHENZOLLERN : I do not know, my Sovereign.
THE ELECTOR : The station I assigned him is called Arnstein!—
Quick! One of you, go down, and fetch him here!
GOLZ : Sir, he will soon present himself before you!
THE ELECTOR : Where is he?
GOLZ : At the Rathaus, so I hear,
where the whole body of senior officers
serving your princely house is now assembled.
THE ELECTOR : Why? For what purpose?
HOHENZOLLERN : That I do not know.
COUNT TRUCHSS : My Lord Prince and Commander, have we leave
to withdraw for a while and go there too?
THE ELECTOR : Where? to the Rathaus?
HOHENZOLLERN : Yes, Sir, the Officers' meeting.
We gave our word that we would join them there.

112

THE ELECTOR (*after a short pause*) : You are
excused.
GOLZ : Come, worthy gentlemen !

[*The officers go.*]

THE ELECTOR : Odd.—Suppose, now, I were the
Dey of Tunis,
at an ambiguous event like this
I'd raise the alarm :
I'd lay the silken cord upon my table,
have the door blocked close with spiked barricades,
and mass before it cannons and howitzers.
But, seeing that it's Hans Kottwitz of Priegnitz
who takes the law into his hands and braves me,
I shall conduct myself like a man of the Marches :
lay hold of one of those three locks of hair
to be seen on his skull, still, glancing silver,
and lead him by it, him and his twelve squadrons
to Arnstein, to his headquarters, back again.
Why should one wake the town out of its sleep?
(*After going over to the window again for a
moment, he walks to the table, and rings.*)

[*Enter two servants.*]

Run down and ask, as though for yourself, what
is happening at the Stadthaus.
FIRST SERVANT : At once, my Lord ! (*He goes.*)
THE ELECTOR (*to the other*) : But you, stay : go in
there and fetch my clothes !

[*The second servant goes and fetches them; the
Elector puts them on, and adds his princely in-
signia. Enter Field-marshal Dörfling.*]
DÖRFLING : Rebellion, my Sovereign !

THE ELECTOR (*still busy, dressing*) : Quiet, quiet!—
This is a thing I hate, as you well know :
men coming into my room, unannounced!
—What do you want?
DÖRFLING : Sir, an event—forgive me!—
of the utmost gravity has brought me here.
Colonel Kottwitz has marched up, without orders,
into the town; some hundred Officers
are gathered about him in the Rittersaal;
a document is going the round of them,
which trespasses on your authority.
THE ELECTOR : Already known to me!—What will
    it be,
unless a move in favour of the Prince,
whom the clear law has sentenced to be shot?
DÖRFLING : It is! By the most high God! You have
    guessed it!
THE ELECTOR : Quite so!—That shows that my
    heart is with them.
DÖRFLING : I hear their mad plan was to face you
    with it
here in the Palace, before today is out,
and if, with unappeased severity,
you insist on the sentence,—this I scarcely
dare to tell you!—by force to set him free.
THE ELECTOR (*frowning*) : Who is it, told you
that?
DÖRFLING : Who told me that?
Someone whom you can trust—my Lady Retzow,
a cousin of my wife's. She dined this evening
at her uncle's—the Constable of Retzow—
and officers, just in from the camp,
spoke openly of the insolent proposal.
THE ELECTOR : I'll have that from a man, ere I'll
    believe it!
My boot shall bar the way to the Prince—simply

with that I'll guard him safe from these young
    heroes!
DÖRFLING : Sir, I implore you, if it is in fact
your will to grant the Prince your gracious pardon,
do it, before some hideous step is taken!
Every army—remember—loves its heroes;
do not allow this spark, now glowing through it,
to kindle a gorging, unquenchable fire.
Kottwitz and those he has gathered do not know,
yet, that I in my loyalty have warned you;
send, before they appear, the Prince's sword
back to him—after all he has deserved it.
By doing so you will give History
one more great deed, one misdeed less, to tell.
THE ELECTOR : First I would have to consult with
    the Prince,
whom arbitrary power, as you know,
did not imprison and may not set free.—
I wish to speak with those gentlemen when they
    come.
DÖRFLING *(to himself)* : Damnation!—He has
armour against all arrows.

[*Enter two heyducks, one of them holds a letter
in his hand.*]

FIRST HEYDUCK : Colonels Kottwitz and Hennings,
    Count Truchss and others
request an audience.
THE ELECTOR *(to the other heyduck, as he takes the
    letter)* :
From the Prince of Homburg?
SECOND HEYDUCK : Yes, Your Highness, my Lord.
THE ELECTOR : Who gave it you?
SECOND HEYDUCK : The Swiss Guard, on duty at
    the door,

who had it from the hand of the Prince's huntsman.

[*The Elector goes to the table, stands there, and reads the letter. When he has finished, he turns and calls one of the pages.*]

THE ELECTOR : Prittwitz! Go and fetch me the death sentence!
—And the safe-conduct for the Count von Horn, the Swedish envoy; I require that too.

[*The page goes. To the first heyduck.*]

Kottwitz, and his attendants,—show 'em in!

[*Enter Colonel Kottwitz and Colonel Hennings, Count Truchss, Counts Hohenzollern and Sparren, Count Reuss, Captains von der Golz and Stranz, and more colonels and other officers.*]

COLONEL KOTTWITZ (*holding the petition*): My revered Sovereign, I beg permission
that, in the name of the whole Army, I may
humbly present to you this Document.
THE ELECTOR : Kottwitz, before I take it, tell me this :
who sent for you to come here, to this town?
KOTTWITZ (*staring at him*): With the Dragoons, Sir?
THE ELECTOR : With the Regiment!
Arnstein is the station I assigned you.
KOTTWITZ : Sir, I was summoned here by your own orders.
THE ELECTOR : What?—Show me the orders.
KOTTWITZ : Here they are, Sir.

THE ELECTOR (*reading*): 'Natalie; given at Fehrbellin;
on behalf of my Sovereign Uncle, Friedrich.'
KOTTWITZ: By God, my Lord Prince, I will not
suppose
the orders are unknown to you?
THE ELECTOR: No! no! Do not
misunderstand.—Who handed you the orders?
KOTTWITZ: Count Reuss!
THE ELECTOR (*after a moment's pause*): On th'
contrary, you are most welcome!
For General Homburg, whom the law has
sentenced,
you are appointed, you and your twelve squadrons,
tomorrow to perform the ultimate honours.
KOTTWITZ (*dismayed*): What, your Highness?
THE ELECTOR (*giving him back the orders*): Is the
Regiment standing
before the palace, still, in the night and mist?
KOTTWITZ: The night, forgive me—
THE ELECTOR: Why has it not turned in?
KOTTWITZ: My prince, it has turned in; as you
commanded,
it has gone into quarters in the town.
THE ELECTOR (*going to the window again*): What?
two minutes ago was it—? Well, by Heaven!
you've lost no time—already found your stabling!—
so much the better! Once more, you are welcome!
What brings you up here, tell me? What is new?
KOTTWITZ: Sir, this petition from your loyal Army.
THE ELECTOR: Give!
KOTTWITZ: But the word that has escaped your
lips
just now, dashes my hopes all to the ground.
THE ELECTOR: Another word can raise them up
again. (*He begins to read.*)

'Petition, that the supreme mercy be extended
to our Commander, under capital sentence :
to General Prince Friedrich Hessen–Homburg.' (*To
the officers.*)
A noble name, gentlemen ! Not unworthy
that you should intercede for it in such numbers !
(*He looks at the document again.*)
The petition is drawn up by whom?
KOTTWITZ : By me.
THE ELECTOR : The Prince has been informed of
what is in it?
KOTTWITZ : No, no, that is the last thing ! It has
been
considered and completed among ourselves.
THE ELECTOR : Allow me, please, your patience for
a moment. (*He goes to the table, and reads the
document through.*)

[*A long silence.*]

Hm ! This is singular !—You, old warrior,
defend the Prince's action? justify his
launching the attack on Wrangel without orders?
KOTTWITZ : Yes, Your Highness, Sir; Kottwitz does
that !
THE ELECTOR : During the battle, that was not your
view.
KOTTWITZ : Sir, I had not then grasped the way
things stood !
I ought to have submitted calmly to
the Prince, who understands war very well.
The Swedes were wavering on their left flank
and, on their right, were bringing up support;
if he had waited, they would have had time
to make a stand again, in the ravines,
and never would you then have won the battle.

118

THE ELECTOR : I see !—It pleases you to put it so.
I had already sent out Colonel Hennings
with orders to attack, take and destroy
the Swedish bridgehead covering Wrangel's rear.
Had you not disobeyed my orders, Hennings
would have succeeded—in two hours set the
    bridges
on fire, planted his men along the Rhyn—,
and Wrangel's forces would have been, to a man,
cut to bits in the rough ground and morasses.
KOTTWITZ : It may suit bunglers, it is not like you
to insist on Destiny's highest garland only :
till today you have taken what was going.
The dragon that was laying waste your Marches
has been sent packing with a bloody head :
what more could you expect from one day's work ?
What harm is done if he, for two weeks longer,
lies winded on the sand and licks his wounds ?
We have now learnt the art of beating him
and are on fire to try it out again :
let us meet Wrangel once more, chest to chest,
sternly,—and you will see the business finished :
him and his whole power hurled into the Baltic !
Rome, Sir, was not built in a single day.
THE ELECTOR : And with what right, fool, do you
    hope for that
when, in the battle chariot, any manjack
may freely snatch the reins out of my hand ?
Do you think Fortune will, as just now, always
reward the disobedient with a garland ?
I do not want a by-blow victory,
rolled me from under a hedge ! I mean to uphold
the Law, that is the Mother of my Crown
and bears me a whole race of victories !
KOTTWITZ : My Lord, the Law, the highest and the
    noblest,

which ought to work in the hearts of your com-
    manders,—
that Law is not the letter of your will :
it is the Fatherland, it is the Crown :
you, yourself, whose head wears it, are nought else !
What, I ask, does it matter by what rules
the enemy is beaten,—provided that
he does, with all his colours, sink before you?
The rule that beats him—that rule is the highest !
This Army, which hangs on you, glowing,—will
    you
take it and turn it into a tool, like
the sword dangling dead at your gold belt?
It was a spirit foreign to the stars,
the poorest spirit, first taught you such a lesson !
—the bad, short-sighted statecraft which, because
    of
some case where feeling proves to have gone wrong,
forgets ten others in which feeling only
has saved the day, for feeling alone could !
Has it been for reward—in money or honour—
that I have shed my blood for you in battle?
God forbid ! It is too good for that !
Look ! all my joy, all my delight I have chosen
—of myself, freely, in stillness, independent—
to seek in *your* excellence and magnificence
and in the glory and growth of your great
name !
That is the pay my heart sold itself for !
Suppose that now, for this unordered victory,
you were to break the Prince's staff,—and I
tomorrow, somewhere between field and forest
shepherding my squadrons, were to stumble
on Victory, again unordered :
by God, I'd be a menial if I
did not, smartly, repeat the Prince's action.

And if, law-book in hand, you said to me :
'Kottwitz, you've forfeited your head!', then *I'd*
  say :
I knew that, Sir; so take it, here it is;
when an oath bound me, skin and hair and all,
to your Crown, I did not keep back the head,—
and nothing could I give you that was not yours !
THE ELECTOR : Against you, extraordinary old man,
I shall never win. Those words of yours,
placed with an orator's cunning, dazzle me—
already, as you know, devoted to you.
So, to end the quarrel, I call in counsel,
who shall conduct my case. (*He rings.*)

[*Enter a servant.*]

The Prince of Homburg—
let him be brought out of the prison, here !

[*Exit the servant.*]

He will teach you, I can assure you, what
discipline and obedience is ! At least
I have a letter from him that rings quite
different from that shaky doctrine of Liberty
you, like a boy, have set forth to me here. (*He goes
  to the table again, and reads.*)
KOTTWITZ : Sends for whom?—Calls in—whom?
COLONEL HENNINGS : The Prince himself?
COUNT TRUCHSS : No, impossible !

[*The officers, disturbed, huddle together and
mutter among themselves.*]

THE ELECTOR : From whom is this, this second
  document?

HOHENZOLLERN : From me, my Lord !

THE ELECTOR (*reading*) : 'Proof that the Elector Friedrich

himself was cause of the Prince's . . .' Well, by Heaven !

I call that cool !

What? The responsibility for this wanton

misconduct in the battle you place on me?

HOHENZOLLERN : On you, my Sovereign; yes, I, Hohenzollern !

THE ELECTOR : Why, by God, this surpasses any fable !

One of you proves me that he did no wrong,

the other that the wrong-doer was I !—

What evidence will you bring for such a statement?

HOHENZOLLERN : O Sir, your Highness will not have forgotten

that night when we all came upon the Prince

sunk in sleep in the garden, beneath the plane-trees :

dreaming, he must have been, of the morrow's victory—

he held a wreath of laurel in his hand.

You, to have quick proof of his deepest heart,

took the wreath from him,—with a smile you twined

about its leaves the chain from your own neck,

and handed wreath and chain, so interwoven,

to the young Princess, to your noble niece,

The Prince, at this vision of wonder, stands

up, all blushing : objects so sweet, and by

so fair a hand offered, he longs to take.

But you, drawing the Princess backwards, hastily

escape him; the doors open to receive you;

maiden and chain and laurel wreath all vanish,

and he remains—with a glove in his hand,

snatched by him, he himself knows not from
   whom—
left alone, in the bosom of midnight.
THE ELECTOR : What glove was that?
HOHENZOLLERN : Sir, hear me to the end!—
The thing was only sport; and yet how much
it meant to him, this I was soon to learn.
For when, as though casually, I slip
out to him through the lower garden gate
and wake him—when he can collect his wits—,
the memory of it pours joy over him;
you cannot imagine anything more moving!
At once he tells me, to the smallest detail,
the whole event, as though it were a dream—
never had he had so bright a dream;
and a firm faith builds itself up in him
that Heaven has here given him a sign :
everything his spirit has just seen
—maiden and laurel wreath and chain of honour—
God will, on the next day of battle, grant him.
THE ELECTOR : Hm! Remarkable!—And the
   glove—? was—?
HOHENZOLLERN : Yes—
That part of the dream—being there, embodied—
at once demolishes and confirms his faith.
First of all, with wide eyes, he stares at it :
the colour, white; and, from its fashion, clearly
a lady's glove—And yet, because that night
he has spoken with no lady in the garden
from whom he could have taken it,—then, when I
break across his imaginings and fetch him
up to the Palace, to attend Battle Orders,
he forgets what he cannot understand
and, absently, sticks the glove in his jacket.
THE ELECTOR : Well? What then?
HOHENZOLLERN : Then he proceeds to the palace

with book and pencil, piously attentive
to hear the Marshal read the plan of battle :
almost at once the Electress and the Princess
appear in the Herrensaal, dressed for their journey.
But who can measure the wild amazement
that grips him, when the Princess searches for
the glove which he has stuffed into his jacket?
The Marshal more than once calls him by name :
'Lord Prince of Homburg !'—'Marshal, at your
    service,'
he answers, struggling to collect his wits;
but, quite shut in by his own wonder—Heaven's
thunderbolt might have fallen, and he still—(*He
    hesitates.*)

THE ELECTOR : Was the glove the Princess's?

HOHENZOLLERN : Yes, of course.

[*The Elector falls into deep thought.*]

HOHENZOLLERN (*resuming*) : He is a stone : there—
    it is true—he stands
pencil in hand, apparently alive;
but all perception in him is extinguished,
as though by magic. Not until the morning,
when already the guns are thundering,
does he came back to life; and then he asks me :
'Tell me, my dear fellow, what was it Dörfling
had to say about me, at Battle Orders?'

DÖRFLING : Sir, it is true : I can endorse that story !
The Prince—yes, I remember—took in not
one word. I have often seen him absent-minded :
not, till that day, right outside his own body.

THE ELECTOR : And now, if I have understood so
    far,
you have been building up to this conclusion :
Had I not played with that young dreamer's plight,

treacherously, he would still have done no wrong:
not been absent-minded at Battle Orders,
not insubordinate during the battle.
Well?—Well?—Is that your meaning?

HOHENZOLLERN : Sir,
I leave it now to you, to draw conclusions.

THE ELECTOR : A dolt is what you are! Half-wit!
  if you
had never called me down into the garden,
I would not, at a twitch of curiosity,
have played, in all innocence, with the dreamer.
Therefore, and with as much right, I assert:
the man who caused his negligence was you!—
The Delphic wisdom of my officers!

HOHENZOLLERN : I am content, Sir; I believe my
  words
have left a weight in the scales of your heart.

[*Enter an officer.*]

THE OFFICER : The Prince, my Lord, will be here
  any moment!

THE ELECTOR : Very well! show him in.

THE OFFICER : In a few minutes!—
Simply that, on his way, he stopped and asked
a gate-keeper to unlock the graveyard for him.

THE ELECTOR : The graveyard?

THE OFFICER : Yes, Your Highness, Sir!

THE ELECTOR : What for?

THE OFFICER : To face the truth, perhaps—I do not
  know;
it seemed he wished to see the vault, which your
command has caused to be opened there for him.

[*The group of officers again close in and mutter
among themselves.*]

125

THE ELECTOR : No matter! Show him in when he
  arrives. (*He goes to the table again and studies
  the documents.*)
COUNT TRUCHSS : There is the guard, already, with
  the Prince.

[*Enter the Prince of Homburg, then an officer and
guards.*]

THE ELECTOR : My young Prince, I have called you
  to my aid!
Colonel Kottwitz here brings me, in your favour,
this document with—look!—the signatures
—a long list—of a hundred noble fellows!
The Army, it is clear, desires your freedom
and has no use for the Court Martial's verdict.—
Read it, please, for yourself,—you will soon see.
  (*He hands him the petition.*)
THE PRINCE OF HOMBURG (*after glancing at it, turning and looking at the group of officers*) : Kottwitz, give me your hand, my dear old friend!
What you are doing for me is more than I
deserved of you in that battle! But now, quick,
go back to Arnstein, where you came from, and
do not stir! I have thought it over, I am
resolved to endure the death allotted me. (*He gives
  the petition to Kottwitz.*)
KOTTWITZ (*in dismay*) : No, never, my Lord Prince!
  what are you saying?
HOHENZOLLERN : He desires death—?
COUNT TRUCHSS : He should not, must not die!
SEVERAL OFFICERS (*pressing forward*) : Sir!—Sir!
  —My Sovereign!—My Commander!—Hear
  us!
THE PRINCE OF HOMBURG : Quiet! That is my in-
  flexible will!

126

The law, which I—in the sight of the Army—
violated, the holy law of war,
I intend to uphold by a free death!
What worth, my brothers, can the victory have
for you—the single paltry victory I
might yet have snatched from Wrangel—set against
the triumph over that most ruinous
of enemies within us, selfish presumption,—
which will be won, gloriously, tomorrow?
Down with the foreigner who would subject us!
and may the Brandenburger take his stand,
free, on his mother country!—it is his,
and the pomp of its fields raised for him only.
KOTTWITZ (*deeply moved*): My son! beloved
    friend! what can I call you?
COUNT TRUCHSS: O God Almighty!
KOTTWITZ: Let me kiss your hand!

[*They press round him.*]

THE PRINCE OF HOMBURG (*turning to the Elector*):
    But you, my Sovereign, who once had for me
a tenderer name, now alas forfeited:
I lay myself, my whole self, at your feet!
Forgive me that, on the day of decision,
I served you with an all too hasty ardour:
from that guilt death is now washing me pure.
Grant to my heart—which, reconciled and cheer-
    ful,
submits now to your judgment—the consolation
that your heart also has resigned all hate:
and, as a sign, in this hour of farewell
graciously concede me one request!
THE ELECTOR: Speak out, young hero! What is it
    you desire?
My word I pledge you, and my knightly honour:
whatever it be, to you it is accorded!

THE PRINCE OF HOMBURG : O Sir, do not, with the
  hand of the Princess,
purchase peace from King Charles of Sweden ! Send
packing, out of the camp, this bargainer
who has proposed a thing of such dishonour :
with grapeshot now write out for him the answer !
THE ELECTOR (*kissing him on the forehead*) : Be 't
  as you say ! See, with this kiss, my son,
I hear and now grant you this last request !
Great though the need was for that sacrifice,
mischance of war alone could wring it from me,
and now there blooms, from each word you have
  uttered,
a victory that shall grind him into dust !
She, I shall write him, is bride to Prince Homburg
who fell to the law because of Fehrbellin :
from whose ghost, striding dead before our banners,
on the field let him win her, if he can ! (*He kisses
  him once more, and embraces him.*)
THE PRINCE OF HOMBURG : Now see ! Now you are
  giving me my life !
Now I would pray down on you every blessing
that, from the throne of clouds, the Seraphim
sprinkle, exulting, on the heads of heroes !
Go out, my Lord, and fight a world of
enemies and overcome them all—for you are
worthy !
THE ELECTOR : Guards ! Here !—Lead him back
  to his prison !

[*Natalie and the Electress appear in the doorway:
behind them, ladies-in-waiting.*]

NATALIE : O Mother, no ! How can you talk to me,
now, of decorum?

The highest decorum, at this moment, is
to love him!—O my poor dear friend!
THE PRINCE OF HOMBURG (*interrupting her*) : Away!
COUNT TRUCHSS (*clinging to his arm*) : No, never,
    Prince! Not that!
THE PRINCE OF HOMBURG : Lead me away!
HOHENZOLLERN : My Lord Elector! Sir!
Have you the heart to—?
THE PRINCE OF HOMBURG (*wrenching himself free*) :
    Tyrants! Would you have me
led in chains to the place of execution?
On!—With this world I have closed my account!

[*Goes, with the guards.*]

NATALIE (*throwing herself upon the Electress's
bosom*) : O Earth, accept me now into your lap!
Why should I ever see another day?
DÖRFLING : O God Almighty! Had it to come to
    this?

[*The Elector speaks confidentially and urgently
to an officer.*]

KOTTWITZ (*coldly*) : Prince and Commander, after
    what has passed,
have we leave to withdraw?
THE ELECTOR : No! Not just yet!
When you have leave to withdraw, I will tell you!

[*He eyes Kottwitz steadily for a moment; then he
picks up from the table the papers brought by the
page, and turns with them to the Field-marshal.*]

Here, the safe-conduct for the Swede, Count Horn!
According to the request of the Prince

my Cousin, which I stand pledged to fulfill,—
prepare for war again three days from now!

[*A pause.—He looks down at the death sentence.*]

Yes, judge for yourselves, gentlemen! In
the past year, through self-centred thoughtlessness,
the Prince of Homburg cost me two fine victories;
and the third,—that too he has gravely impaired.
After the schooling of these days, are you
willing to venture with him a fourth time?
KOTTWITZ and TRUCHSS (*stumbling over each
    other*): What, my adored—my idolized Com-
    mander—?
THE ELECTOR: Will you? Will you?
KOTTWITZ: By the living God,
you, Sir, might stand on the edge of the abyss
and he, I think, now would not even draw
his sword to save your life without an order!
THE ELECTOR (*tearing up the death sentence*):
Then follow me, my friends, into the garden!

All go.

Scene 2

*The Palace, with the stairway leading down into
the garden, as in Act One.—It is again night.*

*The Prince of Homburg, with his eyes bandaged, is
led in by Captain Stranz through the wrought-
iron gate, below. Officers and guards.—In the
distance the drums of the funeral march can be
heard.*

THE PRINCE OF HOMBURG : Now, immortality, you
    are wholly mine !
You shine to me, through the bandage on my eyes,
with the glow of a thousandfold the Sun !
There are wings growing out of my two shoulders,
my spirit soars through ethereal still spaces;
and, as a ship taken by the wind's breath
sees the bright harbour-town sinking away,
to me all life goes under in a twilight :
now I can still distinguish shapes and colours—
and now all lies below me as a mist.

[*The Prince sits down on a bench in the middle,
which is built round an oak-tree. Captain Stranz
moves away from him, and looks up at the stairway.*]

Ah, dame's-violets ! how sweet their scent is !—Can
    you
not smell them?

[*Stranz comes over to him again.*]

STRANZ : Those are stocks, Sir, and carnations.
THE PRINCE OF HOMBURG : Carnations?—How did
    they come here?
STRANZ : I don't know.—
They say a girl planted them here.—May
I pick you a carnation, Sir?
THE PRINCE OF HOMBURG : Dear fellow !—
When I get home, I'll put it into water.

[*The Elector, bearing the laurel wreath with the
gold chain slung about it: the Electress and Princess Natalie: Field-marshal Dörfling; Colonels
Kottwitz, Hohenzollern, Golz and others; ladies-in-*

131

waiting, officers and torch-bearers, appear on the terrace of the palace.—Hohenzollern with a hand-kerchief, steps to the balustrade and signs to Captain Stranz, who thereupon leaves the Prince and goes to speak with the guard in the background.

My friend, what light is this, spreading about us?

STRANZ (*returning to him*) : Prince, would you be so good as to stand up?

THE PRINCE OF HOMBURG : What is it?

STRANZ : Nothing that should cause you fear!— Now let me again open your eyes.

THE PRINCE OF HOMBURG : Has the last hour of my suffering struck?

STRANZ : Yes!—

Hail to you, blessings on you!—you are worthy!

[*The Elector gives the wreath, with the gold chain hanging from it, to the Princess, takes her by the hand, and leads her down the steps.*

Officers, noblemen and ladies follow. The Princess, escorted by torch-bearers, comes and stands before the Prince who, in amazement, rises. She places the wreath on his head and the chain round his neck, then presses his hand to her heart.

The Prince falls in a dead faint.]

NATALIE : O God! His joy is killing him!

HOHENZOLLERN (*supporting the Prince's head*) : Help!

THE ELECTOR : Let
the thunder of the cannon waken him!

[*Gun-fire. A march. Lights are lit throughout the Palace.*]

KOTTWITZ : Hail! Hail to the Prince of Homburg!
THE OFFICERS : Hail! Hail! Hail!
ALL : Victor of the Battle of Fehrbellin!

[*A momentary silence.*]

THE PRINCE OF HOMBURG : No, tell me! Is it a dream?
KOTTWITZ : A dream, what else?
SEVERAL OFFICERS : To the field! To the field!
COUNT TRUCHSS : Into battle!
DÖRFLING : To victory! To victory! To victory!
ALL : Dust take all enemies of Brandenburg!

Curtain

THE UNKNOWN
SOLDIER
AND
HIS WIFE

Two acts of war separated by
a truce

by
PETER USTINOV

First published in Great Britain in 1968 by
William Heinemann Ltd.

First published in the United
States of America in 1968 by Random House Inc.

The Chichester Festival Theatre Co. Ltd. presented *The Unknown Soldier and His Wife* on May 22, 1968, at the Chichester Festival Theatre, with the following cast:

THE SERGEANT	*Mark Kingston*
35914	*George Camiller*
THE GENERAL	*Clive Revill*
THE REBEL	*Michael Burrell*
THE WIFE	*Prunella Scales*
THE ARCHBISHOP	*Peter Ustinov*
14768	*John Hart Dyke*
71696	*Carl Bernard*
THE UNKNOWN SOLDIER	*Simon Ward*
94343	*Anton Low*
THE ENEMY LEADER	*Michael Aldridge*
THE INVENTOR	*David Nettheim*
THE WOMAN	*Ann Kennedy*
REINFORCEMENTS	*Richard Cornish*
	Sandy McDonald
	Christopher Morley
	Charles Rea

Directed by Peter Ustinov

CHARACTERS

THE SERGEANT

35914

THE GENERAL

THE REBEL

THE WIFE

THE ARCHBISHOP

14768

71696

THE UNKNOWN SOLDIER

94343

THE ENEMY LEADER

THE INVENTOR

THE WOMAN

REINFORCEMENTS

FIRST ACT OF WAR

*The curtain rises on a stage bare but for a tomb.
There are a couple of television cameras, protected
by shiny plastic covers against the rain. Soldiers,
at ease, stand with their backs to the audience.
They are wearing camouflage gas-capes. The
setting and the costuming are left to the discretion
of the director throughout, the only admonition of
the author being that the action should be as fluid
and theatrical as possible. Any excess of the imagination is an error on the right side.*

*A new arrival makes his way to the front of the
stage. He carries a bugle.*

*A soldier at the end of the line approaches the
newcomer purposefully.*

He is the Sergeant.

SERGEANT : Bugler, you're late.
BUGLER (*who will later be known as* 35914) : Sorry,
Sar'nt. See, owing to the rain—
SERGEANT : I don't want to hear no shudderin'
excuses. The plungin' facts speak for themselves,
got me? You're on a charge.
BUGLER : Yes, Sar'nt.
SERGEANT : Don't you answer back, or I'll make it
stiflin' for you!
BUGLER : Sar'nt.
SERGEANT : Now. On the signal bein' given from
the television booth up there, you play what?
BUGLER : Last post.
SERGEANT : Last Post what?
BUGLER : *The* Last Post
SERGEANT : *The* Last Post what?

[Pause; the Bugler is perplexed.]

Bugler, I am waitin'. *The* Last Post what?

BUGLER (*tentative*) : *The* Last Post, Sar'nt?

SERGEANT : That's better. Now when I raise my right hand in this manner here, you will raise your bugle to what?

BUGLER : My lips, Sar'nt.

SERGEANT : Now we're getting somewhere at last. You will then play the aforesaid piece of music in a manner appropriate to what type of occasion?

BUGLER : Sad occasion, Sar'nt

SERGEANT : Dodderin' dummit—you don't bleedin' remember, do you? I'll try again. What type of occasion?

BUGLER : Melancholic occasion, Sar'nt?

SERGEANT : One more fancy word out of you, and I'll put you under arrest! Do I convey my meanin'?

BUGLER : Yes, Sar'nt.

SERGEANT : As you were, then. We'll try again. What manner of occasion?

[Silence. The Sergeant shouts.]

A solemn occasion, you half-cock! (*He inclines his head as though tuning a delicate instrument.*) Appropriate to what?

BUGLER : A solemn occasion, Sar'nt.

SERGEANT : What is appropriate to a solemn occasion, then?

BUGLER : The way I play my bugle, Sar'nt.

SERGEANT : The way you play what on your bugle, Bugler?

BUGLER : The Last Post, Sar'nt.

SERGEANT : Got that in yer 'ead, have you?

BUGLER : Yes, Sar'nt.

SERGEANT : You're not very bright, are you?

BUGLER : No, Sar'nt.

SERGEANT : Well, we can't all be bright, can we?

BUGLER : No, Sar'nt.

SERGEANT : That's better. At ease. As you were! At ease. As you were!

[*The General walks over. The Sergeant comes to a thunderous attention.*]

Bugler present and correct, sah!

GENERAL : Good. Good. Try and keep the noise down.

SERGEANT : I impressed that on the bugler, sir.

GENERAL (*with a sad, occasional smile*) : Good man. You will start playing the Last Post when the Sergeant here gives you the signal. I want you to play it as though you really meant it, as befits a sad occasion.

SERGEANT : And solemn, with your permission, sir.

GENERAL : And solemn. Yes indeed. And Solemn. All right, Bugler, on the double!

SERGEANT : Lif right. Lif! Right!

GENERAL : His Grace the Archbishop should be here at any moment. I am told his address to the nation will take about twenty minutes, which is a little longer than I had bargained for. It means we'll have to be right on our toes at the military end— otherwise it'll be a virtual certainty that the pro- gramme will overlap into Children's Hour, which follows us at five sharp.

SERGEANT (*shocked*) : Good gracious me, sir, if I may make so bold—it's a bit shocking, isn't it? I mean, it's not as though we bury the Unknown Soldier every day, is it? I should have thought it'd do the nippers good to see the ceremony. After all, sir, they'll be doin' their military service soon enough . . .

GENERAL: Oh certainly, Sergeant, I quite agree. The television boys have been most co-operative, and I'm sure, if the need arises, they'll let us run over.

[*A dishevelled man, the Rebel, has entered, and is surreptitiously passing out pamphlets to the troop.*]

SERGEANT: Hullo—oh, it's you again, is it? Not content with four years in the fluting brig for desertion, you got to come here of all places with yer filthy coward-like ideas. Get out of it!

REBEL (*laughing*): Still in good voice, Sergeant? That's what I like to hear. Care for a pamphlet?

SERGEANT: Right! Any man takes a bit of paper from this stinking rebel's under arrest, got it?

GENERAL: What seems to be the matter, Sergeant? Oh Lord another troublemaker.

REBEL: Another troublemaker? *The* troublemaker! Don't pretend you don't remember me. At Knossos, in the shadow of the blue hills, you had your first taste of me, didn't you? And you reacted as a soldier should. You ran me through . . . from the back. The last words I remember before I died— 'Death is too good for this man!'

GENERAL: The last words you remember before you died? Knossos? What the devil are you talking about?

REBEL: You remember. You remember Knossos. The One Hundred and Eighteenth Legion.

GENERAL (*with a raucous yell—out of character*): AHHHH! Citizens of Rome, witness my triumph! (*Guiltily he passes his hand over his forehead.*)

142

REBEL (*in triumph*) : You do remember !

SERGEANT (*fuming*) : Christmas, sir, let me get at 'im !

REBEL : Christmas hadn't been thought of yet, but it was imminent. It was imminent.

GENERAL (*sober, but decided*) : Go away, before it's too late.

REBEL : They tell me things have changed—Maximus Severus. They say this is a public park. There's even a rumour this is a free country.

SERGEANT (*losing his head*) : That's right. It's a free country. You're free to come 'ere, and I'm free to spread your guts on the lawn.

[*The Rebel lies down*]

What are you lying down for, you dung droppin'? Frightened, are you?

GENERAL : Sar'nt !

REBEL : Passive resistance.

SERGEANT : Suits me. (*He begins kicking the motionless form of the Rebel, shouting.*) It's a free country ! I'll show you . . . how free it is . . .

GENERAL (*not moving*) : Sar'nt ! Sar'nt !

[*A pretty little wife enters. She is in the last stages of pregnancy.*]

WIFE : Stop it !

[*The Sergeant, who didn't stop for the General, stops for a woman.*]

GENERAL : Sergeant ! You disobeyed an order !

SERGEANT (*aghast*) : I did? I can't think how it happened, sir. I was provocated. (*His sense of duty wins over his ability to find excuses. He stands stiffly.*) Permission to put myself under arrest, sah!

GENERAL (*absently*): I'll deal with you later. (*To the wife.*) The public enclosure is over there, madam . . . that is, if you have a green ticket.

WIFE : I don't need a ticket.

GENERAL : I'm afraid you do.

WIFE : I've a perfect right to be here. Whoever heard of a widow being kept away from her husband's funeral?

GENERAL : I don't think you understand, madam. This is the funeral of the Unknown Soldier.

WIFE : I know. That is the exact description of my husband.

GENERAL : But this is the burial of no specific person, madam. It is a symbolic ceremony.

WIFE : There's a body, isn't there? It must have been alive once.

GENERAL : Of course, but it was selected because it was unrecognizable.

WIFE : That's him! I knew it. He was never recognized by anyone—his face, his character, his personality—it was always the same.

GENERAL (*tactful*): I sympathize with you in your great sorrow, naturally—but I feel bound to point out . . .

WIFE : Oh, spare me your sympathy, man. I've no great sorrow. How the hell can you keep it up after all these centuries? No, I'm just bloody irritated by now. I've had enough of it. Dragging my feet under the weight of the child of an unknown father. Standing in line endlessly to claim my pension, filling in forms—and it wasn't always like that. But before—well, it was the poorhouse or the brothel . . .

REBEL : Poor Virginia.

WIFE : Virginia? Nobody's called me that for centuries!

REBEL : It is your name, isn't it?

WIFE : Not now it isn't . . . but I think it must have been once.

REBEL : I thought so. I don't recognize your face, that's too much to expect . . . but I recognize your condition . . .

[A fierce gleam of sunshine suddenly breaks through the rain clouds. They all notice it. Seconds later, the Archbishop, in full regalia plunges onto the stage. He is also conscious of the change in the weather.]

ARCHBISHOP : Ah! *(Touched by a minor grace.)* I can't help but consider it significant that, at the very moment of my appearance at this scene of ennobling sorrow, a light from above should be shed upon us.

GENERAL : Yes indeed, sir.

ARCHBISHOP *(down to earth)* : In any case, even if there's nothing in it, I believe it will benefit the television.

GENERAL : Oh, undoubtedly, Your Grace.

ARCHBISHOP : Twelve million is the latest figure, I hear.

GENERAL : Twelve million?

ARCHBISHOP : Twelve million viewers. The television experts estimate you will have the highest rating of the century, with the possible exception of the Olympic games.

GENERAL : Well, I must say, Your Grace, that does tend to restore one's faith in certain values which . . .

145

ARCHBISHOP (*a little tartly*) : I am making allusion to that in my address.

REBEL : D'you remember a time before television was invented?

[*The Archbishop is mystified as to the whereabouts of the last speaker.*]

GENERAL : I must apologize, Your Grace.

ARCHBISHOP (*spotting the Rebel on the ground*) : Oh dear, another poor unfortunate who has suffered beyond his means in the recent war, no doubt. We must never lack the humility to minister to those who may possibly find comfort in our words. (*Adopting a gentle tone.*) Yes, indeed I do remember a time before television was invented, my good man.

REBEL : How did you communicate with your flock then?

ARCHBISHOP : It was more difficult, but it was possible. It always has been possible, otherwise we wouldn't all be here today, as Christians. There was the radio.

REBEL : And before that?

ARCHBISHOP : The pulpit.

REBEL : And before that?

ARCHBISHOP : The market-place.

REBEL : And before that?

ARCHBISHOP : The wayside shrine.

REBEL : And before that?

ARCHBISHOP (*puzzled*) : Before that?

REBEL : Before the Cross? Before the Scriptures?

ARCHBISHOP (*gravely*) : There was no before that for me . . . just darkness.

REBEL (*rising*) : Darkness? There was a fierce ray

146

of sunlight then, after the rain, at Knossos. You gazed at the sky . . . at a black cloud with the silver sun edging its way behind it . . . when it shook itself free, blinding us, you rushed among us, shouting . . .

ARCHBISHOP (*with a great shout—out of character*): Victory is ours! Great is Mars, and we are his greatness! (*He grips his head as though in pain.*) I do beg your pardon. I don't know what came over me . . .

GENERAL: I know, Your Grace, the same thing happened to me just now—

WIFE (*who has been staring at the Archbishop, slowly*): Oh, now I remember you—every time it happened, there you were, right on time, with that sickly smile of consolation.

ARCHBISHOP (*a little taken aback, icily*): Some widows have found the consolation I am able to offer, a fount of strength and wisdom.

WIFE: How d'you know I'm a widow? I'm not even dressed as one.

ARCHBISHOP: I thought you said . . .

WIFE: I haven't opened my mouth since you arrived.

ARCHBISHOP: Well, your presence here . . . I must have assumed . . .

WIFE: I don't believe you. You remember, don't you?

REBEL: Of course he remembers.

ARCHBISHOP: Vaguely . . . I must admit . . .

GENERAL (*uneasy*): Do be careful, Your Grace.

ARCHBISHOP: Careful? Why?

GENERAL: I sense a trap.

REBEL: That's unusual for a military man.

SERGEANT (*suddenly roaring*): What's that then! That man! What you got on your feet?

147

[They all direct their looks at the man at whom the Sergeant is pointing.]

14768 : Boots, Sar'nt.

SERGEANT : Call them boots? Look more like shiftin' sandals to me. Gold shiftin' sandals like bleedin' Cinderella!

35914 : We've all got the same, Sar'nt. They look like boots to us.

GENERAL : Regiment! Regiment, two paces forward march! (*The line of men advances two paces. They are seen to be wearing golden sandals.*) Now look here, men . . . I know it's been a long war . . .

SERGEANT (*beside himself*) : Why argue with the chipped marbleheads? A swagger-stick round the vulnerables, that's what they're asking for!

GENERAL (*aside*) : Sergeant, I'll send you to the psychiatrist if you go on like this.

SERGEANT (*quavering*) : Oh no, sir, anything but that!

GENERAL : You just can't talk like that any more in this day and age. Next thing, we'll have a strike on our hands.

71696 : I can only say, sir, speakin' I believe for all the men, when we put them on this morning, they looked like boots to us.

[The men agree.]

GENERAL : And do they look like boots to you now?

14768 : No, sir, but we was up half the night polishin' the ponderous things, the way the Sergeant likes them, so he can see his face in them in the mornin'.

REBEL : Narcissus.

SERGEANT (*as though someone had called his name—out of character*): Yes? Did someone call me?

ARCHBISHOP : Em . . . I neither wish to add to the present perplexities, General . . . nor do I wish to interfere with matters purely military . . . but in the interest of truth, I feel bound to draw your attention to your own footwear.

GENERAL : Good heavens !

[*The General, too, is wearing golden sandals.*]

WIFE : Phew, it's hot . . .

[*The Wife takes her coat off and immediately loses her pregnancy. She wears a flimsy and seductive Roman tunic. The soldiers whistle.*]

SERGEANT : What's going on here? Sir! That woman ! She's lost her child !

WIFE (*hotly*) : I never lost a child ! I lost a husband, but I never lost a child ! I'm a peasant. I've got a pride in my job. I just haven't started a child, that's all. I haven't met Julian yet.

SERGEANT (*electrified*) : Julian ! That moon-struck molecule ! I'll tie a lovers' knot with his arms and throw him in the Tiber if I ever lay my tentacles on him.

WIFE (*violent*) : I'll stuff your short-sword up your scabbard first !

GENERAL : Sergeant ! Pull yourself together ! Tell the men to remove their gas-capes.

SERGEANT : Sah ! Stand by to remove gas-capes. Gas-ca-a-apes, re-move !

[*The soldiers remove their gas-capes. They are*

dressed as Roman legionaries underneath. General surprise.]

REBEL : The crowd ! It's vanished !

GENERAL (*pale*) : Vanished?

ARCHBISHOP : The television cameras are still there !

REBEL : Cameras? Those aren't cameras. Those are our regimental eagles, piled for the night.

[*Sudden laughter from the soldiers while the Rebel rips off his coat, to reveal the uniform of a legionary like the others.*]

GENERAL (*on the verge of panic*) : What are you all laughing at?

35914 : The clothes you wear, Maximus Severus. You dress like a barbarian.

GENERAL : A barbarian? (*Suddenly tremendous, changing in character in spite of himself.*) I'm in command here ! Put your uniforms on at once ! We're on the television in half an hour ! (*Nothing happens.*) Sergeant, arrest them all !

SERGEANT (*compassionate*) : Your wits are frayed by the weight of your decision, Maximus Severus. Pray to the goddess of the night for rest free from phantoms.

GENERAL (*to the Archbishop, hysterical*) : Help us, Your Grace. Pray for sanity !

ARCHBISHOP (*serious*) : I have been asked to pray for prowess in war and wealth and potency, but never have I been asked to pray for sanity.

[*He begins rocking with laughter, in which the men join. He takes off his mitre and throws it gaily into the air and out of sight.*]

150

GENERAL : You too? Oh my God.

ARCHBISHOP (*abruptly stern and menacing*) : What was that? God—in the singular? Beware of thunderbolts, my poor misguided boy. Jove is indeed King of Olympus, father of the gods, but in flattering him it is unwise, most unwise, to ignore the others.

GENERAL (*hardly audible*) : The others?

ARCHBISHOP (*nods sagely*) : Let us pray. O mighty Mars, creator of widows, fount of tears, lend us your ear in your infinite mercilessness, and hear our prayer. Give us this day our daily victim, and teach us to kill without compassion, so that our civilizing mission may go unhindered by cries of mercy or the yells of the despoiled. Blind us to charity, and deafen us to entreaty, for ever, and ever. Amen.

[*The General rips off his cap. He wears a victor's laurels. He throws off his greatcoat. He is dressed as a Roman general.*]

GENERAL (*all smiles*) : Was that a good joke, men?

ALL (*in chorus*) : A very good joke, Maximus Severus.

[*He acknowledges their cheers like an untrustworthy modern wrestler. Quietly a young Roman wanders onto the stage.*]

SERGEANT (*stern*) : Where have you been, Julian?

THE UNKNOWN SOLDIER : There are flowers in this valley which bloom late . . . little flowers we don't have in Italy . . . without much colour, but with a strong and wholesome smell . . . (*He cups his hand to smell the flowers better.*)

GENERAL : Which end of the valley?

THE UNKNOWN SOLDIER : The far end, among the olive trees.

GENERAL : Where the enemy lies encamped?

THE UNKNOWN SOLDIER (*pleasant*) : Yes. Exactly there. I talked to their sentries.

[*A murmur of excitement.*]

GENERAL (*holding up his hand for silence*) : Dressed in your uniform?

THE UNKNOWN SOLDIER (*smiling*) : Oh yes, I haven't changed.

71696 : Our Julian, a hero!

GENERAL : In what language did you converse?

THE UNKNOWN SOLDIER : In the language of signs. Men can always make themselves understood if they want to badly enough.

GENERAL (*excited*) : Well, man, out with it! What did you find out? Will they attack tomorrow?

THE UNKNOWN SOLDIER (*laughing*) : Oh no, I wouldn't have known how to frame such a question. And even if I could have done, I wouldn't have been able to make head or tail of the answer.

GENERAL (*irritated*) : Did you see nothing, at least?

THE UNKNOWN SOLDIER : Oh yes. It's amazing the way the olive trees go almost into the sea down there. I've never seen olive trees grow so close to salt water.

GENERAL (*frankly annoyed*) : But the tents? The activity?

THE UNKNOWN SOLDIER : Tents? Yes, I saw quite a few, but I didn't like to look too closely.

GENERAL : Why on earth not?

THE UNKNOWN SOLDIER : There were people inside them. They may have been undressing.

GENERAL (*exploding*): Great gods! What did you talk about, then?

THE UNKNOWN SOLDIER: About flowers.

GENERAL: I don't believe it!

SERGEANT (*taking over from the defeated General*): How many of them did you kill, Julian?

THE UNKNOWN SOLDIER: Me? I didn't kill any. We found we had a common interest, you see.

SERGEANT: Imperial Rome is at war, man! You know damn well that it is your sacred duty to kill the other fellow before you have time to find out if you have a common interest or not!

GENERAL (*taking over again, with terrible patience*): Julian, I'll give you one last chance to try and understand the meaning of military discipline. I do this only because it takes great physical courage to go up to a barbarian in the uniform of a Roman legionary the way you did.

THE UNKNOWN SOLDIER: Why?

GENERAL: The first lesson, Julian, is . . . never ask questions.

THE UNKNOWN SOLDIER: How will I ever learn if I don't ask questions?

GENERAL: There you are utterly and completely wrong. In order to obey orders, it is best to know nothing. To know everything is impossible, and to know something is merely confusing.

THE UNKNOWN SOLDIER: Since you say it is impossible to know everything, and since you know more than me, it follows that you must know something.

GENERAL (*tense*): You are losing your last chance, Julian. Stupidly. You are losing it stupidly. Your general tells you that field is red, soldier. What is your reply?

THE UNKNOWN SOLDIER: Which field?

GENERAL (*succumbing to his exasperation*) : That field. Any field. They're all red!

THE UNKNOWN SOLDIER (*after a moment*) : I suppose it is—sometimes—when the sun is setting.

GENERAL (*roaring*) : Not when the sun is setting. Now! Now!

THE UNKNOWN SOLDIER (*rational*) : No, sir, not now. Now the field is green.

SERGEANT (*howling*) : Idiot!

GENERAL (*after a moment*) : Julian, watch this. Your general tells you that field is red! What colour is that field?

ALL (*in chorus*) : Red!

GENERAL : Now do you understand?

THE UNKNOWN SOLDIER (*contemplating the field*) : It hasn't made it any redder, if that's what you mean, General.

GENERAL (*with a hopeless gesture*) : Take him away, and kill him as an example.

THE UNKNOWN SOLDIER : Since I'm the most stupid, General, who can I be an example to? They all think the field is red.

WIFE (*in a sudden outburst*) : How can you say that field is red? That's blasphemy, you know, to change the colour of Jove's green fields without permission.

[*The General hadn't thought of that. He looks uneasily at the Archbishop.*]

ARCHBISHOP (*ill at ease*) : The pretty thing may be right. Jove's huge ear is everywhere. (*The stage grows darker.*) See that black thunder cloud which has come between us and the sun? The weather is but the changing mood of the father of the gods.

154

GENERAL (*calling to heaven*): Smile on us, Jove! I meant nothing by my words! The field is green! What colour is the field, men.

ALL: Green!

ARCHBISHOP: See how the top left corner of the cloud suddenly turns down.

GENERAL: Yes . . . Yes, I do . . . like the tongue of a dying bull.

ARCHBISHOP: More like a down-turned thumb at some celestial games.

WIFE (*with trance-like authority*): Julian must not die!

[*They all glance at her, then back at the sky.*]

ARCHBISHOP: See, the thumb begins to turn up . . . and up . . . and up . . .

GENERAL (*delighted*): Yes! Stay the execution!

ARCHBISHOP (*to the wife*): Who are you?

WIFE: A girl from these parts.

ARCHBISHOP (*tenderly*): How often the gods speak to us through the mouths of innocents! Now Julian will not die. He will just be whipped for insubordination as usual. Isn't that wonderful? Aren't you going to thank her, Julian?

THE UNKNOWN SOLDIER: Thank you very much.

WIFE: Why is he to be whipped?

GENERAL: He failed to kill an enemy when he had a golden opportunity.

WIFE: But there were more of them than him. If he'd killed one of them, the others would have killed him.

ARCHBISHOP (*with the patience of a nanny*): If they'd have killed him, there'd be no cause to whip him now, would there? I mean, you can't have it both ways.

WIFE : I don't understand.

GENERAL (*amused*) : She's as bad as Julian.

ARCHBISHOP (*equally amused*) : Prettier, though.

GENERAL (*calling out*) : Whip Julian, and prepare for battle. We march within the hour !

SERGEANT : About turn, lef', ri', lef', ri'—step smartly there !

ARCHBISHOP (*detaining the General*) : Oh, Maximus Severus, almighty Jove may well require a penance for your outrage. It would be best if you fought with your sword in your left hand.

GENERAL (*amazed*) : In my left hand? That's suicide ! Where do you read your instructions?

ARCHBISHOP (*testy*) : Never mind. To each man his calling.

[*There is an ominous roll of thunder. 'I told you so.'*]

You stick to conquests, Maximus Severus, and leave the gods to me.

GENERAL (*calling out*) : I will fight with my sword in my left hand.

[*There is a flash of lightning.*]

ARCHBISHOP : the gods are gratified.

[*The General goes out. The Archbishop is alone with the Wife—except for the Rebel, who lingers unseen.*]

Precious girl ! Come, my little oracle, let me touch you . . .

WIFE : No.

ARCHBISHOP : Why not?

156

WIFE : You frighten me.

ARCHBISHOP : Perish the thought! I only wish to capture a particle of the divine grace which has passed through you.

WIFE : It was common sense more than anything. (*Retreating.*) How many strokes will they give Julian?

ARCHBISHOP (*reasonable*) : Five hundred.

WIFE (*horrified*) : Five hundred!

ARCHBISHOP : Those are the regulations. But don't worry, my sweet child, there's not a man in the ranks who can count comfortably beyond fifty. Come now, gratify my craving. Let me touch you, my darling—my desire to do so springs from a purely religious urge.

REBEL : It's amazing how many religious urges lie at the source of purely secular acts.

ARCHBISHOP : Where have you sprung from, Dementius Praecox?

REBEL : I have been loitering. An artist can always excuse his curiosity on the grounds of a search for material.

ARCHBISHOP : Take no notice of him, my beauty. He's a poor fool of a sculptor they keep around to decorate triumphal arches at the end of minor campaigns.

REBEL : Yes, my beauty, and if you examine the arches carefully, you will see the poor fool's comments on the mortal farce etched on the faces of the heroes.

ARCHBISHOP : The subversive nature of your sculpture has not been lost on us. Why, it is impossible to tell your gods and your men apart. Even if you are an agnostic, at least remember that you are a Roman! The world looks to you for an example.

REBEL : A Roman? Yes, alas. A despicable race. Garrulous, self-important, superstitious, hypocritical. There's so much still to learn, and what do we do? We teach.

ARCHBISHOP : Great Jove! We tolerate you only because, up to now, the gods have tolerated you.

REBEL : The gods tolerate me because they don't exist! Only man exists.

[*There is a loud peal of thunder.*]

ARCHBISHOP (*cringing*) : Fool!

REBEL : That was a peal of thunder, a natural phenomenon with a purely scientific explanation. If, on the other hand, you persist in maintaining the almighty Jove aimed a thunderbolt at me, then, you must admit, he had the unusual experience of missing. (*He holds out his hand.*) And so, my dear, don't be bamboozled by that old man. He is not an agent of the gods, but a man in priest's clothing. Be warned. (*The Rebel goes out.*)

ARCHBISHOP : Insufferable blasphemer! Come, my dear, you must be exorcised, in case his sacrilege has tainted the pristine loveliness of your soul. In the temple of Venus, your patron!

WIFE : What do I have to do?

ARCHBISHOP : Undress. Just slip off your tunic.

WIFE : In front of you?

ARCHBISHOP : Where else? The little demons have entered you by your ears. Together we will winkle the wicked little fellows out of all the orifices where they may be hiding.

WIFE (*escaping*) : You wish to find pleasure in me, not demons.

ARCHBISHOP : In that it is a pleasure for a high priest to winkle out demons, that is quite true.

WIFE : You wish to lie with me !

ARCHBISHOP : Lie with you, stand with you, roll with you . . . the demons defy most positions. Come along now, you have nothing to fear from me. It is more an ecclesiastical formality than anything else.

WIFE : Leave me alone ! (*She runs off.*)

ARCHBISHOP : Come back ! Come here, in the name of all that's holy !

[*He follows her, the The Unknown Soldier staggers on. He is stripped to the waist and covered in blood. The Sergeant helps him to walk.*]

THE UNKNOWN SOLDIER : You overdo everything you put your hands to.

SERGEANT (*with the gentleness of one who knows he has gone too far*) : I lost count.

THE UNKNOWN SOLDIER : You lost count more than once, and every time you started all over again from the beginning. (*He sinks to the ground.*)

SERGEANT : Rest a while, Julian. I'll see to it that you're in the back row of the phalanx.

THE UNKNOWN SOLDIER : That's what I don't understand about this army of ours . . . one moment you're like a bloodthirsty animal . . . next, you're all over me, like a childless aunt. And the others . . . they were happy to watch me being flogged . . . then they come gaping at my wounds, and offering to carry my spear into battle for me.

SERGEANT (*squatting beside him, gentle and reasonable*) : That's what's known as soldierly comradeship, Julian . . . I've been whipped more often than I care to remember . . . I wasn't always a sergeant, you know . . . no, came up through the ranks, I did . . . Would you care to see my scars?

159

THE UNKNOWN SOLDIER : Not now, thank you.

SERGEANT : Any time, any time, just ask. Came a time I no longer minded the whip. Rather liked it, in fact. Proved to me I was a man.

THE UNKNOWN SOLDIER : Don't you have any other proof? I mean . . .

SERGEANT (*confidential and slow*) : Civilians don't have our spirit, lad, because they're never cruel enough to one another to be surprised by another's kindness.

THE UNKOWN SOLDIER : Yes, that's a point.

SERGEANT : You want to think about that. Meanwhile, lie in the sun and let the blood congeal. You'll be a new man in about a month. Report to my tent in a quarter of an hour. I've got a little Ischian wine hidden in my pack. We'll share it.

[*The Sergeant ruffles The Unknown Soldier's hair affectionately, and goes. The Wife runs on stage, her clothes in tatters, followed by the Archbishop, who seems on the verge of a heart attack.*]

WIFE (*falling on her knees*) : Oh, Julian. What have they done to you?

THE UNKNOWN SOLDIER : Why are your clothes torn?

ARCHBISHOP : Because she's a disobedient country girl, who doesn't recognize friendship when she sees it . . . (*Glancing skyward.*) Apollo has almost galloped into the free air again . . . I must prepare to give Victory her wings . . . (*He walks slowly off, holding his heart.*)

WIFE : Your poor back . . . it would have been so easy to say the field was red.

THE UNKNOWN SOLDIER : Easy? I don't think so.

If I admit that, I'd be capable of admitting anything.

WIFE : And can't you?

THE UNKNOWN SOLDIER : Can you? They may flog you yet, for having run away from the high priest. Could you have given in to him?

WIFE : No.

THE UNKNOWN SOLDIER : How old are you?

WIFE : Nineteen. And I have a Roman name. Virginia.

THE UNKNOWN SOLDIER : Where do you live, Virginia?

WIFE : I live on my uncle's farm, over there, on the hill. It's not much of a farm. One room for him, his family and the animals. I spend most of my time in my secret cave near the stream. Come with me. I'll show it you. I'll wash your wounds.

[*He can hardly move, but does.*]

THE UNKNOWN SOLDIER : What do you do in your cave?

WIFE : I dream mostly.

THE UNKNOWN SOLDIER : What else is there for the ignorant to do? We can't read—we can hear, but we can't always understand. but we can fly like birds into a world of colour and of sound, which don't need explanation.

WIFE : And meet above the clouds, where we can't make fools of ourselves.

THE UNKNOWN SOLDIER (*a sudden realization*) : Perhaps that's why they punish me so often.

WIFE : Why?

THE UNKNOWN SOLDIER : I do all my dreaming during the day . . .

[*They go out, walking at the pace of the invalid. There is a noise of marching men. The soldiers enter, the General at their head. He carries his sword in his left hand. The Sergeant brings up the rear.*]

SERGEANT : Lef' ri', lef', halt!

GENERAL : At ease, men. Where's Julian? Didn't you leave him here?

SERGEANT : Yes, General, on this very spot.

GENERAL : Didn't whip him too hard, did you?

SERGEANT : What, me? We were laughing and joking about it! He must be able to move, mustn't he? Otherwise he'd still be here!

[*The sun bursts out from behind the clouds blindingly. The Archbishop rushes on. He carries a dead bird in one hand and a sling in the other.*]

ARCHBISHOP : Victory, victory, victory is ours! Great is Mars, and we are his greatness! Not only has golden Apollo shed his great light upon us, but I have killed a pigeon in flight, which, when I opened it, revealed itself to possess two livers! You all know what *that* means! A miracle!

[*A great cheer goes up.*]

ALL (*in chorus*) : Victory! Victory to Rome!

REBEL (*entering*) : You dropped this I believe, Your Lordship.

ARCHBISHOP : What is it?

REBEL : Another dead bird, Your Lordship, and very probably another miracle as well, for this one evidently was born with no liver at all.

ARCHBISHOP : Where did you find it?

REBEL : I followed you, Your Lordship, and it fell out of your robes.

ARCHBISHOP : Give it here this instant! (*He seizes it in embarrassment.*) You followed me where?

REBEL : To the dovecote in the village, where you killed two domesticated doves and stuffed the liver of one into the other. Almighty Jove turned a blind eye.

ARCHBISHOP : Listen to him, and the earth will open up and send us all headlong into the lower regions. I guarantee it!

[*There is an angry murmur among the men.*]

GENERAL : I will not stand for blasphemy, is that clear, not in the ranks, not before battle. Hey, sculptor, you of the remote passion and the delicate hands, come with us and see at first hand the heroism you so glibly depict on memorials.

REBEL : I am dispensed of active duty as an official war artist.

GENERAL : Seize him! You will be at the apex of our attack, unarmed!

REBEL (*with a wan smile*) : And you will be just behind me, armed to the teeth. You know how to kill; perhaps I can teach you how to die. I am not afraid, because my statues will outlive the Empire.

[*The Unknown Soldier enters. The Wife holds him by the hand.*]

SERGEANT (*rough*) : Where have you been? Picking flowers again?

[*There is a ripple of laughter.*]

163

GENERAL : Join the line, Julian. With Dementius Praecox in the van.

THE UNKNOWN SOLDIER : Narcissus told me I'd be near the back.

SERGEANT : I never !

THE UNKNOWN SOLDIER : You did ! You even offered me some wine.

SERGEANT : Wine ? Where would I get wine from ?

GENERAL : Wine ? I've never heard you wish for wine before, Julian. (*Puzzled.*) Are you afraid ?

THE UNKNOWN SOLDIER : Yes, very.

GENERAL : What has made a coward out of you ?

THE UNKNOWN SOLDIER : The wish to live, I think.

GENERAL : The wish to live ? (*Slowly he turns, and looks at the Wife.*)

WIFE : When will you be back ?

GENERAL : Perhaps never. Why do you wish to know ?

WIFE : I am his wife.

[*Slowly a gale of laughter sweeps the stage, and all are affected except the Wife, The Unknown Soldier and the Rebel. When the laughter threatens to die out, 35914 suddenly remembers, and repeats.*]

35914 : Where have you been ? Picking flowers again ?

[*The laughter surges again, but the General calls for order.*]

GENERAL (*in good humour*) : That's enough, men. We have enjoyed our laugh. Line up. Forward march. Let's have the song of the old whore of Pompeii.

164

[*Great acclaim greets this idea. As they go, they sing a marching song.*]

94343 (*singing*):
There was an old whore of Pompeii
Who had more than had her dayii,
To survive competition,
She got the permission
to charge only ten pence a layii.
ALL (*singing*):
O—
A penny for this, a penny for that,
A penny each for a tit and tat,
A penny for what should have been fat
But was sadly shrivelled and horribly flat.

O—
A penny for that, a penny for this,
A penny each for a hit and a miss,
A penny for what should have been bliss.
Hold your breath as you give her a kiss.

[*The Wife follows them as they march, waving into the distance. The Archbishop just stands there, the dead birds in his hands. A subtle but perceptible change comes over him. The Wife returns, and begins to go out*]

ARCHBISHOP (*intimate and melancholy*): Virginia I will not harm you. The fever's past.
WIFE: Don't you march with them?
ARCHBISHOP: No. I must prepare the triumph and rehearse the lamentations.
WIFE: I'll leave you then.
ARCHBISHOP: Not yet, please. It takes so much longer to understand one's actions than to perform

165

them. I have killed two doves. Why? I only rarely look at birds when they are alive . . . they move about, and flutter . . . they're rather stupid, I suspect . . . I notice them out of the corner of my eye, and I never fear for their safety . . . they know how to save themselves much better than I know how to destroy them. Even if I kill them occasionally for food, I'm not really killing a bird . . . I'm killing a dish, a pie . . . in my mind, it's already steaming on a plate. But to kill these birds as I did without reason, without honour, makes you notice your victim. (*He looks down at the birds.*) Look at the miraculous network of feathers! The little bodies are growing cold in my hands. Their blue eyes are staring at me as though surprised that man, who has been throwing crumbs at them all their lives, should suddenly turn so treacherous. One of them has an olive branch in its beak. (*Deeply disturbed.*) Tell me, Virginia, is it possible to love?

WIFE : Is it possible not to love?

ARCHBISHOP : I deserved such a cruel answer.

WIFE : The months are passing as we stand here talking . . . and we always say the same words . . . and every time I tell you the truth, you always say I am cruel, and always ask for more . . . winter is here . . . can you feel it? And now it's almost spring . . . I feel unwell . . . I must get ready . . .

ARCHBISHOP : So soon?

WIFE (*in pain*): I must get ready . . . (*She goes, with difficulty.*)

[*The Archbishop looks at the birds in silence.*]

ARCHBISHOP : I'd give the rest of my life if you could only fly away . . . (*He kneels to bury them.*)

[*From far away, out of tune, we can hear the song of the old whore of Pompeii. It grows in intensity, but seems in a minor key. The General leads his men on. He is intact, but the soldiers have lost legs, arms, hands, eyes, feet. Behind them are three prisoners in chains. The Unknown Soldier and the Rebel are missing. The General halts; the men likewise. The General raises his sword, of which only the hilt and a few inches of blade remain.*]

GENERAL : Victory!

ARCHBISHOP (*hollow*) : The gods, in their infinite understanding, have blessed our arms.

GENERAL : Bring forward the prisoners! Let the chronicle read that Maximus Severus, tamer of the Illyrians, scourge of the Bulgars, flagellator of the Avars, has won his most golden victory!

[*Very feeble cheer from the men.*]

SERGEANT (*grim*) Wait for it!

GENERAL (*continuing*) : His victory of victories, by putting to flight the . . . what is the name of your people again?

ENEMY LEADER : The Oswingoths.

GENERAL : Oswingoths? Are you sure?

ENEMY LEADER : We are an Indo-European people with an Ugro-Finnish strain, the second cousins, as it were, of the Ostrogoths and the Visigoths, and like all small tribes, we were searching for a peaceful valley to settle in.

GENERAL : You speak remarkably good Latin, if I may say so.

ENEMY LEADER (*apologetic*) : Very few people speak Oswingothic. We all know at least three languages, since we subsist on the mistrust of great peoples for one another. We live as go-betweens. We have to. We are weak in the arts of war.

GENERAL (*flashing*) : Weak? For the purpose of my triumph, you will be a tough, warlike race, and you, as its king, will have the honour of being dragged three times round the walls of Rome behind my chariot.

ENEMY LEADER : That is extremely good of you, but isn't there some other way in which you can give expression to your vanity? Couldn't I, for instance, enter Rome comfortably in a cage?

GENERAL : You fought bravely. You deserve the best.

ENEMY LEADER : I'm quite agreeable to being thrown to the lions.

GENERAL : The lions?

ENEMY LEADER : We are such a poor people that we are naturally averse to waste. Even as you're being eaten by a lion, you have the pleasant feeling that you are at least providing some nourishment, whereas quite frankly to travel three times 'round the walls of Rome behind your chariot seems to me a waste of your time and my body.

GENERAL : Are you trying to insult me?

ENEMY LEADER (*with a sigh*) : I have the feeling that you are the kind of person one succeeds in insulting far more often than one tries. At least be clement to my daughter.

GENERAL (*smiling grimly*) : I am too generous a man to be content with mere clemency. Enough! Take him away!

ENEMY LEADER : Beware if we should ever meet again in freedom!

GENERAL : You believe in reincarnation then?

ENEMY LEADER : I have to. Our people could not live in honour on this earth without a fervent belief in a second chance. You don't need such a belief for the time being, because you are Roman.

GENERAL : You admit our superiority!

ENEMY LEADER : In force of arms, yes. In faith, no. You don't need it . . . yet . . .

[*The General drinks deeply from a flask, waving negligently with the other hand. The Enemy Leader is taken away.*]

ARCHBISHOP : Where is Julian?

GENERAL : Bring the next one forward! No, leave the woman till last! Who are you? Do you have the rank and quality to be dragged round Rome, or are you for the cage, the spittle and the urine?

INVENTOR (*who speaks, surprisingly, with a thick German accent*) : For neither, I think.

GENERAL (*who shows early signs of an eventual inebriation*) : There's presumption for you! What are you, then, to think yourself above degradation? A damned politician?

INVENTOR : An inventor.

GENERAL (*amused*) : Inventor? What have you invented?

INVENTOR : The stirrup.

GENERAL : The what?

INVENTOR : The stirrup. A rider puts his foot in the stirrup to guide the horse, and with the aid of spurs—another of my inventions—sharp pieces of metal worn on the heel—he can accelerate his horse while maintaining entire freedom of manœuvre.

GENERAL (*intrigued*) : I noticed your invention at the height of the battle. Your leader could turn more rapidly than I could.

INVENTOR (*categorical and aggressive*) : The P.M.F. is increased tenfold under certain conditions.

GENERAL : P.M.F?

INVENTOR : P.M.F. Power of Manœuvre Factor.

GENERAL : How would you like to work for Rome?

INVENTOR : How much would I be paid?

GENERAL : You are defeated! Dare you bargain with me?

INVENTOR : I am never defeated while the stirrup lives! Without the stirrup, I give the Roman Empire twenty-five years—thirty maximum.

GENERAL : But we have the stirrup now!

INVENTOR (*tapping his head laconically*) : You think I would be so foolish as to explain my invention to you if I didn't have something up here which will make even the stirrup look ridiculous?

GENERAL : What is it?

INVENTOR : How much will I be paid?

GENERAL : You're not an Oswingoth, are you?

INVENTOR (*for a moment lachrymose and world-weary*) : Oh, never mind where I come from . . . I had trouble at home . . . The Oswingoths did not pay well, but they gave me a hut of my own. (*His aggression reappears.*) They treated me with respect . . . and I demand respect!

GENERAL : A hundred talents a month.

INVENTOR : Two hundred talents a week, with a laboratory of my own, and fifteen literate slaves.

GENERAL (*staggered*) : Fifteen slaves?

INVENTOR : If they are Germanic, I can do with six; if they are Roman, at least fifteen.

GENERAL : Do you dare . . .

INVENTOR : Take it or leave it. Watch Rome go to defeat, or else give my genius the possibility of saving your decadent civilization a little longer.

GENERAL : I will take you to Rome in chains. The Senate will decide.

INVENTOR (*strident*) : For every hour these chains

are kept on, my price will go up by a talent a day!
GENERAL (*shouting*): Take him to Rome without chains!
SERGEANT: Lef', ri', lef', ri'.
INVENTOR (*piercing*): I walk in my own rhythm!

[*The Sergeant looks to the General, who shrugs his shoulders. They go out.*]

GENERAL (*his good humour returning, he holds out his hand to the last captive, a strikingly handsome Woman dressed in furs. She comes forward slowly, impassively*): Here, Your Lordship, is the one captive which justifies the entire campaign. Come, my lovely . . . unlike her father, she will not be dragged round Rome in ignominy . . . she will enter my couch in triumph . . . naked except for my crown of laurels . . .

[*The Wife enters slowly, big with child.*]

WIFE (*eager*): Where is Julian?

[*The General looks at her, embarrassed. He gives the captive Woman his flask.*]
GENERAL: Drink!

[*She does so, obediently.*]

ARCHBISHOP (*quietly*): Go your way, Virginia. I am not fit to console you.
WIFE (*slowly*): He's dead?

[*The General reclaims his flask.*]

GENERAL (*sincere after his fashion*): For a soldier,

171

death matters less than the manner of dying. Rest assured, widow, he died like a Roman.

ARCHBISHOP : Foolishly.

GENERAL : Before the enemy was even in sight, I had drawn my sword to stab the sculptor in the back, the coward's death befitting the crime of sacrilege, when, by some instinct, Julian turned and threw himself before the blade . . . it was too late . . . I impaled them both. There was no time to bury them . . . and (*He laughs.*) there was no one left to fashion a tombstone . . . they lie together the traitor and the fool, like lovers, under the open sky (*In an epic manner.*) When they are found, nothing will be known about the treachery of one, or the folly of the other . . . men will say to themselves, Rome passed this way in all her indestructible majesty, leaving two unknown sons as viceroys in death. (*He is moved by his own eloquence.*)

WIFE (*moving slowly in the direction of the battle, numb*) : How far away are they?

GENERAL (*outraged*) : Do you not dignify your sorrow by shedding tears? Look, I am weeping.

WIFE (*beyond tears*) : Give me time . . . give me time . . . tears are private things . . . I will find them . . . (*She goes out.*)

GENERAL : There's your average foreigner for you. Any Roman matron would be wailing and beating her breast! She has done her best to ruin my evening . . . I've never seen anything less considerate. (*To the Woman.*) Come to my tent. I will find solace in your arms . . .

ARCHBISHOP (*wringing his hands*) : Oh, my son, my son.

GENERAL (*annoyed*) : Why do you call me 'my son'? I am not your son.

ARCHBISHOP : What did I call you? My son? I don't know why I did that. I feel I am sickening for some condition more terrible and more wonderful than death.

GENERAL : What's the matter with you?

ARCHBISHOP : I tried to pray to Jove, but my heart's not in it. I am no longer blinded by his great light —I see only effigies in my mind, accumulating dust. Jove is inadequate.

GENERAL (*his arm around the Woman, laughing*) : If it's hallucinations you're after, get drunk.

ARCHBISHOP : Kill me, Maximus Severus.

GENERAL : What? (*Laughs again.*) Why die for a cause you no longer believe in?

ARCHBISHOP : I no longer believe in Rome.

GENERAL (*harsh*) : Then pretend, as we all do on occasion !

ARCHBISHOP : I no longer can.

GENERAL : What? You do it better than any of us. A pigeon with two livers indeed ! And it's a miracle that I'm still alive fighting with my sword in my left hand.

ARCHBISHOP : If you felt there was no religious reason for the penance I imposed, why did you do it?

GENERAL (*eager to leave*) : For the sake of the men ! Only leaders like you and me can afford the luxury of believing in nothing but themselves. It is the men who must believe in the panoply of gods. Without this fiction of divinity, Rome would be powerless. Great gods, Your Lordship, a great general must be able to make mistakes, huge mistakes, tragic mistakes, without disillusioning the soldiery. There's only one way of doing it—and that is by creating omnipotent and capricious gods, in whose hands we are but playthings. But you know this as well as

I do. Our interests coincide. They always have done. Are you listening?

[*The General, who is on his way out with his captive, is forced to stop by the surprising intensity of the Archbishop's manner.*]

ARCHBISHOP : I hear another voice, dim, distant, as yet indistinct, like a small child crying in my heart.

GENERAL : You are becoming a woman, perhaps?

ARCHBISHOP : Makes jokes at your peril ! The voice is there, Maximus Severus, and it will take over my temple, because it is alive. It is the voice of love.

GENERAL : Voice of love? (*Impatient.*) All right. You can have the girl after I've done with her.

ARCHBISHOP : I am unworthy to touch this sweet woman. My hands would soil her.

GENERAL : What are you talking about? She's a mere barbarian.

ARCHBISHOP : A mere barbarian . . . Maximus, my son, before it is too late, set her free. Speak to her with the charm and tact of which you are sometimes capable. Take her to your tent, but as your guest. Do not outrage her.

GENERAL : Idiot ! What's her body for?

ARCHBISHOP : To tempt you . . . and to be respected.

GENERAL : Are you ill?

ARCHBISHOP : I am cured. (*He smiles.*) I no longer have to believe. I know. I am at peace. I will plant seeds in your mind which will blossom into a harvest, and long after I have gone, I will still be with you.

GENERAL (*to the Woman*) : Come.

174

ARCHBISHOP (*with great gentleness*) : Are you afraid of me now?

GENERAL : Afraid?

ARCHBISHOP : Do you suddenly sense my strength?

GENERAL : You're mad.

ARCHBISHOP : Your pleasure will be cold, your face expressionless, as that of a copulating dog—for that is what you have made yourself.

GENERAL (*furious*) : Enough! (*He places his hand on the hilt of his sword.*) You asked for death a while ago! I am known for my generosity.

ARCHBISHOP : Seek for a mirror to your pleasure in her eyes—all you find there is patience. She will lie under the weight of your coarseness, thinking other thoughts, waiting for the puppy to have done with its petty ecstasies.

GENERAL (*drawing his sword*) : It won't take much to put an end to your voice.

ARCHBISHOP (*as sweet as ever*) : And when you fall into your ugly warrior's sleep, she will look at you with pity—is this little fornicator the emblem of mighty Rome? Is the strength of the eagle in its loins alone?

GENERAL : Aah! (*He runs the Archbishop through with his sword.*)

ARCHBISHOP (*falling to his knees with an echo of the General's shout*) : Aaah! . . . Thank you, Maximus . . .

GENERAL (*aghast*) : What have you made me do?

ARCHBISHOP : I have taught you remorse . . . I have given you a conscience as a parting gift . . .

GENERAL : Why did you make me kill you?

ARCHBISHOP : Because you are weak, my son. There's no weakness more pernicious than the weakness of the strong.

GENERAL (*examining the Archbishop as though he*

were some curious, half-dangerous animal): Why are you smiling?

ARCHBISHOP (*begins to laugh very softly, and shakes his head feebly*): What a question . . .

GENERAL (*slow*): Do you derive pleasure from suffering? (*No reply. The General loses his temper. He stabs the Archbishop again and again.*) There! There! Enjoy yourself! (*The Archbishop rolls over and dies. The General stands there for a moment, panting. He returns his sword to its scabbard.*) Go to my tent. (*The Woman begins to go.*) Say something.

WOMAN: Yes.

GENERAL: Say something else. Tell me I am mad.

WOMAN: I can't.

GENERAL: Why not?

WOMAN: I am your slave.

GENERAL: I despise myself. Do you despise me?

WOMAN: No.

GENERAL (*tired*): You can't give me satisfaction. Go to my tent.

WOMAN: Yes, Maximus. (*She goes out.*)

GENERAL: I will sleep in the grass . . . (*He goes out in the opposite direction.*)

[*It grows lighter. The men gather, severally, as though for an imminent parade. 14768 is the type of hedgehog-browed individual with a curved muscular neck who is usually the runner-up in unit boxing competitions. 35914 is the joker of the unit, optimistic to the point of abnormality. 71696 has quite unnecessary dignity and some sickening middle-class virtues. He is redolent of the quarter-master's stores. 94343 affects whatever appearance happens to be in vogue, since there is safety in conformity. They still bear their wounds.*]

35914 : What time's parade, lads?

94343 : Usual time. There's nothing posted to the contrary.

71696 : By rights we should have a day off. How long's it been, six years?

35914 : I've lost count.

14768 : By rights, once we're talkin' about the letter of the law, we should get ten days off—that's if they don't skimp the old man on his triumph.

71696 : I wouldn't put it past them—to skimp him on his triumph.

14768 : Nor would I. Wouldn't put it past them.

94343 (*anxious*) : Not past them, I wouldn't put it.

[*They all pause.*]

71696 (*to 35914*) : What's up with you? Look as though you'd gapin' seen a ghost.

35914 : It's worse. Look!

[*The Sergeant enters in medieval costume—green tights, crimson jerkin with a coat of arms on it, upturned shoes of immense length, and a rakish cap with an immense feather. The men try to contain their laughter.*]

SERGEANT (*forestalling their laughter with a rising cadence of admonition, he loses his temper*) : You mucous-snotted, ordure-replete set of half-hatched sparrow chicks!

35914 : What's that? The new uniform, Narcissus?

SERGEANT : What's that you called me? Some insult?

35914 (*puzzled*) : That was your name when last we saw you.

SERGEANT : And when was that?

14768 : A few minutes ago . . . after the battle. You remember.

71696 : Ah no, I give it longer than that. Close on an hour, I give it.

94343 : It may have been yesterday . . .

14768 (*violent*) : You'll be sayin' it was last week next!

94343 (*with a sense of the occult*) : Time's a funny thing, you know. I'll be on the safe side. I'll say it was a month ago.

35914 : Once you say it's a month, it might as well be a year . . . or a century.

SERGEANT : Now you're getting warmer. I'll overlook your tunics this once, you're all too gloomy ignorant to know better, but if you go on standin' on one leg much longer, and hiding your arms and hands behind your backs, and winkin' at me, I'll really start showin' you who's the freed-man and who are the fiefs.

71696 : We was wounded.

SERGEANT : What? Them little scratches? Call them wounds? (*Sarcastic.*) Haven't they healed yet, after all this time? Tut-tut. What d'you want me to do? Kiss 'em better?

[*Mysteriously their arms, legs and eyes reappear. They stretch their rediscovered limbs as though they have stiffened with inaction.*]

That's more like it. Now move! Move! Move!

[*They run and stumble off, frightened. The Sergeant spots the figure of the dead Archbishop.*]

What's this, then? Another of you idle malingerers playin' dead? (*He kicks the Archbishop, who sits*

178

up with a start.) Oh, Father Benedict! Beg pardon!

ARCHBISHOP (*suffering*): Oh. Odbert, what a dream! A beautiful pagan in a bearskin, it was . . . Every time she parted her lips to embrace me, a flight of doves fell out of her mouth, and dropped dead at my feet. I gathered their corpses in my arms until I could no longer stand under their weight.

SERGEANT: That must have been when you fell down, my Lord Abbot.

ARCHBISHOP (*whose speech is slurred*): Quite right. Then I remember rejecting them, and gathering the pagan to me. I could feel her warm, firm breasts and the richness of her thighs, and just as I was preparing to enjoy her, a Roman came along and stabbed me in the side for no reason at all.

SERGEANT: That must have been my foot, Lord Abbot.

ARCHBISHOP: Ah yes. You saved me from the devil, Odbert.

SERGEANT: Glad to have been of service to you, sir.

ARCHBISHOP: Oh, my head. The fact is, I don't drink.

SERGEANT: I know that, Father Benedict.

ARCHBISHOP: I am merely on the trail of the damnedest after-dinner cordial . . . a couple more herbs and I'll have it, Odbert, and perhaps one day, it will bear my name.

SERGEANT: I dare say, Father Benedict.

ARCHBISHOP: Yes, Odbert . . . and not only will it give pleasure, but it will ensure the solvency of the monasteries in times of little faith. (*He tries to rise, but cannot, even with the Sergeant's help. Heartfelt—on his knees.*) We live in godless times, my friend.

SERGEANT (*grim*): Indeed we do, my Lord Friar.

ARCHBISHOP : How is the cathedral coming?

SERGEANT : Slowly, my Lord Friar, but I like to think, surely.

ARCHBISHOP : We must finish it soon. Cathedrals are shooting up all over Europe. A city is judged by the height of its spire and the length of its nave. Already I am beginning to think ours is a little on the small side.

SERGEANT : We've no shortage of labour, Father Benedict. We can afford to make mistakes.

ARCHBISHOP (*with fearful sincerity, tugging at the Sergeant's sleeve*) : Odbert, our arches must be more Gothic, our gargoyles more harrowing, our glass more stained than any of our rivals'. There is a faith-race on, my friend, which we cannot afford to lose.

SERGEANT (*lifting him up, and helping him to walk*) : I'll see to it, Lord Abbot. I'll have the men on cathedral fatigues twenty-four hours of the day. We won't be found wanting where faith is concerned.

[*As they go, the General appears from behind an obstacle. He has been listening. He is now a medieval count, a pampered, petulant exquisite in his coal-black wig. He watches them go with manifest displeasure—then hears a noise. His expression changes to one of indecent eagerness. He hides again. The Unknown Soldier wanders on, arm in arm with his bride, the Wife, who is heavily pregnant.*]

THE UNKNOWN SOLDIER (*reciting*) :

O, I sometimes think my heart will burst its banks,
Sweet girl, and that this fragile frame cannot contain

180

Such trumpeting delights forever. Even in idleness,
While carving your name upon some crusty bark, you.
Invade the corner of my eye, and fill my mind
With your dear presence as surely as when we're locked
In love. I cut my thumb, for in all work,
You are my lovely negligence.

WIFE (*reciting*):
Not always was it so. For wert thou negligent, dear boy,
My belly would not now swell with unknown fruit
And cause me to waddle like an ailing duck
While my *mind* is pregnant with images of grace.

THE UNKNOWN SOLDIER:
And we can laugh as well! What a shower of miracles . . .

WIFE:
A shower? Take refuge then.

THE UNKNOWN SOLDIER (*falling to his knees before her*):
                    Not I! Bare-headed
I kneel beneath them, my eyes uplifted, my mouth op'd wide
To drink in pleasures while those pleasures last.

WIFE (*sadly*):
Ay, there's the truth, for nothing lasts.

THE UNKNOWN SOLDIER: Nothing lasts
But memory and hope.

WIFE:
                    And memories of hope.

THE UNKNOWN SOLDIER:
And hope of memories when we are old.
My love for thee encompasses all seasons in a second,

181

Stretches beyond the confines of mortality, baffles
    time,
Cheats age, and scoffs at Providence itself . . .
Have I not known thee for a thousand years, and
    more?
Yet could I love thee then as I love thee now?
Has it not taken a luxury of time, to know
What now we know?

WIFE :

                  To feel what now we feel?
When first we met, it was the brief love
The moth feels for the flame. A mere winking of
    an eye
And all was over. We had lived, and loved.
You had even died. But I could never guess then
What I had lost.

THE UNKNOWN SOLDIER :

                  Lost but found again.
For what is love but endless rediscovery?
To see thee once is to see thee for all time
And to see thee not at all. A thousandth look
Is but a confirmation of the first, and yet is
    different.

WIFE :

I know only this, in all simplicity. I am a book
Thou hast chosen from the vast library of
women.
Open me. I lie open. The wind may lose my place,
But not another reader. I, like all volumes, have
    secrets
To be read between the lines, but the words are
    these as well.
Unread, I am not worth the binding.
Unfinished, I am not worth beginning.
Read, I surrender what rewards I may.
Understood, I am a life's companion.

Rewritten, I may yet be improved upon.

Lent to an illiterate, I go to waste.

I cannot bring myself to life. Only he who reads me well

Will know what is written there, and, knowing what is written,

Will know also that which destiny has failed to write.

But be not hard. Judge me not always by perfection's rote.

Think, instead, and humbly, how wonderful it is

The pages are not blank. One final word :

Read not with impatience, for though life, they say, is short,

At moments it seems long, and time will turn my pages

Soon enough . . .

THE UNKNOWN SOLDIER :

My eyes are weary from so much study.

Let me put you by, then, to read again

The early chapters at some later hour. I close the book.

And seal my pleasure with a kiss . . .

[*They kiss with increasing fervour. The General looks out of his hiding-place.*]

GENERAL (*aside, reciting*) :

How? How's this? The ignorant know bliss

While I, in my noble loneliness, do search for fancies,

To cajole my sad and complicated mind—

The colloquy of poets, the plucking of a casual string,

The ponderous baggage of Westphalian philosophers,

The simple songs of peasants, even those degrading
    practices—
Love of wayward women and of fearful boys—
The wild excesses of the chase, love's substitute—
All are mobilized to satisfy my spirit's hunger,
To slake my parched soul's dismal thirst.

[*The lovers break. They see the General.*]

THE UNKNOWN SOLDIER :
Most Noble Count!
GENERAL :
        Kiss on, youth! And may the soft breeze
Waft a few particles of revivifying pollen
Upon this dying plant. You spoke to each other in
    verse.
Why?
THE UNKNOWN SOLDIER : I was speaking normally,
sir.
GENERAL : Normally? Lass, could you speak to me
as you spoke to this youth?
WIFE : No.
GENERAL : Try.

[*The General prepares to listen, taking up a
romantic stance. The Wife and The Unknown
Soldier look at each other in embarrassment.*]

No?
WIFE : No, I'm truly sorry, sir, I can't.
GENERAL (*suspicious*) : You hadn't learned it by
heart, had you, from some learned volume—stolen
from my library?
THE UNKNOWN SOLDIER : We can't read, sir.
GENERAL : Why, then, did you compare yourself
to a book?

WIFE : It was a . . . a manner of speaking, sir.

GENERAL : It was a manner of singing. You can't remember any of it, can you?

THE UNKNOWN SOLDIER (*after a look at the Wife*) : No, sir.

GENERAL : You mean all that is lost?

WIFE : It comes out differently, sir, every time we see one another.

GENERAL : If you are left alone, is that it? In other words, I'm not wanted—not wanted in my own sixty thousand acres! (*His eyes half-closed.*) I seem to remember you from some other field . . . a field which sprouted rosemary and thyme . . . you came forward with that same irritating look of impervious innocence, a bunch of ridiculous little flowers gathered in your fist . . .

THE UNKNOWN SOLDIER : I have often gathered flowers, sir.

GENERAL (*slow—his eyes half-shut in reminiscence*) : And you . . . that swollen womb is nothing new . . . That look of health, that indecent sparkle . . . that galling smell of the open air and of clean linen . . . you ask a question . . .

WIFE : This will be our first child, sir.

GENERAL : Curious . . .

[*The Sergeant marches on with his men. They carry bows and arrows.*]

SERGEANT : Lef', ri', Lef', ri', halt! Three hearty cheers for the Count of Rochentière. Hip hip . . .

ALL (*in chorus*) : 'Ray!

SERGEANT : You can do better than that! Hip hip . . .

ALL : 'Ray!

GENERAL (*a languorous falconer's hand aloft*) : I

am touched by your loyalty. Where are you going?

SERGEANT : To the archery range, may it please you, to test the Professor's new weapon.

GENERAL : Good. Good. Test it well, for it is fiendish.

SERGEANT (*spotting The Unknown Soldier*) : What are you doing here then? (*A murmur among the men.*) Where you been?

THE UNKNOWN SOLDIER : Dead, I believe.

SERGEANT : Fall in then!

GENERAL : Do not be hard on him, Odbert. The lad's a poet.

SERGEANT : A what? Yes, sir. Very good, sir.

[*The Inventor enters, wearing the macabre black cap of medieval men of learning, and metal-rimmed glasses. He carries a device looking like a crossbow, but seemingly twice as heavy. He has difficulty in transporting it.*]

INVENTOR (*as German as ever*) : I thought you were going to send some men to fetch the weapon! I am engaged here as a man of learning, not as a manual labourer!

SERGEANT : Beg pardon, Professor. You, the poet, take the weapon, and fall in!

[*The Unknown Soldier takes the weapon. He falls momentarily to his knees.*]

THE UNKNOWN SOLDIER : Ooh! It's heavy!

INVENTOR (*rasping*) : It is not heavy! It is an infantry weapon, therefore it is light!

SERGEANT : Lef', ri', lef', ri' . . .

[*The men, including The Unknown Soldier, march off.*]

INVENTOR (*beaming*): With my new weapon, Count, you will soon be master of the known world.

GENERAL: I am gratified, Professor . . . but how to conquer the unknown world?

INVENTOR (*irritated, after a momentary hesitation*): One thing at a time please. (*He goes out.*)

[*The General turns to seek the Wife.*]

GENERAL: Now that we are alone, my dear . . .

[*He fails to find her. The Archbishop re-enters behind him.*]

ARCHBISHOP: Ah, there you are, my son. I have been waiting for you in the chapel. Will you not confess today?

GENERAL: I do not feel like confessing today, Father, I have too much on my mind.

ARCHBISHOP: My son, you must. I cannot allow you to squander your fortune on pardons when there is an easier, cheaper way.

GENERAL: Does the money for the pardons ever get halfway to Rome?

ARCHBISHOP: Ten Hail Marys for that crack, my son. Kneel with me here, if you will. I will draw my cowl over my head to preserve the necessary anonymity. I have things to tell you.

[*They kneel.*]

GENERAL: You have things to tell me?

ARCHBISHOP: I must confess you first.

GENERAL: My mind is troubled, Lord Abbot. I have had women—enjoyed them in the vulgar

187

parlance—yet I did not enjoy them. They come to make my bed—anonymous women, their arms full of sheets. They are my serfs. I exercise my rights. All passes joylessly, in silence.

ARCHBISHOP : All this since yesterday?

GENERAL : Since this afternoon, I believe. Lads too —they make a change.

ARCHBISHOP : Heavens! Is there no end to your appetites?

GENERAL : I have found no vice which appeases me for longer than the time it takes to perform it.

ARCHBISHOP : My son, there is no alternative to the hair shirt and the scourge.

GENERAL : The hair shirt is bad for the skin.

ARCHBISHOP : Better the skin should suffer than the soul.

GENERAL : Men only see the skin.

ARCHBISHOP : Our Father sees them both. Come, my son, I will thrash you lightly.

GENERAL : I have not finished my confession.

ARCHBISHOP : Is there more then? Is it possible?

GENERAL : My waking hours drift into night—my sleeping hours, if I ever sleep, drift into day. I sometimes wake the cooks at night to banquet all alone—and I sometimes retire at noon. I may walk in sleep or lie abed awake—where dreams begin and actions end I am not sure. I wonder, therefore, if I perform these horrid deeds at all, or whether they are not all done in my head, for my solitary delight.

ARCHBISHOP : Are you sure of this?

GENERAL : I can be sure of nothing now.

ARCHBISHOP : Men of high station deserve the benefit of our doubt. Since you are half-drowned in dreams my son—I command you to dream that you have been soundly whipped by me.

[*The General writhes and howls as though he is being flogged.*]

Not now, my son. Your fustigation can wait. You have given me an earnest of your intention to relish every blow, and that is enough to go on with. I need to talk to you.

GENERAL : What is it?

ARCHBISHOP : You need a change of air, my son. Your skin is flaky, your complexion sallow, while your mind festers with depravity.

GENERAL : What do you suggest?

ARCHBISHOP : I have no suggestion; Rome has.

GENERAL : Rome?

ARCHBISHOP : His Holiness himself! On his behalf I can promise you, in writing—listen carefully—a remission of all sins, past, present and *future*. You realize what this means? A passport to paradise!

GENERAL (*dry*) : What are his conditions?

ARCHBISHOP : Why do you speak so quickly of conditions?

GENERAL : Because I am a man, and so is His Holiness. Why are you so disappointed?

ARCHBISHOP : I expected at least a moment of unmitigated delight.

GENERAL : I will express delight when and if I feel it. What are his conditions?

ARCHBISHOP : Take a crusade to the Holy Land, my son.

GENERAL : A crusade? You call that a change of air? Mosquitoes, pestilence and sores?

ARCHBISHOP : All *future* sins?

GENERAL : A crusade may last for years! Armand de Queslin and Raymond de la Baule never came back at all!

ARCHBISHOP : They are in heaven at this moment, and better off than here. I guarantee it!

GENERAL : I may miss ten, fifteen hunting seasons.

ARCHBISHOP : Copulation to your heart's desire, free of moral charge.

GENERAL : No more chamber music!

ARCHBISHOP : The music of gold cascading into coffers.

GENERAL : No.

ARCHBISHOP (*an appeal to reason*) : My son, Christianity needs you.

GENERAL (*slowly*) : And before it was Imperial Rome, wasn't it?

ARCHBISHOP (*slowly*) : You remember, do you?

GENERAL : Oh yes . . . memory comes fitfully, in flashes . . . I remember then being a victim of your faith. You made me stab you, and after that I knew no peace. I had killed an unarmed man at his own request. Can one go further in servility? No, I will not go to the Holy Land.

ARCHBISHOP : Can't you see that you have had your revenge already, my son? His Holiness, in his infinite understanding, offers you a pardon for sins as yet uncommitted, and yet you say, with reprehensible arrogance, that he is only a man. If he is a man, how much less of a man am I, and what is my pardon worth? I can no longer absolve you. You cheat at every confession.

GENERAL : You came here as my confessor, with endorsed credentials!

ARCHBISHOP : But since then you have worn away my faith as surely as water wears away a rock. You have had your revenge, my son. I came to lift you off the ground; you have brought me to my knees. I will not exonerate you before God. You are on your own.

190

GENERAL (*slowly*) : Religion is blackmail. It holds a man's opinion of himself to ransom.

ARCHBISHOP : It assesses the value of a man's opinion to himself.

GENERAL : Religion is superstition. It makes a man conscious of the alternatives.

ARCHBISHOP : Religion is the work of God . . .

GENERAL : Perfected by the devil. I will go to Jerusalem.

ARCHBISHOP : Deo gratias ! (*Chanting.*)

Alleluia . . . Alleluia . . .

We go to the land of our Lord

To clash with the infidel horde.

And if we should die,

To heaven we'd fly—

Father Benedict gave us his word.

Alleluia . . . Alleluia . . .

[*The men file in, carrying crossbows and religious symbols. They chant with the Archbishop. He leads them in a procession. He goes off majestically with the court, while the men go round in diminishing circles, the song growing feebler as the sun now beats fiercely on them. They fall exhausted, one by one.*]

SERGEANT (*comatose, once they have fallen*) : Right. Fall out ! Wait . . . for . . . it ! Fall out ! (*He falls to the ground.*)

35914 (*feeble*) : You've got some water, by the holy cross ! Why can't we have a sip ?

SERGEANT (*feeble*) : It's holy water, for the daily benedictions. You lumber-headed blunderbumpkins won't never be able to tell the secular water from the divine, will you ?

94343 : We seen you take a swig.

SERGEANT : I was testin' its freshness, got it? In *case* we're reduced to using it. I never ask the men to do nothing I'm unwilling to do myself.

35914 : How was it then?

SERGEANT : Un-ruddy-drinkable. Satisfied?

THE UNKNOWN SOLDIER : No, I'm not satisfied . . .

SERGEANT : Eh?

THE UNKNOWN SOLDIER : They didn't even give me time to say good-bye.

SERGEANT : When you get back, my boy, there'll be a large bouncin' lad to greet you. That'll be a nice surprise, won't it?

REBEL : A large bouncing lad of about twenty-five years old, the way this campaign's going.

SERGEANT : I don't want no rumination from you. I got my eye on you. If it wasn't so flamin' hot, I'd settle you.

REBEL : Well, it is so flaming hot. You can't even see to keep your eye on me. Every time you blink, the perspiration rolls in.

THE UNKNOWN SOLDIER : Death is a waste of time.

[*They all stir, despite their stupor.*]

All men die at night, and it holds no fear when it goes by the name of sleep. What holds fear is dying.

[*The Wife appears.*]

WIFE : Why do you speak of death? Have you forgotten . . .

THE UNKNOWN SOLDIER : I have remembered. To die is but search for you again.

SERGEANT (*gruff*) : Who are you talkin' to?

THE UNKNOWN SOLDIER : What would you write to me, I wonder, if you could write?

WIFE : I am not lonely, because I am alone. The men have gone. The hunting horns are silent. There is no mischief anywhere. Even the beasts of the forest wander into the pasture unafraid. There's nothing to confess. And what would you write?

THE UNKNOWN SOLDIER :

I'd write, I'd write . . . let me see . . .

I'd write that I am lonely because I am not alone. My loneliness travels with me. Six thousand men carry it

And I carry theirs for them. I share my secrets

As I share my water and my food.

WIFE : But why? These men were never friends of yours.

THE UNKNOWN SOLDIER : Where there is no choice, all men are friends. (*Pause.*) Why are you silent?

WIFE :

I feel another journey coming.

The child begins to stir, and I know my cue for tears.

I will not cry. I will not cry at all. Now or then.

ARHCBISHOP (*entering*). Why are you crying, my child ?

WIFE (*angry, turning her head away*) : Crying? I am so angry with my man !

ARCHBISHOP : Angry, child? Can he help his absence any more than I can help my presence?

WIFE : Why are you here to bother me?

ARCHBISHOP : They deemed I was too old to die before my time. Rest assured, your man will return . . .

THE UNKNOWN SOLDIER : I have marked my place in the book. Even if it drops from my hand, I will know every detail of what went before.

WIFE : Why should you die?

THE UNKNOWN SOLDIER : A coward can survive. He finds out nothing. He merely stays alive.

WIFE : Is that not enough?

THE UNKNOWN SOLDIER : No.

SERGEANT (*crawling over to The Unknown Soldier*) : Here, take a sip of water, man. You're ravin'!

THE UNKNOWN SOLDIER : I don't want it.

SERGEANT (*as violent as he can manage*) : Take it! That's an order! You're under-bloody-mining us all!

[*Calls of 'Take it,' 'Go on,' etc., are heard. The General enters in full armour. hardly able to move.*]

GENERAL : Water, for the love of God!

SERGEANT : Platoon! To your feet!

[*They struggle to their knees.*]

GENERAL : Forget the the protocol! Just give me water.

SERGEANT : It is blessed.

GENERAL : I don't care if it's perspiration of a saint, I must have it!

SERGEANT (*as he gives the General his flask*) : It's the last we have.

[*The General drains it.*]

GENERAL : Is there no more?

[*The men look at each other, dismay and hatred suddenly written on their faces. A weird sound is heard.*]

The infidel! Every time I put this armour on, I feel a pressing need to relieve myself.

SERGEANT: We can get you out of there in half an hour.

GENERAL: With the enemy so close? Are you mad? No, no, it must be a nervous reaction to the imminence of battle. It will pass. Where did the sound of the trumpet come from?

SERGEANT (*pointing right*): From over there.

ALL (*pointing in all directions but one*): There, there, there.

GENERAL: Then we will advance in the opposite direction. With a little luck we may outflank them.

SERGEANT: Form up! Shoulder crossbows!

[*The men form up with the greatest difficulty.*]

Any order of the day, sir?

GENERAL: Instruct every man to pray for my safety.

SERGEANT: You heard that, men. Start praying!

[*They go off like a hideous parody of the Crucifixion.*]

Right, prayers over. Someone give us the song of the old hermit of Chartres.

REBEL: I'll sing it. I've written new words for it. (*He sings.*)

There was an old hermit of Chartres
Who fell in love with a tartre.
The cunning old fox
Contracted the pox
And became a good Christian martre.
Alleluia! Alle-lu-ia!

195

[*They disappear. The Arabic trumpet sounds a louder and more imminent note.*]

ARCHBISHOP (*to the Wife*) : Come with me. Do not stand here, staring into the distance. What can you see, child?
WIFE : I'll tell you soon enough.

[*There is a sound of the clash of arms, shrieks and screams. It rises to an electronic intensity and dies on a sob. The victor appears. He was known as the Enemy Leader in Roman times. He is now in the gorgeous robes of an Arab chieftain. With him is his daughter, veiled. He claps his hands. A couple of Arabs carry in the suit of armour and set it down.*]

ENEMY LEADER (*tapping the armour with his scimitar*) : Are you still in there, Christian? You have had the incalculable misfortune to fall into the hands of the Emir Ibrahim Bin Yussuf Al Hadj, the richest of your opponents, and the most devout.

[*The General enters. He wears only a loincloth, and his hands are tied. He looks minute alongside his armour. The Unknown Soldier enters with him, also tied.*]

Oh, there you are ! How you have shrunk in defeat, little fellow.
GENERAL : I am Archibald, Count of Rochentière.
ENEMY LEADER (*sarcastic*) : Who would have thought it.
GENERAL : A ransom can be arranged.
ENEMY LEADER : Not with me. No money can speak

for you. (*Curious.*) Ah, after all, you have one soldier with you who did not run away. Do you plead for your leader's life, fellow?

THE UNKNOWN SOLDIER : Yes, I plead for any man's life.

ENEMY LEADER (*staring at him*) : But I know you . . . not so much your face as your expression . . .

Yasmina, my daughter, do you remember him?

WOMAN (*unsure*) : No . . .

ENEMY LEADER : A tree . . . a tree beside a mountain path . . . we passed in chains, you and I . . . a couple of Roman soldiers staring at the sky like lovers . . . (*He turns slowly to the General, snarling.*) And you! Three times round the walls of Rome . . . now I know you! Showered with rose petals by that belching, puking, stinking Roman mob! The rocks and pebbles hammering my head. I hoped that every second would be my last, but still I lived on.

GENERAL : Stop it! Those were different times . . .

ENEMY LEADER (*full of loathing*) : Different times!

GENERAL : There were no great moral issues. We all behaved like animals. We knew no better.

ENEMY LEADER : Did we not? I asked you whether you believed in a life after death and you mocked me. Now have you learned to believe? I still do, alas. I cannot kill you for ever!

[*He lunges at the General. The Unknown Soldier steps forward.*]

THE UNKNOWN SOLDIER : No! (*He accepts the blow on the shoulder and sinks to the ground.*) No more death . . . (*He dies.*)

WIFE : Now try to console me.

ARCHBISHOP : I look into your eyes, and see that I cannot.

WIFE : No, you cannot . . . (*She goes out slowly.*)

ARCHBISHOP (*he vanishes*) : Oh my God, to what folly have I lent your name?

ENEMY LEADER (*slow*) : You have found a man to die for you, and it has appeased my anger. Who was he?

GENERAL (*shaking*) : I never knew his name.

ENEMY LEADER (*with opulent oriental melancholy*) : With what economy he expressed himself, and made us look like fools! We will build a fountain from which fresh water will play eternally. Our finest craftsmen will encrust it with rubies and emeralds, symbolizing blood and hope. It will be known as the fountain of the Unknown Warrior, the words 'No more death' will be inscribed upon it, and it will be a place of pilgrimage.

GENERAL : All this for a simple soldier?

ENEMY LEADER (*with a return of cunning*) : All this for a simple soldier. And for the Count? What did he do to you after I had been taken to Rome, Yasmina?

WOMAN : He respected me for a day or two.

ENEMY LEADER : How strange—and then?

WOMAN : Then he took me to his bed after all.

ENEMY LEADER : He made you his wife?

WOMAN : No. He sold me into slavery. He had a wife already.

ENEMY LEADER : I see. He likes many women, as we do. The life of the harem would suit him down to the ground, don't you think?

GENERAL : I have all the women I want in my castle.

ENEMY LEADER : Did nobody warn you that it is dangerous to refuse the hospitality of an Arab? We are extremely sensitive people. Generosity is

a part of our religion. I invite you to share my
harem with me for life.

GENERAL : I am, of course, profoundly touched.

ENEMY LEADER : As a eunuch.

GENERAL : You must be joking!

ENEMY LEADER : I am prepared to laugh, Christian.
Take him away!

[*The Arabs bustle the screaming General out. The
Enemy Leader laughs.*]

Is the joke a good one, Yasmina?

WOMAN : Very good, O my father, but I can't
help wondering . . .

ENEMY LEADER : Yes?

WOMAN : What will he do to you next time?

ENEMY LEADER (*nervous, for once*) : You are right,
my treasure . . . (*As they go.*) Once he is castrated,
we must treat him with every consideration.

[*The General screams.*]

Oh, my dear Count, you will partake of some
sherbet with me?

[*The sky darkens again. The men wander on,
dishevelled, in rags.*]

SERGEANT : Where are we?

REBEL : It's cold now . . . we must be near home . . .

[*The Archbishop appears, now dressed as a puritan,
with conical black hat, austere coat and pumps.
He carries a small portable pulpit, which he erects.*]

SERGEANT : Beg pardon, sir, could you tell us where
we are?

ARCHBISHOP : Thou art lost, thee and thine.

35914 : We know we're lost, with all due respect. We'd like to know where we are.

ARCHBISHOP : Upon the road to redemption, if thou wilt hear my lesson.

14768 : Redemption? In what land is that?

ARCHBISHOP : In the kingdom of heaven.

35914 : We don't want to go there, sir. We've managed to avoid that.

ARCHBISHOP : Thou standeth in need of salvation, brother. We have sinned exceedingly, and there is no health in us. The coffers of righteousness are empty, the vaults of Satan full to overflowing. Let us begin our war upon the master of darkness at the beginning, at the hour of birth. The newborn child must needs be covered at once, lest the sight of his own nakedness lead him into immediate temptation . . . at times of lactation, the dress should be so arranged that only the nipple protrudeth, never seeming to be the crown of that odious rotundity which is the field for some of Beelzebub's most notorious pranks. The infant should be blindfolded, and guided to the milk-giving valve, so that no heinous association may develop in later life. I see a question?

SERGEANT : May it please Your Honour, we're just a platoon of soldiers on our way home from the Crusades. If you'd just answer our question, we'll be on our way . . .

[*The entire cast begins to assemble during the Archbishop's harangue. They are dressed simply, and without palpable personality.*]

ARCHBISHOP (*aghast*) : From the Crusades, sayest thou? Repent, repent then ! Monstrous instruments of a Popish plot! And home, say you? Home is the world for Christian brothers. In my company, thou art in the company of almighty God, and therefore thou art home!

[*The men look at one another in perplexity.*]

14768: Home is where my wife and children are.
ARCHBISHOP: What sayest thou? And what would'st thou do with thy wife, pray?
14768: If you must know, I would lay with her . . . it's been about twenty years . . . I enjoy her company . . .
ARCHBISHOP: Lay with her? My brother, the devil is well and truly entrenched in thee! Out, out I say!
14768: Out what?
ARCHBISHOP: Out, Satan! Our sisters are in this world for the sacred purpose of procreation, and no other—at no time may they be enjoyed. (*He suddenly sees the Wife.*) Thy ankle is showing, sister!

[*A murmur of anger rises among the crowd.*]

Thou never knowest where Satan will show himself next!

REBEL (*with a shout*): We *are* home! It's Father Benedict! He's gone round the bend!
SERGEANT (*angry*): Don't you know better than to interrupt a sermon?
REBEL: Father Benedict! The bird with two livers! Is this the result of your guilty conscience?

[*The men seem about to manhandle the Rebel.*]

201

ARCHBISHOP : Yeah! Yeah, remind me of my sins, brother. I carry the sins of the world upon my back, among them mine own! Let him speak! It is good to suffer so!

REBEL : And he's taking you in again?

14768 : Stone him!

71696 : Hang him!

SERGEANT : Burn him! The devil's got inside him!

ARCHBISHOP : Leave him be! Let us sing a hymn, in unison. Harmony too is the work of Satan, to say nothing of counterpoint, canon and fugue. Those rocky protuberances of music are ledges upon which the dark one can conceal himself unmolested! We have the sins of centuries to erase, dearly beloved! The debit of the human race is such that it will take all our courage and all our gravity to rediscover the paradise we have lost. Take heart! Cover the statues, whitewash the churches, dress the naked on the murals, and above all—above all—close the theatres—for ever!

The entire cast, who have placed Puritan hats on their heads during this speech, and murmured 'Amens' and 'Alleluias', now gaze upward as the curtain slowly falls. Their eyes follow the curtain with awe and a bewidered sense of occasion.

Curtain

SECOND ACT OF WAR

The stage has an atmosphere of cool precision about it, and no wonder, for the Archbishop sits there sipping chocolate, his ample wig cascading down his shoulders. He is enjoying the company of the beautiful female who has been known hitherto as simply the Woman.

WOMAN: How is it, my Lord Archbishop, that, apart from your wig, which betokens adherence to another age, there is nothing about you to suggest the thinker, let alone the divine?

ARCHBISHOP (*affable*): La, madam, we live in the Age of Reason. In an age of reason, it behoves men to behave reasonably.

WOMAN: Men, yes, but clergymen?

ARCHBISHOP: Clergymen most of all, for they have the reputation of being the least reasonable of men. Have you noticed how they rail against common practices such as adultery?

WOMAN: Would you defend libertines then?

ARCHBISHOP: Are not the words liberty and libertine derived from the same source, madam? Does not indeed libertine have a feminine grace to it, leaving liberty but a pallid masculinity—yet we, cowardly creatures that we are, tend to lay down our lives for the one and condemn the other.

WOMAN: Are you not afraid of being overheard, my Lord?

ARCHBISHOP: By women! I ask nothing better. By men? I am a man. By other clerics? I waited until I was at the top of my particular tree before I gave free reign to my thoughts. (*He sighs humorously.*) And thus I wasted the best years of my life. (*Smiling.*) Do I confuse you? May I make amends by complimenting you upon your chocolate? It is as delectable as you are.

WOMAN: Is that a declaration, sir, or an expression of regret?

ARCHBISHOP (*aside*): With that wit she reads between my lines—although I must say, the spaces I leave there are enormous. I will dissemble. (*To the Woman.*) Were I to be over-conscious of the grey hairs which lie concealed beneath this wig, then I own, madam, it would be an expression of regret. And yet, if I am to pay heed to the youthful heart which still lies hidden beneath the cloth, I'll grant it is a declaration.

WOMAN (*aside*): Vanity knows no age. As man's body weakens, it is the only one of his attributes which grows stronger by the minute.

ARCHBISHOP: May I have some more chocolate?

WOMAN (*aside*): His desires are insatiable. And yet, if the younger clerics were like he, the churches would be full to overflowing. (*She rings a bell.*) Sir, how did you come by such light thoughts?

ARCHBISHOP: I came to them by artistry, madam, for nothing requires more art in its diffusion than conventional morality. For example, I make you conscious of your own morality, madam, by compelling you to reject my advances.

WOMAN: And if I surrender to you, sir?

ARCHBISHOP: Then I will happily admit failure, madam, and pray for better luck next time. Come, shall we to your bedchamber?

WOMAN: But I have ordered more chocolate, sir!

ARCHBISHOP: After I have drunk my chocolate, madam.

[*The Wife enters, carrying the chocolate. She is a plump and appetizing soubrette.*]

WOMAN: You speak with a rare cynicism, my Lord.

ARCHBISHOP : Madam, it is the language of our times. The Puritans sought to bend the world into the image of paradise, but being human, all they succeeded in doing was to emulate hell. The great wind of freedom which sweeps through the world is mankind's sigh of relief . . . relief at life rediscovered . . . with all its transitory pleasures and teasing condiments.

WOMAN (*aside*): With what indecent haste he drinks his beverage! I must induce him to ask for a third cup.

ARCHBISHOP (*aside*): That is, without a doubt, the worst chocolate I have drunk in years. What sacrifices a man must make to punctuate his gallantry, for the greatest enemy of the rake is haste.

WOMAN : Will you not partake of another cup, sir?

ARCHBISHOP : Another cup, madam, would be to abuse your time and my taste buds. Chocolate, like love, palls when taken in excessive doses. (*Rising.*) Shall we then pass from one to the other?

[*A bugle blows as the Archbishop leans over his quarry.*]

WOMAN : It is my husband, with his regiment.
ARCHBISHOP : How like a soldier, to be forever in the wrong place at the wrong time.

[*The General enters in a bright and preposterous uniform.*]

GENERAL : Madam, I have returned!
WOMAN : And I, sir, am the happiest and most impatient of women!

GENERAL (*seizing her, with a laugh*) : Impatient, say you?

WOMAN (*rejecting him*) : To hear your news.

GENERAL : Fifty days' march across Flanders and back again in search of the enemy—and no sign of him.

ARCHBISHOP : He, no doubt, spent fifty days in search of you.

GENERAL : Ah, my Lord Archbishop, I did not see you. (*Aside.*) What does this scurvy cleric here?

ARCHBISHOP (*aside*) : If he fails to see me in a room, is it any wonder he has difficulty finding the enemy in the whole of Flanders?

GENERAL : It is a strange kind of war indeed, with no sign of the enemy.

ARCHBISHOP : Shall we say it is a safe kind of war?

GENERAL : Is that an insinuation, sir?

ARCHBISHOP : It is a congratulation, sir.

GENERAL : If you were an officer . . .

ARCHBISHOP : I am not, sir; I oppose graver dangers.

GENERAL : Such as constipation from too much chocolate?

ARCHBISHOP : Constipation of the body, sir, is curable. That of the mind, not.

GENERAL (*aside*) : This fellow rails with a spirit something less than sacred. (*To the Archbishop.*) Have you designs upon my wife, sir?

ARCHBISHOP (*aside*) : For coarseness of expression, this varlet takes the wafer. (*To the General.*) Not to have designs upon your wife, sir, were to be insensitive to beauty. And yet, not all designs become cathedrals.

WOMAN (*aside*) : I blush—for the cathedrals.

GENERAL : Why do you blush, madam?

WOMAN : Alas, sir, it is a pleasant lot for a woman

of quality to know that when her husband makes reference to the enemy, he is alluding to none other than her own dear father?

GENERAL (*rattled*): Madam, madam, we have explored this territory many times before, and found it sterile. The fact that your revered father, the King, and I find ourselves opposed on the field of battle is but one of many inconveniences which arise from a marriage of convenience. (*A trumpet sounds.*) What is that?

ARCHBISHOP (*shading his eyes and looking out over the audience*): The enemy at last! *He* has found *you*.

GENERAL (*drawing his sword*): Outnumbered—and surprised!

ARCHBISHOP: That you are surprised is never surprising.

WOMAN (*tragic*): Father! O that this woman's heart of mine would break! To see the noblest of men locked in mortal combat!

GENERAL: What's this? How now? A white flag? Does he surrender?

WOMAN: Surrender! Never! Father, rather die than see your honour smirched by the vile upstart I call husband by your Royal decree!

[*The father, the Enemy Leader, enters in a uniform of absurd dignity, feathers all over the place. The Unknown Soldier carries his bag.*]

ARCHBISHOP (*since the General and the Wife still look out over the audience*): Ahem. At the risk of surprising you again—His Majesty is with us.

ENEMY LEADER: I come in peace, most elevated, splendid and resourceful Prince.

WOMAN: Father!

207

GENERAL : Silence, woman! Most noble, august and utterly serene Majesty, is this then surrender?

ENEMY LEADER : Surrender? Never!

WOMAN (*grateful*) : Oh, Father!

ENEMY LEADER : Silence, girl!

GENERAL : Is it the gesture of men of honour to appear in line of battle at the hour of lunch?

ENEMY LEADER : Let no man say I cut short meals in pursuit of glory. On this occasion, however, our interests coincide, and under the flag of truce I came as quickly as I could.

GENERAL (*surprised*) : Our interests coincide? How's this? Explain yourself, Your Majesty.

ENEMY LEADER : I am aware that on the face of it, there is no love lost between us.

WOMAN : Oh, Father!

GENERAL
ENEMY LEADER } (*together*) : Silence!

ENEMY LEADER : We both claim the throne of Heligoland, the electorate of Potsdam, and the morganatic Grand-Duchy of Hessen-Essen and Plessen. Pleasant as this war of succession has been, it is time to put an end to it by mutual consent before it puts an end to us by force of circumstances. I have since discovered however, that our patrols met on numerous occasions without our knowledge.

GENERAL : What say you?

ENEMY LEADER : They met, and in lieu of killing each other as prescribed in the articles of war, they fraternized, comparing notes on conditions of life, payment, and the like.

GENERAL : Have you proof of this?

ENEMY LEADER : This man, my servant. Come forward, man. (*To the General.*) Speak slowly, he is a fool.

GENERAL (*very slowly*) : Is this true, man? Did you fraternize with my soldiers? (*Pause.*) Make friends? (*Pause.*) Pow-wow?

THE UNKNOWN SOLDIER (*grinning*) : Oh yes, sir, we did, but not more than once or twice a day. There wasn't the opportunity, you see.

GENERAL : And why did you not tell your officers of this?

THE UNKNOWN SOLDIER : We reckoned they'd have put a stop to it.

GENERAL (*exploding*) : But why is this man still alive? He should have been shot as an example!

ENEMY LEADER : Are you willing to shoot your entire army as an example if you are not sure that I am going to do likewise?

GENERAL (*suddenly*) : But I know you, soldier. You always went off and chatted with the enemy, didn't you?

THE UNKNOWN SOLDIER : I've always been interested in people, sir, if that's what you mean.

GENERAL : And flowers . . . and poetry . . .

ENEMY LEADER (*dry*) : He died for you once, and now you wish to shoot him.

GENERAL : Great heavens, I know you too!

WOMAN (*suffering*) : I warned you, Father.

GENERAL : The degradation of a life spent in a smelly harem, surrounded by vast women bathing in curdled milk!

ENEMY LEADER : You used to sing for us after supper in a pure and exquisite coloratura voice.

[*With a roar, the General draws his sword. The Enemy Leader does likewise.*]

WOMAN : Father! Husband!

ENEMY LEADER : Do keep quiet, Annabel. Your relationship to us has been established quite a while ago. (*To the General.*) I recognized you at your wedding, dog!

GENERAL : Why did you allow me to go through with it?

ENEMY LEADER : Because the world has shrunk. A king needs enemies to justify his appetite for conquest—and what greater evidence of esteem is there than to keep enmity in the family. I could think of no greater compliment to you.

GENERAL : You were afraid of me this time! That's why you bribed me with your daughter.

ENEMY LEADER (*haughty*) : It is ungentlemanly to draw attention to the truth in such a cavalier fashion.

GENERAL : It's true then!

ENEMY LEADER : I only admit it because the days of our hostility are over, as are the days of elegance in battle. (*They resheathe their swords.*) The business of stopping battles for meals, which began as an exquisite courtesy, has become an acute embarrassment. There is not enough bread to go round—and in the absence of bread, the only substitute is thought.

WOMAN : If there is no bread let them eat—(*She stops abruptly.*)

ARCHBISHOP : What, my daughter?

WOMAN : I was going to say something dreadful.

ARCHBISHOP : Rest assured—it has already been said.

ENEMY LEADER : Our soldiers have begun to read. We encouraged them in our infinite blindness—believing in a kind of abstract enlightenment as a mark of progress. But—sooner than you imagine—mark my words—they will master thoughts as well,

210

ideas, theories. And how will a decent war be possible with literate soldiery?

GENERAL : You're mad! A soldier with theories?

ENEMY LEADER (*to The Unknown Soldier*) : Who is your favourite author, man?

THE UNKNOWN SOLDIER : I don't know many, Your Majesty.

ENEMY LEADER : But you can read?

THE UNKNOWN SOLDIER : Slowly, Your Majesty. I still confuse the effs and the esses.

ENEMY LEADER : And have you any preferences as to reading matter?

THE UNKNOWN SOLDIER : Oh yes. Your Majesty. But there's still so much I haven't read, I don't like to express myself.

ENEMY LEADER : Feel free, man, feel free.

THE UNKNOWN SOLDIER : Well, Your Majesty, if that's an order—then, I'd say, of the little I have read, I like Voltaire best of all.

GENERAL (*staggered*) : Voltaire?

WOMAN : Voltaire? Who's that?

ENEMY LEADER : Quiet, Annabel. You are too well educated to know. (*To The Unknown Soldier.*) And do you understand him?

THE UNKNOWN SOLDIER : No, sir, not entirely. That's perhaps why I like him. I am compelled to read him again and again, Your Majesty.

ENEMY LEADER : And what book in particular is your favourite? There's hardly room in your pack to take the collected works into battle.

THE UNKNOWN SOLDIER : Oh, a little volume, Your Majesty—I hope I pronounce it right—called *Can-deed*.

GENERAL (*exploding*) : Where did you get it?

THE UNKNOWN SOLDIER : One of your soldiers was kind enough to lend it me, sir, on patrol. Now that

I've finished it, I hope to be able to return it to him, if we're lucky enough to go on patrol again.

GENERAL (*beside himself*): What kind of book is this *Candide*?

ENEMY LEADER (*amused*): You have not read it?

GENERAL (*stoutly*): I have read about it. That is why I have not read it.

ENEMY LEADER: It is about the victory of a simpleton over the hazards of a world governed by kings, princes and prelates. I will lend you a copy.

ARCHBISHOP (*dryly*): I have a copy here.

[*The General seizes it.*]

ENEMY LEADER: We must sign the peace treaty without delay. Already our men are intermingling on the parade ground.

GENERAL (*looking out over the audience*): Exchanging reading matter! (*Furious.*) My court of honour looks like the campus of a university? What's come over them? They're even laughing! Let us adjourn to the apartments of state. Madam, do you partake of some chocolate with His Lordship while your royal father and I do draft the treaty.

ARCHBISHOP (*as they go*): More chocolate! Six more cups and she'll be mine!

[*When they have gone, The Unknown Soldier avidly opens his pack, brings out a slim volume, and sits down to read it, slowly, with fiendish application. He understands a phrase with the greatest difficulty, and roars with laughter. The Wife enters with a tray to take away the chocolate.*]

WIFE (*robust*): Get up off the good chair, you lout!

212

[*They look at one another. The Unknown Soldier slowly rises. Long pause. Her voice is small, with ill-disguised emotion.*]

Oh, it's you . . .

THE UNKNOWN SOLDIER (*awkward*): After all this time, is that all you're going to say?

WIFE: What do you expect me to do! Rush into your arms?

THE UNKNOWN SOLDIER (*almost inaudibly*): I half-expected it, I must say.

WIFE: What are you doing, dressed up like that?

THE UNKNOWN SOLDIER: I'm a subject of His Majesty.

WIFE: Since when?

THE UNKNOWN SOLDIER: All my life, all this life.

WIFE: What are you doing? Reading?

THE UNKNOWN SOLDIER: Mm.

WIFE: That's new.

THE UNKNOWN SOLDIER: It's new, yes. Five years ago it was only the alphabet. Now it's every other word, sometimes two in three. Can you read?

WIFE: I can write my name.

THE UNKNOWN SOLDIER: That's a start. (*Pause.*) What are you doing here?

WIFE: I'm in service with the Prince—or rather, with the Princess. We hardly ever see the Prince.

THE UNKNOWN SOLDIER: Well, it was bound to happen, I suppose.

WIFE: What?

THE UNKNOWN SOLDIER: Our meeting again. (*Pause.*) Remember we used to spout poetry at each other? I can't do it any more. Since I started reading, I can't phrase a thought properly, the way I used to.

WIFE: I don't want to remember it.

THE UNKNOWN SOLDIER : Why not?

WIFE : I was someone else then, I was younger.

THE UNKNOWN SOLDIER : No, you weren't.

WIFE : I was younger. That's why I can't bring myself to rush into your arms.

THE UNKNOWN SOLDIER : Don't you want to?

WIFE : God knows I want to.

[*They embrace.*]

THE UNKNOWN SOLDIER : What's the matter?

WIFE : We're an old married couple, that's what's the matter. We're an old married couple at birth, every time, every time . . . and you keep on getting yourself killed. I can't keep up with you, and that's the truth. It's too silly.

THE UNKNOWN SOLDIER : You may be right. But I'm a bit slow, you know. I need time to think things over.

WIFE : Time? Centuries.

THE UNKNOWN SOLDIER : Centuries is time.

WIFE : What's your name now?

THE UNKNOWN SOLDIER : Engelbrecht.

WIFE : Serves you right.

THE UNKNOWN SOLDIER : What's yours?

WIFE : Ernestine.

THE UNKNOWN SOLDIER : That's pretty.

WIFE : You know it's hideous. (*She rushes into his arms.*) Oh God, how you annoy me!

[*They kiss.*]

THE UNKNOWN SOLDIER : Thank heaven I've found you.

WIFE : Thank heaven, yes, but for how long? You're bound to do something stupid again.

THE UNKNOWN SOLDIER : I don't consciously do stupid things.

WIFE : D'you think I'd love you if you weren't what you are? You'll go under again when I'm six months gone. And I'll be hawking your child around, begging for alms.

THE UNKNOWN SOLDIER : What's he like?

WIFE : Who?

THE UNKNOWN SOLDIER : Our son.

WIFE : How d'you know it's a son?

THE UNKNOWN SOLDIER : Stands to reason. It's me that needs replacing, not you.

WIFE : He's fine. Sometimes he's thin and under-nourished, sometimes he's huge and demanding. Last time he insisted on being breast-fed until he was two years old. It was agony. But always he's the spitting image of you—with that soft welcoming look—and I'm beginning to think I'm a fool to go through these endless labour pains just in order to bring forth another one—a lad who will one day go into his father's business—that of being an unknown soldier.

THE UNKNOWN SOLDIER (*trying to be bright*) : Oh, come on, I'm not ready to retire yet.

WIFE : That's the trouble.

THE UNKNOWN SOLDIER (*sighs*) : I reckon someone's got to do it, once it's become an established practice. Like someone's got to be the hangman. It's un-pleasant, but someone's got to do it while there's hanging.

WIFE (*very wistful*) : The hangman comes home for supper. (*She sees his dejected look at the irrefuta-bility of her argument, and is moved.*) Oh, come with me to my room . . . I need you in my arms, you fool!

THE UNKNOWN SOLDIER : When?

WIFE : Now!
THE UNKNOWN SOLDIER : But I'm on duty.
WIFE : So am I.

[*A song begins to swell in volume as men and flags and lanterns begin to appear.*]

CHORUS (*singing*) :
Lift up your eyes, and face the light,
You men accustomed to the night.
The scarlet banner of revolt has burst
Through the cloudbanks of despair.

[*As the menace increases, The Unknown Soldier and his Wife seek comfort from one another.*]

WIFE : I hate it when men sing together. It's always a sign of going away.
THE UNKNOWN SOLDIER : I don't recognize the music —or the words.
CHORUS (*singing*) :
Lift up your eyes, prepare to fight.
Freedom's torch is burning bright.
Snuff out the lives of the accurs'd,
Hold their heads up by the hair !

[*The men burst in.*]

71696 (*a new personality*) : Where's your revolutionary cap, citizen?
THE UNKNOWN SOLDIER (*laughing*) : Why don't you call me by my name then?
94343 : Our names keep us apart in the shadow of religion and superstition. The name of citizen unites us in secular equality.
WIFE (*nervous*) : Come with me. We've got some work to do.

14768 : What work is more pressing than revolution, citizen?

[*The Unknown Soldier laughs.*]

Why do you laugh?

THE UNKNOWN SOLDIER : At your joke, friend. It so happens my most pressing work is to press His Majesty's shirts.

[*There is an outcry among the men.*]

REBEL (*calming the fury of the men*) : Do it then, albeit for the last time. Revenge is good and wholesome, but to degrade the condemned would be merely savage. Let kings die in spotless linen. It is the only perfection they know.

THE UNKNOWN SOLDIER (*annoyed*) : What's all this talk about kings dying? What are you lads up to?

WIFE : Come away from here, Engelbrecht.

THE UNKNOWN SOLDIER : No. I've got to get to the bottom of this.

REBEL : The revolution has swept away centuries of tradition in the blinking of an eye, in the changing of a thought, in the twinge of a nerve. We took even ourselves by surprise. For the first time in history, the people have seized the power nature intended as their birthright! Now before we build the new life on the eroded soil of society, we must dispose of the garbage from the banquet of kings and emperors which has come to an end at last!

[*The men cheer and harangue him.*]

THE UNKNOWN SOLDIER : It's all wrong, you know, to do all this without asking!

217

REBEL (*powerful, staying the fury of the men*): Take him away, woman, and let him into your secrets. He is so overwrought that, if you do not turn his passion in your direction, he may well overthrow the revolution by himself.

[*The men's anger is canalized into laughter.*]

WIFE (*pulling at The Unknown Soldier*): Come on. Come away.

14768 (*who is not so easily sidetracked*): I demand his head!

REBEL (*patient*): You will have it, citizen, I have no doubt. But in time. Let us concentrate on heads with brains in them. Where is the captive? (*The Inventor comes on in chains.*) Ah. The citizens arrested you in your workshop, I understand. You were building a cannon for the King and a new type of breech-loading rifle for the Prince. You were serving two masters.

INVENTOR (*scornful*): He who serves only one master is a slave; he who serves two is already relatively free.

REBEL: There is a degree of logic in your cynicism.

INVENTOR: On the contrary, there is a degree of cynicism in my logic. I have chains on my wrists. Why? The men who judge me until yesterday fired the rifles I designed, whichever side they were on. There is no difference in morality between us, only a difference in salary.

REBEL (*powerful*): You cannot blame a working-man for wishing to eat.

INVENTOR (*powerful*): And you cannot blame an intellectual for wishing to eat more than the working-man!

71696 (*furious*): I demand his head!

218

REBEL : What are your terms for working for us?

71696 (*in the outcry*) : He should die, and now you're freeing him?

REBEL : To kill him will serve no purpose except to put an end to years of research and knowledge which we can use. I ask you, citizens to close your minds to the ugly thoughts this creature expresses.

INVENTOR (*released*) : My terms are to free me of my shackles. I don't even insist that you put them on yourselves. *Now* tell me I am incapable of generosity!

REBEL : Kindly stick to technicalities at all times. Free this citizen!

14768 (*obeying*) : I think it's revolting.

REBEL : Rest assured, citizen, I agree with you.

71696 : Then why . . .

REBEL (*violent*) : Because there are a hundred other kings left. We have only set one foot in the door of the vast ballroom of state. Shall we rub our hands in self-congratulation and talk of world revolution when all but the first small gesture remains yet to be made? Where we had one enemy before, we now have countless enemies. And he will win who walks forward with the purity of his ideals in one hand and science in the other!

INVENTOR : Admirably expressed, if I may say so.

REBEL : What have you for us?

INVENTOR : An idea I have cherished for some years, and held back against the rainy day, as it were. It came back to me owing to the crowded condition of my cell. This . . . (*He spreads out his plan*) . . . device is a semi-automatic decapitator which is able to sever five heads every eight minutes during a normal working day. This represents a figure of three hundred and twenty victims in a working day or two thousand two hundred and forty a week. I don't know if it's your intention to work on Sunday's.

REBEL: There will be a day of rest—on any day but Sunday. Have you made provision for the trials in your assessment?

INVENTOR (*a little disappointed*): Oh, there are to be trials? I see . . . (*Ingratiating and apologetic.*) Naturally, I couldn't take trials into my calculations, which are of a necessarily abstract and technical nature.

REBEL (*puzzled*): This invention of yours reminds me of something.

INVENTOR (*hasty*): Oh, I know it bears a superficial resemblance to a French contraption, but theirs does not go far enough. It only dislodges one head at a time. Owing to the extreme rigidity of my frame and the length of my blade. I can dislodge five at a time. There is no comparison between the two humane exterminators. (*Suddenly mournful.*) Yet, life is never without its ironies. The simple fact that the revolution broke out in France and not here means that my device will go into the history books as a guillotine and not as a Schwalbenbrecher.

REBEL: I understand your deception, citizen.

INVENTOR: It is wonderful to be understood . . . (*Risking it.*) citizen?

REBEL: Take your places at the bench. The republican court is now in session.

INVENTOR (*sotto voce*): You mean, I was not on trial? Then, with your permission, I will go to my workshop to prepare!

[*The Wife enters. She is pregnant.*]

REBEL : Are you on trial, citizen? If so, take your place in the dock.

WIFE (*anxious*) : I'm not on trial, but I heard a rumour my man was.

REBEL : Rumours these days are usually correct. You may be seated if you wish to see justice dispensed.

WIFE : But ... don't you remember me?

REBEL (*cold*) : Yes, I remember you.

WIFE : My man saved your life!

REBEL : You expect me to save his? I am not a man any longer, but an instrument of the people's justice. Take a seat if you wish. Enter the dock, Archbishop.

[*The Archbishop is led on.*]

94343 : On a point of order! Is it not citizen Archbishop?

REBEL : He will be citizen Archbishop if acquitted. If not, he will remain plain Archbishop, and an enemy of the people.

ARCHBISHOP : It is strange that today a friend of God should by definition be an enemy of the people.

REBEL : God does not exist.

ARCHBISHOP : Since when?

REBEL : Since yesterday at the tenth hour, when Decree 914 of the Republican Code was passed unanimously.

ARCHBISHOP : I see. Well, it's just as well to know this.

71696 : Reason is the only God.

ARCHBISHOP : So there is a God after all, if it is Reason. Strange still that if Reason be God, that a man of Reason should be an enemy of the people.

221

REBEL (*to* 71696, *irritated*): Citizen, await your turn to speak. You have no experience in argument.

71696 (*dogged*): Citizen, I know my rights.

ARCHBISHOP (*aside*): To know one's rights is one thing. To exercise them, quite another. I fear our friend is not long for this committee, or for this world.

REBEL: Are you an Archbishop?

ARCHBISHOP: I am.

REBEL: Do you believe in God?

ARCHBISHOP: I do.

[*A buzz of excitement among the committee members.*]

Is it so surprising to find an Archbishop who believes in God?

REBEL: Are you willing, from this day on, to accept Reason as your God?

ARCHBISHOP: Certainly. I see nothing incompatible between God and Reason. God has never required me to do other than to behave reasonably.

REBEL: Are you prepared to desecrate your altars, to strip your abbey of all religious symbols?

ARCHBISHOP: In that most religious symbols are inferior art, I will not weep to see them go. If you really feel that the people have overnight attained such a degree of mental sophistication that we can dispense with all Christian symbolism, I am quite willing to attempt the experiment.

94343: Why do you give in to our ideas so easily? Are you afraid of death?

ARCHBISHOP (*smiling*): Of course I am afraid of death. I am only a man, after all—and that's why I'm gratified that I have not had to give in, as you

222

say, to a single one of your ideas. I have not even compromised. You have not required me to. It would have been different if you had asked me to believe in *nothing*. You have not done so, precisely because you know full well that you cannot ask the people to believe in *nothing*. They will not follow you if you do. You must cautiously transfer their belief from one deity to another, and if I arrive at the conclusion that the two deities are, in fact, the same one, I see no reason to quarrel with you. You may think you are desecrating; All you are really doing is redecorating.

94343 : Are you accusing us of being Christians then?

ARCHBISHOP : I would not dream of being so impolite, citizen. I am merely saying that we are, all of us, reasonable.

REBEL (*smiling in spite of himself*) : Thank you, citizen. I move for his immediate acquittal. All citizens in favour kindly signify your approval in the usual manner.

71696 : I ask for death.

94343 : I second that.

35914 : No opinion.

14768 : No opinion.

REBEL : You are acquitted.

ARCHBISHOP : Thank you very much.

71696 : I protest!

REBEL : As chairman, I have the casting vote under Clause 8, Subsection 24A.

94343 : You have no right . . .

REBEL : There is no time for technicalities, we have work to do, citizen! (*He raps his gavel.*) Next prisoner.

[*The Archbishop sits beside the Wife, who moves*

away slightly. The Enemy Leader enters. He is bound.]

What is your profession?
ENEMY LEADER : King.
REBEL : Do you repent?
ENEMY LEADER : What for, you scum? For being what I was born?
94343 (*rising, furious*) : What's that he called us?
ENEMY LEADER : My time is valuable. Don't waste it. Where do I go to die?
REBEL : You will be told soon enough. Have you anything to say?
ENEMY LEADER : A great deal, but not to you. Now kindly take my head off. There are ladies waiting.
REBEL : Do you require religious consolation according to your beliefs?
ENEMY LEADER : As a king, I can offer it myself?
REBEL : Are we unanimous? (*Nobody dares to stir.*) Death. Stand aside there.
ENEMY LEADER : Thank you for your courteous brevity.
REBEL : Next prisoner.

[*As the Enemy Leader steps aside, the General, now the Prince, enters the dock.*]

What is your profession?
GENERAL : You know perfectly well.
REBEL : Do you repent?
GENERAL : Why? You think it easy to rule? (*He laughs.*) Good luck to you all—and I thank you, gentlemen, for taking a weight off my shoulders— get it? A weight off my shoulders?

[*He and the Enemy Leader laugh heartily.*]

ENEMY LEADER : Damn good. I must remember that. Weight off my shoulders.

[*The General steps down.*]

REBEL : We have not finished with you yet !
GENERAL : I have finished with you, however.
94343 (*hysterical*) : Death ! Death ! I won't be laughed at like that !

[*This provokes renewed laughter from the monarchs.*]

ENEMY LEADER : How did we ever fight decent wars with such animals ?
REBEL (*rapping his gavel rhythmically*) : Kindly re-enter the dock !
GENERAL : I refuse. You are determined to kill us. Therefore you can no longer threaten us. Please hurry up. There are already four thousand souls in a prison I built to contain sixty. Conditions there are intolerable. No doubt it is due to your adminis-trative inexperience, but you simply must execute at the rate you arrest, otherwise there will be out-breaks of the plague, and as Prince, that is the last blight I wish on my subjects.
REBEL (*betraying a little irritation*) : We are quite aware of the problems. Do you desire religious consolation ?
GENERAL (*gay*) : From the Archbishop ? My wife may accept.
REBEL : Death. Next prisoner.

[*The Woman enters the dock. The Wife gasps.*]

Profession ?

WOMAN : None.

REBEL : Do you repent?

WOMAN : Repent? What for? I have had an enviable life. The only fear which forever haunted me was that of old age. Now, thanks to your generosity, this fear is removed from me, for which I humbly thank you.

WIFE (*in tears*) : Oh. Your Highness!

WOMAN : I will not need that army of face creams, Ernestine. I bequeath them to you.

REBEL : Have you anything to say?

WOMAN : I am a woman, gentlemen. I have already talked excessively all my life.

REBEL : Do you require religious consolation?

WOMAN : I am not certain, gentlemen, that the consolation I would derive from his Lordship the Archbishop would be of a purely spiritual nature, and so, in the interest of my soul, which will presently be under more august scrutiny, I had best abstain here on earth.

[*The General and the Enemy Leader applaud her statement.*]

GENERAL : Excellent speech.

ENEMY LEADER : Absolutely first class.

REBEL : Death. Next prisoner.

[*The Sergeant takes the Woman's place. A murmur of hostility.*]

Profession?

SERGEANT : Sergeant, as you know full well.

REBEL : Do you repent?

SERGEANT : Repent? Have you lost your reason, lads, or something? I only did my duty.

94343 : You struck me across the face with the butt of a blunderbuss 'cos you said I wasn't peelin' potatoes fine enough!

SERGEANT : I told you to peel the shiftin' spuds, not cut them in half! I will not have waste!

94343 : Four teeth lost—and teeth is harder to come by than potatoes!

14768 : You kept the water from us in the desert!

71696 : You stole our food from us in Greece!

REBEL (*rapping his gavel in order to cut short the fugue*) : Order! Order in the revolutionary court!

94343 : Death!

14768 : Death!

71696 : Death!

35914 : Oh, I don't know . . . it seems too late to kill him now . . . I've thought of it so often, but now—I mean, it'd be like killing a chicken you've begun to call by name, isn't it?

REBEL : Have you anything to say?

SERGEANT (*in a weak voice*) : Yes. Yes, I got a lot to say.

REBEL : Make it brief.

SERGEANT : What's come over you all? I was like a father and a mother to you all . . . when I knocked out your teeth . . . who picked them up?

94343 : You did, to throw them away.

SERGEANT : They was no good to you any more, was they?

14768 : I'm going to vomit if he goes on.

REBEL : Have you finished?

SERGEANT : I haven't hardly begun.

REBEL : Do you require religious consolation?

SERGEANT : And another thing . . .

GENERAL : Sergeant.

SERGEANT (*stiffening*) : Sah!

GENERAL : Answer the question.

227

SERGEANT : I didn't hear no question, sah!

GENERAL : Do you require religious consolation?

SERGEANT : I don't want to die, sah, with your permission.

GENERAL : You are to die, Sergeant. That's an order.

SERGEANT : Sah!

GENERAL : Why are you trembling, man?

SERGEANT : It's never 'appened to me before, sir.

REBEL : Death. Stand down. Next prisoner.

[The Unknown Soldier enters the dock.]

WIFE *(emotional)* : What are you doing there?

THE UNKNOWN SOLDIER *(smiling)* : I don't know. Ask the lads.

REBEL : Profession?

THE UNKNOWN SOLDIER : Soldier.

WIFE *(violent)* : What's come over you all! You know him as well as I do—better! Profession : Unknown Soldier. Why all the stupid questions? What kind of a revolution is this?

REBEL *(rapping his gavel)* : The authority of the court will be respected.

THE UNKNOWN SOLDIER *(tapping his stomach)* : You're not . . . again?

WIFE : Of course I am. I always am.

THE UNKNOWN SOLDIER *(incredulous)* : That's quick.

REBEL *(insistent)* : Do you repent?

THE UNKNOWN SOLDIER : What for?

REBEL : I take it that is an answer. Have you anything to say?

THE UNKNOWN SOLDIER : What about?

ARCHBISHOP : May I intercede for him, citizen?

REBEL : Can he not speak for himself, citizen?

ARCHBISHOP : I think no, citizen.

94343 : I object!

REBEL : On what authority do you wish to intercede on his behalf?

ARCHBISHOP : On the authority of Reason, citizen.

REBEL (*laying down his quill*) : Very well.

ARCHBISHOP : For what crime is the man arraigned before the people's court?

REBEL : That is a good question. Without such men as this, Kings would be impotent, tyrants would be powerless, the revolution would have taken place long ago. Today, in his hour of triumph, when all men have rushed for their armbands and their Phrygian bonnets, he is still dressed as a soldier of the King. When arrested, he was pressing the King's shirt!

[*A murmur of anger from the court.*]

ARCHBISHOP : You yourself have not put a Phrygian bonnet on your head, nor are you wearing an armband. Are we to assume from that that you are less enthusiastic a revolutionary than your fellow members of the revolutionary tribunal?

REBEL : I am its chairman.

ARCHBISHOP : Were you always a revolutionary? Were you born one?

REBEL : What do you mean?

ARCHBISHOP : Wasn't there a moment at which you saw the light?

REBEL : Yes, as a student.

ARCHBISHOP : Well now, if this man were to choose this moment to see the light? If he were to denounce the King, for instance. Wouldn't that ensure his acquittal?

REBEL (*smiling sadly*) : Of course. But you know him as well as I do. You know very well he won't.

ARCHBISHOP (*to the Unknown Soldier*): Young man, you remember me.

THE UNKNOWN SOLDIER (*smiling*): Oh yes, Your Lordship, Father Benedict, the Puritan . . .

ARCHBISHOP (*hastily*): Yes, yes, all that. Now, I order, you, as your father in God, to denounce the King. Don't ask why. Just do as I tell you. Repeat after me : I denounce the King.

THE UNKNOWN SOLDIER : What for?

ARCHBISHOP : You are entirely innocent. You know it. I know it. Every citizen on the revolutionary tribunal knows it. We just cannot afford to have you misunderstood once again !

35914 : Go on, denounce the King !

14768 (*edgy*) : Denounce him, damn you !

THE UNKNOWN SOLDIER : I don't understand what all this is about. Why are all the lads sitting up there with those hats on? Is it a new uniform, or something? Will we all be getting them?

WIFE (*writhing*) : Oh, I can see it coming again . . . For my sake . . . for our child's sake . . . denounce the King !

THE UNKNOWN SOLDIER (*affectionate*) : Don't be silly, my sweetheart. You don't even know His Majesty. How can I denounce him for your sake?

94343 (*bursting out*) : I can't stand it no more. He's always throwing himself in front of swords. Maybe that's what he wants. Let's give it him then. Death ! Death ! Death !

71696 : He brings bad luck, that's what I say. Something always goes wrong when he turns up— something you can't forget afterwards. Death !

ENEMY LEADER (*impatient*) : Come along, man, denounce me ! What difference does it make now?

230

THE UNKNOWN SOLDIER : I couldn't do that, Your Majesty, not after the great kindness you've shown me. It wouldn't be right.

ARCHBISHOP : The King has ordered you to denounce him !

THE UNKNOWN SOLDIER : He's no longer the King though, is he? They took him off the throne, if I understood it right. I mean, it wasn't as a king he showed me great kindness, but a man. It's as a man I owe him a lot.

REBEL (*quiet*) : Do you require religious consolation?

THE UNKNOWN SOLDIER : If it'll help the Archbishop here, I'll take anything he has to offer.

ARCHBISHOP (*faltering*) : What did you say?

WIFE : I want to die in his place.

REBEL : You are not on trial.

WIFE : I want him to know what it's like to survive ! I want him to do the mourning for a change !

REBEL : Sit down or leave the court.

WIFE : Damn the revolution ! Long live the King ! There, arrest me !

REBEL (*glacial*) : You are pregnant. The death sentence may not be carried out on a pregnant woman, since you are carrying a potential revolutionary in your womb. Article 73, Subsection 18. You can shout to your heart's content, citizen. As for your husband, he has been given every chance to save himself. Either through an inability to understand the revolution or a refusal to do so, he has refused to avail himself of the opportunity. This leaves the revolutionary court no alternative but to condemn him to death. There are now sufficient criminals for the sentences to be carried out. You will be buried in a communal grave with no trace of your identities.

WIFE (*furious*): This time he's dying before witnesses.

REBEL: Order! Order!

WIFE: Don't interrupt me, damn you! You know he's my husband and that I'm his wife. Even if he's to be unknown as usual—do I get my pension?

REBEL: Citizen, how can you speak of money at such a time?

WIFE: I've shocked you! Death of this useless sort has become a habit in our family, and anything that becomes a habit is shocking to those who face it for the first time. I want to know—and I want my man to know—do I get my pension this time as a soldier's widow?

REBEL (*taking refuge in an unnatural calm*): There are no pensions for the dependants of criminals. You will receive the pittance due to expectant women, Article 77, and afterwards free milk.

WIFE (*screaming*): Free milk! The one thing I can produce myself, I get free! What's the difference between all your governments?

REBEL: Order!

WIFE: Fraternity? If my brother banged a hammer all the time I was talking to him, I'd slap his face for him, I would.

REBEL: Take her away!

WIFE: Take her away! So much for liberty!

WOMAN: Ernestine!

WIFE (*suddenly sober*): Yes, ma'am.

WOMAN: Think of your child. You can't change anything. Go away. Let us die in peace.

[*For a long while, the Wife and The Unknown Soldier look at one another—a silence respected by the court. Then she goes quickly.*]

REBEL : Take them away.

INVENTOR (*like a maître d'hôtel*) : This way please. Now, if you will lie down here, with your face downward—in any order.

[*They go off, saluting the public with bravado. The Inventor remains on the stage, looking off.*]

ENEMY LEADER'S VOICE : I refuse to lie with my face downward. What do you take me for, a slave?

INVENTOR : All my calculations are based on a downward position.

ENEMY LEADER'S VOICE : What are you doing, man, face downward?

THE UNKNOWN SOLDIER'S VOICE : Well, I'm not a king, sir. I'm just an ordinary man.

ENEMY LEADER'S VOICE : Turn over at once. That's an order!

THE UNKNOWN SOLDIER'S VOICE : Yes, sir.

SERGEANT'S VOICE (*suddenly hysterical*) : I've got a new idea for my defence! I denounce the Prince! I denounce the King!

[*He is drowned in derisive voices. The Archbishop wanders to the front of the stage, deeply troubled. The Rebel joins him.*]

INVENTOR : Ready? A little to the left, madam. No, to your left. It won't last long. *Eins. Zwei. Drei!* (*The blade falls.*) It works!

[*A cheer from the men. The next scene is punctuated by Eins, Zwei, Drei, the formal cheer, and the rise and fall of the blade.*]

ARCHBISHOP : You cannot disguise the fact that you are as troubled by events as I am.

REBEL : I make no attempt to disguise anything. I believe in the revolution. That is enough.

ARCHBISHOP : When will it end, this massacre of the innocents? Eins, Zwei, Drei, day after day.

REBEL : It is not for me to decide. The tribunal has a communal responsibility.

ARCHBISHOP : And do you think *you* will survive your responsibility?

REBEL (*slow, smiling*) : I think . . . not.

ARCHBISHOP : You will be called on to die in your turn?

REBEL : No doubt. The people tire of the same faces.

ARCHBISHOP : And will you remain as impassive under the blade as before it?

REBEL (*casual*) : There is no life without a sense of death. Man lives his own death in his imagination all his mature life. Sometimes I die well—sometimes not so well. It will depend on the weather. But by then—there won't be much I regret leaving behind. My dog . . . the taste of coffee . . . the smell of apples . . .

ARCHBISHOP : Things created by reason?

REBEL : You realized yourself that we have no quarrel with God. We oppose Him merely because He has become the tool for ambitious men. It was time to liberate Him.

ARCHBISHOP : Perhaps you're right.

REBEL : Only perhaps?

ARCHBISHOP : Doubts are the spurs of thought. The more I know what I am supposed to think, the less I know what I really think. There goes that blade again ! I can hardly stand it any more !

REBEL : And I hardly noticed it.

ARCHBISHOP : Does that callousness signify to you that your revolution has succeeded?

REBEL : It has failed.

ARCHBISHOP : Then how can you pretend to support it?

REBEL : And can you, as a Christian, maintain that Christianity has succeeded? (*The Archbishop is silent.*) Ideas cannot be judged by their success or failure in practice. The idea of liberty is really only clear in captivity. Equality is only understandable in an autocracy. Fraternity has a meaning in a civil war. The poor pregnant wife was right, of course. Ideals do not lend themselves to practical application in normal times. They are vibrant only when they are unattainable.

ARCHBISHOP : And love?

REBEL (*with a shrug*): Love may be possible in secret, I don't know. But on the scale of policy, it is sanctimony. Do you love God more while preaching to a faceless multitude, or in the silence of your cloister?

ARCHBISHOP : And yet there are great communal experiences.

REBEL : They are political. Even Christ's miracles were political. What convinced the multitude was not a sentiment of love, but the fact that there were suddenly enough loaves and fishes to go round.

ARCHBISHOP : But can we live at all if we face such facts without illusion? Do they not harden the heart? The blade falls again! You don't even flinch.

REBEL : I don't even hear it. The revolution has failed, as it was bound to. And yet I am more of a revolutionary than ever. I know of no idea more beautiful, more sacred than a compulsory faith in man—who is, forever undeserving of such faith. Like you in your meditations, I knew my cause was right only when I was in isolation, waiting for the day. That longed-for day brought its compromises, the dream is tainted by the need to administer. From the pure seed of a divine idea, a political forest has sprouted.

ARCHBISHOP : There is no solution, then.

REBEL : You Christians are more cynical than we. Your solution is not of this world. You safely relegate it to the kingdom of heaven.

ARCHBISHOP : While you aim at paradise on earth? May God help us all ! As though we hadn't learned our lesson with the Puritans !

REBEL : Ah yes, but we are the Puritans. Our ideals are impossible. That gives us our solemn sense of failure. Ours are the faults not of vice, but of excessive virtue. The blade has fallen again, as though to prove my point, and this time it was you that didn't hear it.

ARCHBISHOP : I was frankly thinking of something else. It was the mention of the Puritans that did it.

REBEL : What?

ARCHBISHOP : I thought of the temptations of the flesh. I had not entertained it for so long, that it burst upon me as a new and sparkling idea. (*He sighs.*) It is hard for a Christian to survive in a godless society. The first casualty in a godless society is always the devil. And without the devil, a Christian is lost ...

[94343 *appears between them.*]

94343 : Citizens, you are both under arrest.

REBEL (*unsurprised*) : On what grounds, citizen?

94343 : Under suspicion of having communicated with one another.

REBEL : By what means?

94343 (*the most terrible of accusations*) : By means of words.

236

ARCHBISHOP : I miscalculated again. I was sure he would be the first to fall from grace.

REBEL : Rest assured . . . he now holds my job . . . he will be the next.

94343 : No more talking! Enter the dock.

[*The Rebel enters the dock.*]

Your profession?

REBEL : The saddest profession in the world. Aging revolutionary.

94343 : Do you repent?

REBEL : Yes. I betrayed the revolution.

94343 : How?

REBEL : It is for you to tell me, citizen. I have not seen the indictment.

94343 : We will take that as an admission.

REBEL : It was intended as one.

94343 : Do you require religious consolation?

REBEL : No.

94343 : Have you anything to say?

REBEL (*automatic*) : Long live the glorious revolution of the people! Death to the tyrant!

94343 : Death.

14768 : Death.

71696 : Death.

35914 : Death.

94343 : Next. What is your profession?

ARCHBISHOP : How must I answer such questions? I no longer know. I have heard them so often, I no longer understand them. I am a man.

94343 : I asked your profession, not your sex.

ARCHBISHOP : I am a man. In conscience I can't say more.

[*Two figures enter in terrifying unison, like*

237

monstrous Samurais. The one on the left is dressed in the uniform and shako of an operetta Hussar. The one on the right wears the swollen mortarboard and lifeless tassel of a Balkan lancer. The clank of metal appendages accompanies them. They both wear ferocious moustaches. They come to a noisy halt. They are the General and the Enemy Leader.]

GENERAL and ENEMY LEADER : We have returned!

94343 (*nervous*) : You have no business here! Clear the court!

GENERAL (*rasping, affected. His speech is occasionally afflicted with a distressing stammer*) : Is this stupid farce still going on then? And are you still alive, Archbishop? Bravo! Although it seems we are just in time to rescue you.

ARCHBISHOP : Yes, yes indeed, Your Excellencies. The nick of time, I assure you. Whom do I have the honour of addressing?

GENERAL : We are the Archduke Boris-Emmanuel the Eighth.

ARCHBISHOP : Both of you?

GENERAL : We are using the royal 'we'.

ENEMY LEADER (*who also has his speech defect—a glut of sibilants, with its attendant splashes, and a hail of saliva*) : We also have that right. We are Nikolai-Ludwig of Posen and Pilsen, hereditary overlord of more places than we are able to recollect without assistance.

GENERAL : We are, not unnaturally, cousins as well as brothers-in-law. We are married to one another's sisters. Our parents, too, are cousins. Everything under the sun has been done to preserve our hereditary deficiencies, which distinguish us from mere people in the singular.

ENEMY LEADER : Now, hurry up, you swine, and

get into uniform, where you belong! War is on the point of breaking out again.

ARCHBISHOP (*alarmed*): War? Again? May one ask between whom?

GENERAL (*leaning on the Enemy Leader's shoulder*): Between us. Didn't you know, we are mortal enemies? We have seen his summer manoeuvres.

ENEMY LEADER (*smiling wickedly*): We have seen his winter manoeuvres.

GENERAL (*with the same complicity*): It promises to be one of the most interesting wars yet fought.

REBEL: What's the matter with you, citizens? Where's your revolutionary spirit? The court is in session, and you allow the solemn proceedings to be interrupted with only a feeble word of protest? Clear the court!

ENEMY LEADER: We thought you were a prisoner?

REBEL: I am under sentence of death. I insist that the sentence be carried out by the will of the people!

GENERAL: Like a scorpion, this pin-headed socialist does away with himself rather than face the inexorable march of progress.

ENEMY LEADER: Poor fool! Your world of high ideals is dead forever.

REBEL: Once born, it can never die!

GENERAL: You wish us to prove it to you? Schinkelmann!

[*The Inventor enters, well-dressed in the period of 1910. He wears a hard collar, pin-stripe trousers, bowler hat and pince-nez. He clicks his heels together with a snap. He carries a pointer.*]

INVENTOR: Highnesses! At your service!

GENERAL : Tell these peasants what has happened to the world while they have been asleep in their committee.

INVENTOR (*the perfect schoolmaster*) : I guessed that would be Your Highness' wishes! (*He claps his hands.*) Lanterna magica!

[*A screen descends from the top of the guillotine frame.*]

Take out your pens and papers, and don't copy from your neighbours! First slide, please!

[*A slide appears. It shows an old-fashioned railway engine in motion. A gasp from the men.*]

14768 : What's that?

INVENTOR : I was expecting this question. This is a steam engine; this iron giant on two parallel rails can propel a thousand civilians or two thousand soldiers at sixty miles an hour.

71696 : But where are the horses?

INVENTOR : The horses are inside the boiler.

[*He begins to laugh.*]

71696 : Don't they get burned?

[*The Inventor, the General and the Enemy Leader laugh.*]

INVENTOR : Ach, it's too good! Next slide, please!

[*A Victorian battleship appears. The men show consternation.*]

This is a dreadnought! A ship which can destroy

240

a city of twenty thousand people in ten minutes with its guns. It travels fifteen sea miles in the hour thanks to its boilers. (*He points.*) The steam escapes through the funnels.

35914 : How does it work? Like a kettle?

INVENTOR (*surprised*) : This boy shows promise. Yes, like a huge kettle!

35914 : Which blows the steam against the sails?

[*Great laughter.*]

ENEMY LEADER : Say what you will, the peasant is the salt of the earth!

INVENTOR (*still laughing*) : Next slide.

[*An ancient airplane appears. The men panic.*]

This is an airplane, which can fly like a bird with as many as two men aboard for up to two hours!

94343 : It flies? With men in it?

INVENTOR (*pointing*) : You can see the men clearly in the photograph.

GENERAL : Well, Rebel?

REBEL : If birds can fly, why shouldn't man? It was only to be expected eventually. But who pays for all this progress?

INVENTOR : Next slide.

[*Some miserable children appear in a factory scene.*]

With child labour, production is rising, the market is booming. There never has been such prosperity in all of history!

REBEL : You put children to work?

ENEMY LEADER : Not just any children, working-

241

class children. They know their station. They expect nothing else, and they are happy with their
lot.

ARCHBISHOP : They receive religious instruction?

GENERAL : Free!

ARCHBISHOP : That sounds like progress indeed.

INVENTOR : It is not merely child labour, that is a
detail! Next slide!

[*A long row of native porters appears in a tropical
setting.*]

We have empires on which the sun never sets, in
which we have found unlimited resources beneath
the soil and unlimited resources on the soil to
drag those riches to the surface!

ENEMY LEADER? : Well, Rebel? Do you understand
how feeble ideas are against resources?

REBEL : It will not always be so. If the sun never
sets on your empires, it follows that it never rises
either. You will destroy your own prosperity out
of force of habit. Rome did it. Summer does not
last forever, and it is not spring which lies in wait
for you, but autumn.

[*The men look at one another in perplexity.*]

INVENTOR : Next slide!

[*A machine gun appears.*]

This is a machine gun, which can fire a hundred
bullets in a minute, and kill as many men if correctly aimed!

94343 (*Suddenly, with devotion*): Long live their
Highnesses!

[*The Archbishop launches himself eagerly into the fray.*]

ARCHBISHOP : Hip! Hip! Hip!
ALL : 'Ray!

[*A bugle sounds.*]

14768 : There's the bugle, lads! Come on! At the double!

[*The men go out.*]

REBEL (*to the Archbishop*): You, too? (*He goes, quickly.*)
ENEMY LEADER : After him!
GENERAL : Don't bother, Cousin. He has nowhere to go but the world, and that is shrinking.
ENEMY LEADER : If it is shrinking as you say, we must have something to fear after all . . .
GENERAL : Oh yes, dear Cousin . . . each other . . .

[*They go out, laughing slightly. There is an explosion.*]

ARCHBISHOP : What was that?
INVENTOR : From the sound of it, it was a bomb. A home-made one.

[*The Rebel runs in and out. He stops when he hears the newspaperman.*]

THE UNKNOWN SOLDIER : Archduchess Carmensita assassinated! General mobilization! Read all about it!
ARCHBISHOP : How was that? How ghastly! I'm afraid my money is rather out of date.

INVENTOR : Here. Two papers, please.

ARCHBISHOP : Who was the Archduchess Carmensita?

INVENTOR : I don't know. There are so many of them. What interests me is the mobilization.

ARCHBISHOP (*melancholy*) : At moments, I feel we are like children who never grow up.

INVENTOR (*sinister*) : Thanks to me, the toys grow up instead.

[*They go out. The Wife wanders on, dressed as a streetwalker.*]

THE UNKNOWN SOLDIER : Why d'you choose this pavement? D'you do it just to annoy me?

WIFE : Annoy you? That's rich. I'm earning my living same as you are.

THE UNKNOWN SOLDIER : There are plenty of other pavements. This is a big city.

WIFE : That goes for you too.

THE UNKNOWN SOLDIER : Aren't you ashamed of yourself?

WIFE : Oh, how high and mighty we've become! What d'you think? I've been reduced to this before because of you. It's better than the workhouse. I can choose my own clothes, and I can sleep till noon.

THE UNKNOWN SOLDIER : But what happens the rest of the time?

WIFE : It's good for you to imagine. I've lived longer than you have, remember. I got to ninety-three one time, and I've reached eighty quite often. You're a quite small part of my life, come to think of it. I know your son much better than I'll ever know you.

THE UNKNOWN SOLDIER (*bleak*) : How is he?

WIFE : Last time he was born blind and backward. The doctor said it must have been the shock of seeing you go.

[*The Sergeant enters. He wears a black armband.*]

THE UNKNOWN SOLDIER (*horrified, miserable*) : War declared ! Read all about it !

[*The Sergeant buys a paper.*]

Blind and backward !
SERGEANT : Let's have the change, then ! What's the matter with you?
THE UNKNOWN SOLDIER : Sorry, mister.
SERGEANT : You'll be in the army soon, my lad. That'll wake up your ideas for you ! (*He looks at the paper.*) War, eh? Just as well. I'll give it three weeks with all the modern weapons we got. (*He goes out.*)
THE UNKNOWN SOLDIER : Blind and backward? Well, that does it. I'm not going this time. I'm going to register as a conscientious objector.
WIFE : You? (*She laughs.*) Isn't it marvellous. My lad a conshie !
THE UNKNOWN SOLDIER : Well, I might as well be for all the use I am. In all these thousands of years, I've never killed anyone. I only go out there in order to get killed. You're right. It's silly.
WIFE : D'you expect me—or anyone else for that matter—to look up to you if you don't go do your bit?
THE UNKNOWN SOLDIER : My bit? What the hell are you talking about? I want to stay with you for a change. I want to see the boy !

WIFE : There isn't no boy, and there won't be another one if I can help it.

THE UNKNOWN SOLDIER : Then why are you so keen for me to go, if you don't care for me?

WIFE (*irritated*) : Oh, you know us, surely, after all this time. In spite of all my good resolutions, something always goes wrong sooner or later. I find myself that way.

THE UNKNOWN SOLDIER : It may be someone else this time.

WIFE (*hotly*) : Someone else? What do you take me for?

[35914 *enters as a working-man.*]

Hello, honey.

35914 : Sorry, no time now. Going to join up! See you when I come back on leave.

THE UNKNOWN SOLDIER : Read all about it!

35914 (*cheerful*) : I've had all the bad news I can take for one day. (*He goes out.*)

WIFE : There's a real man.

THE UNKNOWN SOLDIER : I don't understand you any more.

WIFE : Think of the neighbours if we hitch up again. How can I hold up my head if everyone knows my husband's a coward?

THE UNKNOWN SOLDIER : Oh, we've got neighbours now?

WIFE : The world's much fuller than it was. People talk. From balconies, on the stairs, in the shops. They come in to borrow things, without knocking. There's no private life no more. That's why I want you to go, dear. Only don't volunteer for nothing this time. I want you back, d'you hear me? Keep your head down. Be the last over the top, dear.

246

[*The Soldiers pass—all dressed as civilians, but with rifles and suitcases. The Sergeant leads the way.*]

ALL (*singing; very sentimental*):
Every hour, round the clock
I will think of you,
If every hour, round the clock
You will think of me.
Every key must fit a lock,
And every lock a key.
My key's lock is only you,
If your lock's key is me.

[*They go out.*]

WIFE (*in tears*): Give your son a dad to be proud of!

[*They kiss passionately.*]

THE UNKNOWN SOLDIER: Wait for me, lads!

[*The Wife follows slowly, waving her little handkerchief and wiping her tears. The General wanders on, in a bad humour. He is in khaki. The Inventor follows him. He is in a lab coat.*]

INVENTOR: I think I have something at last, Your Highness.
GENERAL: You think you have something? You *think*? Great God almighty, Professor, three Christmases have come and gone, and still we have found no low trick with which to break the enemy's resistance.
INVENTOR: We have had to stop work from time

247

to time, Your Highness, to improvise counter-measures to his new weapons.

GENERAL : How does he get all the new weapons before us, Professor?

INVENTOR : That is the luck of the game, Your Highness.

GENERAL : Game, man? You call it a game when all we stand for could be brushed aside in a minute? We might even be forced to spend the remainder of our days in exile—do you realize that? Archduke of nothing more than a floor in a four-star hotel!

INVENTOR (*piqued*) : If you don't want my invention, I can easily take it elsewhere.

GENERAL : Good gracious me, no. Can't you understand a joke?

INVENTOR : I can understand a joke which makes me laugh. Yours does not!

GENERAL : What is this invention of yours?

INVENTOR : Never mind.

GENERAL : Now you're sulking again. Oh dear. What d'you want, a title? Sandwich?

INVENTOR : A title? Sandwich?

GENERAL : We'll make you a baron if this invention works.

INVENTOR : What's the use of being a baron when I'm a genius?

GENERAL : We realize that . . .

INVENTOR : Whatever you give me, it will only be a fraction of what I can take whenever I want it! (*He sways.*)

GENERAL : I realize that, Baron Schinkelmann.

INVENTOR : I don't know what came over me. I have not slept for weeks, working on this confounded invention.

GENERAL : Nobody is more conscious of your

patriotism then we. Now, let's hear about it, Baron Schinkelmann.

INVENTOR : I don't know how to thank you, Your Highness. You do me too great an honour.

GENERAL : It will be the first of many if you bring us victory.

INVENTOR : I have invented a new poison gas, Your Highness. No gas mask known to man can stand up against it. It pollutes crops, food, kills livestock, destroys everything it comes into contact with. It is lethal. That is why I have called it Lethanol.

GENERAL (*smiling*) : Why not Schinkelmannol?

INVENTOR (*with dignity*) : Your Highness, I also invented the hypodermic needle and the safety pin. I have no wish to be remembered by a gas.

GENERAL : When can we have this?

INVENTOR : By Christmas.

GENERAL : Not before?

INVENTOR : By Christmas.

GENERAL : Very well. Not a word to the Archbishop, is that understood?

INVENTOR : Of course not, Your Highness.

GENERAL : We are well satisfied, Baron. To work, to work.

[*The Inventor clicks his heels, bows, and walks out. The General goes his way. Since the beginning of their scene, the stage has been growing darker, lit by occasional flashes. The Soldiers have been creeping onto the stage, their rifles cradled in their arms.*]

94343 : 71696!

71696 : What?

94343 : We can't go no further than this. It's suicide!

14768 : Sergeant isn't even here. He's gone sick again.

71696 : Fact he ain't here don't make no difference to our orders.

35914 : You make me puke, 71696. Ever since you got the bronze victory medal, you've been a public danger.

94343 : Sah! Listen.

[*From far away, we can hear a ragged male choir singing 'O Tannenbaum'.*]

It's the enemy.

35914 (*glum*) : Yeah. That reminds me. A merry Christmas, everyone.

ALL : A merry Christmas.

[*The Unknown Soldier crawls forward with a tiny twig.*]

14768 : What you got here?

THE UNKNOWN SOLDIER : Christmas tree. (*Laughter.*) Sergeant's coming up, boys.

[*Everyone groans.*]

SERGEANT : Right. Break off the advance. There's something big in the air.

35914 : Something new.

[*Suddenly there is a strange tearing note, and a report.*]

That's it, lads! That was one of our shells. Didn't sound like a normal one to me.

94343 : Listen! They've stopped singin'.

SERGEANT : 654321987.

THE UNKNOWN SOLDIER : Yes, Sar'nt.

SERGEANT: Lift yer head up, and see what that was.

35914: Don't be a fool!

THE UNKNOWN SOLDIER (*half looking up*): That's odd. Looks like a smoke screen.

SERGEANT: Can't be a shiftin' smoke screen if we're not going into the attack, you dollop.

THE UNKNOWN SOLDIER: That's what it looks like. It's white.

35914: Hey! Can you smell something?

94343: Yes, like lavender.

71696: More like a wet dog now.

35914: Yes, like a stale face-flannel.

14768: Like cats in a damp corridor.

SERGEANT: It's gas! That's what it is!

[*There is general commotion and cries of 'Gas!'.*]

THE UNKNOWN SOLDIER (*unconcerned*): Well, we'll soon know, because it's coming this way.

SERGEANT: It's doin' what?

35914 (*holding up his hand*): The wind! It's changed direction!

SERGEANT: Put on your gas masks!

[*Before they have a chance to, they begin to cough, and the scene takes on the aspect of a weird, convulsive ballet. While it is still going on, the General walks on from one side, the Enemy Leader from the other.*]

GENERAL: Allow us to congratulate you.

ENEMY LEADER: You had bad luck. If the wind hadn't changed, our positions would have been reversed.

GENERAL: We have the honour of capitulating.

251

ENEMY LEADER : We have the honour of returning your sword.

GENERAL : No hard feelings?

ENEMY LEADER : Of course not. It was fun while it lasted. What news from home?

GENERAL : Revolution.

ENEMY LEADER : Same with us.

GENERAL : Will you be going into exile?

ENEMY LEADER : Where else?

GENERAL : We will see each other there then.

ENEMY LEADER : We moved our fortune to a neutral country when the war didn't end that first Christmas.

GENERAL : So did we! We really have too much in common to quarrel like this.

ENEMY LEADER : We only quarrel in public, dear Cousin.

GENERAL : You will think us a very poor host, I'm afraid. We still have several thousand bottles of champagne in which to toast your victory, but unfortunately there's nobody left to serve it . . .

[*They walk off arm in arm. The lights come up, and the men are in their gas-capes again. They push the tomb back into place. The Sergeant walks on, exactly as he was in the beginning.*]

SERGEANT : All right! Everybody back into place as you was in the beginnin'. Move! Don't know what came over you all? Only a few minutes before we're on the air. Move!

[*The Archbishop rushes on.*]

ARCHBISHOP : What happened? I seemed to lose touch with you all.

252

SERGEANT : We can go into that later, Your Grace.
We've got a ceremony to get through now.

[*The Wife enters.*]

Ah, there you are, little lady, we'll have to decide
what to do with you now, won't we? There's someone missin'.

[*The Rebel enters.*]

Ah, it's you, yes. Late as usual. Lie down where
you was, out of it.

[*The General enters, still adjusting his tie.*]

GENERAL : What hit us? It was like a sudden blackout.

[*The Enemy Leader comes on, wearing a sheep-
lined duffel-coat.*]

What are you doing here? You were always my
enemy before.
ENEMY LEADER (*smiling*) : Oh, that was long ago.
But I still am your enemy in a way. I'm the director
of the television coverage. I stand between you and
your public. Every false note, every half-truth, and
I magnify it out of all proportion, in colour.

[*The Inventor comes on.*]

INVENTOR (*livid*) : It's a scandal ! This country calls
itself a modern state, and my chauffeur can't even
park my car in the V.I.P. enclosure because I
haven't got a red sticker. (*Shouting.*) I was never

sent a red sticker! I have had to walk a mile through the crowd!

GENERAL (*beginning to lose his head*): I'm very sorry, Professor, it's not my fault. I have to organize . . .

INVENTOR (*furious*): Organize! Why don't you use my computers? I don't know why I stay here. Every week I have offers to go and work elsewhere, where they don't make mistakes! (*He breaks off, and mutters, as an echo.*) Where they don't make mistakes . . .

[*The Unknown Soldier totters on, slowly and unsteadily. He is in tatters, and covered in blood. There is a petrified silence. The Wife is the first to break it.*]

WIFE: Oh, my darling!

THE UNKNOWN SOLDIER (*restrains her. He speaks with clarity, but it's clearly an effort*): Don't come near me . . . sweetheart . . . you'll get your clothes all dirty . . . and then, I'm only held together with bandages . . . if you touch me . . . I might fall apart . . .

SERGEANT (*finding his tongue*): Why isn't you in yer coffin as per instructions?

THE UNKNOWN SOLDIER: I decided . . . not to die this time.

SERGEANT: Decided not to die? It's not for you to decide this, that, or the copulatin' other. You know yer orders!

THE UNKNOWN SOLDIER: I decided . . . not to die.

GENERAL (*shaken*): Is that quite fair? All the arrangements for your funeral have been made. You know that. In a few minutes, you'll be on television.

THE UNKNOWN SOLDIER: I'm sorry, General. There it is.

ARCHBISHOP: It is not given to everyone to have a ceremony as fine as this in his honour, you know . . . and it is in your honour.

THE UNKNOWN SOLDIER: I came here . . . as quick as I could . . . and then I thought . . . what if I don't make it in time? They'll have their ceremony just the same . . . there's no need for a body . . . There's a lid on the coffin . . . there's never been no need for a body . . .

GENERAL: Are you seriously suggesting we should cheat the public?

THE UNKNOWN SOLDIER: You cheat the public every time you declare war. Why not now?

[*The Sergeant runs amok.*]

SERGEANT: Let me get at 'im. Give me a rifle, someone. I'll finish 'im off. It won't take much!

[*The soldiers deny him their rifles, and struggle with him.*]

GENERAL: Sergeant! Sergeant!

[*The Sergeant suddenly goes limp.*]

SERGEANT (*pathetic*): I can't go on, sir . . . I never seen the like . . . I'm givin' up, sir . . . I'm givin' . . . (*He tries to stand up.*) Permission to . . . (*He falls.*)

THE UNKNOWN SOLDIER: There. I've killed a man at last . . . There goes my clean sheet . . . after all this time. Sir?

GENERAL (*upset*): Yes?

THE UNKNOWN SOLDIER: May I make a suggestion?

GENERAL : What is it?

THE UNKNOWN SOLDIER : You've got an empty coffin, haven't you . . . now you've got a corpse . . . what with the soldiers and the flags and the drums . . . he deserves it much more than I ever did.

GENERAL : What do you say, Archbishop?

ARCHBISHOP : Well, it's a little irregular. I mean, the sergeant was hardly unknown, was he?

WIFE (*emotional*) : My man wasn't unknown either. You all know him. You've known him for centuries. He's just known as the Unknown Soldier!

ARCHBISHOP : Yes, that's quite true.

GENERAL : Men, place the sergeant in the tomb.

[*The men begin to do so.*]

ENEMY LEADER : We have three minutes to go.

[*The Wife grips her stomach and starts writhing.*]

THE UNKNOWN SOLDIER : What is it, doll?

WIFE : It's started.

GENERAL : Not here, for heaven's sake!

THE UNKNOWN SOLDIER : I'm going to see my son!

[*A nurse enters. It is the Woman.*]

GENERAL : Take her away.

WOMAN : It's too dangerous to move her now.

WIFE : Oh. Your Highness.

WOMAN (*gentle, laying her down. The soldiers offer their greatcoats*) : Yes. Her Highness. Doing something useful at last . . .

GENERAL : But the ceremony? You'll have to keep the cameras away from this area.

ENEMY LEADER : We shoot whatever's newsworthy.

ARCHBISHOP : Am I to understand that my address to the nation . . .

ENEMY LEADER : We try to give the public what it wants.

REBEL : You see, this is the real revolution at last. The one man who has never changed, the one constant factor throughout history, has woken up.

INVENTOR : Woken up? What are you talking about? A man has refused to die, that's all. What is so surprising about it?

REBEL : He is in charge. We are awaiting his decision, awaiting his orders.

INVENTOR : I am not awaiting his orders! The next time you will all be unknown soldiers, I have seen to that! This man is incapable of decision! It is I who can destroy the world!

REBEL : He can prevent you.

INVENTOR : I can order him to press the button!

REBEL : He can refuse.

INVENTOR : I am a genius! I harness the power of the earth and sky!

REBEL : He is a simple man. He harnesses the imagination.

[*The Wife cries out.*]

THE UNKNOWN SOLDIER : Professor, you're an intelligent man . . . with all your knowledge . . . you must know something about childbirth.

INVENTOR : I beg your pardon? Childbirth? (*He looks at the Wife for the first time, as she lies, surrounded by a wall of soldiers.*) Ach, you are doing it all wrong. You are not making it easy for her that way. Higher with the legs. Lower with the head. More pillows. Quick. Now give her one of these pills to suck. They are called Laborine. I

I   257

invented them for just such an emergency . . .

ENEMY LEADER : Five, four, three, two, one. We're on the air!

[The red light on the camera lights up.]

ARCHBISHOP *(amplified electronically)* : Fellow countrymen. Who was the Unknown Soldier? Was he tall or short, fair or dark? We know not. Did he come from North or South, East or West? We know not. All we know about him is that he died in battle as many others did, to defend his country and his religion, and our right to be free!

[A child starts crying fitfully. The soldiers form a little cluster around the Wife. The Enemy Leader looks up at the control room.]

ENEMY LEADER *(sotto voce, but projected urgently)* : All cameras concentrate on the childbirth—cut off the Archbishop's mike!

ARCHBISHOP : Let us then reflect, our hands on our hearts, our eyes on the . . . *(He continues his speech, in silence.)*

INVENTOR : Easy! Easy, nurse! So . . . let nature take its course! Good! . . . Nature is doing surprisingly well, all by itself! . . . So . . . so . . . It works!

[The child begins to wail. The Unknown Soldier begins to laugh incredulously. His delight is contagious. The Archbishop goes on obliviously with his silent invocation to the nation. Suddenly a siren sounds. Panic. Only the Archbishop it too wrapped up in what he is saying to notice.]

258

REBEL : What is it?

INVENTOR (*hysterical*) : I gave no order!

94343 : What is it then?

71696 : The balloon goin' up, I wouldn't be surprised.

35914 : It may only be a factory . . . on a time signal . . . or the fire department!

14768 : Listen!

[*There is silence, except for the child's crying.*]

INVENTOR : There is no use listening! We will never hear it coming . . . are you completely heartless! To interrupt a childbirth?

GENERAL : What is it, Professor? As commander-in-chief, I deserve to know.

INVENTOR : It may be the enemy.

GENERAL : I knew we should have attacked him first!

INVENTOR : It may be a short-circuit in the early warning system . . . It may be a short circuit in the system warning us of a short circuit in the early warning system . . . it could be almost anything, ad infinitum, et cetera . . .

GENERAL : Right! Where's the Sergeant?

REBEL : He's dead for good this time . . . there's no place for him in a society advanced enough to destroy itself.

[*The Unknown Soldier appears with the child in his arms.*]

GENERAL : Right. Form up. Put down that child, man.

REBEL (*to the Unknown Soldier*) : You lead us!

[*Enthusiasm from the men.*]

259

GENERAL : That's rank disobedience!

REBEL : Look where centuries of obedience has got us!

THE UNKNOWN SOLDIER : Come then, my darling. Well, there's nowhere left to hide, lads . . . I reckon the only way to go is out in the open. If we don't find an enemy to share our common interests . . . then we don't deserve to survive . . .

35914 : Common interests . . . flowers?

THE UNKNOWN SOLDIER : No . . . living this time.

ENEMY LEADER (*to the audience*) : Normal service will be resumed after this message . . .

[*The lights fade on the still garrulous Archbishop.*]

THE UNKNOWN SOLDIER (*with a sad smile to the audience, who are suddenly lit up*) : Well, don't expect me to do everything just because I'm not dead. It's up to you too, all of you. Come on, lads . . .

He leads his men out through the auditorium. The sirens grow in volume.

Curtain

THE
SECRETARY
BIRD

A Comedy

by
WILLIAM DOUGLAS HOME

© *1969 by William Douglas Home*

The Secretary Bird was first presented at the Mowlem Theatre, Swanage, on May 9, 1963, with the following cast :

HUGH WALFORD	*Anthony Roye*
LIZ WALFORD	*Patricia Leslie*
MRS GRAY	*Betty Woolfe*
MOLLY FORSYTH	*Dona Martyn*
JOHN BROWNLOW	*Robert Dean*

Directed by Anthony Roye

Later John Gale (Volcano Productions Ltd.) presented it at the Savoy Theatre, London, on October 16, 1968, with the folowing cast :

HUGH WALFORD	*Kenneth More*
LIZ WALFORD	*Jane Downs*
MRS GRAY	*Katharine Parr*
MOLLY FORSYTH	*Judith Arthy*
JOHN BROWNLOW	*Terence Longdon*

Directed by Philip Dudley
Setting by Hutchinson Scott

CHARACTERS

HUGH WALFORD

LIZ WALFORD

MRS GRAY

MOLLY FORSYTH

JOHN BROWNLOW

SYNOPSIS OF SCENES

The living-room of the Walfords' country house.

ACT ONE

SCENE 1. *Friday night*

SCENE 2. *Saturday morning*

ACT TWO

SCENE 1. *Saturday night*

SCENE 2. *Sunday morning*

ACT ONE

Scene 1

*The living-room of the Walfords' country home.
Friday night.*

*It is a charming room, much lived in, comfortable,
well-furnished, homely. Double doors in a small
alcove lead to the hall, and french windows in a
bay to the garden.*

*When the curtain rises, Hugh and Liz, his wife,
are sitting at a card table playing Racing Demon.
They play quite slowly as the curtain rises, then
they quicken steadily, and then the pace gets fast
and furious. Eventually Hugh cries 'Out!'. He
gathers all the cards together from the middle of
the table and divides the packs, one colour for
himself and one for Liz.*

HUGH : How many in your 'talon', darling?

LIZ (*who has just counted them*) : Seven.

HUGH : Bad luck. I had a damned lucky run. How
many are you? (*He counts his output as he divides
the cards.*)

LIZ (*counting*) : Nine.

HUGH : That makes you eighty-four. I'm thirty-
eight. That's—eight and five—thirteen. And carry
one—four—four and six—ten—one hundred and
three. I've done it. One game all, my darling. Now
for the decider. Damned close games, they've been.
Let's see, you were a hundred and ten in the first
game. I was eighty-seven. And, in this one, I'm a
hundred and three, and you're eighty-seven. Cut
to me, my darling.

LIZ : Do you mind if we don't—not tonight. I'm
feeling tired.

HUGH (*noting her strange mood, but providing an excuse*): Poor darling. Yes—of course, you must be. Up and down from London in the same day. Have a drink? (*He rises.*)

LIZ : Oh, all right—a small whisky.

HUGH : That's right. (*He pours.*) And I'll have a large one. Beats me why you never took the train, instead of that damned car. It's sixty miles each way. Where did you lunch?

LIZ : At the hairdresser.

HUGH : Sandwiches, I'll bet.

LIZ : Of course.

HUGH : Under the drier?

LIZ : Where else?

HUGH : Never ring your wife up at the hairdresser a fellow once told me—because she won't be there.

LIZ : Did you ring me?

HUGH : No.

[*There is a pause, during which Hugh stops pouring the drinks. Then he speaks with his back to her.*]

What's his name?

LIZ (*considering whether to tell him and then knowing she's got to in the end so may as well do it now*): John Brownlow.

HUGH : How long have you known him?

LIZ : Six months.

HUGH : Where'd you meet?

LIZ : At dinner with the Chilean Ambassador.

HUGH : Was I there?

LIZ : Yes.

HUGH : Six months—March. (*He gives Liz her drink.*)

LIZ : I expect so.

HUGH : Where's the Embassy?

LIZ : Don't ask me—you were driving. Somewhere by the river, I think.

HUGH : I remember. I was shouting rather loud that night. I had a row with someone in the Government about South Africa.

LIZ : That's right. We'd been to quite a lot of cocktail parties.

HUGH (*pouring his own drink*) : He kept saying that my facts were wrong, which irritated me, as he'd never been there and I had—for three weeks, what's more.

LIZ : In the Game Reserve.

HUGH : He didn't know that.

LIZ : Yes, he did. I told him so at dinner.

HUGH : That's what I call loyalty.

LIZ : I didn't know that you were going to have a row with him.

HUGH : Don't tell me he's the fellow.

LIZ : No.

HUGH : He's English, is he?

LIZ : Yes.

HUGH : More than that fellow was! That cuts the field down. Not the fellow on my right, over the coffee—he was Uruguan. And the fellow on my left was this ass in the Government. Then opposite —round the Ambassador—were lots of diplomats. Is he a diplomat?

LIZ : No—he's a stockbroker.

HUGH (*sitting*) : How old?

LIZ : Not very.

HUGH : Not compared to me! Good-looking?

LIZ : Very.

HUGH : Fair or dark?

LIZ : Fair.

HUGH : Tall or short?

LIZ : Tall.

HUGH : Spectacles?

LIZ : Yes.

[*All Liz's answers can, of course, be interchangeable according to the appearance of the actor playing Brownlow.*]

HUGH : Sober?

LIZ : Yes.

HUGH : I've got it—the chap in the cummerbund. What was his name again?

LIZ : John Brownlow.

HUGH : That's right—charming fellow. Said he liked my books. We dropped him at the end of Eaton Square on the way home—the Sloane Square end.

LIZ : Yes—that's right.

HUGH : Yes, of course. A very civil fellow—I remember now. What happened next?

LIZ : He rang me the next morning.

HUGH : After I'd started on the treadmill . . .

LIZ : You'd gone to Newmarket.

HUGH : What did he say?

LIZ : He asked me out to lunch.

HUGH : And you went?

LIZ : Yes.

HUGH : And it all started over sole and spinach?

LIZ : Turbot. (*She starts playing Seven Patience.*)

HUGH : And he took you in a taxi to a mews off Eaton Square to help him choose a new chintz for his bedroom curtains?

LIZ : No—you've jumped the gun—he went back to the City.

HUGH : Oh—a pro! And then?

LIZ : He asked me out to dinner the next week.

HUGH : Why wasn't I there?

LIZ : You were dining with your publisher.

HUGH : And you were going with your parents to the opera.

LIZ : That's right—but Daddy got a cold.

HUGH : Your mother didn't.

LIZ : She was playing Scrabble with him.

HUGH (*watching her playing Seven Patience*) : Is your mother in on this?

LIZ : Of course not—she thought I'd gone home.

HUGH : When you were choosing chintzes.

LIZ : No, I wasn't.

HUGH : Well, what were you doing?

LIZ : Dining.

HUGH : Where?

LIZ : In Charlotte Street.

HUGH : And then?

LIZ : And then he dropped me at the flat, and you came in about eleven.

HUGH : That's right. (*He rises.*) Like a refill?

LIZ : No thanks.

HUGH : I would. (*He goes over to get the drink.*)

LIZ (*after a pause*) : How did you find out?

HUGH : Miss Forsyth saw you in the travel agency.

LIZ : I know—I saw her. Did you put her on to me?

HUGH : Of course not—I had no idea.

LIZ : You're very unobservant. But men are.

HUGH : Yes, so they tell me . . .

LIZ : Do you mean to say you've noticed nothing, all this spring and summer?

HUGH : I've been busy on my book.

LIZ : Yes, that's the trouble.

HUGH : One has got to live.

LIZ : I'm sorry.

HUGH : I did think to myself once—when I was playing golf in May—so far as I remember—that

269

your hair was getting quite a beating-up this year. But then I got a 'birdie' and forgot about it.

LIZ : What about the time you found me crying in the summer-house?

HUGH : That didn't worry me unduly.

LIZ : Well, it should have.

HUGH : I don't see why. Women cry when they're happy—like men whistle.

LIZ : In your books, I dare say.

HUGH : And in real life.

LIZ (*rising*) : I don't.

HUGH : Yes, you do. You cried that time we saw the Northern Lights in Ullapool.

LIZ : That was the whisky.

HUGH : Never mind—you cried.

LIZ : So you decided I'd seen the Northern Lights that evening in the summer-house in Ascot Week?

HUGH : No—I just thought you'd seen a blue-tit feeding its young—or a baby rabbit.

LIZ : Well, I hadn't.

HUGH : And you hadn't got a treble at the races?

LIZ : No.

HUGH : I'll buy it.

LIZ : I was crying because he'd asked me for the first time in the Paddock Bar.

HUGH : Ah—the plot thickens—asked you what?

LIZ : To choose his curtains.

HUGH : And what did you answer?

LIZ : Yes.

HUGH : You see—I was right. Women do cry when they're happy.

LIZ : Hugh, I wasn't happy.

HUGH : Oh, I beg your pardon.

LIZ : I was miserable.

HUGH : Poor darling.

LIZ : Fifteen years of faithfulness to you to end like that with one word.

HUGH : In the Paddock Bar.

LIZ : We drank champagne.

HUGH : Most proper.

LIZ : And he clicked his glass against mine—and his eyes were full of laughter.

HUGH : What the devil had he got to laugh about?

LIZ : His latest conquest.

HUGH : Oh, so he's an old campaigner—is he?

LIZ : Yes—he's had three wives.

HUGH : His own—or other people's? (*He sits.*)

LIZ : Other people's first—and then his own.

HUGH : What happened to them? Thrown aside when he got tired of them?

LIZ : He's a romantic.

HUGH : So that's what he is!

LIZ (*rising*) : It's no use trying to pretend you don't know all about him. He's well known to be the most attractive man in London.

HUGH : Greater London? Or just Mayfair?

LIZ : You're being silly.

HUGH (*rising*) : Well, you're making sweeping statements. You're talking as if you'd combed the streets round Shepherd's Bush and in the Elephant and Castle area and made comparisons. I saw a smashing speed-cop on the Chiswick over-pass last Friday for example. How does he compare with him?

LIZ : You've seen them both—make up your own mind.

HUGH (*thinking it out*) : Balancing the motor-bicycle against the cummerbund—That's a nice picture, isn't it?

LIZ : What was Miss Forsyth doing at the travel agent's?

HUGH : Fixing up her holiday—she's off to Italy

271

on Sunday for a fortnight—Venice, Florence, Rome
—she's a Renaissance fan. Perhaps you'll meet her
—you were booking on the Milan car-train, weren't
you?

LIZ : John was, yes—he's got business there.

HUGH : One couchette, she said.

LIZ : That's right.

HUGH : Is he a very big man?

LIZ : All right, you win. (*She sits on the sofa.*)

HUGH : How long are you going for? (*He moves
behind Liz.*)

LIZ : A fortnight.

HUGH : Starting when?

LIZ : On Sunday morning. He's got meetings in
Milan on Monday.

HUGH : For a fortnight?

LIZ : No, of course not.

HUGH : Were you going to tell me?

LIZ : Not until we were abroad.

HUGH : What were you going to tell me when you
left? The hairdresser's no good on Sunday.

LIZ (*Starting to play Patience again*): Mother—I
was going to lunch with Mother, for your benefit,
at Kew. But, actually, I'm going to meet John
there—and drive to Lympne—and then fly over to
Le Touquet, where I would have rung you from . . .

HUGH : From where I would have rung you.
(*Watching her play.*) Two on three.

LIZ : Oh, yes.

HUGH : And put the King up.

LIZ : All right, I'm not blind.

HUGH : You're home now.

LIZ : No, I'm not.

HUGH : Bad luck. (*He watches her for a moment
in silence.*) Is this to be the start of the affair?

LIZ : Never you mind.

HUGH : I do mind.

LIZ : Only in so far as it might give you a good plot for your next book.

HUGH (*sitting*) : One shouldn't look a gift-horse in the mouth.

LIZ : Exactly.

HUGH : And you are my wife.

LIZ : Yes, at the moment—but I won't be for long.

HUGH (*after a pause*) : What does that mean?

LIZ : Just exactly what it says.

HUGH : You want a divorce.

LIZ : Yes.

HUGH : Why? Aren't you coming back after the fortnight?

LIZ : No.

HUGH : Why not?

LIZ : Because I love John.

HUGH : And you want to marry him?

LIZ : Yes, Hugh.

HUGH : And then get thrown aside when he gets tired of you?

LIZ : I'll risk that.

HUGH : I won't.

LIZ : I'm afraid you'll have to. If you won't divorce me, we'll have to live in sin, that's all.

HUGH : Put those damned cards down—put them down, I said.

[*Liz stops playing.*]

You're getting old, Liz.

LIZ : That's right.

HUGH : And I'm over fifty.

LIZ : That's right too.

HUGH : And we've got teen-age children.

LIZ : Two.

HUGH : And we both love them—and they love us.

LIZ : That's right.

HUGH : And you're going to throw all that away for one flash fellow in a cummerbund.

LIZ : He isn't flash.

HUGH : He reads that way to me.

LIZ : He's everything that you aren't

HUGH : You'll forgive me saying so—but that's no contradiction.

LIZ : He's romantic—he's warm-blooded—he's—alive.

HUGH : It therefore follows that I'm unromantic, cold-blooded and dead.

LIZ : You said it.

HUGH : Thank you very much.

LIZ : I didn't mean it literally, darling. (*Rising.*) You know just what I meant. I'm much younger than you are. Oh, I know I'm as much to blame as you are—I mean—I married you knowing that you were too old for me! But I thought I could get away with it. I can't, Hugh. I've found that out now, since I met John—I just can't.

HUGH (*persisting*) : I'm sorry to be so persistent, but is this to be the start of the affair—this couchette on the Milan train—or have the tapes gone up already?

LIZ : Why should I tell you?

HUGH : Because I'd like to know how far the rot's set in.

LIZ : I'm going to marry him, Hugh—that's how far it's set in.

HUGH (*after a pause*) : When was Ascot?

LIZ : June, some time.

HUGH : The third week—that's right. (*Rising.*) And

it's the third week in July now. A month in fact, since you said 'Yes'. And you're in love with him. What's more, you're quite prepared to go to Milan without telling me—except when it's too late. (*Moving to the drinks table.*) Now, let me see—if I was working out a plot like that, with characters behaving like that. I'd reckon they'd be in it right over their gumboots. Right?

LIZ : You're always right, Hugh—aren't you—when it comes to sex. That's what the critics all agree about whatever else they may say—'Mr Walford, with his quite uncanny "insight" into every woman's heart leads us enchantingly . . .'

HUGH (*interrupting*): What sort of curtains are they?

LIZ : Bright red velvet.

HUGH : And you chose them the week-end that I was fishing down in Stockbridge and you went allegedly to the Palladium with your old nanny.

LIZ : Yes. I rang her up—and said I had 'flu, so she took her sister.

HUGH : And you hung them the next week-end when you went allegedly to stay with Mabel Stourton down in Kent after her nervous breakdown.

LIZ : That's right. I invented all that—Mabel never had a nervous breakdown. She was playing golf at Rye that week-end, and she won the competition, what's more.

HUGH : Good for her.

LIZ (*sitting*): I was afraid you might have seen it in *The Times*.

HUGH : I did.

LIZ : You did !

HUGH : That's what I said.

LIZ : But weren't you surprised?

HUGH : No.

LIZ : No! A woman with a nervous breakdown winning six and five!

HUGH : She played extremely well—I went and watched her.

LIZ : Watched her!

HUGH : From a decent distance. She did one chip straight from Heaven, landed full pitch in the hole —an 'eagle'.

LIZ : So you've known the whole time?

HUGH : Yes.

LIZ : Since when?

HUGH : Since Mrs Chilean Ambassador said 'Do you know John Brownlow' and you said 'No'—and shook hands. Your eyes were dancing like a pair of stars.

LIZ : You were behind me.

HUGH (*moving to the sofa and sitting*) : They were dancing all the evening like they used to when we were engaged. And every time I tried to walk between you after dinner in the drawing-room to the drinks table, I had to break some sort of barrier.

LIZ : What nonsense!

HUGH : No, I did. Some kind of ray—like burglars do in banks—and alarm bells were ringing everywhere—and police cars dashing by—and sirens hooting—every portent you could want, in fact, except a thunderstorm.

LIZ (*rising*) : Why didn't you say anything?

HUGH : I did—I quarrelled with that bloody Under-Secretary about South Africa.

LIZ : But then you offered John a lift, when we left.

HUGH : Why not? It was raining and he hadn't got a coat.

LIZ : But, if you knew . . .

HUGH : I should have let him get pneumonia.

LIZ : You should have said something. You might have stopped it in time.

HUGH : It was too late when it started.

LIZ : No.

HUGH : Yes—nothing would have stopped it.

LIZ : If you'd taken me away . . .

HUGH : Where to?

LIZ : The South of France—or Spain—Marbella . . .

HUGH (*rising and moving to the drinks table*): Wouldn't have done any good. It would have made it worse in fact. You would have seen the fellow sitting with you every night at dinner—fondling his brandy at the table—sitting in the lounge behind a big cigar and swotting up *The Times* when you went up to bed—having a night-cap on the terrace in his dressing-gown—watching the moonlight on the sea—then turning round and turning into me. It would have made it worse.

LIZ : It couldn't be worse than it is now.

HUGH : Poor old girl—you've got it badly haven't you?

LIZ : You make it sound like measles!

HUGH (*moving to Liz*): Let me top it up for you.

LIZ (*giving him her glass*): All right.

HUGH (*going to refill both glasses*): Well, it was bound to happen in the end.

LIZ : Why?

HUGH : Why? Old Mother Nature! Look at red deer. Every old stag looks up from the heather one fine day—and sees a pair of antlers on the sky-line —then a pair of ears—and then a handsome head and thick set neck—and then a glossy body, rippling with muscle—and he knows he's had it . . .

LIZ : Not without a fight.

HUGH (*giving Liz her drink*): Oh yes, he fights all

right. But he's an animal. (*He fetches his own drink.*) He didn't go to Eton. But it doesn't do him any damned good—just prolongs the agony and makes the hind just that much keener on the other fellow—most unwise. Imagine me and Brownlow with our antlers locked together, roaring round and round the drawing-room at the Chilean Ambassador's, with you up on the piano with your nostrils quivering—and your ears flapping to keep off the flies. It wouldn't make a very pretty picture, would it? Let's be civilized at least—and take defeat with dignity.

LIZ : So you accept defeat?

HUGH : Of course I do. It had to happen as I say. The only questions were 'when' and 'in what form'. Now we've had the answer to both questions and we've got to make the best of it. Damn funny! Fifteen years of marriage—then it happens, just like that! One moment you're going upstairs, married to the eyebrows—solid as the Bank of England. The next, you're split right down the middle like a ruddy atom—back where you were in your twenties—all alone and screaming for your mother.

LIZ : Speak for yourself.

HUGH : That's exactly what I'm doing. (*He sits.*) Do you know, I damned near took that butler's hand and went out of the room in tears. Instead, I swallowed four Martinis in as many minutes— much more sensible at my age—and much more constructive. Why don't stockbrokers commute instead of dining out with South American Ambassadors?

LIZ : He stays in London during the week.

HUGH (*after a pause*) : What about the children.

LIZ : His? Or ours?

278

HUGH : Ours.

LIZ : What about them?

HUGH : Were you going to tell them?

LIZ : No—I thought it'd come much better from you—as you were the injured party.

HUGH : You mean that you funked it?

LIZ : Naturally, I didn't want to even see them till I'd made the final break and it was too late to go back on it.

HUGH : What if I pick that telephone up now— and get them back from school?

LIZ : You wouldn't do that, would you?

HUGH : No—I'm not that bitter.

LIZ : You'll get their custody, of course, but I hope you'll let them come and stay with John and me when we're married.

HUGH : In the Mews flat?

LIZ : No—in Gloucestershire. He's got a country house there.

HUGH : Big or small?

LIZ : Quite big enough.

HUGH : What acreage?

LIZ (*with a shrug*) : Five hundred.

HUGH : Farm?

LIZ : Yes.

HUGH : Well to do, then.

LIZ : Comfortable.

HUGH : In spite of alimony three times over.

LIZ : He gets by. Sheila and Dick'll like him.

HUGH : Good.

LIZ : He's very good with children.

HUGH : Other people's? Or his own?

LIZ : Both.

HUGH : What's he chalked up so far?

LIZ : Three—one by each wife.

HUGH : Boys or girls?

LIZ : Both.

HUGH : Hermaphrodites?

LIZ : Two boys—one girl.

HUGH : Living with him?

LIZ : No—with their mothers.

HUGH : So you'll be alone.

LIZ : Yes.

HUGH : Strolling round the park, knee deep in bluebells.

LIZ : Bluebells don't grow knee-high.

HUGH : Brussels-sprouts then . . .

LIZ : Ha ! Ha !

HUGH : It's all physical you know.

LIZ : Yes—at the moment—anyway.

HUGH : It always will be.

LIZ : No.

HUGH : Yes, darling.

LIZ : You're jealous.

HUGH : Naturally, but that's not why I'm saying it. I'm saying it because you wouldn't want to leave me if it weren't . . .

LIZ : Wouldn't I ?

HUGH : No. As a lover, I may be inadequate, I'll grant you that—

LIZ : That's big of you !

HUGH : —but, every other way, I'm what the doctor ordered—kind, amusing, unpredictable in conversation and behaviour, interesting, well-read and generous.

LIZ : That's not enough—not for a woman.

HUGH : You've been satisfied for fifteen years.

LIZ : No, Hugh, I haven't.

HUGH : You've been happy.

LIZ : Negatively.

HUGH : Nonsense.

LIZ : It's not nonsense, Hugh—it's true. Oh, I've

been happy, but I haven't been alive. If vegetables
are happy, I've been happy—but that's all.

HUGH : You've hidden it well.

LIZ : Thank you.

HUGH : You were happy when we married.

LIZ : Yes.

HUGH : And on our honeymoon.

LIZ : Yes—at the start. And then I started Sheila—
and that was a different thing—and then I started
Dick—and so was that. And then I had to bring
them up and that was new and satisfying and
exciting. But now that's all over—they've grown
up.

HUGH : Not quite.

LIZ : Well, very nearly. And now there's just you
and me.

HUGH : And I lack glamour.

LIZ : If you put it like that—yes.

HUGH : And Brownlow doesn't.

LIZ : No. Don't think I'm blaming you—I'm not.
It's just the way things go. You're older than me—
much much older. And it's not surprising that
you've reached the age when you don't want or
need the things that I do.

HUGH (*after a pause*) : So it's physical, as I said.

LIZ : All right then, it is.

HUGH : It won't last.

LIZ : I'm afraid I disagree.

HUGH : It didn't with the other ones.

LIZ : They weren't up to it.

HUGH : Maybe they got bored.

LIZ : Nonsense they're all in love with him still.

HUGH : Have they signed an affidavit?

LIZ : It's quite obvious.

HUGH : You've met them, have you?

LIZ : No. I've seen their letters though.

281

HUGH : They all keep up their correspondence, do they?

LIZ : Yes—they're all great friends still.

HUGH (*with the first note of bitterness in his voice*) : Pity that he's not a Moslem.

[*There is a pause. A train is heard in the distance.*]

LIZ : I'm so sorry.

HUGH : That's all right.

LIZ : We'll always be friends, won't we, Hugh? Like John is with his exes. It's the only civilized way of behaving. And it won't upset the children. They'll be able to respect us both still. And do half the holidays with each of us.

HUGH : Not these next holidays, I hope.

LIZ : No, after the divorce is through, I mean.

HUGH : Mrs John Brownlow the Fourth!

LIZ : No need—all the exes married again.

HUGH : Well done them. (*He pauses.*) Where's Brownlow now?

LIZ : In London.

HUGH : In the Mews flat?

LIZ : I imagine so.

HUGH : Poor devil—on a Friday night in London. Ring him up and ask him down here. Go on. Does he play golf?

LIZ : Yes, I think so.

HUGH : Well then, I'll have a round tomorrow morning with him—if he'd like to. Then he can come on to lunch and stay till you push off on Sunday morning. What's the number? I'll do it, if you're shy.

LIZ : Don't be ridiculous—it's quite out of the question.

HUGH : Why—it'll clear the air. I'm sure he hates

282

this hole and corner stuff as much as you do. Anyway, I'd like to vet him. Otherwise, I'd always feel I hadn't been responsible.

LIZ : You may not like him.

HUGH : 'Course I will, dear. 'Any friend of yours etc.' What's the number? (*He lifts the receiver.*)

LIZ : I'll do it upstairs from my bedroom. (*She takes the receiver from him.*)

HUGH : All right, but he'll be asleep soon—the poor fellow !

LIZ : I'm just going up. (*She replaces the receiver.*)

HUGH : Good. You look tired dear—I should take some Metatone to Italy if I were you. I'll get some on my way down to the Club House in the morning.

LIZ : Thank you. Well, I'll say good night.

HUGH : Good night, Liz.

LIZ : Good night, Hugh. (*She moves to the door.*)

HUGH : Tell him to meet me at the Club House between half-past ten and quarter to eleven. We'll play a dozen holes and then be back around a quarter to one. What's his handicap?

LIZ : Don't ask me.

HUGH : Never mind, dear. I will.

LIZ (*turning at the door*) : It won't make you any happier, Hugh.

HUGH : What won't?

LIZ : Asking him down.

HUGH : I'll get some exercise though. (*He sits.*)

LIZ : You'll be punishing yourself that's all. It won't do any good. And it'll merely be embarrassing for all of us.

HUGH : I can't see why. If I'm prepared to go through with it, there's no reason why you two should funk it. I'm the only loser, after all. Besides, the whole affair wants talking over.

LIZ : Talking over?

HUGH : The divorce, I mean. Who's going to cite who—and so on, and so forth.

LIZ : You're going to cite John naturally.

HUGH : No, on the contrary. I'd like to give you a divorce.

LIZ : That's too old-fashioned for words, darling.

HUGH : Maybe so. But that's the way it's going to be.

LIZ : You mean that you'll go to Brighton with some blonde?

HUGH : No, darling—I won't go to Brighton—and the blonde'll come to me.

LIZ : Here!

HUGH : Yes—why not?

LIZ : But what will Mrs Gray say?

HUGH : Quite a lot, in Court—I hope! About what she saw when she brought the breakfast in—'The Master, he was sitting up in bed, my lord, with one arm round the lady and the other, roving like. And when I says "Good morning", he says, "Make a note of it, then, Mrs Gray."' And, as I don't defend it, you can marry John as soon as it's made absolute.

LIZ : You're very generous, Hugh.

HUGH : It's the least that I can do for you, my dear.

LIZ : Who will you choose? A lady from some strip-club?

HUGH : No. Why ask a stranger—when it's possible to ask a friend.

LIZ : Who have you got in mind—the Vicar's wife?

HUGH : Miss Forsyth, —probably.

LIZ : Miss Forsyth! Don't be silly—she's your secretary.

HUGH : Maybe she is—but she's most faithful. And she's been in love with me for years.

LIZ : Well, if you're determined to talk nonsense, I'll say good night.

HUGH : Liz.

LIZ (*turning*) : Yes, Hugh?

HUGH : What's this fellow Brownlow got that I've not got? In one word—or two—if you find it more convenient.

LIZ : Good night. (*She moves towards the door again.*)

HUGH : No, I want to know, Liz. I'm not joking.

LIZ : That's a nice change.

HUGH : Come on, darling. Out with it. Cards on the table—please—I want to know.

LIZ (*moving*) : He treats me like a man should treat a woman.

HUGH : Cave-man stuff, you mean.

LIZ : You know exactly what I mean, Hugh.

HUGH : And he flatters you as well, I bet.

LIZ : He tells me that I'm beautiful, if that's what you mean. He appreciates me.

HUGH : And I don't.

LIZ : One wouldn't notice it.

HUGH : Don't be a damned fool, Liz. Of course you're beautiful—you always have been.

LIZ : Women like to be reminded of those sort of things.

HUGH : I can't see why. You've got a mirror, haven't you?

LIZ : It doesn't talk, Hugh.

HUGH : I'd have thought it did, in your case.

LIZ : Well, it doesn't say the right things.

HUGH : Unlike Brownlow.

[*Liz moves to the card table*]

Yes. I see it all now. (*He rises and moves to the drinks table.*) Cave man Brownlow in skins with a club in one hand and a carrot in the other, taking you away from me in my old Jaeger dressing-gown and carpet slippers. Technique—that's it, isn't it— technique. I've always lacked it. Maybe I'm too sensitive—or too insensitive. Or maybe I'm just lazy. (*He refills his glass.*) Don't let me detain you, darling—I'm just thinking aloud.

[*Liz moves to the door, then turns back*]

Or maybe I'm just queer. That's a good thought, isn't it? Sailing for half a century under a false flag!

[*Liz smiles at this, but Hugh does not see it as his back is still turned*]

(*Facing her.*) One for the stairs?

LIZ : All right, but just a drop.

HUGH (*pouring a drink for her*): Do you think that's the answer? If it is, I must confess that everything drops into place at once. The fact that I'm so popular with women readers—and the fact that I'm reacting to the break-up of my marriage like this. I'm an ineffectual old queer whose life's entirely centred round himself and his romantic novels. I don't give a damn for you, or Brownlow, or divorce, or Dick, or Sheila. All I care about is continuity and comfort. I'm a hedonist, in fact, my darling. Quite a good word, isn't it? (*He hands her the drink.*)

LIZ : What does it mean?

HUGH : A pleasure-lover—a narcissist. Someone who sees everything, including marriage, in relation to himself. And Brownlow's just the opposite, I should imagine—thinking only of you. I'll bet he concentrates like no one's business. You needn't tell me if you'd rather not.

LIZ : That's most broadminded of you.

HUGH : I once knew a don at Oxford who couldn't understand all the fuss about sex, as he said it only took place about three times a year at the outside. I wouldn't wholly subscribe to that view, but I can see what he meant. Maybe men are like steaks— rare, medium or overdone. If so, I know which I am.

LIZ : I'll second that.

HUGH : I'm sorry—obviously I've been most inadequate. (*He moves to the card table.*) And you've been very noble, putting up with it for so long. But as I've already said, the break was bound to come one day. So run along, my darling, now—and ring the fellow up.

LIZ : You're sure you want him, Hugh?

HUGH : Yes, naturally I want to meet the fellow. I've a proprietary interest in you, after all, my dear. Like handing one's tank over in the last war to another squadron officer. I'll turn the lights out.

LIZ : Thank you. If I'd known that you were going to take it like this, I'd have told you earlier. I hated all the deceit.

HUGH : Never mind that—everything's all right now.

LIZ : Good night, Hugh. (*She kisses Hugh, gives him her glass, and goes out.*)

HUGH : Good night, Liz . . . (*He puts the glasses on the table and turns off the lights. Then he goes to turn off the desk lamp.*)

[*The telephone tinkles a little, as Liz makes her call*

from upstairs. Hugh looks at the instrument, then up at the ceiling, then picks up the receiver.]

HUGH (*at the telephone*): Hullo—sorry to butt in, Liz, but I'd like to ask the fellow something. Brownlow, are you there? . . . Oh, good. I'm Liz's husband, Hugh. She's told you about golf tomorrow morning, has she? . . . And is it all right? Oh, good—that's first class. I was wondering if you'd have time to call at Harrods and pick up an eight-ounce jar of caviare on your way down . . . You would? Good man. And put it down to me—Hugh —well you know the other name by now, I shouldn't wonder! . . . Good, well, see you at the Golf Club between half-past ten and quarter-to-eleven. You can't miss it. There's a great big sign up, saying 'Stonewall Golf Course' with an arrow pointing in the right direction more or less. Well, I'll look forward to it. We've a lot to talk about I gather. Well, good night, so sorry to butt in. All yours, my darling. (*He is about to put the receiver down and then picks it up again.*) By the way, what handicap do you play off? . . . Hullo, hullo, what's happened to the fellow, Liz? . . . Oh, why did he do that, I wonder? . . . You keep saying that, but why? Why should he be embarrassed— if I'm not? Yes, all right, darling—leave the water in for me—I'll be up quite soon. Sleep well. (*He hangs up, stands thinking for a while, with his drink, and then goes back to the telephone and dials.*) Miss Forsyth? Mr Walford here . . . Oh, good—not asleep, I hope? . . . Oh, I'm so sorry. I won't be a second and then you can get back to the programme. Could you catch the train tomorrow morning that arrives here at twelve-twenty? . . . You could—good—well, I'll be playing golf, and we'll pick you up on our way home for lunch. (*He is about to put it down when he adds an afterthought.*) And bring your sleeping-bag—we may be working late.

Hugh replaces the receiver, as—

the Curtain falls

Scene 2

When the curtain rises it is Saturday morning, between half-past twelve and one and Liz is finishing off the flowers. She has done the drawing-room flowers, those she is doing now are for the bedrooms. Mrs Gray enters with an ice bucket, which she puts on the drinks table.

LIZ : Oh, thank you, Mrs Gray—I could have done that.

MRS GRAY : Don't you worry, dear. You've other things to think about, poor lamb.

LIZ : What an extraordinary remark to make.

MRS GRAY : Well, it's made now—and I feel better for it.

[*Liz starts for the door with two small vases of flowers.*]

Let me take those.

LIZ : I can manage.

MRS GRAY : No—no—you've your guests to think about, dear. And there's nothing doing in the kitchen at the moment, with the first course being caviare—according to what Mr Walford said.

LIZ : Oh, well—it's very sweet of you . . .

MRS GRAY : No trouble at all, dearie.

LIZ : That one's for Miss Forsyth in the spare room. And that one's for Mr Brownlow in the spare room dressing-room.

MRS GRAY : But he's in Mr Walford's dressing-room, Ma'am.

LIZ : Who is?

MRS GRAY : Mr Brownlow.

LIZ : Really, Mrs Gray—who said so?

MRS GRAY : Mr Walford, Ma'am—as he was going off for golf. 'Put Mr Brownlow in my dressing-room', he says, 'And move my things into the spare room dressing-room.'

LIZ : Mr Walford said that?

MRS GRAY : Yes. And when I said—'Well, that's a funny thing', he said, 'Wait till you see Miss Forsyth, Mrs Gray, and you won't think so.' Then he winked at me.

LIZ : And have you moved his things?

MRS GRAY : (*putting the vases on the drinks table*) : Yes, and it's taken me all morning.

[*Liz decides not to ask her to move them back, and lights a cigarette*]

I'm sorry for you dear—I really am. All these years looking after him—and bringing up the children—and he brings a bit down here, as bold as brass and cracking jokes about it.

LIZ : She's his secretary, Mrs Gray.

MRS GRAY : That's what he told me, but it doesn't make it any better.

LIZ : You know Mr Walford by now, surely Mrs Gray, and he was joking, as you say.

MRS GRAY : That's what I thought at first. But when I thought it over afterwards, when I was hoovering—I didn't think so. Not after that wink. I've seen men wink like that before and I don't like it. You know—trying to get round you, like a naughty schoolboy who's been stealing apples. Still, as he's a writer, I suppose you have to make allowances, but in his own . . .

LIZ : That's just it, that's the explanation. He's right in the middle of a book now, and Miss Forsyth types them all for him. And sometimes he gets inspiration in the night—and so—to save disturbing me—and everything . . . (*She finishes lamely.*)

MRS GRAY : You'll go to Heaven—you will, bless you !

LIZ : Well, I'm sure we'll meet there, Mrs Gray.

MRS GRAY : I hope so, anyway—I've done my best. (*She goes to pick up the vases.*) I'll tell you something, dear. When Mr Gray tried it on once with me, I hit him with a bottle—well, you've seen the scar, dear—his war wound, he calls it—and the best name for it too.

[*There is the sound of two cars arriving.*]

LIZ (*moving to the door*) : I'll open the door for you.

MRS GRAY : Thank you. Like a brand it is, I always tell him—like they put on cattle in the Argentine or Texas on the tele. Every time—he has a shave, he sees it in the mirror and he knows who he belongs to. Here's the car, dear. (*She moves to the window.*)

LIZ : Yes, well, run along.

MRS GRAY (*trying to linger*) : It's this one for Miss Forsyth and this one for Mr Brownlow. There's another car.

LIZ : That's Mr Brownlow's. He drove down from London.

MRS GRAY : And there's no flowers for the Master?

LIZ : No.

MRS GRAY (*still lingering*) : And quite right, too. (*She moves to the door.*) I call it a shame, I do. (*She moves back to Liz.*) What's this Mr Brownlow like?

LIZ (*pushing her out gently*) : He's very nice.

MRS GRAY : Well, you get off with him, dear. That's the ticket. Make him jealous and see how he likes it.

LIZ : Run along, please, Mrs Gray, or they'll think I forgot to do the flowers.

[*Mrs Gray goes out. Liz shuts the door behind her and moves to the sofa table.*]

HUGH (*off*) : Well in you go, Miss Forsyth. Mind the step. We don't want you arriving on all fours.

[*Hugh enters through the french windows with Miss Forsyth. She is younger than Liz, and very good-looking.*]

Let's see, Liz, you don't know Miss Forsyth, do you? (*He returns to the windows for John.*)

MISS FORSYTH : Hello, Mrs Walford.

LIZ (*shaking hands*) : I do hope you had a good trip down.

MISS FORSYTH : Yes, thank you.

HUGH (*to John*) : Mind the step.

[*John Brownlow enters through the windows. He also is good-looking, and not unduly flash.*]

And I think you two know each other? (*He does an introductory gesture with his hands.*)

LIZ : Hullo, John.

JOHN : Hullo, Liz.

HUGH (*coming forward to Liz with a couple of parcels in his hands*): Here's your Metatone, my darling. Give it to Miss Forsyth, otherwise you're certain to forget it. To be packed, Miss Forsyth. Mrs Walford's off to Italy tomorrow morning. Pack it with a tea-spoon in the square red jewel case, wouldn't you think, darling?

LIZ : I should think so.

HUGH : And then you can get your hands on it, whenever you feel like a swig. At Domodossola— or in the Great St Bernard Tunnel, if you go that way.

LIZ : Yes, thank you, Hugh.

HUGH : And here's the caviare that Brownlow very kindly brought down with him.

LIZ (*seizing this excuse to retire*): Oh yes—I'll take it in to Mrs Gray.

[*She moves to the door and goes out.*]

HUGH (*as Liz goes*): Don't let her have too much— it's wasted on her.

[*By now Liz has gone, ignoring this, so Hugh turns to Brownlow.*]

Mrs Gray's our house-keeper-cook-charlady combined—and Gray's our gardener. Now, you two haven't met before, I take it.

JOHN : No, I think not.

HUGH : Well, Miss Forsyth is my secretary, Brownlow.

JOHN : Ah, yes.

HUGH (*to Miss Forsyth*) : And my wife was telling me last night that Mr Brownlow is the most attractive man in London.

JOHN : Nonsense.

HUGH : Not to speak of the most modest. (*He moves to the drinks table.*) Now then who'd like a drink? Miss Forsyth?

MISS FORSYTH : Thank you, Mr Walford.

HUGH : Gin and tonic? Sherry? Gin and bitter lemon?

MISS FORSYTH : Sherry please.

HUGH : You, Brownlow?

JOHN : Could I have a gin and tonic, Walford?

HUGH : Why not? I'll join you. Thirsty work in those damned bunkers. I know what a camel feels like in a sand-storm now. Now, let me see, have you been here before, Miss Forsyth?

MISS FORSYTH : No

HUGH (*moving to Miss Forsyth and handing her a glass of sherry*) : Well, we must make the most of it.

[*Liz enters, overhearing this remark.*]

(*Moving to the drinks table.*) Ah, there you are. What are you drinking, darling?

LIZ : I think I'll have a glass of sherry. Don't bother, I'll do it. (*She pours herself a sherry.*)

HUGH : Do you like ice, Brownlow?

JOHN : Yes, please.

HUGH : Is there any?

LIZ : Yes, of course there is.

HUGH (*cheerfully*) : I say—what a surprise! And a slice of lemon!

JOHN : Thank you.

HUGH : Dead on time, Miss Forsyth's train was, darling.

LIZ : Oh, good.

HUGH : Hadn't been there half a minute when it came in and we saw Miss Forsyth tripping down the platform looking like a lovely flower—a passion flower, to be precise.

MISS FORSYTH : You're being silly, Mr Walford. (*She sits on the sofa.*)

HUGH : On the contrary, I'm being accurate. (*To John.*) Your drink. You read 'Maud' don't you, Brownlow?

JOHN : Maud?

HUGH : 'Maud' Tennyson. Let's see—how does it go? Ah yes—(*He quotes at Miss Forsyth.*)

'There has fallen a splendid tear from
     the passion-flower at the gate.
She is coming, my dove, my dear—she
     is coming my love, my fate
And the red rose cries . . .'

[*Hugh pauses to try and remember how it goes on and Liz takes the opportunity to interrupt him.*]

LIZ : Who won your golf?

HUGH (*surrendering and going back to mix his own drink*) : Need you ask, darling?

LIZ : You, John?

JOHN : Well, yes—actually I did.

HUGH : I never had a hope.

JOHN : Don't listen to him. I was flat out.

HUGH : Were you, old chap? Well, you didn't show it—that's all I can say. We only played nine holes because we had to meet Miss Forsyth's train and he won five and four.

LIZ : Well done, John.

HUGH : On a strange course, too. Technique, that's what I told him in the Club House, wasn't it? Technique. The fellow who's got better technique than the other fellow always wins, whatever game it is, and whatever the handicap. Well, good luck all.

MISS FORSYTH : Good luck.

JOHN : Cheers.

LIZ : Good luck.

HUGH *(to John)* : Taking your clubs with you on the Milan train?

JOHN : Well, yes—I thought I would.

HUGH *(to Liz)* : You'd better take yours, darling. Make a note of it, Miss Forsyth. Metatone and golf-clubs. Mrs Walford's going on a holiday with Mr Brownlow, leaving in the morning. Well, you knew that, didn't you?

MISS FORSYTH : Well, yes, I did.

HUGH *(to John)* : She saw you in the travel agency.

JOHN : Oh, really.

HUGH : Yes—on Thursday—booking the couchette —more ice?

JOHN : No, thanks.

HUGH : You, Miss Forsyth? *(He moves above the sofa.)*

MISS FORSYTH : Well, just half a glass.

HUGH *(taking Miss Forsyth's glass to the drinks table)* : And she put one and one together and decided that it made two. So she came and told me, like the loyal girl she is.

MISS FORSYTH : It sounds too interfering for words put like that.

HUGH : What nonsense. It was most efficient. Mr Brownlow and my wife are going to run away, Miss Forsyth.

MISS FORSYTH : Oh dear—I'm so sorry.

HUGH : Don't be—they're in love with one another.

JOHN : Really, Walford!

HUGH : And I'm giving my wife a divorce and then they'll get married.

LIZ : Really darling—you're being too embarassing for words.

HUGH (*coming back with a glass in each hand*) : I can't see why. It's only civil to put Miss—Good Heavens, anyone'd think that we were in the office —what's your Christian name again, dear?

MISS FORSYTH : Molly.

HUGH : That's right—well done. May I call you Molly, as we're on holiday?

MISS FORSYTH : Of course.

HUGH (*handing Molly her glass*) : Your sherry, Molly.

MOLLY : Thank you, Mr Walford.

HUGH : Hugh's the name.

MOLLY : Hugh.

HUGH : Gin and tonic, John?

JOHN : No thank you, Walford.

HUGH : Hugh's the name still.

JOHN : No thanks, Hugh.

HUGH : Good! That's it. That's the ticket. Now we're all friends. No more tension. (*He slaps Liz on the shoulder.*) No more thunderclouds. The cumuli have broken up—the sun's come through —the birds are singing. And I want a spot more gin-and-tonic! What about you, darling?

LIZ : I'm all right, thanks.

HUGH : Well, I'll take your word for it—what time's lunch?

LIZ : One.

HUGH (*looking at his watch*) : Good—time to see the garden. How about a walk round, Molly—with your sherry?

MOLLY : I'd love to.

HUGH : Good girl. Liz is a great gardener. She's got green fingers. I'm just the destroyer—passion-flowers and bind-weed—ivy and delphiniums—they all fall to my axe. Do you have window-boxes in your flat, John?

JOHN : Yes.

HUGH : What do you grow in them?

JOHN : Geraniums.

HUGH : Did Liz plant them?

JOHN : Yes.

HUGH : Oh well—you're all right. I'll bet they're climbing round the bath-taps now! Ready, Molly?

MOLLY (*getting up*): Yes—indeed.

HUGH : Right. Through the door the way you came in. Mind the step—it may be trickier than when you came in—with the sherry. Coming, John?

[*Molly goes out to the garden.*]

JOHN : I'll stay here if you don't mind.

HUGH : Not a bit, old fellow, not a bit. And help yourself if you feel thirsty. All right, darling?

LIZ : Yes, of course I'm all right.

HUGH : Good. Well, have another glass of sherry and relax yourself. You look a bit strung up. (*To John.*) She's pretty, don't you think?

JOHN : Of course I do.

HUGH : No, I mean Molly. (*Moving to John and leaning confidentially to prevent Molly hearing.*) Hot stuff too, they tell me. At least, that was the *on dit* when she worked in my publisher's office. And she's got a passion for me. Funny, isn't it—considering I'm old enough to be her father. Still, one never knows with women—they're rum things.

298

LIZ : You're being very rude, Hugh. —

HUGH : Rude, dear—why—I like rum—Oh, I see —yes—sorry. Coming, Molly. (*He nips out to the garden.*)

(*Off.*) Sorry, dear—let's start on the herbacious border first . . .

LIZ : It's too pathetic, isn't it?

JOHN (*moving to the drinks table*) : And damned embarrassing.

LIZ : Do you know that he's put you in his dressing-room? (*She puts her drink on the table.*)

JOHN : Good God!

LIZ (*Picking up the waste-paper basket and putting in the wrapping and pieces from the flowers*) : And himself in the spare-room dressing-room next to Miss Forsyth.

JOHN : That's just bluff—don't let it worry you.

LIZ : It doesn't worry me. It worries Mrs Gray, though. It'll be all round the village by this evening.

JOHN : Well, it will be by tomorrow evening anyway.

LIZ : She thinks that she's his mistress. She came in and tried to mother me this morning just before you got here. Called me 'dearie' and 'poor lamb'.

JOHN : She doesn't know about us, then?

LIZ : Of course not.

JOHN (*sitting on the sofa*) : I thought that your husband might have told her in that charming open way he has.

LIZ : Why did you come down, John?

JOHN : You told me to.

LIZ : I know—I thought I couldn't stand it by myself until tomorrow, once I knew he'd found out.

JOHN (*rising*): Poor darling. Did you have a dreadful night?

LIZ : I never slept a wink.

JOHN : It evidently suits you. You're looking wonderful.

LIZ : I'm not, John.

JOHN (*gently*): Yes, you are. Have some more sherry?

LIZ : No thanks. Was the golf a nightmare?

JOHN : Not too bad.

LIZ : Were you on time?

JOHN : Yes.

LIZ : What did Hugh say when you met?

JOHN : 'Good morning—I'm Hugh Walford.'

LIZ : What did you say?

JOHN : 'I'm John Brownlow.'

LIZ : Is that all?

JOHN : It seemed to cover everything. Well, most things, anyway. (*He sits on the sofa.*)

LIZ : And then?

JOHN : We went inside and paid our green fees. At least, he did.

LIZ : You let him pay yours?

JOHN : He wouldn't hear of anything else.

LIZ : And you really beat him, five and four?

JOHN : Yes.

LIZ : Was he very bad?

JOHN : He did some good shots—but they weren't very straight.

LIZ : And yours were?

JOHN : Straighter—and he found a lot of bunkers.

LIZ : And you didn't?

JOHN : I was lucky.

LIZ : Poor Hugh.

JOHN : Now, don't start getting sentimental.

LIZ : But he's so good usually.

JOHN : I dare say—but I'm better.

LIZ : Yes, of course you are. And did he talk about us?

JOHN : Not a word.

LIZ : Not even in the car?

JOHN : We were in different cars.

LIZ : Well, in the Club House?

JOHN : No.

LIZ : Aren't men extraordinary!

JOHN : Some men, I dare say.

LIZ : You're just as bad. You should have talked to him.

JOHN : I did.

LIZ : About us?

JOHN : No.

LIZ : Why not?

JOHN : Well, what is there to say, for God's sake?

LIZ : Quite a lot I should have thought.

JOHN : Not anything he doesn't know already.

LIZ : I just think you ought to tell him that you love me.

JOHN : Darling, that goes without saying.

LIZ : Oh, does it?

JOHN : Yes, of course it does. No, if we're going to have a 'man to man' together, it'll be about the damn fool way that he's behaving.

LIZ : Don't be hard on him. He's never grown up.

JOHN : Well, it's time he did.

LIZ : Perhaps, but you do like him, don't you?

JOHN : Yes—he's charming. But I like you better. Put that glass down. Put it down, I said. Now, come . . .

[*Liz puts her glass on the table.*]

Now come here. (*He kisses her.*) Darling.

[*Hugh comes in and watches them embracing.*]

(*Breaking the embrace and looking into her eyes.*)
Liz, my darling.

LIZ : Johnski—oh, my darling Johnski.

[*Liz and John kiss. Hugh moves down and taps
Liz on the shoulder.*]

HUGH : Hold it just a second—if you don't mind.
Sorry, old chap, didn't mean to butt in, but it's
Molly. She's got bogged down on the croquet lawn
in her high heels. (*To Liz.*) Have you got a pair
of sandals handy?

LIZ : There's some in the flower-room. I'll get them.

HUGH : Thank you, darling.

[*Liz goes out.*]

(*To John.*) There's a touch of lip-stick on your
left cheek.

[*John takes out a handkerchief and dabs at his
right cheek.*]

Left, I said—old chap—

[*John gets the right spot.*]

That's better. (*He strolls to the table, picks up two
photographs.*) Really puts her back into it, old Liz,
doesn't she? She damn near broke my neck the
first time that I met her. In a Land Rover, it was—
in Scotland, north of Carlisle somewhere—we'd
been out fishing and I stopped to light a cigarette
and she was on me like a panther. Everything

went—matches—cigarette-case and the button on my shirt collar. I reckon I was lucky not to finish up in hospital. Still, it was worth it. (*He gives John the photographs.*) This is Dick—and this is Sheila. You'll be seeing quite a lot of them in future, I imagine. Sheila's very like her mother—goes right off the deep-end. She'll be a push-over for any over-sexed young bounder in jeans. Dick's more like me—full of charm but just about as lively as a tortoise. I expect he'll write books if the pencil's not too heavy for him.

[*Liz enters with the sandals.*]

LIZ : Will these do, Hugh?

HUGH : Perfect, darling.

LIZ : I hope they'll fit her.

HUGH (*taking the sandals and moving to the window*) : May be just a shade big. Still, the thought's there. Thank you, darling. I'll call you if she's sunk in any further and wants jacking up. (*He goes out.*)

LIZ : What's he been saying to you?

JOHN : Telling me about your first kiss, that's all.

LIZ : Our first . . .

JOHN : In a Land Rover in Scotland—north of Carlisle—after fishing.

LIZ : John—he didn't . . .

JOHN : Yes, he did—and I don't find it very funny.

LIZ : Did he?

JOHN : I'm afraid so, riotously.

LIZ : I'd had neat whisky with the fishing lunch as I was so wet.

JOHN : There's no need to make excuses.

LIZ : He's too naughty.

JOHN : He's too childish, if you ask me.

LIZ : I agree but never mind. He's got to keep up his morale somehow and that's the way he likes to do it.

JOHN : He'll be telling me about your honeymoon, I shouldn't wonder, next.

LIZ : I shouldn't either. (*Seeing that John has the photographs.*) Did he talk about the children?

JOHN : Yes. He said that Sheila's going to be a push-over like you.

LIZ (*taking the photographs*) : And Dick?

JOHN : Dick's full of charm like him—but just about as lively as a tortoise.

[*Liz's mouth twitches.*]

It's not funny, Liz.

LIZ : No, John, you said that. (*She replaces the photographs.*)

JOHN : Let's go back to London. Come on, I can't stand this. Come on—let's get out of it. We'll have lunch on the way in some pub.

LIZ : No, John.

JOHN : Why not?

LIZ : We can't run away.

JOHN : I can't see why not. We're going to in the morning, anyway. So let's just put it forward twenty-four hours.

LIZ : No, John.

JOHN : But why not?

LIZ : It'd be the end, that's why not. If we can't take this, it means we can't take anything. We'd both be starting off with a defeat and that's not what I want to build our marriage on. We've got to go through with it.

JOHN : I suppose you're right.

LIZ : Of course I'm right.

JOHN : O.K., that's settled. But get this into your head. (*He takes her by the wrist.*) If things get on your nerves, don't blame me.

LIZ : That hurts, John.

JOHN : It's meant to—to impress on you that staying here's your choice, and not mine.

LIZ : Let me go please.

[*John lets her go.*]

JOHN : I can't tell you how I missed you last night.

LIZ : Have a carrot?

JOHN : What?

LIZ : I mean a nut. I'm sorry, darling. I'm not concentrating. Everything's so confusing.

JOHN : No it's not. It's clear as crystal. Come here.

[*Liz moves to John and they are about to embrace again.*]

HUGH (*off*) : Mind the step.

[*Liz moves away from John. Molly enters.*]

MOLLY : Thanks so much for the sandals.

LIZ : Not at all.

MOLLY : I think the garden's lovely.

[*Hugh enters with Molly's shoes.*]

HUGH : Molly likes the blue delphiniums best. You should have a look at them, John.

JOHN : I'd like to.

LIZ : Not now Hugh—if you don't mind. It's almost lunchtime. (*To Molly.*) Would you like to see your room?

MOLLY : Yes—thank you.

LIZ : Hugh—will you show John his?

HUGH (*moving to the drinks table*) : When I've topped myself up. Molly, my dear, don't forget your running shoes.

MOLLY : Oh, no. (*She turns back.*) Thanks so much.

[*Molly goes out.*]

HUGH : Not at all, dear—I liked carrying them.

[*Liz moves to the door.*]

(*To Liz.*) She came out quite easily. A good strong pull and then a squelch and there she was.

[*Liz goes out.*]

(*To John.*) I know just how a thrush feels now when it gets hold of a nice juicy worm. One for the stairs?

JOHN : No, thanks. (*He moves to the door.*)

HUGH : Come on.

JOHN : Oh, all right, Walford.

HUGH : Hugh's the name still.

JOHN : Hugh then—I'm your guest, I know, but I feel bound to tell you, you're behaving like a lunatic.

HUGH (*philosophically*) : Maybe, but it's a mad world, isn't it? And I can never quite decide which side of the asylum wall's the inside.

JOHN (*ignoring this*) : Liz and I are going off together and, although I'm sorry—looking at it from your point of view—there's nothing you can do about it.

HUGH (*on the old tack*) : Do you know the one

about the pigeon? (*He goes to John and gives him his drink.*)

JOHN : Pigeon?

HUGH (*moving to the sofa and sitting*): That's right. And the lunatic. You brought the subject up not me. It illustrates my point about the difficulty of deciding who's sane and who isn't. Well, this lunatic was walking in the garden with a nurse, when this pigeon flew over. And it got him in the eye with a direct hit. In the lunatic's eye, got the picture?

JOHN : Yes.

HUGH : Good. And the nurse said 'Hang on, I'll nip inside and get a bit of toilet paper!' Are you with me?

JOHN : Yes.

HUGH : Well, here's the punch line. And the lunatic said, 'Are you crazy, nurse, by the time you get back that bird'll be a mile away'. Makes one think, old fellow, doesn't it? What was it you were saying? Ah yes—about you two pushing off. Don't worry about that. I've got the message. That's why I'm behaving like I am. I'm trying to keep everybody happy. That's why I asked Molly down. To make a foursome, so that no one'd feel left out. I'd better show you your room now, or we'll be in trouble. (*He rises, takes John's glass and goes to the drinks table.*) You're in my dressing-room—I hope you don't mind. Well, of course, you don't—why should you? It'll save a lot of mileage one way and another. And a lot of passage-navigation in a strange house in the dark's no fun at all. I knew a fellow once who used to go downstairs to dinner in a strange house with his valet following behind and sticking drawing-pins in every board that creaked. He's dead now—and I'm not surprised.

The chap—I mean. I wouldn't know about the valet. Probably still with us, as he must have got a lot of exercise.

[*Hugh moves to the door. John follows.*]

Right—off we go Camp One.

[*Hugh opens the door, Liz enters.*]

Hullo, darling. Molly settled in all right?
LIZ : She seems quite happy.
HUGH : So she should be. After you, sir.
JOHN : Thank you. (*He goes out.*)
HUGH : Did you put the champagne on the ice, dear?
LIZ : Mrs Gray did.
HUGH : Well done her—two bottles, I hope. I'm in festive mood.

[*Hugh goes out. Liz collects dirty sherry glasses fom the table. Mrs Gray enters with two bouquets, one of lilies and one of roses.*]

MRS GRAY : These just came, Ma'am.
LIZ : Who for?
MRS GRAY : One's for you, the lilies.
LIZ : For me !

[*Mrs Gray shows Liz the bouquet of lilies.*]

MRS GRAY : That's right, dear—from Mr Walford.

[*Liz looks at the label.*]

LIZ : And the roses?

MRS GRAY : For Miss Forsyth.

LIZ (*hastily, having seen her label*) : Put them in some water in the flower-room, Mrs Gray. (*She goes to the drinks table.*)

MRS GRAY : They're a picture, dear—and no mistake—I've seen them on the coffin at a funeral once, but I've never handled them before. 'Course these are lovely, too—I've got to say so. But it doesn't mean that I'm not shocked.

LIZ : Please, Mrs Gray, it's almost lunchtime.

[*Mrs Gray turns for the door. Hugh enters.*]

HUGH : Ah, so they've arrived. Where are you going to put them, darling?

MRS GRAY (*indicating Miss Forsyth's bouquet of roses*) : I know where I'd like to put this lot, sir—and that's in the dustbin.

HUGH : Mrs Gray, you're jealous.

MRS GRAY : Me—jealous—at my age—I like that.

HUGH (*persisting in pulling her leg*) : You like that! (*Indicating the lilies.*) And you'd like a bunch of these. Now, wouldn't you? Confess! Right, you shall have one, Mrs Gray.

MRS GRAY : It's no use trying to get round me.

HUGH : We'll see!

MRS GRAY : I'm plain disgusted with you if you want to know—and that's a fact.

[*Mrs Gray goes out. Hugh goes over to the telephone.*]

LIZ : How could you, Hugh?

HUGH : Quite easily—Interflora. I rang up Constance Spry before I started for the Golf Club. (*He dials.*)

LIZ : Who're you ringing now? (*She sits on the sofa.*)

HUGH : A girl friend.

LIZ : Aren't you satisfied with one?

HUGH : No. I've become insatiable. (*He is holding on.*) She's smashing Molly—isn't she? And most accommodating. So they tell me. Rumour has it she went through my publisher's office like a circular—and still good friends with everyone—That's what I'm looking for—I'm through with love—it lets you down—it's unreliable. From now on its champagne and dalliance for me—and laughter. Life's too short to dig down any deeper. Hullo, Constance Spry? . . . Ah, good—Hugh Walford speaking—I rang earlier this morning . . . Yes— indeed they have—and they're lovely. Thank you very much. I'd like to have the same again in lilies, if you don't mind . . . That's right Mrs Gray—A— Y. The same address, yes . . . What? The card? Oh, yes—what did we have the first time? . . . 'All my love, Hugh'. Yes, that's all right if you put a 'Walford' on the end. I don't know her so well as I know Mrs Walford. And slip in a dozen roses as well. To John Brownlow . . . Yes, I did say John . . . Yes, same address and same card. Without 'Walford' on the end. Just 'all my love, Hugh' . . . Thank you so much. Have a nice week-end. Where are you going to? . . . Yes—I see. Well, be careful of the jelly-fish. Good-bye, dear. (*He hangs up.*) What a nice girl—I can think of much worse things than being bedded out by her. Well, everybody's fixed up now—except for Mr Gray and he can pick his own. So let's hope there'll be no more jealousy.

LIZ : How many gin-and-tonics have you had?

HUGH : I've lost count, but thanks for reminding me. (*He goes to the drinks table.*)

LIZ : You're being very silly, Hugh.

HUGH : We all are, aren't we? What about a touch more sherry?

LIZ : No thanks.

HUGH : Come on, you're behaving like a disapproving governess.

LIZ : And you're behaving like a spoilt child.

HUGH (*refusing to be ruffled*) : Come on.

LIZ : No, I said.

HUGH : What were you planning for this afternoon?

LIZ : Don't ask me—you invited them.

HUGH : I thought a little snooze myself to set the caviare. And then I thought I might take Molly swimming in the Jessel's pool.

LIZ : You've asked them, have you?

HUGH : They're in the South of France. But David said we could go any time. Provided that we put the lilos in the changing-room and locked the door.

LIZ : I'm sure you'll do that.

HUGH : What do you and John plan doing?

LIZ : I don't know—I haven't asked him.

HUGH : You could watch the racing on the television or play croquet.

LIZ : Thank you.

HUGH : Or perhaps he's got his own ideas. A nice chap, isn't he? Damned near the perfect athlete, I should say. It's not surprising he's collected all those wives.

LIZ : Hugh.

HUGH : Yes, my darling.

LIZ : If you think that your extraordinary behaviour's going to have the least effect on me, you'd better think again.

HUGH : I will if necessary.

[*Molly enters in trousers, looking a dish.*]

Ah, Molly—well, well—that's a sight for sore eyes. Can I tempt you? (*He indicates the drinks.*)

MOLLY : No, thanks—I've had quite enough.

HUGH : I've just been telling Liz—I thought I'd take you swimming in the afternoon when I've had my siesta.

MOLLY : Oh, how lovely. Is it near here?

HUGH : Five miles—through the lanes.

MOLLY : What fun. I hope you're coming, Mrs Walford.

HUGH : No, she isn't. John and Liz are going to play a little gentle croquet.

[*John enters.*]

MOLLY : I love croquet.

HUGH : So they tell me. Here you are, John. Just time for a quick one.

JOHN : No, thanks.

HUGH : Come on. You'll be swilling down that damned Chianti next week, longing for a decent drop of gin-and-tonic. (*He goes to the drinks table.*) Molly's going off to Italy tomorrow too.

JOHN : Oh really—what part?

MOLLY : Venice—Florence—Rome . . .

HUGH : She likes a bit of sculpture, don't you, Molly?

MOLLY : Well—yes.

HUGH : And a bit of achitecture—and a bit of painting—and a bit of everything, in fact. I've just been telling Liz, we're going swimming in the afternoon at a friend's pool.

JOHN : Oh, that sounds just the ticket. It's the perfect day for it.

HUGH : Well, it's the perfect day for everything. That's why I'm leaving you and Liz here with the croquet lawn at your disposal.

JOHN : Oh, fine.

LIZ : If you'd rather go and swim, John—we'll all go together.

HUGH : No, no. You stay here. You're going to get a lot of swimming when you're in Italy. But poor old Molly hoofing round the Doge's Palace and me in my study—we're the ones who want to take advantage of the sun. I just can't wait to go in at the deep end—can you, Molly—you in your bikini and me in my water-wings!

[*Mrs Gray enters with the lilies in a vase.*]

MRS GRAY : I've brought them in, dear. They're so lovely that I couldn't bear to waste them for another minute.

LIZ (*indicating the sofa table*) : Put them down there Mrs Gray—and I'll find the best place for them. Thank you. Is lunch ready?

MRS GRAY (*at the sofa table*) : Nearly, Ma'am.

HUGH : Have you arranged Miss Forsyth's roses?

MRS GRAY : No, sir.

HUGH : Why not?

MRS GRAY : I've not had the time, sir. (*She moves to the door.*)

HUGH (*thundering*) : Find time, Mrs Gray.

MRS GRAY : Yes, sir. (*She goes out, quaking.*)

HUGH : Women like a bit of domination. Keep the voice as low as possible and kick them in the teeth and you're in clover. I'm so sorry, but she's jealous.

MOLLY : I don't understand.

HUGH : What don't you understand, my dear?

MOLLY : Who's sent me roses.

HUGH : I have.

MOLLY : You have!

313

HUGH : Yes—two dozen.
MOLLY : But whatever for?

[*Mrs Gray enters with roses in one hand and a vase in the other.*]

HUGH : Because I find you very charming—that accounts for the first dozen. And I find you most attractive. That covers the second. May I? (*He kisses her on the cheek.*) Thank you.
MOLLY : Oh, how lovely. Are they really for me? (*She takes the roses.*)
HUGH : Every one of them, my dear. (*He takes the roses.*)
MOLLY : Oh, thank you.

[*She embraces and kisses Hugh.*]

HUGH : Fifteen all, my service—

[*Hugh kisses Molly, then takes the vase from Mrs Gray.*]

Thank you, Mrs Gray.
MRS GRAY : That's quite all right, sir.
HUGH : You can have a teaspoonful of caviare as a reward and half a glass of champagne.
MRS GRAY : Thank you, sir.
HUGH : Don't mention it.
MRS GRAY : And lunch is in, Ma'am.
LIZ : Thank you, Mrs Gray.

[*Mrs Gray goes.*]

MOLLY : And who gave you those, Mrs Walford?
LIZ (*lying*) : Mr Brownlow.

314

MOLLY : They're lovely, too—but I like roses best.
HUGH (*letting Liz get away with it*) : I thought you
would, dear. I find lilies just a shade funereal. (*He
improves the arrangement of the roses.*) They're
beautiful of course—but faintly sad—like a
memorial. A kind of 'thank you' for the past.
Whereas I always think of roses as a promise for
the future; don't you, John?
JOHN : I've never thought about it.
HUGH : Oh well, you will, you will.
LIZ (*coldly*) : We'll find a place for those two vases
after lunch, Hugh. (*She moves to the door and
waits.*) Come along, Miss Forsyth.

[*Molly waits for Liz to go first.*]

No, no, after you, dear.
MOLLY : Thank you.

[*Molly goes out, followed by Liz. John moves to
the door, but hesitates, as Molly did. Hugh beckons
him forward.*]

HUGH : No, no, after you, Johnski !

John starts to go out, as—

the Curtain falls

ACT TWO

Scene 1

The same. Late on Saturday night.
Moonlight can be seen in the garden through any
openings in the window curtains. Another fine vase
of red roses stands on a table, waiting to be pin-
pointed.
When the curtain rises, John, Liz, Hugh and Molly
are playing bridge. The men wear dinner-jackets,
and John has his cummerbund. The women are in
evening gowns. Hands are being arranged.

HUGH : One no trump.
JOHN : Double.
MOLLY : Two hearts.
LIZ : Three Clubs.
HUGH : Three Hearts.
JOHN : Four Clubs.
MOLLY : Four Hearts.
LIZ : Double.
HUGH : Content.
JOHN : No.
HUGH (*to Liz*) : Your lead, Liz—four Hearts.
MOLLY (*to Hugh*) : Oh, dear—I hope you've got
something.
HUGH : You'd be surprised, my dear.

[*Liz leads, Hugh puts down his hand.*]

Four Hearts, and if you get it, that's the rubber.
(*He rises.*) Anybody thirsty?
LIZ : I'd like a bitter lemon if there is one.
HUGH : Molly?
MOLLY : No thanks, I'm far too excited.
HUGH (*moving to the drinks table*) : Good girl. Take
it steady, my dear—and count trumps. There tend

to be around thirteen in most packs. You John?
JOHN : No, thanks?
HUGH (*pouring Liz's drink*) : Who took that trick?
MOLLY : I did.
HUGH : Well done keep it up. There's lots more where that came from.
LIZ : Be quiet, Hugh—you're cheating.
HUGH (*giving Liz her drink*) : Sorry, darling.
LIZ : Thank you.
HUGH : There's a lot of people walking the Embankment, so they say, who never took trumps out.

[*Liz, Molly and John continue to play.*]

LIZ : Hugh, if you don't stop talking, I'll throw my hand in.

[*Mrs Gray comes in carrying her bouquet of lilies.*]

HUGH : Come in, Mrs Gray. Don't worry Mrs Walford at the moment—we're playing four hearts doubled. Have a drink while you're waiting?
MRS GRAY : No, sir—thank you all the same.
HUGH (*moving to the drinks table*) : Well, you won't mind if I do.
MRS GRAY : Thank you for the lovely flowers, sir.
HUGH : Not at all. (*He pours himself a drink.*) I'm glad you liked them.
MRS GRAY : They're lovely. But you never should have done it. Mr. Gray says they're the most expensive flowers that you can buy—especially in London.
HUGH : He's got something there. (*There is a pause while the bridge continues.*) Well, let's do my department while we're waiting, shall we? I'll have my usual cup of tea at seven-thirty.

MRS GRAY : Yes, sir.

HUGH : And I'm sure that that'll suit Miss Forsyth as she's got to be in London early. Molly, my dear —are you very busy?

MOLLY : I'm just thinking.

HUGH : Sorry.

MOLLY : Why, what is it? You've distracted me now!

HUGH : What train are you catching in the morning?

MOLLY : Ten-five.

HUGH : Yes, I thought so. That's the only one there is. And Indian or China?

MOLLY : China, please.

HUGH : Good. That'll save a lot of trouble, won't it, Mrs Gray? One teapot and two cups at seven-thirty in the spare room. And a Rich Tea biscuit, or two.

MOLLY (*referring to a finesse that has succeeded*) : Got it! And the rest are mine. (*She throws her cards face up on the table.*)

HUGH : Well done, dear.

MOLLY : Well, all the finesses came off.

HUGH : Most unusual.

MOLLY : What's that make it?

HUGH : Four Hearts doubled—two hundred and forty. And five hundred for the rubber. And another fifty for the insult.

MOLLY : Oh, how lovely.

[*There is a pause.*]

HUGH (*to Liz*) : Darling—(*indicating Mrs Gray's presence.*)—Mrs Gray. I've done the early morning order for my section—what about you? (*He moves to the French windows.*)

318

LIZ : Just knock on my door at half-past seven, Mrs Gray—as usual.

MRS GRAY : Yes, Ma'am.

LIZ : John—do you like early morning tea?

JOHN (*rising*) : No, thank you—never touch it.

LIZ : Well, then—breakfast—nine on, down here. How would that suit everybody?

MOLLY : Perfect, yes.

JOHN : Fine.

HUGH : Dressing-gowns for those who haven't been to Early Service.

LIZ : Thank you, Mrs Gray. Good night.

MRS GRAY : Good night, Ma'am. Good night, Sir. Good night, Miss.

MOLLY : Good night, Mrs. Gray.

MRS GRAY (*mellowed towards Hugh since the flowers*) : Good night, sir.

HUGH : Good night, Mrs Gray.

[*Mrs Gray goes out.*]

Well, that's the way to treat an Amazon—say it with flowers. Now, what's the damage, John?

JOHN (*getting out his money*) : I make it twenty.

LIZ : Oh—I've left my money upstairs in my other bag.

HUGH : Don't worry, darling, I'll fix it.

[*John gives Hugh a ten-shilling note.*]

Thank you, John. (*He passes it on to Molly.*) That's Liz's debt to you my dear.

MOLLY : But what about you?

HUGH : Never mind me—it's the last time I'll be paying up for her—apart from alimony. Please forgive me, Molly, if I talk shop for a moment, as

319

there won't be much time in the morning. I'll be
giving Liz a divorce, John—I don't know if she
told you?

JOHN : Well, yes, she did mention it this afternoon.

HUGH : Oh, good. And I'll be as generous as possible, of course—allowing for the children and the
Chancellor. And you're pretty well endowed, from
what I gather—and she's not expensive.

LIZ : Darling, anyone'd think I was your daughter
from the way you're talking!

HUGH : Quite a lot of people have thought that, my
darling—in the past. That's been the trouble. Any
of your past wives been much younger than you,
John?

JOHN : The second one was.

HUGH : How old?

JOHN : Seventeen.

HUGH : Oh dear—that's stretching it a bit. What
was she : Mexican?

JOHN : No, Austrian.

HUGH : How long did she last?

JOHN : Two years.

HUGH : What went wrong?

LIZ : Hugh, really! Anyone'd think you were a
psychoanalyst.

HUGH (*moving about*) : I sometimes think I should
have been one—writing makes one very analytical,
you know—one couldn't be one if one weren't. One
sees everything from outside quite impersonally—
one's own life just the same as other people's. For
instance, I can see four people in this room quite
clearly—not three. Maybe that's what makes me
difficult to live with. Look at Liz, poor darling, she's
been living with a typewriter to all intents and
purposes for fifteen years. And typewriters aren't
good in bed—apart from all their other failings—

twisted tape and three-quarters instead of question marks! (*He has arrived beside John's flowers.*) I hope you like them, John—you never thanked me for them. When did they arrive?

JOHN : This afternoon.

LIZ : When you were swimming at the Jessels' pool.

HUGH : Ah, yes, I see—and you forgot about them—fair enough. Or were you annoyed?

JOHN : No, of course not.

HUGH : Sure?

JOHN : Of course I'm sure.

HUGH : You didn't mind the note?

JOHN : No.

HUGH : 'All my love, Hugh'! Took that in his stride, Liz, did he?

LIZ : Yes, of course, Hugh.

HUGH : I'll bet he didn't. (*Moving to the desk.*) I'll bet he snorted and then tore it up and threw it in the basket. Any takers? (*He picks up a crumpled card from the waste-paper basket.*) Hullo, hullo—what's this, John, old fellow? (*Reading.*) 'All my love, Hugh.' Crumpled, thrown away, rejected, spurned—I hoped you'd stick it in your wallet underneath the dollar-clip, and look at it each night before you went to bed, and thank God that there's no ill-feeling.

JOHN (*moving to Hugh*) : I'm afraid I didn't take it very seriously.

HUGH : Why not? That was a mistake.

JOHN : I just thought you were being funny.

HUGH : Dear, oh dear! What made you think that —just because I write light novels. Dear, oh dear—you mustn't be so superficial, John, you really mustn't. Even my son Dick knows clowns tread water in their own tears all their lives, and he's a schoolboy. I was being serious, old chap. Those

roses represent my olive branch, my pipe of peace
—and, since they won't survive for long, this little
card's my draft peace treaty.

[*Hugh holds out the card and John takes it.*]

JOHN : Thank you. (*He takes the card and puts it
in his wallet.*)
HUGH (*watching John*) : Thank you. I apologize
for giving the impression I was being funny. That's
the penalty for being different in a uniform world
—I can't help it. It's the way I'm made.
LIZ (*rising*) : I think I'll go up, if you don't mind.
What about you, Molly?
MOLLY : Well, I ...
HUGH : No, no—Molly doesn't want to go yet, do
you, Molly? We're going to go and listen for a
nightingale out in the orchard—planned it all this
afternoon, when we were swimming, didn't we—
she's never heard one. (*He picks up a light cardigan,
off the arm of the sofa.*) Come along, my dear, is
this yours? You may need it.
MOLLY (*getting up*) : Yes. (*She moves to Hugh.*)
HUGH (*helping her on with it.*) : Good. (*To Liz.*)
Don't go up yet, darling—stay and talk to John.
It is your last night, after all, at home. We won't
be long, and we must have a night-cap; just to show
there's no ill-feeling. (*To Molly.*) Ready, dear?
MOLLY : Yes, Hugh.
HUGH : Good. Lead on. Mind the step.

[*Molly goes out through the french windows.*]

(*Moving to John and whispering.*) Amazing—she
spends half her life in Berkeley Square and yet she's
never heard a nightingale.

[*Hugh follows Molly out.*]

LIZ : He's going to do it, John.

JOHN : Do what?

LIZ : Provide me with the evidence. He ordered tea for two from Mrs Gray at seven-thirty.

JOHN : Yes—I heard him. That's what made me lead the wrong card.

[*John and Liz clear the cards.*]

LIZ : It's disgusting—in his own house!

JOHN : Still, if that's the way he wants it done—why should we worry?

LIZ : He's my husband, John.

JOHN : Yes, darling.

LIZ : After fifteen years! He's never looked to right or left before. And now he's ready to jump into bed with that appalling girl.

JOHN : I don't think she's all that appalling.

LIZ : No, of course you don't—you're a man—and men have got no taste. You're animals, that's all you are. If you think something's pretty, that's enough for you—you're utterly, completely superficial—all of you!

JOHN : Thanks very much.

LIZ : Whereas a woman can see through a girl like that at once. She's money-grubbing, over-sexed—in fact, she's almost certainly a nymphomaniac.

JOHN : Well—I'm not arguing.

LIZ : How can he even contemplate it, John?

JOHN : Don't ask me.

LIZ : If he wants to give me a divorce—and there's no reason why he should when he can easily divorce me—but still, if he wants to, out of a mistaken sense of chivalry—why can't he go to Brighton like a normal person, with a normal woman—instead of indulging in this beastly exhibition in his own home with that dreadful little creature.

JOHN : I don't think she's all that dreadful.

LIZ : Don't keep saying that!

JOHN : I'm sorry, darling—but I see old Hugh's point.

LIZ : Trust you!

JOHN : And in fairness I must say so—I mean, why go off to Brighton with a lady in a leopard-skin coat in her fifties, when you've got a girl who's obviously keen on you, who won't be doing *The Times* crossword all night in an arm-chair by the gasfire. Why go off to the Municipal Baths when you've got a private swimming pool?

LIZ : You're talking just like Hugh.

JOHN : I'm sorry. I'm afraid the most attractive man in London's letting you down. What on earth made you say that about me?

LIZ : I got furious with Hugh pretending he'd never heard of you.

JOHN : So you indulged yourself in wishful thinking.

LIZ (*ignoring this argument*) : Do you realize Hugh's over fifty, John?

JOHN : That's right.

LIZ : What do you mean—'that's right'?

JOHN : I was confirming your assessment of his age, that's all.

LIZ : And Molly's twenty-five, at the outside.

JOHN : That could be right, too.

LIZ : Can't you see it's quite out of the question?

JOHN : On the drawing-board, perhaps—but not in practice. Maybe he's just what she's looking for—some women like them old—and vice-versa.

LIZ : You must stop him, John.

JOHN : I hardly think I'm quite in a position to.

LIZ : If you don't. I will.

JOHN : I see—how do you propose to do that?

LIZ : By appealing to his better nature.

JOHN : Well, good luck to you.

LIZ : If you stay down here, talking to him, after we've gone up—and you must—otherwise he'll get into that spare room dressing-room, and he might lock the door—then I'll come down again, and you must go to bed, and leave us.

JOHN : I'll be glad to, darling.

LIZ : Yes, of course you will—you're all alike, you men—you stick together like glue. If you had an ounce of guts, you'd talk to him yourself and make him so ashamed he'd curl up on the sofa for the night instead of going upstairs to that . . . (*She pauses to find an adequate word for Molly's inadequacy.*)

JOHN (*cutting in*) : You're jealous, Liz.

LIZ : Me—jealous?

JOHN : Yes.

LIZ : Don't be silly.

JOHN : Well, possessive, if you like—but it's the same thing. You can't bear to see what's been your property for years on someone else's mantelpiece. You've got to face it, though—you've got to learn that Hugh's entitled to conduct his life exactly as he pleases once you've left him. If he wants to keep a harem here, you haven't any right to stop him. If you can't accept that, we'd better call the whole thing off—because it's not on.

LIZ : No, John—you don't mean that, do you?

JOHN : I'm afraid I do.

LIZ : No, darling—say you don't. Please say you don't. You've got to say you don't.

JOHN : All right—but pull yourself together—otherwise you'll lose the pair of us.

LIZ : You didn't mean that, darling?

JOHN : We'll see.

LIZ : What do you mean by that?

JOHN : Exactly what I say—you're either Hugh's or mine—you can't be both. You've got to make the break—the final break.

LIZ : I've made it, John.

JOHN : All right—but don't keep looking back—or it'll make you dizzy.

LIZ : I can talk to him, though—can't I?

JOHN : I suppose so—if you must.

LIZ : I must, John.

JOHN : All right—but remember what I've said. It's Hugh—or me. And, if it's me—it isn't Hugh in any way—not even as a self-appointed supervisor of his sex-life. (*Trying to lighten the atmosphere.*) How would that be as a bit of dialogue in one of his books?

LIZ (*sulkily, hearing footsteps outside*) : You'd better ask him.

[*Molly enters from the french windows.*]

MOLLY : We heard one.

LIZ (*forcing civility*) : Oh, well done.

MOLLY : It was too lovely.

[*Hugh enters.*]

HUGH : Singing fit to bust itself—you ought to hear it, John.

JOHN : I'd like to.

HUGH : Take him down there, darling—just beyond

the summerhouse—the far end of that clump of saplings.

JOHN : Don't you bother—I'll go.

HUGH : No—I don't want you ploughing through the border like a wounded buffalo. You take him, darling—it's worth hearing.

MOLLY (*offering her woolly*) : Would you like this?

[*Hugh moves to the drinks table.*]

LIZ : Thank you. (*To Hugh.*) Where are you going, Hugh?

HUGH : To get the drinks. What would you like, my darling?

LIZ : Nothing, thank you.

HUGH : Come on—we must have a farewell drink together. That's one reason why I've got this bottle on the ice. (*He picks up a champagne bottle.*)

LIZ : Oh, all right—just a drop, though. (*She goes out through the french windows.*)

HUGH : You, John?

JOHN : Half a glass'll do me. (*He moves to the window, trips on the step, and goes out.*)

HUGH : Right, sir. Mind the step. (*Shouting to John.*) And sing a bit yourself if it won't play. They can't stand rivalry. What would you like, my dear?

MOLLY : A drop of champagne, please.

HUGH (*starting to open the bottle*) : I've given you a dreadful reputation with those two—I hope you don't mind.

MOLLY : Oh dear—what have you said?

HUGH : Well, I've left Liz with the idea that you're most accommodating.

MOLLY : And did she believe it?

HUGH : I sincerely hope so.

MOLLY : It won't work.

HUGH : I wonder. (*The cork pops.*) Anyway, it's very nice of you to play.

MOLLY : I don't appear to have had much alternative.

HUGH (*pouring*) : I told her you'd been right through my publisher's office like a circular.

MOLLY : Thanks very much.

HUGH : And that you were still friends with all of them.

MOLLY : Well, that's nice, anyway.

HUGH : And that you had a passion for me.

MOLLY : Oh, how did you guess?

HUGH : And that I'm going to give her evidence for the divorce by being found in bed with you by Mrs Gray tomorrow morning, when she brings the China tea and Rich Tea biscuits in at seventhirty.

MOLLY : I love Rich Tea biscuits . . .

HUGH : Oh, well, that'll be a point of contact. And I'm sleeping in the spare room dressing-room communicating with your room. (*He picks up two glasses.*)

MOLLY : I guessed that when I heard you singing before dinner.

HUGH : And you musn't lock the intervening door.

MOLLY : Why not?

HUGH : Because I'm too big to get through the keyhole.

MOLLY : So you're going to pay a social call? (*She takes her glass.*)

HUGH : Yes.

MOLLY : What time?

HUGH : Any time that suits you.

MOLLY : Seven twenty-seven.

HUGH : Not before that!

MOLLY: No, Hugh.

HUGH: Why not?

MOLLY: I'll be asleep.

HUGH: I thought of that. So I planned coming in before you went to sleep tonight.

MOLLY: Oh, did you?

HUGH: Yes—with champagne and what Mrs Gray's left of the caviare.

MOLLY: What purpose would that serve?

HUGH: A very good one. Liz is sure to come along and peep into the dressing-room at some time in the night or other—and it wouldn't do for her to find me there, snoring my head off, would it?

MOLLY: Why not?

HUGH: You know damned well why not.

MOLLY: But it would do if she heard you snoring your head off in my room—through the intervening door?

HUGH: Precisely—are you playing?

MOLLY: What do I get out of it?

HUGH: Champagne and caviare.

MOLLY: And nothing else?

HUGH: No—not unless you want it. If you want a grape, or something, naturally I'll nip down for it.

MOLLY: Thank you.

HUGH: Is it on then?

MOLLY: How loud do you snore?

HUGH: Depends on whether I'm alseep, or not.

MOLLY: When you're asleep.

HUGH: Not too bad. You'll merely think you're crossing prematurely to Boulogne tomorrow in a heat haze.

MOLLY: That sounds rather restful.

HUGH: Yes, it could be—Well?

MOLLY: All right, Hugh.

HUGH : You're a good girl.
MOLLY : Don't forget that.

[*Liz enters.*]

HUGH : Hullo—did you hear it?
LIZ : Yes.

[*John enters.*]

HUGH : A good sound, isn't it, John? (*He hands John a glass.*)
JOHN : Fabulous, yes. (*He takes the glass.*)
HUGH : Funny way of getting through the night. Still, if we all did that, I reckon it'd save a bit of trouble. Think of Johnski, sitting on the bed-post in his mews flat, with his cummerbund contracting and expanding and his Adam's apple going sixteen to the dozen. (*He raises his glass.*) Well, good luck in Italy—and in the future.

[*Liz takes the glass from Hugh.*]

JOHN : Thank you—and the same to you.
HUGH : Don't worry about me. I'm going to have myself a ball. I'm feeling like a convict coming out of Dartmoor after fifteen years. (*To John.*) I see why you've cut down your marriages to size, old chap. It's definitely not an institution that wants over-emphasizing—not unless you want to finish up a vegetable. (*To Liz.*) That's what I've been for years, Liz. I was thinking in my bath tonight—a bloody vegetable. Well, that's no damned good for a novelist. He ought to be outside the kitchen garden, in among the roses and the lilies of the valley.

LIZ : Are you coming, Molly?

MOLLY (*rising*) : Yes—I think I will. (*To John.*) Good night. (*She moves to the door.*)

JOHN : Good night, Miss Forsyth.

MOLLY : Good night, Hugh. (*She goes out.*)

HUGH : Good night, my darling.

LIZ : Good night, John. (*She goes out.*)

JOHN : Good night, Liz.

HUGH : Good night, Liz, sleep well.

[*John moves to the drinks table.*]

HUGH : One for the stairs?

JOHN : No, thank you.

HUGH (*moving to the drinks table*) : Come on! Give them time to take their faces off, good Heavens! (*He pours some more into John's glass.*) Nothing's killed romance so much, in the last fifty years, in my opinion, as men going up to bed at the same time as women. Well, it stands to reason. Who wants some great purple-faced baboon lying in bed behind them when they're working on the Ponds Cold Cream! And what man's going to be a demon lover after hearing bottles clicking on a glass-topped dressing-table like machine-gun fire for half the night? I wouldn't be surprised if it's not that that's got the sexes all botched up. You mark my words, young fellow, if it goes on, by the year two-thousand—I'd reckon you'd need a radar set to tell the sexes apart. Our grandfathers weren't fools, you know. They came upstairs, topped up with brandy and they found their women waiting for them—whether they were theirs or someone else's they were waiting for them. Do I make myself clear?

JOHN : Amply.

[John rises, but Hugh puts his hand on John's shoulder and they sit side by side on the sofa.]

HUGH : I'll tell you something, Johnski. Sometimes Liz'll sit on that damned dressing-table stool till after midnight—firing intermittent bursts with those damned bottles on the glass top. And then, by the time she's berthed alongside me—I'm sunk without trace. (*He puts his hand on John's leg.*) You watch that, my boy, in Italy—she doesn't like it. Take my tip and stay downstairs in the hotel until they turn the lights out in the lounge—don't take the lift—go up the stairs by easy stages, smoking a last cigarette and, even then, you'll be too early nine times out of ten. I'll tell you what to do then—get into the bath—that's if she's out of it—if not, it's naturally a different story—if she is, though, jump in and lie soaking in it—never mind the indigestion—till she calls you. Then don't answer. She'll call again in a few minutes, 'Hugh, sorry, I mean John, what—are you doing, darling?' —and don't answer again. Then she'll call a third time. This time answer casually, though. Just say, 'Coming, darling'. Then get out and dry and nip into the bedroom. It's the only way to stay on top —perhaps I could have put that better. But you see what I mean?

JOHN : Yes, I take the point.

HUGH : It's over-rated, isn't it?

JOHN : What?

HUGH : Sex, in general.

JOHN : Well, that's a point of view.

HUGH : Which you don't share?

JOHN : No, not entirely—not at all, in fact.

HUGH : You're quite a dab hand at it, so they tell me?

JOHN : Who do?

HUGH : No one old chap. Don't misunderstand me.
It's just my assumption—based on what I know
about you.

JOHN : On my marriages, you mean?

HUGH : Yes—three—would that be right?

JOHN : Quite right.

HUGH : Why did you marry them?

JOHN : Instead of living with them, do you mean?

HUGH : Yes, that's right.

JOHN : I'm a marrying man.

HUGH : Fair enough. Why leave them, then?

JOHN : Quite simple. I got bored with them.

HUGH : In what way?

JOHN : All ways.

HUGH : Mentally and physically?

JOHN : Yes, both.

HUGH : But which, predominantly?

JOHN : Well . . .

HUGH : I'll tell you—physically.

JOHN : Perhaps.

HUGH : You wanted a change.

JOHN : Possibly.

HUGH : Like someone who's been playing damned
well on St George's for a long time and he thinks
he ought to have a go at Prince's!

JOHN : If you like.

HUGH : You're a professional, in fact—an expert.
You're so highly skilled that every now and then,
you want to try your woods and your long irons on
a different set of bunkers and a different set of
greens.

JOHN : You put things very picturesquely.

HUGH : But why become a Member each time, old
boy? Why not pay your green fees and then have
whatever rounds you feel like?

JOHN : Members have a lot of prestige.

HUGH : For example?

JOHN : A good conscience.

HUGH : Bless my soul, you really meant that, didn't you?

JOHN : Of course I did.

HUGH : Do you know, if I put you in a book—a fellow with three wives and a fourth on the drawing-board—and made you say the reason why you acted like an amateur Mohammedan was conscience, no one would believe me. They'd think it was a bad joke, but the truth is it's a very good joke—the best sort of joke of all, because it's true. I love you, Johnski, you're honest and straightforward and I love an honest and straightforward man. You're worth a bench of Bishops. Every time you love a woman, you get married. Do you know, you should be canonized.

JOHN : Are you being sarcastic?

HUGH : No. You've taught me so much in the last ten minutes. But what about Liz?

JOHN : What about her?

HUGH : I don't want you getting bored with her.

JOHN : I won't—don't worry.

HUGH : You thought that before—with all the other ones.

JOHN : Yes, that's true. But I'm older now.

HUGH : And wiser?

JOHN : Much, much wiser.

HUGH : Well, you've had some cramming, certainly.

JOHN : Besides, it isn't only physical with her.

HUGH (*putting his arm round John*) : I doubt if she'd agree. You see, old fellow, let's face it. I'm a pretty poor performer in that line. You don't mind me talking to you like this, do you?

JOHN : I'm beginning to get used to it.

334

HUGH : That's most broadminded of you. Well, what I was going to say was that—in that particular sphere, you make rings round me, I should imagine—like you do at golf. Don't think I'm criticizing you, for Heaven's sake—I'm merely stating facts. That being so—once you turned up behind that cocktail glass at that damned Embassy and hit it off with Liz—the game was up. There wasn't anything that I could do about it except smooth your passage so to speak. We're on two different wavelengths—yours is physical and mine is mental, broadly speaking. And the trouble from my point of view is that my batteries are running down. Well, they're bound to for a lot of reasons— age, for one, and lack of distilled water for another, and a little too much distilled whisky for a third ! It therefore follows that my signals, on my wife's receiving set, are getting weaker, even if you weren't jamming me—and yours are coming over, loud and clear. And that's why I concede defeat with no hard feelings. (*He raises his glass.*) Good luck. God speed. (*He kisses John on the top of the head.*)

[*Liz enters.*]

Hullo, darling what's the matter?
LIZ : I came down to get my travellers' cheques. (*She goes to the desk.*)
HUGH : Oh, yes—you'll need them. And your passport. Don't forget your passport.
JOHN : Well, I think I'll go to bed.
HUGH : Poor Johnski never got a word in edgeways. That's what happens when the most attractive man in London meets the most long-winded man in Hampshire head-on !

JOHN : Good night, Liz.

LIZ : Good night, John.

HUGH : Don't forget your roses.

JOHN (*embarrassed*) : I'll take them in the morning.

HUGH : No, no take them up. I'll be most hurt if you don't take them.

[*John collects the flowers and moves to the door.*]

John, what time are you due at Lympne?

JOHN : Twelve-thirty, isn't it, Liz?

LIZ : Yes, I think so.

HUGH : Oh, well, if you leave about a quarter to ten you'll do it easily. (*He moves to the door.*)

LIZ : Where are you going, Hugh?

HUGH : To get the caviare—good night, John. (*He goes out.*)

JOHN (*calling after him*) : Good night.

HUGH (*off*) : Sleep well.

LIZ : What has he been saying?

JOHN : Quite a lot—I'll tell you upstairs, darling.

LIZ : John, I've locked my door.

JOHN : Whatever for?

LIZ : Because I'm tired.

JOHN : Oh. I see—all right—good night. (*He turns for the door, carrying the flowers.*)

LIZ : Let me take those up—you look too silly carrying them.

JOHN (*as dignified as possible in the circumstances*) : I'm all right, thanks.

LIZ : Aren't you going to kiss me?

JOHN : No. (*He goes out.*)

LIZ (*moving to the door*) : Johnski . . .

[*Hugh enters, leaving the door open, and carrying the caviare and a spoon.*]

HUGH : Found them, darling?

LIZ : Yes—I've got them.

HUGH : And the passport?

LIZ : Yes.

[*Hugh adds the champagne bottle and two glasses to the tray, then turns to the door.*]

HUGH : Right, there we are. Two glasses, pot of caviare, nice warm spoon, champagne. Good night, darling.

LIZ : Hugh . . .

HUGH (*stepping back to her, still*) : Yes?

LIZ : Shut the door—I want to talk to you.

[*Hugh shuts the door, and turns round, holding the tray.*]

HUGH : I don't think there's much left to say.

LIZ : Put that tray down—you look too silly carrying it. (*This repetition is due to her frayed nerves.*)

HUGH : I'm all right, thanks.

[*He remains standing, holding it. She nearly loses her temper, but decides not to.*]

Well, what's on your mind?

LIZ : You—making a fool of yourself.

HUGH : Me?

LIZ : Yes—you—taking caviare and champagne upstairs to a girl, at your age.

HUGH : Never mind my age. It's hers that matters.

LIZ : If the whole thing wasn't so pathetically ridiculous, I'd laugh. But as it is, I merely feel like crying.

HUGH : Cry away—It'll do you good, my darling.

LIZ (*again repetitive*): You're behaving like a spoilt child.

HUGH (*looking down at the tray*): Really! I must be a thoroughly precocious one, in that case! Listen, I'm providing evidence for you. Please don't think that I wouldn't rather take up a jug of hot water and two asprins. At my age, it's no joke—this kind of thing—like fielding in the Father's Match at long leg at Dick's private school. Will that be all—or do you want to go on being beastly to me?

LIZ: I'm not being beastly to you, Hugh.

HUGH: In that case, I'll put down my tray. (*He puts the tray on the sofa table*)

LIZ: I'm trying to make you see sense, that's all. You won't do any good by going on like this.

HUGH: It's worth a try, though, isn't it?

LIZ: No—I've made up my mind—and nothing's going to change it. I'm in love with John, and John's in love with me—and there's precisely nothing you can do about it—anyone can do about it. I'm so sorry, Hugh—but these things happen—you admitted that yourself—they happen and it's no use trying to prevent them.

HUGH (*after a pause*): How hard did you try?

LIZ: Extremely hard—I really did—ask John.

HUGH: I'll take your word for it. (*He pauses.*) You don't think if I wore a cummerbund . . . ?

LIZ: No, darling.

HUGH: What about a term or two at Gordonstoun or somewhere? You know, shinning up Ben Nevis on a nylon rope—or jumping off a cliff and chasing the Sports Master under water . . .

LIZ (*her lips twitching, trying to hide it from him.*): I'm not laughing.

HUGH: What about a course of monkey glands,

then? I'm told they do wonders. It'd only take a fortnight, and when you got back from Italy you'd find me swinging through the branches in the garden, howling for my mate.

LIZ : I'm still not laughing.

HUGH : That's the trouble—where's it got to?

LIZ : What?

HUGH : Your sense of humour?

LIZ : Love's no laughing matter, darling. That's one reason why all this has happened, actually—you've always thought it was.

HUGH : It could be—couldn't it?

LIZ : Not for a woman, no.

HUGH : You laughed that night I fell out of bed on our honeymoon in Avignon, and cut my backside on a tooth-glass.

LIZ : I know I did.

HUGH : Well?

LIZ : One can't live on that for fifteen years.

HUGH : I could give a repeat performance if pressed. Has John ever laughed?

LIZ : Of course he has.

HUGH : No—I mean in the mews flat—behind the red velvet curtains?

LIZ : Never you mind.

HUGH : That means 'no', Oh, my poor darling—and you want to live with that for ever—you'll be sewing a crêpe border round your nightgown next!

LIZ (*moving up to the door*) : If you're going on like this, I'll say good night.

HUGH : Well, *on y soit qui mal y pense*. (*He goes to pick up his tray.*)

LIZ : Hugh—you aren't really serious?

HUGH (*with the tray*) : I am, my dear—I'm going right through with it, if it kills me. (*He walks towards the door.*) I want you two going off to Italy without a worry in the world—in the full knowledge that I've given you your evidence, and you can marry John the moment the divorce comes through. I'll ring young Rubinstein on Monday morning and get him to start the ball rolling. (*He has reached the door, and stops in front of her.*) I'll call it off if you'll stay with me.

LIZ : I don't like blackmail.

HUGH : All right, then—forget about the blackmail and just stay with me.

LIZ : I can't.

HUGH : Why not?

LIZ : Because I love John.

HUGH : O.K. Turn the lights out, will you? Good night, darling—wish me luck. (*He steps into the doorway and turns.*) And if I should holler in the night, don't hesitate to dial nine-nine-nine!

Curtain

Scene 2

The following morning, a fine day.
Breakfast is set for four on the table, and three chairs placed round it.
When the curtain rises, Mrs Gray is discovered setting out coffee on the sofa table. John enters, dressed for travelling.

JOHN : Good morning, Mrs Gray. (*He picks up* The Sunday Times *from the sofa arm.*)

MRS GRAY : Good morning, Mr Brownlow. Breakfast's ready and the coffee's nice and hot.

JOHN : Good. Thank you. Mrs Walford down yet?

(*He moves to the desk.*)

MRS GRAY : She went off to Early Service, sir.

JOHN : Oh, did she? (*He puts a section of the paper on the desk, then moves to the french windows.*) What a lovely day. By Jove—that border's looking wonderful.

MRS GRAY : Can't you talk to him, sir?

JOHN : Talk to who?

MRS GRAY : Mr Walford. It's not right—and you're a man. And men talk to each other easier than women do. And you're a friend of Mrs Walford's, aren't you?

JOHN : Yes, indeed.

MRS GRAY : Is that why you're taking her to Italy —to get her right away from him?

JOHN : Well, I suppose you could put it like that.

MRS GRAY : It's not right. Mrs Walford's always been a good wife to him—never looked to right or left—not since I've known her. And that's fifteen years. We came here—Mr Gray and me—the week they got back from their honeymoon. And, ever since then, it's been such a happy place—him with his books—her with her garden and the children. Well, of course, they've had their ups and downs— who hasn't in the writing world! I've seen him so down sometimes I've been worried for him—but she's always cheered him up and got him writing again. And now this—I don't know what's come over him, I really don't. I said to Mr Gray last night, 'I don't know what's come over him', I said.

[*John, hoping to divert the flow, moves to the sofa table and helps himself to breakfast. Liz enters through the french windows, unseen by either of them.*]

341

And he said, 'Maybe there's more to it than you think, Jean'. 'Well', I said, 'I hope not, Jim, it's bad enough already.' That was last night. Then, when I took up the tea at half-past seven to the spare room, and saw him and that hussy sitting up in bed together—bold as brass—with one arm round her shoulder and the other . . .

[*John turns round with his plate and coffee to take his seat at the table, and sees Liz.*]

JOHN : Hullo, Liz.

LIZ : Good morning, John. Good morning, Mrs Gray.

MRS GRAY : Good morning, Ma'am—breakfast's all ready.

LIZ : Thank you.

[*Mrs Gray goes towards the door with her empty tray. Liz looks at John, and makes up her mind.*]

Mrs Gray . . .

MRS GRAY : Yes, Ma'am?

LIZ : I overheard what you were saying then to Mr Brownlow.

MRS GRAY : Yes—I was afraid you had, Ma'am, and I'm sorry.

LIZ : Don't be. It was no surprise to me. And thank you for your indignation and support—but it's misplaced. I've got to tell her, John—I'm sorry. But it isn't fair to Hugh to let her think like that. It's my fault, Mrs Gray—entirely—Mr Walford's blameless.

MRS GRAY : Blameless !

LIZ : Well, let's say he's not to blame initially. (*She puts her hand on John's shoulder.*) The fact is that

342

I started it. I fell in love with Mr Brownlow and he fell in love with me and, when the divorce comes through, we're getting married.

MRS GRAY : Jim was right, then, after all.

LIZ : Jim?

MRS GRAY : Mr Gray—I've just been telling Mr Brownlow he was telling me last night there might be more to it than what I thought.

LIZ : Yes, Jim was right.

MRS GRAY : I don't know what to say, dear.

LIZ : Well, perhaps that's just as well, because I don't suppose you think a great deal of me—after what I've told you.

MRS GRAY : If it's love. dear—I'm not blaming you. Because it can't be helped. There's nothing anyone can do about it—not a woman anyway. I learnt that when I married Jim. I couldn't stand the sight of him—not for a minute—but I loved him so I married him.

[*Mrs Gray goes out. Liz closes the door.*]

LIZ (*returning to John*) : I'm sorry, John—that must have been embarrassing for you.

JOHN (*rising*) : For me—what about you! When you came in—and heard all that about the tea tray ! (*He takes her hand.*) How was Early Service?

LIZ : All right. Darling, did you mind me telling Mrs Gray?

JOHN : No, I feel better now it's out.

LIZ (*going over to the sofa table*) : Yes, so do I.

JOHN : Poor Jim—she does talk, doesn't she?

LIZ : Yes, she's a dear, though. (*She picks up the coffee-pot.*)

[*John eats his breakfast. Liz suddenly puts down*

the coffee-pot, her shoulders heaving silently—then she bursts into violent sobs. He hears her, and jumps up.]

JOHN (*moving to Liz*) : Liz, my darling—what's the matter?

LIZ : Nothing—leave me alone, darling. I'll be all right in a minute. Please sit down and go on with your breakfast—I'll be all right. Please.

[*As John moves away Liz whips round, furiously.*]

How could he, John—how could he! In his own home, with that girl—in front of Mrs Gray. How could he!

JOHN : Well, he told you he was going to, didn't he?

LIZ : Yes, but I never thought he meant it—did you?

JOHN : P'raps he didn't.

LIZ : What do you mean?

JOHN : P'raps he really didn't mean it.

LIZ : Don't tell me it happened by mistake.

JOHN : Perhaps it didn't happen.

LIZ : But she saw them.

JOHN : In bed, yes—but what does that prove?

LIZ : Quite enough for a Divorce Court Judge.

JOHN : Ah, yes, exactly—that's what I mean.

LIZ : You mean Hugh got into bed just before Mrs Gray brought in that tea tray?

JOHN : Well, it's not impossible.

LIZ : Would you have?

JOHN (*after a pause*) : Darling—what a question!

LIZ (*moving to John*) : Would you have, John?

JOHN : No—not in the circumstances.

LIZ : In what circumstances.

JOHN : Well, the set up. Wife unfaithful—damned

344

attractive girl. I would have taken full advantage of it, I'm afraid. But I'm not Hugh.

LIZ : What do you mean by that?

JOHN : Well, we're different. He said so himself last night. My wave-length's physical, and his is mental—broadly speaking—that's what he said. And he also said his batteries were running down.

LIZ : He said that?

JOHN : Yes—through old age—lack of distilled water, and a little too much distilled whisky.

[*Liz's mouth twitches, unseen by John.*]

So, don't worry, darling—not that you've the smallest right to, as I told you last night. It was all a put-up job. He nipped in from the dressing-room, beating the tea tray by a short head.

LIZ : But I listened at the dressing-room door, last night—and he wasn't in there.

JOHN : How do you know?

LIZ : Well, he wasn't snoring.

JOHN : P'raps he had a night off. Don't be silly, darling. He went in this morning, just before the maid came in in the approved style.

LIZ : That was seven-thirty.

JOHN : Yes—that's what I'm saying.

LIZ : Well, it's half-past nine now, and he's not down yet.

JOHN : He's dressing, darling—don't be silly.

LIZ : Well, let's hope so.

[*Hugh enters, in his Jaeger dressing-gown and carpet slippers, and gay as a cricket.*]

HUGH : Morning, Liz, good morning, John. (*He moves to the window.*)

JOHN (*rising*) : Good morning. (*He sits.*)

HUGH (*looking into the garden*): Isn't it a lovely day you'll have a perfect crossing to Le Touquet. So will Molly, bless her, in her little Channel steamer. What time are you going, darling?

[*Liz makes no reply.*]

JOHN : Half an hour.

HUGH : Oh, well, there isn't any violent hurry. What's old Ma Gray trundled up for breakfast? I could eat an ox. All packed up, darling?

LIZ : Yes, thanks.

HUGH : Good. And you, John?

JOHN : Yes.

HUGH (*helping himself to breakfast*) : Good. All the little bits and pieces? Cuff links—shaving soap—ties — dressing-gown — cords — toothbrush — cummerbunds—you get them all in?

JOHN : Yes, I think so.

HUGH : Well done—what about you, darling? Bras—bikinis—nylons—Metatone—suspender belts—foundation cream—eight dozen pairs of shoes—hair-curlers—Kleenex—all in order?

LIZ : Yes, Hugh, thank you.

HUGH : What's the matter, darling—had a bad night?

LIZ : No, I'm quite all right, Hugh.

HUGH : Good. Sleep well, John?

JOHN : Yes, thanks.

HUGH : Well done. What time are you due in Milan?

JOHN : Eight tomorrow morning.

HUGH : Oh, good. You'll see the mountains in the early morning from the window of the couchette

when you're snaking down to Milan. I'm referring
to the train, old boy.

[*There is a long pause, as he eats his breakfast.*]

Are the berths in a couchette, one above the other?
JOHN : I'm not sure—I think so.
HUGH : Which do you prefer? I like the top one
myself.
JOHN : So do I.
HUGH : That's lucky. Liz prefers the bottom one,
don't you my darling? Always has. I've never
understood why. All you get down there's a close-
up of a pair of hairy legs and flat feet, shinning
up a ladder. Whereas, on the top, you've got a bit
of privacy—apart from pairs of trousers on coat-
hangers clipping you across the jaw at intervals.

[*Molly enters in a dressing-gown, again looking
a dish.*]

Ah, there you are, my darling—come along and
help yourself.
MOLLY : Good morning, Mrs Walford.
HUGH : Molly said 'Good morning', Liz.
LIZ : What—oh, good morning—I'm so sorry, I
was thinking about something else.
MOLLY : Good morning, John.
JOHN : Good morning, Molly.
MOLLY : Isn't it a lovely morning. I feel I could eat
a horse.
HUGH : Remember that your train's at ten-five,
darling.
MOLLY : That's all right—I've packed.
HUGH : Well, as I'm going to run you to the station,
I'll nip up and get dressed. (*To Molly.*) No hurry,

dear—you haven't got to shave, but I have. See you again, John—before you go. I'll be down in a jiffy. Gray'll bring the luggage down, if you ring, darling. (*He moves to the door.*)

LIZ : All right, Hugh.

HUGH : And make sure that you've packed the Metatone. (*He goes out.*)

JOHN (*to Molly*) : You're going to have a nice, smooth crossing.

MOLLY : Yes, I think so. You're flying to Le Touquet, aren't you?

JOHN : Yes, and then we catch the car-train at Boulogne. I don't suppose you go on that one.

MOLLY : No, mine's passenger.

JOHN : Of course—it would be—if you haven't got a car.

LIZ : I'm going to go and get my things together, darling.

JOHN : Right.

LIZ : Good-bye, Miss Forsyth—just in case you're upstairs, getting ready.

MOLLY : Good-bye, Mrs Walford—thank you so much. I've enjoyed it so much—it was sweet of you to have me.

LIZ : Not at all—I'm so glad you could come. I hope you'll have a lovely holiday.

MOLLY : Thanks so much.

LIZ : John, time's getting on.

JOHN : I know.

[*Liz goes out.*]

JOHN (*turning to Molly*) : It's all bluff, isn't it?

MOLLY : What is?

JOHN : You're not the girl that you pretend you are—and Hugh pretends you are.

MOLLY : What kind of girl is that?

JOHN : 'The kind of girl that goes right through the office like a circular'—I quote.

MOLLY : Who told you that?

JOHN : Well, Hugh told Liz—and she repeated it to me. Tell me it isn't true.

MOLLY : What does it matter to you—one way or the other?

JOHN : I'm incurably romantic.

MOLLY : You'd prefer me to have had a dozen husbands—rather than a string of lovers?

JOHN : Definitely.

MOLLY : What a Puritan you are. You should have been a Covenanting Minister in Scotland in the old days—doing dreadful things behind the shelter of the law.

JOHN : So you think I do dreadful things?

MOLLY : Well—running off with Liz.

JOHN : I am in love with her, you know.

MOLLY : So's Hugh.

JOHN : I'll have to take your word for it.

MOLLY : You don't believe me?

JOHN : Well, let's say he doesn't shout it round the market-place.

MOLLY : You think he should?

JOHN : If he wanted to keep her—yes. I think it would have been wise.

MOLLY : He's not ostentatious.

JOHN : You're telling me.

MOLLY : No. He's unselfish. Liz's happiness comes first with him—and not his own. If he's decided she'll be happier with you, that's all that matters.

JOHN : So he lets her go without a fight.

MOLLY : I don't suppose he thinks that fighting leads to happiness.

JOHN : That's not the way to keep a woman.

MOLLY: It could be the way to keep one happy, though.

JOHN: I'd question if he's made her happy recently.

MOLLY: Until you met her. I'd say he managed quite well.

JOHN: I don't mean that. I mean in this house since we arrived here yesterday. I wouldn't say that his behaviour—with you last night, for example—was conspiciously geared to make her happy.

MOLLY: He was helping over the divorce.

JOHN: By having tea with you in bed this morning!

MOLLY: Yes.

JOHN: You're pretty brazen, aren't you?

MOLLY: I'd rather use the word 'straightforward'. It's more flattering. And, anyway, what right have you to criticize me? The divorce'll go through now, provided Mrs Gray does her stuff—and you don't get caught by the Queen's Proctor out in Italy and he starts intervening.

[*John looks at her interestedly. Molly notices this and continues somewhat automatically.*]

I think that's a lovely word, don't you? I visualize a little man in horn rims and a bowler hat, creeping down corridors in car-trains—intervening madly all night.

JOHN: You look smashing in that dressing-gown.

MOLLY: You said that quite mechanically.

JOHN: Oh, did I?

MOLLY: Yes—like one of those machines on railway platforms, slip a woman in the slot and watch it turning out a platitude.

JOHN: You get more charming every minute.

MOLLY: That's much better. That came out quite

naturally—although you didn't mean it—and it therefore sounded quite sincere! I'm sorry for you, John.

JOHN : Sorry for me!

MOLLY : Yes—I find you pathetic.

JOHN : Thank you very much.

MOLLY : Well, look at you, three honeymoons at your age and another in the offing! Talk about commuting! You don't need a marriage licence—what you want's a season ticket!

JOHN : So you disapprove of my divorces?

MOLLY : No, your marriages. You never should have married any of them.

JOHN : Oh, why not?

MOLLY : Because you didn't love them.

JOHN : On the contrary, I did.

MOLLY : All right then, you did, but for the wrong reasons. Perfect ones for an affair, I'll grant you that. But not for marriage. That's why I'm not married. I'm still looking for a man that I can love for the right reasons.

JOHN : Such as?

MOLLY : Humour—kindness—mutual affection—understanding—tolerance.

JOHN : Like Hugh.

MOLLY : No, not like Hugh. I don't love Hugh that way. But Liz does. And that's why you won't do any better with her than you have done with the other three.

JOHN : I love Liz.

MOLLY : Yes, of course you do—but only physically. And that's the way she loves you too. And that's the trouble. You're like two people playing bridge with far too many trumps between them and too few outside tricks in the other suits. It makes it very difficult to get one's contract.

JOHN: It depends how well one plays, I should imagine.

MOLLY: I dare say—but you've already lost three rubbers in those circumstances, haven't you.

JOHN: Why are you laughing at me?

MOLLY: Well, why not? It's high time someone did. The truth is that you definitely shouldn't have a wife who loves you physically. You see, you love yourself enough for two already—and a wife who loves you physically makes three—and three's a crowd!

JOHN: Do you write Hugh's books for him?

MOLLY: What you need's a woman who can laugh at you—and sew your buttons on—and do the ordering. Instead of turning into a blancmange each time you look at her! I know you think there's no such woman in the world. But you should have a look around you just to make sure.

JOHN: I'm surprised that you don't run a marriage agency.

MOLLY: Well, your account'd be worth having, wouldn't it!

[*Hugh enters.*]

HUGH (*in the doorway*): Now, come along, you two, it's zero hour. Good God, you're not dressed yet?

MOLLY: Oh dear—how long have I got?

HUGH (*looking at his watch*): Fifteen minutes.

MOLLY: Well, good-bye John—if I miss you.

JOHN: Good-bye, Molly.

HUGH: Gray'll bring your case down.

MOLLY: Thank you. (*She goes out.*)

JOHN: I'd better go, too.

HUGH: What time are you leaving?

JOHN : Any time now. I'll nip up and get cracking. (*He moves to Hugh.*) Hugh . . .

HUGH : Yes?

JOHN : Sorry about all this.

HUGH : That's all right, old fellow. These things happen.

JOHN : I'll look after her all right.

HUGH : I hope so.

JOHN : And I'll stick to her.

HUGH : Good show.

JOHN : I know you don't believe me—you think it's just physical. It's not, though—it's for the right reasons.

HUGH : Such as?

JOHN : Humour, kindness, mutual affection, understanding, tolerance . . .

HUGH : I'm glad to hear it.

JOHN : I'll prove it to you.

HUGH : That's right. That's the idea. Run along, or you'll miss your Skyways.

[*John turns for the door.*]

John . . .

[*John turns.*]

JOHN : Yes?

HUGH : Don't let her forget the Metatone—morning and evening—one dessert spoon, in a glass of water.

[*Liz enters, wearing a hat and carrying a small case.*]

LIZ : John, it's nearly time to go. (*She puts down the case and hat.*)

JOHN : Right, darling—I'll be with you in five minutes. (*He goes out.*)

LIZ : Well, good-bye, Hugh.

HUGH : Good-bye, old girl.

LIZ : You'll tell the children, won't you?

HUGH : Yes, of course. Dick's coming out from school next weekend. I'll tell him then.

LIZ : And Sheila?

HUGH : I'll go down and see her during the week.

LIZ : Please don't make me out too awful.

HUGH : Why should I do that, my darling?

LIZ : What excuses will you make for me?

HUGH : None. I'll just tell the truth.

LIZ : You're good at doing that, too, aren't you?

HUGH : Well, I do my best.

LIZ : In that case, p'raps you'll tell me where you spent last night.

HUGH : What purpose would that serve?

LIZ : I want to know.

HUGH : Why?

LIZ : Because I'm a woman.

HUGH : So is Molly—

LIZ : I dare say—but you've already told me she's accommodating—so what's wrong with telling me about the latest chapter? I told you about John.

HUGH : No, you didn't—Molly did.

LIZ : I told you about the mews flat, then.

HUGH : No—you didn't. I told you.

LIZ : Well, I confirmed it.

HUGH : Granted.

LIZ : Then it's only fair you should confirm this.

HUGH : I'm afraid I disagree. The mews flat was a basic piece of puzzle in the jig-saw of our marriage. Last night, thanks to the incredibly broad base of the divorce laws in this country—was irrelevant. The only thing that matters was that Mrs Gray saw us in bed together, drinking China tea and eating Rich Tea biscuits. Anything that happened before that—or after that—or both— is quite beside the point. I've given you the evidence for the divorce—that's all that matters. You'd better tell Gray if you want to take your golf clubs.

LIZ : I have told him.

HUGH : Good. (*After a pause.*) John's going to bore your pants clean off.

LIZ : What makes you think so?

HUGH : He does.

LIZ : He's not in the least bit boring.

HUGH : Maybe not in bed. But you can't stay in bed for ever—not unless you're an invalid. In which case, you're better off in bed alone! He's a bore my darling Liz—a great big cracking bore. He hasn't got an idea in his head, except one— and it's not a new one. It's been going on since Adam knocked off gardening and started talking to that very superficial serpent. And it's not a basis for the future.

LIZ : I'd have thought that history'd contradicted that for some time.

HUGH : Only population-wise—and any given pair of rabbits can do better, if it comes to that. I'm talking about plain, straightforward sex, my darling, with or without an end-product, and it's not the same as marriage, which is less enjoyable, I dare say, but a great deal more rewarding in the long run and most definitely not a thing to be embarked on lightly—that's why rabbits have no time for it—I should imagine.

LIZ : What's all this in aid of, Hugh—your new book?

HUGH : I'm not saying I won't use it later—but it's aimed at you at the moment.

LIZ : Well, I'm afraid it's not hitting the mark.

355

HUGH : A pity. If you weren't so infatuated it would. You'd realize that although Johnski may be a prize rabbit with the walls of his hutch papered with rosettes, he's also going to be a wash-out as a husband.

LIZ : Give me one good reason.

HUGH : Certainly. He's got no sense of humour. If he fell out of bed and cut himself on a tooth-glass he wouldn't laugh. He'd stick a Band-aid on it and go back to square one. Life's too short to spend it with a fellow like that!

LIZ (*cutting in*) : Can I get a word in edgeways?

HUGH : Please do.

LIZ : Thank you. Every word you say displays your ignorance of women and of life in general. I don't know how you've got away with it for all these years. I really don't. But just because the cardboard figures in your silly little books say cardboard things, you think you're Socrates, or someone— whereas in reality you've no more idea of what love is to a woman than a monk has.

HUGH (*half to himself*) : Abelard?

LIZ : You see that's you all over—always trying to be funny. Here you are, saying good-bye to some- one you've been married to for fifteen years and all you do is make facetious little literary cracks like some dehydrated old Don.

HUGH : I'm sorry, but it slipped out when you started talking about monks. And Abelard was the first one that came into my head. You've read the book, of course.

LIZ : You read it to me.

HUGH : So I did. You didn't mean that sort of monk, though, did you?

LIZ : No, I didn't.

HUGH : You mean the conventional kind—beads

and gardening and Bible-reading during meals—
and great big bare toes, flapping up and down like
croissants.

[*Liz's lips twitch.*]

P'raps I'd better take the veil—or whatever it is
that monks do. Maybe that's my future, darling—
tending vines on top of some hot mountain, in a
dressing-gown, and getting plastered alone in my
cell on Saints' day. Will you come and see me,
darling, sometimes? Just to keep me up to date on
Dick and Sheila and the Derby winner and John's
latest dirty story from the Stock Exchange? Oh,
well, it's no use talking—he'll be down in a minute.
So, if you're determined on it, I can only wish you
luck. And, as I say. I've given you the evidence
for the divorce—and so it's all plain sailing. (*He
walks away to the desk to get a cigarette.*)

[*She looks at him, and makes up her mind.*]

LIZ : I don't want one.
HUGH (*turning to Liz*) : What did you say?
LIZ : I don't want a divorce.
HUGH : Why not?
LIZ : You know why not perfectly well.
HUGH : Because John lacks humour?
LIZ : No, because you've got too much. You've
killed it, Hugh.
HUGH : Killed what—I don't like killing things.
LIZ : My love for John. It's dead. It died the
moment you found out about it. And you buried it
the moment that you asked him down here, and I
saw you both together. And you stuck the tomb-
stone in position last night.

HUGH : Last night?

LIZ : When you talked about your monkey glands, and when you went up to the spare room dressing-room with caviare and champagne on that beastly little tray. You made it all seem sordid—in a moment, what had been so beautiful before—so secret and so precious and so heavenly—you made a joke of. It became just every day and common-place—the sort of thing that other people do and keep on doing all the time in beastly little flats and hotels up and down the country when it's raining. Fat, complaisant men in sock-suspenders and huge leather belts like hoops and hard-faced women taking off suspender belts like someone ripping plaster off a boil. It all became so sordid and you killed it, Hugh.

HUGH (*after a pause*) : I'm sorry, darling.

LIZ : Never mind—it can't be helped—it's done now. (*She goes and picks up the hat.*)

HUGH : So you're going to stay at home with me?

LIZ : Yes, if you'll have me.

HUGH : I'll have you, darling. You're certain, are you?

LIZ : Yes, Hugh.

HUGH : You won't change your mind again.

LIZ : No, never.

HUGH : Then why are you putting on that bloody silly hat?

LIZ : Because I'm still going to Italy with John, but I'm not going to marry him. You've killed my love for him, all right, but you can't stop me finding him attractive. So, I'm going off to Italy.

HUGH : To have an affair with him?

LIZ (*defiantly*) : Yes.

HUGH : Like all those other people in the rain?

LIZ : It won't be raining.

HUGH : You're not, you know.

LIZ : I am, Hugh.

HUGH : No—you're not. Or, if you do, you wont be seeing me again.

LIZ : You mean that you won't have me back?

HUGH : That's right.

LIZ : But why not?

HUGH : Because I won't want you.

LIZ : You won't want me!

HUGH : No—and I'll tell you why—because I've found a substitute—the perfect substitute. A pretty girl who loves me for all the right reasons. And, what's more, she's got a sense of humour.

LIZ : And I haven't?

HUGH : No. You had one once, I'll grant you—but you've lost it, since that dinner with the Chilean Ambassador. And I can't live with somebody who hasn't got a sense of humour.

LIZ : You propose to live with Molly?

HUGH : If she'll have me.

LIZ : Marry her, you mean?

HUGH : Why not?

LIZ : You're old enough to be her father.

HUGH : What's that got to do with it?

LIZ : It's laughable.

HUGH : That's just why the idea appeals to me so much.

LIZ : You've gone mad, Hugh.

HUGH : No, I don't think so—merely been rejuvenated. Nothing like a shake-up when you're in a rut. And we've been in one now for seven or eight years, my darling, and I've managed to climb out of it, thank God. Time's getting on—we'd better call the others, or they'll miss all their connections.

LIZ : So that's final is it? You won't have me back?

HUGH : Not on your terms, no.

LIZ : On what terms, then?

HUGH : If you take that silly hat off, and give up your trip to Italy, I'll think about it.

LIZ : Think about it—is that all?

HUGH : It's something, isn't it? I'll finish my book in a week or two. Then I thought I might push off on a holiday.

[*Liz half hears this.*]

Would you like to come with me?

[*Liz looks round, blankly, at him.*]

We could drop in on Avignon and find out if they've replaced that tooth-glass yet!

[*Liz turns away to hide her smile. Hugh watches her. John enters and moves down to Liz.*]

JOHN : Well, here we are, my darling—dead on time. Gray's put your cases in the car.

[*Liz takes off her hat.*]

HUGH : Well he'd better take them out again.

[*John looks up.*]

LIZ : John, I'm not going.

JOHN : What! You're pulling my leg!

LIZ : No—I'm not, John.

JOHN : Here—what's going on?

HUGH : She's changed her mind, old fellow—that's all—women do you know.

JOHN (*moving to Liz*) : Is that right darling?

360

LIZ : Yes, John.

JOHN : But—why?

LIZ : I don't know—don't ask me, please.

JOHN : But you still love me, don't you?

LIZ : Yes, but not for the right reasons.

JOHN : Oh, my God.

[*Molly comes in, dressed for the road.*]

(*Moving to Molly.*) Have you been talking to Liz?

MOLLY : No—apart from saying good-bye. Why, what's happened?

JOHN : You tell me.

HUGH : She's going to stay with me, and see how things work out.

MOLLY (*moving to Liz*) : I'm so glad.

LIZ : You—glad?

MOLLY : Yes, why not?

LIZ : Aren't you in love with Hugh?

MOLLY : Not so you'd notice.

LIZ : You mean that you wouldn't marry him if he proposed to you?

MOLLY : Of course not.

LIZ : But why not—Hugh said . . .

MOLLY : Because it wouldn't be for the right reasons.

JOHN : If I hear that phrase again, I'll scream.

HUGH : You'll miss your plane, John—if you don't get moving.

JOHN : Come on, Liz—he's bluffing. He's been leading you a dance. All he's been doing is to try to make you jealous. He's succeeded, I admit—but now his bluff's been called. (*Pulling Liz by the wrist.*) So let's get moving.

LIZ : No, John.

JOHN : But why not?

LIZ : I can't explain—I've told you. Don't keep asking questions. I'm not coming—that's all.

JOHN : Well, in that case, I'd better say good-bye.

LIZ : Are you still going off to Italy without me?

JOHN : Yes, I've got to. I've got business in Milan.

LIZ : Business in Milan—yes, of course you have. Good-bye, John.

JOHN : Aren't you going to kiss me?

[*Liz looks at Hugh. Hugh nods.*]

LIZ : All right. (*She moves to John.*)

JOHN : Good-bye, darling.

[*John and Liz kiss.*]

HUGH (*rising and moving to John*): Bye-bye, Johnski. Thanks for coming down. It was a great help.

JOHN : Good-bye, Molly.

MOLLY : Good-bye, John.

[*John starts to go to the door.*]

HUGH : Why don't you drop her at the station— just outside the lodge gate?

JOHN : All right.

MOLLY : Are you sure you don't mind?

JOHN : No—of course not. We'd better go, though. It's just on ten. (*He goes out.*)

MOLLY (*moving to Liz*): Well, good-bye, Mrs Walford.

LIZ : Good-bye, Molly.

MOLLY : Good-bye, Mr Walford. (*She turns for the door.*)

HUGH : Aren't you going to kiss me?

362

MOLLY : All right. (*She kisses him.*) Good-bye, Hugh.

HUGH : Good-bye, my darling.

[*Molly goes out. Liz moves to the window. There is the sound of a car revving up and driving away. Hugh goes to the door and calls.*]

(*Calling.*) Mrs Gray !

[*Mrs Gray enters.*]

MRS GRAY : Yes, Mr Walford?

HUGH : Ah yes, Mrs Gray. Could you ask Mr Gray if he'd take Mrs Walford's suitcase upstairs to her room again?

MRS GRAY : Yes, sir.

HUGH : And could you move my things back from the spare room dressing-room into my own, please?

MRS GRAY : Yes, sir. And will you both be lunching at home?

HUGH : Yes, I think so. (*He looks at Liz.*) Won't we, darling?

[*Liz does not reply.*]

That's right—both at home for lunch. Thanks so much, Mrs Gray.

[*Mrs Gray goes out. Liz stands looking out of the window, still—after the car. Hugh goes to the desk and picks up the playing cards.*]

We're one game all. (*He replaces the cards, picks up the card table from behind the drinks table, unfolds it and places it in front of the sofa. He*

*goes to the desk for the cards, then to the table for
a chair. He sits on the chair and cuts the cards—
one pile on Liz's place, one on his own.)* So let's
have the decider.

[*Liz moves to the sofa and sits. They start to play.
We hear a distant train, then Liz's shoulders heave,
and she stars sobbing.*]

Don't cry, please. Please don't cry, darling. He's
the wrong man for you. He's not on your wave-
length. Or if he is, it's a pirate station. He'd have
ditched you in a few years, if not earlier. You don't
believe me, do you? All right, I'll have to prove it
to you. (*He goes to the telephone and dials.*)

[*Liz stops crying, out of interest.*]

(*On the telephone.*) Hullo, that the station? . . .
Ah yes, good. Good morning. Mr. Walford here.
Tell me—did someone from here drop a lady for
the ten-five—very pretty, in a lemon-coloured
coat? . . . Nobody . . . And the ten-five's gone out,
has it? . . . It has. I see. Thank you. I'm so sorry to
have troubled you on such a lovely morning. Good-
bye. (*He hangs up and returns to the card-table.
He gathers up his cards and hers. Then he puts her
cards in her hand gently*) I think we'd better start
again, don't you?

Hugh begins to shuffle. So does Liz, as—

the curtain falls

THE SERVANT
OF
TWO MASTERS

(IL SERVITORE DI DUE PADRONI)

by
CARLO GOLDONI

Adapted by David Turner
from a literal translation
by Paul Lapworth

Michael Codron presented *The Servant of Two Masters* at the Queen's Theatre, London, on December 18, 1968, with the following cast:

DOCTOR LOMBARDI, a lawyer	*Ken Wynne*
BRIGHELLA, an innkeeper	*Ronald Radd*
SILVIO, son of Lombardi	*Clive Francis*
PANTALONE of Bisognosi, a rich merchant	*Graham Crowden*
SMERALDINA, Clarice's maid	*Michele Dotrice*
CLARICE, daughter of Pantalone	*Morag Hood*
TRUFFALDINO, a servant	*Tommy Steele*
BEATRICE RASPONI, of Turin	*Julia Lockwood*
FLORINDO ARETUSI, of Turin	*Edward de Souza*
1st PORTER	*John Rapley*
2nd PORTER	*Bunny May*
OLD WAITER	*John Crocker*
YOUNG WAITER	*Kenneth Shanley*
3rd WAITER	*John Rapley*
SERVANTS	*Hazel McKay* *Amanda Duckett*
MUSICIANS	*Peter Honri* *Tony Reiss* *Adrian Harman*
ICE CREAM SELLER	*Bunny May*

Directed by Toby Robertson

Scenery and costumes by Alan Barrett

Music by Ben Pearce Higgins

CHARACTERS

PANTALONE of *Bisognosi*

CLARICE, *his daughter*

DOCTOR LOMBARDI

SILVIO, *his son*

BEATRICE, *of Turin, dressed as a man, under the name of Federigo Rasponi*

FLORINDO ARETUSI, *of Turin, her lover*

BRIGHELLA, *an innkeeper*

SMERALDINA, *Clarice's Maid*

TRUFFALDINO, *servant to Beatrice, then to Florindo*

1st PORTER (*also Servant to Pantalone*)

2nd PORTER

OLD WAITER

YOUNG WAITER

3rd WAITER

1st SERVING MAID

2nd SERVING MAID

ICE CREAM SELLER

In the original London production of this play the stage setting represented a Venetian courtyard with Pantalone's house indicated on the O.P. side and Brighella's Inn on the P.S. The main acting area became an exterior or interior as required.

Music was used extensively in the production, both played by live musicians on and off stage, and recorded on tape. Music was used to create atmosphere, to cover transition from scene to scene, and as accompaniment to sung or spoken dialogue. The points at which music was used are indicated.

The street scene between Scenes Four and Five in Act One using one or two extra minor characters may be cut.

ACT ONE

Scene 1

*A room in Pantalone's house. Pantalone, Dr
Lombardi, Silvio, Brighella, Smeraldina.*

DOCTOR (*he turns to Pantalone*) : Signior Pantalone, we are met here for the happy occasion of
the betrothal of my dear son, Silvio.
PANTALONE : We are, Doctor.
DOCTOR : Then bid your daughter come forth,
sir, . . . *et ergo accidat.*
PANTALONE : Smeraldina. Fetch your mistress.

[*Music: Serenade.*]

SMERALDINA (*bobs*) : Sir. (*She goes out.*)

[*Music continues. Clarice enters followed by
Smeraldina.*]

ALL : Ah.

[*While Clarice comes gracefully in, the Doctor
speaks to his son.*]

DOCTOR : To her, my son. Give her your hand.
SILVIO (*moves to Clarice*) : Clarice . . . here is my
hand . . . and with it, take my heart.
PANTALONE : Well, go on, daughter. Don't be shy.
Simple ceremony . . . and you're engaged.
CLARICE : Silvio . . . here is my hand. I promise to
be your wife.
SILVIO : And I to be your ever loving husband.
ALL : Ah.

371

DOCTOR and OTHERS : Bravo! Excellent.
DOCTOR : Brighella, you will swear you have borne
witness to this.

[*Servant enters with a tray—jug of wine and two
glasses. Pantalone takes them and gives the smaller
glass to the Doctor—keeping the bigger one for
himself. Clarice and Silvio kiss.*]

BRIGHELLA : I will indeed, sir. I hereby witness the
betrothal between your dear son Silvio and the
lovely lady Clarice, and if I may say so, sir, I don't
think there had better be a very long engagement.
PANTALONE   } (together) : { Clarice!
DOCTOR   }   { Silvio!

[*The lovers break apart.*]

PANTALONE : I respect your sentiments, my dear
Brighella. I've no desire for there to be a long
engagement this time.
DOCTOR : This time? What is that you say? This
time?
PANTALONE : Ah, well, there's something a little
delicate, something that we never quite got round
to speaking about. I think this is the proper time
to tell him Clarice, don't you?
CLARICE : Silvio knows already.
PANTALONE : And you're quite happy about it?
SILVIO : Why, of course, sir.
DOCTOR : What is it then? What is it?
PANTALONE : Sorry, well, it's simply this. My
daughter Clarice has been engaged before.
DOCTOR : What?
PANTALONE : Don't worry. She never saw the feller.
It was all done by proxy, you understand.

DOCTOR : I see. But then hasn't this fellow a claim to her?

PANTALONE : No. You see . . . The poor chap's gone to a better place . . . passed over.

DOCTOR : Dead?

PANTALONE : Yes, he had the call—and he went.

DOCTOR : I see. And who was this gentleman?

PANTALONE : A certain Signior Federigo Rasponi of Turin.

DOCTOR : And what did he die of?

PANTALONE : Killed in a duel. They say it was because of his sister—to save her honour or something. Anyway he was struck down—fatal blow.

BRIGHELLA : It came as a very nasty shock to me, I can tell you, sir.

PANTALONE : You knew him?

BRIGHELLA : Oh yes. I was three years in Turin afore I settled here.

PANTALONE : Then you have the advantage of me, sir. I never clapped eyes on the fellow. Everything was done by letter.

BRIGHELLA : Yes, I knew him very well, what's more, I knew his sister too. A proper tomboy, she was—ride a horse like this (*Miming riding astride.*) Not like this. (*Miming side saddle. Laughs.*) Ha, Ha ! A right lass . . . And the brother was proud of her . . . too proud to my mind . . . Would never let her marry . . . And now he's dead. Ah, well, we never know what fate has in store for us do we, sir?

DOCTOR : No—no—no. The ways of the Lord are many and devious.

PANTALONE : So, doctor, seeing that my dear daughter has never been within one hundred miles of her late fiancé, there can be no possible harm done, can there?

DOCTOR : I agree. A clear case of *Corpore Absente*
... *Virgo Intacta.*

[*Both raise their glasses to Clarice, who curtsies.*]

PANTALONE : Quite, eh? But let us not talk of sadness. (*He collects Doctor's glass and gives both to
servant who goes out.*) My dear Brighella, the
gentle doctor here is of my disposition. We decided
against any guests or relations. We don't want
lavishness, do we? (*To Brighella.*) So how about
preparing us some tasty dish or other?
BRIGHELLA : My privilege and pleasure, sir. And
you could do no better than to eat at my Inn in
the square over there, sir.

[*They hear three loud knocks.*]

PANTALONE : Someone knocks, Smeraldina, see who
it is.
SMERALDINA : At once, sir. (*She goes out.*)
PANTALONE : I only hope it's not a relative. They'll
stay all day and drink every bottle in the cellar.
CLARICE : Father, with your permission ...
PANTALONE : Yes, my dear?
CLARICE : If you have a visitor, Silvio and I would
like ...

[*Smeraldina returns.*]

PANTALONE (*to Clarice*) : A moment. A moment.
(*To Smeraldina.*) Yes, what is it?
SMERALDINA : Sir, it's the servant of some stranger
or other. He says nothing to me. He says he wants
to give you a message.

374

PANTALONE : Let him come in. Let's hear what he wants.

[*Smeraldina leaves.*]

PANTALONE : Yes, my dear . . . you were saying?
CLARICE : If you have a visitor, Silvio and I would like to withdraw.
PANTALONE : What? Withdraw? Go off by yourselves? You'll stay here.

Scene 2

The same.

Truffaldino enters, followed later by Smeraldina.

TRUFFALDINO : Greetings, respects and heartiest salutations to one and all. (*To audience.*) And I must say a very nice quality of person we've got here . . . very nice indeed. (*Looking at Clarice.*) Who's the lovely lady then? What are you doing tonight, sweetheart?
PANTALONE : How dare you, sir. That is my daughter.
TRUFFALDINO : Congratulations, sir. Well done.
PANTALONE : I beg your pardon.
SMERALDINA : Signora Clarice is engaged to be married.
TRUFFALDINO : Oh well, it's not my day, is it? And what might your role be in this *ménage*, may I ask?

SMERALDINA : I'm Smeraldina, her maidservant.

TRUFFALDINO : Maidservant, eh? What are you doing tonight?

PANTALONE : Enough of that, sir. Leave her alone. Just tell me, who are you? What do you want, and where do you come from?

TRUFFALDINO : Who? What? Where? Three questions all at once. (*He touches his head.*) It's too much for me.

PANTALONE (*aside to Doctor*) : The man's a numb-skull . . . a blockhead.

DOCTOR (*aside to Pantalone*) : A comical fellow to be sure.

PANTALONE : Now look here, sir. Who are you?

TRUFFALDINO : My name, sir, is Truffaldino. By trade, a servant . . . a humble servant to my master. (*To Smeraldina.*) What time do they let you out?

PANTALONE : Your master, sir? Your master? Who is he?

TRUFFALDINO : Why, he's the gentleman who is waiting outside to come in and pay you his respects.

PANTALONE : This gentleman, sir? What's his name?

TRUFFALDINO : His name? That's fair—straight-forward. One question at a time. I'll answer that. He is none other than the right worthy Signior Federigo Rasponi of Turin.

ALL : What !

TRUFFALDINO : That went well !

PANTALONE : Come here, sirrah. That name. Say it again. I couldn't have heard you correctly.

TRUFFALDINO (*aside*) : The poor old fellow's hard of hearing. (*He yells into Pantalone's ear.*) Signior Federigo Rasponi of Turin.

PANTALONE (*pushing his finger into his ear*) : Get

away. What the . . . (*To Doctor.*) He's mad,
absolutely mad. (*To Truffaldino.*) I'll have you
know, sir, Federigo Rasponi of Turin is dead.

TRUFFALDINO : Dead !

PANTALONE : Dead as a doornail.

TRUFFALDINO : My master . . . dead ?

PANTALONE : Quite, quite dead.

DOCTOR : No shadow of doubt.

TRUFFALDINO : But I've only just left him outside.
He was very much alive then. Accident, was it?
(*Suddenly dawns on him.*) Just a moment ! Dead,
sir? You've killed him.

PANTALONE : What?

TRUFFALDINO : While I had my back turned, talking to the lady here . . . one of you slipped out and
done him in. Who was it?

DOCTOR (*approaching Truffaldino*) : Now look
here . . .

TRUFFALDINO : Don't you come near me . . . I've
heard all about you city folks . . . you Medicis, you
Borgias . . . Vendetta, was it? Knifed him in the
back while I was being affable, did you? I must
see it for myself. (*He goes out.*)

PANTALONE : Well, what do you make of that?
What is he? A rogue or an idiot?

DOCTOR : He's a bit of both, if you ask me.

BRIGHELLA : Rogue, no; idiot, yes.

SMERALDINA : No, simple and good, that's how I
put it. (*To audience.*) I liked him.

PANTALONE : And what's all this about Signior
Federigo?

CLARICE : Heaven help me, if it is true.

PANTALONE : We've letters, girl, telling us he's dead.

SILVIO (*to Clarice*) : Even if he is alive, he'll have
come far too late. (*Taking her hand.*) You are
mine.

[Truffaldino returns.]

ALL (*startled*): Aha!

TRUFFALDINO: Aha! Oh, gentlemen. You naughty pair. (*Wagging his finger.*) You naughty, naughty pair.

PANTALONE (*aside*): He's raving . . . absolutely raving.

DOCTOR (*aside*): Agreed.

TRUFFALDINO: Allow me to learn you your manners. Gentlemen what are proper gentlemen have respect for servants. They don't go playing around with them.

PANTALONE: We must be careful—he might be dangerous. What's the matter, sir, the world's been treating you badly, has it?

TRUFFALDINO: Did you or did you not tell me that Signior Federigo was dead?

PANTALONE: What of it?

TRUFFALDINO: He's still very much alive, thank you very much. Still waiting outside in the street to come in and pay you his respects.

PANTALONE: Signior Federigo?

TRUFFALDINO: Signior Federigo.

PANTALONE: Rasponi?

TRUFFALDINO: Rasponi.

PANTALONE: Of Turin?

TRUFFALDINO: Of Turin.

PANTALONE: Ha. Those who are mad ought to go into hospital.

TRUFFALDINO: Now look, sir . . . Before I resort to bad language, I'll put it to you again: if you go outside in the street you'll see him—Signior Federigo Rasponi waiting on the corner . . . And if you tell me once more he's dead, I shall be forced to use a certain word.

PANTALONE (*lifting his hand*) : You are asking for a beating, sirrah !

DOCTOR : Calm, Signior Pantalone, calm. Tell him to ask this so-called Signior Rasponi to come in.

TRUFFALDINO : At last ! In future, gentlemen, I trust you'll know how to handle men of quality, honourable fellows from Bergamo like myself. (*To Smeraldina.*) Young lady, we'll talk again ! I go ! (*He goes.*)

CLARICE (*quietly*) : Silvio, I tremble with fear.

SILVIO (*quietly*) : Whatever happens, you're mine.

DOCTOR : Now let the truth be revealed.

PANTALONE : 'Tis some cock and bull story to swindle me.

BRIGHELLA : Rely on me, sir. I'm the only one here who's ever seen Signior Federigo. I'll soon tell you if it's him.

SMERALDINA (*to audience*) : He's not a liar, that servant; he's as good as gold. I can sum up men, don't you worry . . . *and* I know when they're nice. (*To Pantalone.*) Sir, by your leave. (*She goes.*)

Scene 3

The Same. Beatrice enters in man's dress.

BEATRICE : Signior Pantalone?

PANTALONE : Sir?

BEATRICE : Allow me to issue a rebuke.

PANTALONE : Eh?

BEATRICE : I send my servant to you with a message and you keep me standing in the street for a whole half hour.

PANTALONE : Excuse me, sir, but truly who are you?

BEATRICE : I am Federigo Rasponi of Turin.

PANTALONE : You are Federigo Rasponi of Turin!

[*All show astonishment.*]

BRIGHELLA (*aside*) : What's all this about? This isn't Federigo, it's his sister, Beatrice. What's she up to I wonder?

BEATRICE : You have heard, no doubt, that I am dead?

PANTALONE : That sums it up . . . yes.

BEATRICE : Killed in a duel?

PANTALONE : Exactly.

BEATRICE : Thanks be to Heaven, I was only wounded.

PANTALONE : Wounded!

BEATRICE : And I am come here to Venice to claim the money you owe me.

PANTALONE (*clutching at the Doctor*) : Oh, no—no, no—no, no—no, no.

[*Smeraldina enters, takes Beatrice's hat, stick and gloves, and goes out.*]

DOCTOR : Calm now, Signior Pantalone, calm! (*Moving to Beatrice.*) Tell me, Signior, have you authority, recommendation, testimonial, signature, stamp or stigmata about you, to prove to us your identity?

BEATRICE : Your doubts are just. Here are four letters from business correspondents, people Signior Pantalone knows well. (*Gives Doctor four letters.*) You will recognize the handwriting and assure yourselves of who I am.

380

[*Brighella coughs loudly.*]

(*She sees Brighella and her face drops. She makes a mute 'ah'. Aside.*) Brighella here? He recognizes me. Should he reveal who I am, I am lost. I must forestall him. (*Aloud to Brighella.*) Friend, you seem to know me.

BRIGHELLA : That I do . . . I believe you know me too. Brighella Cavicchio's the name.

BEATRICE (*she moves to Brighella*) : Yes I remember you well . . . Tell me : what are you doing here in Venice? (*Aside.*) Do not give me away.

BRIGHELLA (*aside*) : Have no fear. (*Then aloud.*) Why, sir, I run the inn in the square over there. I am ever at your service.

BEATRICE : Splendid. In that case, I shall be staying there.

BRIGHELLA : Honoured guest you'll be, sir.

[*Beatrice turns and walks to Pantalone.*]

(*Aside.*) What's her game, then?

BEATRICE (*to Pantalone*) : Satisfied, Signior?

PANTALONE : I've examined them . . . (*He blinks weakly.*) . . . er . . . yes . . .

BEATRICE : As a further proof, Signior Brighella knows me and will vouch for who I am.

BRIGHELLA : That I do, . . . rest assured.

BEATRICE : What is my name?

BRIGHELLA : Your name?

BEATRICE : The truth, sir.

BRIGHELLA : Rasponi!

BEATRICE : You hear? I am Federigo Rasponi of Turin . . .

CLARICE : No. He can't be.

BEATRICE : Tell me, sir, who is this young lady?

381

PANTALONE : Why, sir, this is Clarice, my daughter. (*Aside.*) Now for some fun !

BEATRICE : Clarice? Then she is the one who is promised to me in marriage?

PANTALONE : Just so, sir, just so.

SILVIO : No, sir. Never, sir, never.

BEATRICE : Pray, sir, who are *you*?

SILVIO : Signora Clarice, sir, is betrothed to me.

BEATRICE : To you?

SILVIO : Yes, sir, she's mine.

BEATRICE : How dare you, sir. You are speaking of my promised bride . . .

CLARICE (*rushing to Pantalone and gripping him*) : Oh, Father.

PANTALONE : There now, Clarice, there . . . Dear Signior Federigo, I must reveal all . . . I truly believed that you were . . . er . . . how shall I put it?

BEATRICE : Dead?

PANTALONE : That's the word . . . So I offered my daughter to Signior Silvio here, and at the very last moment you have turned up. But there's no damage done. You have got the prior claim, sir. There you are ! Clarice is yours.

CLARICE : What?

BEATRICE : Come, Clarice, come to the arms of one who adores you !

SILVIO : Stop !

BEATRICE : Eh?

SILVIO : Do you think, sir, that I would ever allow that? You might be Federigo Rasponi . . . but I am *Silvio Lombardi*.

DOCTOR : Well said, my son . . . Long live the Lombardis.

SILVIO : Exactly ! Now should Signior Pantalone here do me this wrong, why then I shall have my revenge. Whosoever tries to take my Clarice from me, must first face me with the sword . . . and then sir, we will fight to the death. Clarice, sir, is mine.

[*Silvio leaves. The Doctor follows him and calls after him.*]

DOCTOR : I'm proud of you, my son. Proud. (*To the rest*). Long live the Lombardis. (*He hurries after his son.*)

BEATRICE : Dearest Lady Bride, all this must be very distressing for you.

CLARICE : Don't come near me. Why can't you go back to where you came from?

BEATRICE : But we have signed a contract—we are bound to each other for life.

CLARICE : Oh, Father! Must I marry him?

PANTALONE : That you must.

CLARICE : Oh!

PANTALONE : So dry your eyes, and try to make yourself presentable.

CLARICE : Oh!

PANTALONE : Go to your room.

CLARICE : Oh!

PANTALONE : Obey your father.

CLARICE : Oh!

PANTALONE : Go.

CLARICE : Oh . . . no . . . . (*She leaves weeping.*)

Scene 4

The Same.

BEATRICE : Signior Pantalone, we must do all we can to treat her gently. In truth, sir, I pity the girl.

PANTALONE : So do I, sir, so do I. But I am a man of business. I've made a contract . . . contracts must be honoured.

BEATRICE : Exactly, sir.

BRIGHELLA : Well now, if you're going to stay at my inn, I'd better go and make the necessary arrangements. So you're going to marry Signora Clarice, are you? That will be nice!

BEATRICE : That is enough, my man.

BRIGHELLA (*going up steps*): Excuse me! (*To Pantalone.*) Your servant, sir. (*He goes out.*)

BEATRICE : And now, sir, to business. Shall we examine our accounts?

PANTALONE : Yes, let us do so. The books are in order. I shall have them delivered to your room at the Inn, shall I?

BEATRICE : If I am not about, give them to my servant, will you?

PANTALONE : Your servant?

BEATRICE : Don't worry. He is thoroughly reliable. You can trust him with anything.

[*A servant enters with Beatrice's hat, stick and gloves, hands them to her, and then goes out.*]

PANTALONE : Very well, then, I'll do as you say. I shall see you soon . . . Son-in-law.

BEATRICE : At your service, dear Father.

Music starts and they both go out.

General entrance to music.

Boy wheeling Ice Cream cart enters calling 'Ices— Ices—get your lovely ices!' Smeraldina enters with straw mat and carpet beater. She beats mat.

Serving-girl with empty shopping basket enters, crosses and beckons three musicians to enter, playing as they come. Girl then goes out. Truffaldino enters and grabs an ice-cream off cart. Boy grabs it back and wheels cart out, followed by the musicians.

Truffaldino acknowledges Smeraldina who goes out with mat and beater. Old waiter enters and dusts table. Truffaldino mimes short conversation and goes out. Old waiter goes out.

Brighella, wearing hat, enters and sits, laughing.

Beatrice enters with hat and stick and crosses Brighella, not seeing him.

Music fades.

Scene 5

Street before Inn.

BRIGHELLA (*laughing*): Oh, Madam, you really fooled them, didn't you?

BEATRICE (*turning*): Shhh!

BRIGHELLA: You do like your little practical jokes, don't you?

BEATRICE: This is no joke, this is something serious.

BRIGHELLA (*rising*): Oh?

BEATRICE (*taking Brighella aside*): Do you know who killed my brother, Federigo?

BRIGHELLA: Well I heard tell it was Florindo Aretusi.

BEATRICE: Florindo, my lover.

N

BRIGHELLA : Yes, Madam.

BEATRICE : His family told me that he had fled here to Venice, so I decided on the instant that I would follow him. I took my brother, Federigo's clothes to support my disguise, and his letters of credit . . .

BRIGHELLA : Here, you're not going to trick Signior Pantalone out of his money, are you?

BEATRICE : Trick? The money is mine. My brother dead, I am his heir.

BRIGHELLA : Then why not tell him the truth?

BEATRICE : Think, Brighella, think. Should I tell him that I want the money to help Florindo, why, they would try to hasten me to either an asylum or a nunnery. I'll not be bothered with any of them. I want freedom.

BRIGHELLA : Truly, Madam, you've a rare spirit.

BEATRICE : Then help me, Brighella, please.

BRIGHELLA : Trust me, I'll help you. (*He kisses her hand.*) Oh, that manservant of yours . . .

BEATRICE : What about him?

BRIGHELLA : He seems a bit of a blockhead to me.

BEATRICE : Maybe—but he is loyal. To me, loyalty is everything.

BRIGHELLA : True, very true . . . This way . . . *Sir*!

Music : 'Beatrice'
Beatrice goes out followed by Brighella.

Scene 6

The same. Truffaldino enters as the music fades.

TRUFFALDINO : I'm right fed up, I am. I do nothing but hang around all day long, doing nothing. I wouldn't mind but I'm starving hungry too. Ever since I met this master of mine on the road from Turin, not a morsel has passed these lips. I'm so hungry I feel quite faint. Mind you, it's my own fault. I chose the wrong master. He never eats, my one. Have you noticed, he's got no stomach on him to speak of . . . it's all . . . plenty of that (*He mimes walk with stomach tucked in.*) You should always choose a master with plenty of . . . (*Mimes big stomach.*) Mind you, there's masters and masters, you know. There's them as got respect for servants, give them a decent place to sleep, decent food . . . but my one . . . he's not in the place five minutes, and he's off, visiting and leaving me hanging about. Well, I'm hungry, I'm fed up and I'm broke, and it's rotten being a servant. I'm going to change my job. I want something more exciting—something out of the humdrum. But what can I do? I'll have to be a servant. I'm not trained up for anything else.

Music. Truffaldino crosses and leans against wall.

Scene 7

The same. Florindo Aretusi is seen strolling along the back. He wears a top hat and carries a sword-stick. He is talking over the music as he comes.

FLORINDO (*off*): Thank you, Gondolier. Come along, Porter, it must be along here, and turn right. (*As he enters.*) Ah, here we are, Villa Brig-hella. Come along, come along.

[*Porter enters. He is bent double under a large trunk and carries a wicker basket, and a long carpet bag with a butterfly net stuck through the handles.*]

PORTER : Ugh—ugh—ugh . . . the weight's killing me. (*He drops the lot.*)

FLORINDO : Careful, man, careful.

PORTER (*sits on trunk exhausted*) : No good, I'm done for.

FLORINDO : But the inn's only just over there. It's only two or three steps . . . pick it up, pick it up.

PORTER : Sorry, it's me for the knacker's yard . . . Ruined.

TRUFFALDINO (*aside*) : This looks like my chance to earn a halfpenny or two.

[*Music fades.*]

Can I be of any assistance, Sir?

FLORINDO : Ah, yes. I'm trying to get my things into this inn.

TRUFFALDINO : Say no more, sir. Leave it to me. Always a privilege and always a pleasure, sir. (*He moves to the porter who is still seated on the trunk.*) Get off.

PORTER : Eh? Who are you?

TRUFFALDINO : You heard. Get off.

PORTER : Oh, I can't get up. He's done me an injury he has.

TRUFFALDINO : Hard luck. (*He pulls the trunk from under the porter who falls to the ground. Truffaldino picks up everything and heads towards the inn.*) Won't be a moment, sir. (*He goes out with luggage.*)

FLORINDO : Good man. (*To porter who has picked himself up.*) What are you waiting for?

PORTER : Your token of appreciation, sir.

FLORINDA : You know, that's what I thought you might be doing. There you are, and good luck to you. (*Gives him coins.*)

PORTER : Thank you, sir. Very civil of you. (*Looking at coins.*) What's this? Three ha'pence. Ruddy top-hatted stinker. (*He goes out.*)

Scene 8

The same, Truffaldino returns.

TRUFFALDINO : I have taken the liberty of booking you in, sir.

FLORINDO : Good man.

TRUFFALDINO : A very nice room you've got, sir, . . . very superior. I've also done a tour of the kitchens : lovely food and very big helpings . . . Oh, yes, highly recommended, sir.

FLORINDO : Now look here. What's your name?

TRUFFALDINO : Truffaldino Battochio de Bergamo. Vecchio, sir.

FLORINDO : Well now, Truffaldino, may I ask what you do?

TRUFFALDINO : Do, sir?

FLORINDO : For a living.

TRUFFALDINO : Me, sir? I'm a servant, sir.

FLORINDO : Are you working for any one at the present moment?

TRUFFALDINO : At the present moment, I am working for no one at all.

FLORINDO : So you are without a master, then?

TRUFFALDINO : I am as you see me, sir, without a master. (*Aside.*) Well, the other fellow's not here, so I tell no lies.

FLORINDO : Would you care to serve me?

TRUFFALDINO : Serve you, sir? Why not? (*Aside.*) If the pay's better, I'll swop. (*To Florindo.*) May I enquire what would be my rerumination, sir?

FLORINDO : Your what?

TRUFFALDINO : My rerumination, sir.

FLORINDO : Oh, I see, your wages, (*Laughs.*)

TRUFFALDINO : Yes, sir.

FLORINDO : Well now, what would you expect?

TRUFFALDINO : Well, my other master gave me a pound a month and all found.

FLORINDO : Good. I'll do the same.

TRUFFALDINO : If you didn't mind, sir, I did feel I ought to better myself.

FLORINDO : Well? (*Taking snuff.*)

TRUFFALDINO : Shall we say a penny a day for snuff.

FLORINDO : Agreed. (*Offers Truffaldino pinch of snuff, who takes it, and puts remainder back in snuff box.*)

TRUFFALDINO : Thank you, sir. I'm yours, sir.

FLORINDO : Now then Truffaldino, this is the first thing I'd like you to do . . .

TRUFFALDINO : I'm all ears, sir.

FLORINDO : I'd like you to go down to the post office . . .

[*Truffaldino gives colossal sneeze. Florindo looks at him coldly.*]

Bless you! I'd like you to go down to the post office . . .

[*Truffaldino sneezes again.*]

I'd like you to go down to the post office . . .

[*Florindo looks sharply at Truffaldino who does not sneeze.*]

and see if there are any letters for me. My name is Aretusi—Florindo Aretusi.

TRUFFALDINO : Florindo Aretusi. I've got it, sir.

FLORINDO : That's it. Good man. Now then, if there are any letters for me, I'd like you to bring them back to me here immediately.

TRUFFALDINO : You can rely on me, sir.

FLORINDO : I'm sure I can.

TRUFFALDINO : And in the meantime, would you consider ordering a small meal, sir.

FLORINDO : Yes, yes, I'll see to it. Off you go.

TRUFFALDINO (*going off*): Florindo Aretu . . . (*Huge sneeze.*)

FLORINDO : Well, he's something of a joker perhaps, but nothing too displeasing. Do you know, I think I'll try him out for a day or two. Innkeeper! Innkeeper! (*He goes off.*)

Scene 9

The same.

TRUFFALDINO : I thought I handled that very well. I told him my other master gave me a pound a week and all found. He didn't. He gave me a guinea. Well, whichever way you work it out, he's a better proposition than the other fellow. I mean, my other master was a bit soft round the gills, you know . . . a bit girlish. I would have had to have watched myself with that one. Oh well, I've a new master now, so off to the post office for him.

BEATRICE (*off*) : Truffaldino!

TRUFFALDINO : Ay, Ay! It's the beardless wonder!

[*Enter Beatrice and Brighella.*]

BEATRICE : Ah, Truffaldino, I'd like you to go this instance, to the boat, take delivery of my trunk and bring it back to the inn.

TRUFFALDINO : Which inn?

BRIGHELLA : This inn.

TRUFFALDINO (*aghast, aside*) : I've got them both staying there now.

BEATRICE : Hurry along, man. Don't moon about.

TRUFFALDINO : Like lightning, sir.

BEATRICE : Ah! Just a moment.

TRUFFALDINO : Yes, sir.

BEATRICE : While you're about it, go to the post office and see if there are any letters for me.

TRUFFALDINO : At the gallop, sir.

BEATRICE : Hold it.

TRUFFALDINO : Yes, sir.

BEATRICE : You'd better ask if there are any letters for Beatrice Rasponi as well.

TRUFFALDINO : Beatrice Rasponi. I take it the lady's your wife, sir?

[*Brighella laughs.*]

BEATRICE : She is my sister. (*Nods to Brighella.*) She was to have come with me but at the last moment she was indisposed.

TRUFFALDINO : Oh, I am sorry to hear that, sir.

BEATRICE : Certain friends of hers may have written to her, so bring any letters there are, and I'll give them to her when I return. Hurry along now, hurry along.

[*Truffaldino goes out. Beatrice re-enters the inn. Truffaldino comes back. Brighella is by the table.*]

TRUFFALDINO (*to audience*) : Here, what with the shortage of jobs . . . (*He sees Brighella and breaks off.*) Owdo.
BRIGHELLA : Owdo.
TRUFFALDINO : Are you the landlord here then?
BRIGHELLA : Yes, I am, and remember, if you want to eat well, you had better behave well.
TRUFFALDINO : I was waiting to hear you say that.
BRIGHELLA : Right then. Off you go then.
TRUFFALDINO : I beg your pardon?
BRIGHELLA : I said, off you go.

[*They both start to go out then turn.*]

TRUFFALDINO ⎱
BRIGHELLA ⎰ (*together*) : Off you go!

Brighella goes out.

Scene 10

TRUFFALDINO (*coming back*) : There's enough people looking for one master . . . I've got two now. Well, it stands to reason I can't serve both of them, can I? And why not? It'd be something, wouldn't

it. Two masters—double wages—double rations—
and if I was found out—double trouble. And what
if I was found out? If one of them sends me packing, I can always stay with the other one. When
all's said and done, it's something to boast of, isn't
it? Something out of the humdrum. Two masters,
just like that. (*He makes a gesture of juggling.*)
Right. I'm resolved. I'm off to the post office for
both of them.

[*As he turns to go, Silvio enters.*]

SILVIO (*aside*): At last I have found the servant
of Signior Federigo Rasponi. (*To Truffaldino.*)
Fetch me your master.

TRUFFALDINO: Which one?

SILVIO: Which one? What do you mean, which
one?

TRUFFALDINO: I beg your pardon, sir. He's in the
inn.

SILVIO: Then you fetch him (*Pushing Truffaldino
backwards.*) And tell him from me that if he is a
man of honour, which I doubt, he will come forth
immediately and meet me face to face.

TRUFFALDINO: Face to face?

SILVIO: Face to face. I hate him. So you fetch him
before I break every bone in your miserable little
body.

TRUFFALDINO: Oh well, it's a fifty-fifty chance. I'll
send the first one I find.

SILVIO: Don't dawdle, Sirrah, or I'll beat you.

Truffaldino goes out.

Scene 11

The same.

SILVIO : Oooo, I am resolved. Ooo, I am. Either Federigo here renounces all claims to my dear Clarice, or we shall put it to the test, life against life.

[*Florindo and Truffaldino enter.*]

TRUFFALDINO : That's him, sir . . . only be very careful. He looks very dangerous to me.
FLORINDO : But I don't know him.
TRUFFALDINO : You don't know him.
FLORINDO : No.
TRUFFALDINO : Oh well, off to the post office. (*He goes out.*)

[*Florindo draws his sword stick. Silvio already has drawn his.*]

FLORINDO : Sir.
SILVIO : Sir.
FLORINDO : You asked for me, sir.
SILVIO : I, sir?
FLORINDO : Yes, sir.
SILVIO : I beg your pardon, sir, but I do not know you, sir.
FLORINDO : But my servant told me that you threatened to issue a challenge.
SILVIO : He must have made a mistake, sir. I asked to see his master, sir.
FLORINDO : I am his master.
SILVIO : Are you?

395

FLORINDO : Certainly.

SILVIO : Oh. Do forgive me, sir, do forgive me. But your servant is the very image of a man I saw this morning.

FLORINDO : Eh?

SILVIO : His double, in fact. It's quite clear, sir, that I have made a terrible mistake, and I do crave your pardon, sir.

FLORINDO : You mean you mistook my servant for another?

SILVIO : Yes, well, I must have done, sir.

FLORINDO (*crossing to him and sheathing his sword stick*) : Ah well, there's no harm done. Mistakes often happen. (*Laughs.*)

SILVIO (*sheathing his swordstick*) : You are a stranger here, are you not?

FLORINDO : Yes I am. I'm from Turin.

SILVIO : Turin.

FLORINDO : Yes, from Turin.

SILVIO : But the man I wish to speak to—he comes from Turin.

FLORINDO : Oh. Well, I'm sorry to hear it. Still, since he is a fellow countryman of mine, perhaps I can make peace between you.

SILVIO : Would you know a certain . . . Federigo Rasponi?

FLORINDO : Federigo Rasponi?

SILVIO : You know him?

FLORINDO : Well, I used to, only too well.

SILVIO : He intends to snatch from me—the woman I love.

FLORINDO : What's that?

SILVIO : My beloved—my betrothed. But I'll not let him, sir. No, I will kill him first.

FLORINDO : Kill him? But how can you kill him? He's dead.

SILVIO: Ah yes, sir, so it was given out. But he gave us proof, he showed us letters . . .

FLORINDO: What! Not dead but—

SILVIO: No, sir. He lives.

FLORINDO: So—I did not kill him then.

SILVIO: He arrived in Venice this morning, sir, Safe and sound.

FLORINDO: Federigo—here in Venice. I fly from justice and I come face to face with my enemy.

SILVIO: Sir, when you meet him, which you are bound to, as he is staying at this inn here . . .

FLORINDO: Here?

SILVIO: Yes, sir. I beg you to do me a tiny little service . . . Now, sir, when you see him, tell him, for his own good (*Half draws sword stick.*) You understand me, sir, for his own good he must abandon all ideas of this marriage. (*Sheathes sword again. Brings heels together and bows.*) My name, sir, is Silvio Lombardi. You have my respect and my friendship.

FLORINDO: I am honoured, sir, and privileged, sir. (*Aside.*) And what is more, absolutely perplexed.

SILVIO: Would you grant me, Sir, the favour of telling me your name?

FLORINDO: My name? Why yes, my name is . . . (*Aside.*) I must not reveal myself! My name is Arazio Ardenti, ever at your service.

SILVIO: Signior Arazio, I am yours to command.

FLORINDO (*clicking heels*): Sir.

SILVIO (*clicking heels*): Sir.

FLORINDO: Your servant ever.

SILVIO: Dispose of me as you will.

FLORINDO (*clicking heels*): Sir.

SILVIO: Sir. (*Clicks heels too hard, hurts himself, and limps out.*)

Scene 12

Florindo alone.

FLORINDO : What's this? Can the dead arise? Perchance I did not touch a vital spot . . . I had not time to watch him breathe his last. No, he lives. Federigo Rasponi lives. What to do now? Ah, my beloved Beatrice,

[*Music.*]

has he walled you up in a nunnery . . . then come here seeking his revenge? Well, dead or alive, what matter is he to me now? I'll to Turin . . . back to my Beatrice. Immured as a nun . . . my Beatrice . . . never!

Music fades as Florindo goes out.

Scene 13

Truffaldino enters with another porter who is carrying Beatrice's trunk on his back. The porter, bent under his load, cannot see his way.

TRUFFALDINO : Straight on, mate. Hard right. Straight down. Left wheel.
FLORINDO (*off left*) : Ah, Truffaldino!
TRUFFALDINO : Hold on. That's master number two, and this luggage belongs to master number one. What to do . . . Think . . . Got it. Into action. Back.
PORTER : Back?

TRUFFALDINO : Back, you fool. Into reverse.

PORTER : But I can't go back.

TRUFFALDINO : Keep going. Wait for me on the corner.

[*Porter goes out the way he entered. Florindo enters.*]

FLORINDO : Ah, Truffaldino.

TRUFFALDINO : Sir?

FLORINDO : I must leave for Turin. Will you come with me?

TRUFFALDINO : When?

FLORINDO : Now, immediately.

TRUFFALDINO : How about my dinner?

FLORINDO : Ah! First we eat, then we go.

TRUFFALDINO : In that case, a pleasure to accompany you, sir.

FLORINDO : Good man. Now, then, have you been to the post office?

TRUFFALDINO : I have, sir.

FLORINDO : Have you got any letters?

TRUFFALDINO : I have, sir.

FLORINDO : Give them to me.

TRUFFALDINO : Right, sir. (*He takes three letters from his pocket and drops them. Aside.*) Strike! I've mixed them up. There's one letter for one master and two for the other, but which is which? I can't read.

FLORINDO : Come along, sirrah, give me the letters.

TRUFFALDINO (*marching up to him*) : A matter to report, sir.

FLORINDO : And what's that?

TRUFFALDINO : On the way to the post office I met a colleague—another servant. 'Going to the post office' he said. 'Me', I said. 'Yes' I said. 'Save me

399

a journey' he said. 'See if there are any letters there for my master.' 'Anything to oblige an old chum' I said. So there we are, sir. One of those letters isn't yours.

FLORINDO (*taking the letters*): Ah well, that's all right, we'll soon get that sorted out . . . Let's see now. Florindo Aretusi. What? 'Beatrice Rasponi'. (*Aside*) Beatrice. Here in Venice?

TRUFFALDINO: That must be the one for my colleague, sir.

FLORINDO: Who is the colleague of yours?

TRUFFALDINO: I've told you another servant . . . going under the name of . . . (*He taps his forehead twice. The answer pops out of his mouth.*) Pasquale.

FLORINDO: Pasquale?

TRUFFALDINO: Yes, sir, Pasquale.

FLORINDO: I see. And who is the master of this Pasquale?

TRUFFALDINO: Master, sir?

FLORINDO: Yes. What is his name?

TRUFFALDINO: I've no idea.

FLORINDO: No idea? But you must have some idea. When you went to collect the letters from the post office, you must have given a name.

TRUFFALDINO: Very well reasoned, sir.

FLORINDO: Well? What is it?

TRUFFALDINO: I've no idea.

FLORINDO: You've no idea?

TRUFFALDINO: My friend wrote it down on a piece of paper.

FLORINDO: A piece of paper? What did it say?

TRUFFALDINO: I'm sorry, sir, but I can't read.

FLORINDO: Well, where's the paper?

TRUFFALDINO: I left it with the man at the post office.

[*Florindo moves left, holding his brow.*]

FLORINDO : Oh, my God.
TRUFFALDINO (*moving right. Aside*) : I'm making it up as I go along.
FLORINDO : Now look here . . .
TRUFFALDINO : Yes, sir?
FLORINDO : This servant, this Pasquale.
TRUFFALDINO : Pasquale, sir?
FLORINDO : Where does he live?
TRUFFALDINO : I've no idea.
FLORINDO : No idea? Well, perhaps you'd be kind enough to tell me how you can give him back this letter?
TRUFFALDINO : That's a point.

[*Both laugh.*]

FLORINDO : Well?
TRUFFALDINO : He told me to meet him on the town square.
FLORINDO : Did he?
TRUFFALDINO : Under the clock . . . Now sir, if you'll give me the letter, I'll set about finding him.
FLORINDO : No. I shall open it.
TRUFFALDINO : What. But you can't read . . .
FLORINDO : Silence.
TRUFFALDINO : But it isn't . . .
FLORINDO : Silence! (*He marches to the side of the stage tearing open the letter and saying aside.*) This letter is written to the woman I love . . . Beatrice and I are one. Shall I not read it then? Yes.
'Dear Lady,
     Your sudden departure from the town has caused much gossip. Everyone knows you have gone in search of Signior Florindo. The magistrates

have found out that you are wearing men's clothing and have left nothing undone (*He looks up amazed—then turns letter over.*) left nothing undone to trace you and make an arrest'. Oh, I see. (*Laughs.*) 'Take care, Madame, and Heaven bless you.

I remain your humble and devoted servant,

Maria della Doira.'

TRUFFALDINO (*to audience*): No manners, you know, no manners! Fancy . . . reading other people's letters. He's a real nosey parker, that one.

FLORINDO (*aside*): So—Beatrice has left home . . . wearing men's clothing . . . trying to follow my footsteps. Oh, my beloved—my dearest—how faithful—how devoted. Truffaldino!

TRUFFALDINO: Sir?

FLORINDO: Quickly. Go and find your Pasquale, and ask him where his master lives. Bring me news of it . . . Away now.

TRUFFALDINO: The letters, please, sir.

FLORINDO: Oh, yes. There you are.

TRUFFALDINO: How am I going to explain its being opened, sir?

FLORINDO: Oh, don't worry about that.

TRUFFALDINO (*aside*): Don't worry about that, he says.

FLORINDO: On your way. No time to be lost.

TRUFFALDINO: Still going to Turin, are we?

FLORINDO: Turin? No . . . certainly no.

TRUFFALDINO: Well, how about my dinner, then?

FLORINDO: I've got more important things to think about than your dinner . . . Go and find your Pasquale. (*Aside.*) Beatrice is here in Venice, so is Federigo, she must be found before she meets her brother. (*To Truffaldino.*) Truffaldino, on your way—no time to be lost.

TRUFFALDINO : But sir . . .
FLORINDO : Don't loiter about. Away with you.
(*He leaves.*)

Scene 14

The same.

TRUFFALDINO : What about that, then? Still, at
least I'm glad he's not leaving. I'm anxious to see
how I can manage my two servant jobs. I mean,
it's a challenge to industry. If I pulled it off, I
might get an award from the Doge. The problem
is this letter. I can't very well deliver it open, can
I? Well, first we fold it, then we seal it . . . It's
not difficult if you've got a little knack. My old
granny once taught me how to seal letters with
chewed bread. How about that? Chewed bread.
The only problem is I haven't any bread.

[*The young waiter enters with a basket of bread
on his right shoulder. He crosses the stage in front
of Truffaldino, whistling.*]

TRUFFALDINO : 'Owdo.
WAITER : 'Owdo.

[*As he crosses Truffaldino mimes taking a bit of
bread from basket. Actually he has it in his pocket.
Waiter goes out.*]

TRUFFALDINO : Well, we've got the bread. Extend
the forefinger and thumb of your right hand, take

a piece, place it in the oral position, and chew.
(*He does so.*) Oh, it's lovely. (*He panics.*) I've
swallowed it. (*He takes another bite.*) Don't be a
fool, Truffaldino. One last chance, lad. (*He
struggles with himself.*) It's going—it's going—It's
no good. Nature's calling. Don't do it, Truff, don't
do it.

[*Business trying not to swallow bread. Truffaldino
finishes kneeling facing audience—sticks out his
tongue and the bread chewed to paste is on his
tongue.*]

Paste! I'm a great one for the household hint and
the practical tip.

[*There is a loud whistle from the second porter
offstage.*]

PORTER (*off*): 'Ere! 'Ow much longer I got to
wait then?
TRUFFALDINO (*sealing letter with the paste as he
talks*): It's the porter. I'd forgotten all about him.
Straight in here, mate.

[*The porter enters again with trunk on his back.*]

Straight on . . .

[*The porter heads for the edge of the stage—just
as he gets there . . .*]

Hard left.

Porter wheels left.

Scene 15

The same. Enter Beatrice.

BEATRICE : Ah, my trunk.
TRUFFALDINO (*to porter*) : Left again. Right on as far as you can go.

[*Porter and trunk go out.*]

BEATRICE : You got it here safely, then?
TRUFFALDINO : Everything's safe with me, sir.
BEATRICE : Have you been to the post office?
TRUFFALDINO : Yes, sir. And I've got a letter for your sister, sir.
BEATRICE : Ah, good. (*She takes it.*) This letter's been opened.
TRUFFALDINO : Opened, sir? Impossible, sir.
BEATRICE : Opened, and sealed up again, with . . . what is this?
TRUFFALDINO : Bread. I wonder how that came about?
BEATRICE : You don't know, eh? You good for nothing! Who opened it? Answer.
TRUFFALDINO : Kind sir, I crave your pardon. Allow me to confess the truth.
BEATRICE : What?
TRUFFALDINO : Er . . . When I got to the post office I found out there was actually a letter there for me too . . . from my dear old Granny. And as I can't read, I opened your letter instead of hers.
BEATRICE : If you can't read, why bother to open them at all?
TRUFFALDINO : I was anxious to feel the notepaper that Granny's loving hands had touched.

BEATRICE : In that case, I admire your sentiment.

TRUFFALDINO : So do I.

BEATRICE (*aside*) : Good kind Maria. What a faithful servant you are. (*To Truffaldino.*) Well, my man, as my trunk has arrived, here is the key. (*Gives him key.*) Open it up and give my clothes an airing.

TRUFFALDINO : Certainly, sir. One key, one trunk.

Beatrice goes out.

Scene 16

The same. At once Florindo enters.

FLORINDO : Now then, my man, have you put my trunk in my room?

TRUFFALDINO : Yes, sir.

FLORINDO : Well, here is my key. (*Gives Truffaldino key.*) Give my clothes an airing. Now, then, what about this Pasquale?

TRUFFALDINO : Pasquale?

FLORINDO : Yes, Pasquale.

TRUFFALDINO : Pasquale who, sir?

FLORINDO : Your friend, the servant. You were to meet him in the town square, under the clock, and ask him who he serves under. You remember?

TRUFFALDINO : Oh, Pasquale . . . the town square . . . under the clock. What's the time, sir?

FLORINDO : What's the time?

[*A clock chimes one offstage.*]

It's one o'clock.

TRUFFALDINO : Well, there we are, sir. I'm not supposed to meet him till 2.30.

FLORINDO : Not till then?

TRUFFALDINO : 2.30 sharp. So that just about gives us time for a small meal, sir.

FLORINDO : What?

TRUFFALDINO : I believe it is customary around mid-day, sir.

FLORINDO : Yes. I suppose it is.

TRUFFALDINO : Well, if you'll kindly follow me this way, sir.

FLORINDO : What?

TRUFFALDINO : Order the food, sir.

FLORINDO : Oh, yes, yes, yes. Very well. (*Looking out front.*) What a remarkably pretty clock !

[*He enters the inn.*]

TRUFFALDINO : Yes, it's lovely, sir. (*With utmost speed.*) For what we are about to receive may nothing stand in the way. (*He dives into the inn.*)

Scene 17

A room in Pantalone's house.

Clarice and Pantalone can be talking offstage before entering together.

PANTALONE : Daughter—daughter—I'll not be bamboozled—I'll not be undermined by sentiment. You'll marry Federigo. I've given my word. It's as simple as that.

407

CLARICE : I'll not marry Signior Federigo.

PANTALONE : Oh dear, oh dear, what's a man to do? Look daughter, this Signior Federigo is a pleasant enough chap surely?

CLARICE : Not to me.

PANTALONE : Why no?

CLARICE : I hate him.

PANTALONE : Hate him? Nonsense . . . you just get that Silvio out of your noddle and you'll soon find that Signior Federigo is the finest figure of a husband any girl could wish for.

CLARICE : I'll not forget Silvio. I love him.

PANTALONE : I'm not talking of love—I'm talking of marriage.

[*Clarice howls.*]

Oh, shut up please. I'll not have my heart softened by you or anybody.

Scene 18

The same. Smeraldina enters down steps and stops half-way.

SMERALDINA : Sir. Master! Signior Pantalone!

PANTALONE : Yes? What is it?

SMERALDINA : Signior Federigo is here. He wishes to speak with you.

PANTALONE : Show him in.

[*Smeraldina goes out again.*]

PANTALONE : Come on, daughter. Less of the fairy fountains for heaven's sake.

CLARICE : But, Father, please . . .

PANTALONE (*giving her a handkerchief*) : Have a good blow.

Scene 19

Smeraldina enters followed by Beatrice down steps.

SMERALDINA : Signior Federigo Rasponi.

[*She goes out.*]

PANTALONE (*to Clarice*) : Your husband's here.

BEATRICE : Signior Pantalone.

PANTALONE (*to Beatrice*) : My respects, sir.

[*Clarice sobs.*]

BEATRICE : Your daughter, sir . . . Why is she sobbing?

PANTALONE : Why? Well, shall we say the news of your death has left a lasting impression.

BEATRICE : Signior Pantalone, do something for me. Leave me alone with her for a while. I might be able to comfort her.

PANTALONE : Very well. (*Aside.*) I'll try anything. Daughter, your husband to be would speak to you in private.

[*Clarice howls.*]

She's all yours, sir. I'll take my leave. (*He bows and leaves.*)

Scene 20

The same.

CLARICE : Oh, I'll not marry . . . never . . . not even if they drag me to the altar.

BEATRICE (*aside*) : I have not the heart to see her suffer so—I shall tell her all immediately. (*Coughs.*) There is something I must confide. Clarice! You do not want me and neither do I want you!

CLARICE : What?

BEATRICE : Even if you offered yourself to me I wouldn't know what to do with you.

CLARICE : I don't understand.

BEATRICE : You love another. So do I.

CLARICE : You do?

BEATRICE : Yes, prepare yourself for a surprise.

CLARICE : What is it?

BEATRICE : I am not Federigo Rasponi.

CLARICE : Not?

BEATRICE : I am Beatrice, his sister.

CLARICE : Sister? What are you saying? You are a woman.

BEATRICE : Indeed I am . . . Every inch a woman.

CLARICE : Oh! How can you stand there and torment me?

BEATRICE : You don't believe I am a woman . . . Very well, since you insist, I shall give you proof.

CLARICE : Proof?

BEATRICE : Yes, my dear . . . (*Turns up stage.*)

410

CLARICE : Oh ! ! Oh, I believe you.

BEATRICE : Ah.

CLARICE : Oh ! But your brother? What is the truth about your brother?

BEATRICE : My brother is dead.

CLARICE : Oh good ! Oh !

BEATRICE : He was killed by my lover, who has disappeared. I am trying to trace him, wearing this disguise. I have confided this secret because I could not bear to see you so affected but I beg you by all the sacred laws of friendship, do not betray me.

CLARICE : Never.

BEATRICE : You are on your honour to tell no one.

CLARICE : Oh, I promise, on my honour. None. Silvio?

BEATRICE : No, I forbid it. The fewer who know the better.

CLARICE : Well then, I shan't say a word.

BEATRICE : Thank you . . . Well now, are we not friends?

CLARICE : Indeed we are, and if ever I can be of any help, you have only to command me.

BEATRICE : And I too swear eternal friendship.

Scene 21

The same. Pantalone enters and sees them.

BEATRICE : Give me your hand as a sign of your love and loyalty.

CLARICE : Most gladly.

BEATRICE : You'll not break your promise to me?

411

CLARICE : I take my oath on it.

[*They kiss each other on both cheeks.*]

PANTALONE : Promise? Oath? Kisses! What's this? And so soon! Bravo! You're a bit of a speedy worker, aren't you? Well, there's one thing quite clear to me now, we must get you two married immediately.

CLARICE : Married!

BEATRICE : There's no need for such haste, sir, I do assure you.

PANTALONE : Oh, isn't there? I can see the twinkle in your eye, m'boy . . .

CLARICE : But, Father . . .

PANTALONE : Hush, girl. You needn't be so shame-faced. Daddy understands. You're both in a hurry so the wedding will be tomorrow . . . Oh, yes, we don't want any disturbances in church, do we, so I'll just go and have a word with Signior Silvio. Make him understand.

CLARICE : Oh Father, keep him calm! Don't let him desert me.

PANTALONE : Desert you? You don't want two husbands do you? Greedy guts! Ha, ha, ha, I'll be back presently. As you were, Federigo. (*He goes.*)

CLARICE (*to Beatrice*) : Oh, now you've made things worse than ever.

Music : Tarantella.

Beatrice and Clarice go out.

Scene 22

The courtyard. Silvio comes in with drawn sword and comes down to Pantalone's house, when the Doctor appears.

Music fades as Doctor speaks.

DOCTOR : Silvio my boy. What are you doing?

SILVIO : Oh, Father. I am outraged! I am humiliated! I am slighted. I am affronted!

DOCTOR : Hold your temper. Don't be so hasty lad.

SILVIO : But Pantalone must give me satisfaction.

DOCTOR : Leave him to me. I'll deal with it.

SILVIO : But, Father . . .

DOCTOR : Obedience my boy! Do as I say!

SILVIO : Very well, Father, I'll obey you. (*He moves to leave then turns.*) But, Father, as the name of our family is sacred to us, should Signior Pantalone persist in his insult, then I shall deal with him. Death is the only answer! (*He goes out.*)

DOCTOR : Oh my poor boy! How I pity him! *Damnum sine injuria*. How he suffers without remedy! However, the law is on my side. My son shall marry Pantalone's daughter.

[*There is a noise offstage.*]

Aha! I shall now inform Signior Pantalone of his legal obligations.

[*Pantalone enters and crosses in front of Doctor to centre of stage.*]

413

Aha!

[*Pantalone jumps and turns to see the doctor.*]

The man with whom I wish to speak.

PANTALONE : Ah, Doctor, I was just on my way to visit you.

DOCTOR : You are going to assure me that after all your daughter will be marrying my Silvio.

PANTALONE : Now look, sir, my daughter is in love with . . .

DOCTOR : With my son—exactly. Now let me put you right concerning the law.

PANTALONE : The law?

DOCTOR : The law on marriage is absolutely plain and straightforward. It is, in a nutshell—*Consensus et non concubitus fecit verum.*

PANTALONE : Eh?

DOCTOR : Latin.

PANTALONE : But I don't know Latin.

DOCTOR : It means your daughter is free to choose the man she loves. The law will uphold her. The wishes of the daughter are paramount.

PANTALONE : They are?

DOCTOR : They are.

PANTALONE : Anything else to say?

DOCTOR : I've said my last word.

PANTALONE : Finished?

DOCTOR : Finished.

PANTALONE : My dear Doctor . . .

DOCTOR : And don't you worry about the dowry. It's not your money I'm after, I assure you.

PANTALONE : Shall we start again?

DOCTOR : Eh?

PANTALONE : My turn, now?

DOCTOR : Your turn.

PANTALONE : You say that all my attempts to give my daughter to Signior Federigo will come to nothing if she should not love him?

DOCTOR : Exactly. I could not have put it better myself.

PANTALONE : Fancy that! And I don't speak Latin!

[*Both laugh.*]

Well, let me inform you, sir, that he has captured her heart.

DOCTOR : Who?

PANTALONE : Federigo Rasponi.

DOCTOR : Federigo Rasponi?

PANTALONE : I have just left them in there, exchanging promises, oaths, and fond embraces.

DOCTOR : But only this morning she was in love with my son. Oh, it's shameless!

PANTALONE : You're not casting aspersions against my daughter, I hope?

DOCTOR : Not against your daughter . . . against you . . . you! : How have you achieved it then? Threats? Intimidation? Menaces? Oh, there are laws against all that, I'll tell you. I'll have an injunction set against the marriage. I'll have you sued for breaking of contracts, breach of promise . . . blackmail of daughters . . . public slander of my family. *Nemo non hat habet . . . Dunc*! (*He goes.*)

PANTALONE : You do what you like . . . I'm not afraid of you. (*To audience.*) My daughter's going to marry a Rasponi, God bless her! A Rasponi in the family! The Rasponis have got quality, and they've got riches! Do you think I'd let her marry a Lombardi when she has a chance like this? One Rasponi is worth a thousand Lombardis!

[*During the last sentence Silvio enters with drawn sword.*]

SILVIO : What's that you say?

PANTALONE : One Rasponi is worth a thousand Lombardis . . . (*He turns and sees Silvio.*) Oh . . .

SILVIO : Then, know, sir, that I, Silvio Ottavio Pietro Antonio Giovanni, youngest son of the thrice illustrious house of the Lombardis, do demand of you, sir, instant satisfaction. Now draw, sirrah, draw!

PANTALONE (*tugging at his stick*) : But it doesn't draw!

SILVIO : Oh, do be quick about it, sir. This hand of mine is itching to run you through. Now draw, I say!

PANTALONE : Oh heavens! (*He draws a pistol out of his pocket.*)

SILVIO : Oh, so that's it, is it? A pistol against a sword. The odds are all on your side, sirrah, but a Lombardi, sir, is no coward, no, he is not, so I'll still take you on. Set to!

PANTALONE (*with trembling hand trying to pull back the hammer*) : Oh God, how does it work?

Scene 23

The same. Beatrice dashes on with swordstick (sheathed) in hand.

BEATRICE : Stay! Father-in-law, I beg you, grant me the honour of taking up this challenge?

PANTALONE : Granted.

BEATRICE : Or would you rather kill him yourself?

PANTALONE : No. You go ahead.
BEATRICE : *En guarde*, Lombardi !
SILVIO : A pleasure, Rasponi !
BEATRICE : I warn you, sir, I have been taught by
the best fencing masters in Turin . . . Care to think
again?
SILVIO : Never ! To hell with Turin and all the
Rasponis, say I !

[*Pantalone fires pistol. Silvio falls to floor in surprise. Pantalone staggers saying 'It worked—it
worked!'*

*Beatrice and Silvio start fighting. Silvio lunges
across. Pantalone gets in the way. Silvio chases him
off.*]

PANTALONE (*as he is chased off*) : Help—help—not
me—Him—help . . . etc. (*He goes.*)

*Silvio and Beatrice fight. Beatrice knocks his
sword out of his hand and points hers at his throat.*

Scene 24

The same. Clarice rushes to left of Beatrice.

CLARICE : Stop ! Stop ! Don't !
BEATRICE : He challenged the house of Rasponi ! !
CLARICE : Oh no, please.
BEATRICE : You would have me spare his life?
CLARICE : I beg you.
BEATRICE : You in return will remember your
promise to me.

CLARICE : I swear.

BEATRICE (*to Silvio*) : Well, Silvio Lombardi—
You're a lucky fellow ! Be grateful to her !

Beatrice marches off stage quickly.

Scene 25

The same.

CLARICE (*rushing to Silvio*) : Oh, my darling
Silvio . . . Are you safe?

SILVIO : You deceiver.

CLARICE : What?

SILVIO : This oath that you have just sworn . . .
What is it?

CLARICE : Oh forgive me. I can't tell. I promised
secrecy.

SILVIO : With him? So ! We have it now . . . You
little cheat ! You little fraud ! You little Jezebel !

CLARICE : I shall die if you go on like this !

SILVIO : Then die ! Because I would rather see you
dead than lead a life of lies.

CLARICE (*picking up his sword*) : Very well ! If
that's what you want, I'll die. (*Pointing the sword
to her breast.*) One day, you'll know how much I
loved you ! Sword, come !

Scene 26

The same.

Smeraldina rushes on with basket of vegetables.

418

SMERALDINA: What! What the devil you doin'? (*She snatches the sword from Clarice. Then to Silvio.*) Drive her to this would you! To hell with you, that's what I say. Go on! Clear off! Rubbish!

Clarice bursts into tears and rushes off stage.

Scene 27

The same.

SMERALDINA: What do you think you're at then? ... Stand by? ... Let her do herself in?

SILVIO: But it was all a pretence. She's a two-faced perfidious wretch.

SMERALDINA: Oh, go calling her names now, will we? I know your game: soon as a woman starts having a mind of her own you men start ruining her reputation.

SILVIO: That's not true.

SMERALDINA: It's all very well for you men to scandalize women . . . when given half the chance, you're off committing all the infidelities you can. Why are we women always condemned . . . and why are you men always excused? I'll tell you why: 'cos the laws are made by them men. I mean, if women made the laws, things'd be different. All right, if I ruled, I'd put every man what's unfaithful up to public show, I would. I'd make him carry an oak branch in his hands . . . second thoughts, perhaps not . . . do that and we

419

wouldn't be able to move for trees, would we?
You men! (*Looking as if she's going to be sick,
she goes off.*)

Scene 28

The same. Music. Silvio is alone.

SILVIO : Oh, Clarice, you have deceived me! I
must be revenged. Fate did make me stumble
before my rival. Yet in spite of fate, all my thoughts
are vengeance. Federigo shall die . . . Yes, Clarice,
when next you see your lover, he will be steeped
in his own blood! I swear it! (*He leaves.*)

Music ends.

Scene 29

A Room in the Inn. Enter Truffaldino.

TRUFFALDINO : You'd never believe it . . . Two
masters and none of 'em's had their dinner yet . . .
Of course you know what will happen, don't you?
They'll both want serving at the same time. I'll
be in a right mess then . . .

[*Enter Beatrice.*]

BEATRICE : Ah, there you are, Truffaldino. I'm
ready for dinner.

420

TRUFFALDINO : Everything comes to him who waits !

BEATRICE : Tell the Innkeeper I'll want a table for two. I've asked Signior Pantalone to join me.

TRUFFALDINO : And what would you like to eat, sir?

BEATRICE : Oh, I don't know. Not a lot. Quality rather than quantity, I think.

TRUFFALDINO : Why not leave the ordering to me, sir?

BEATRICE : Oh?

TRUFFALDINO : I'm a bit of an expert in the food line, sir.

BEATRICE : Well, why not? You go ahead. Excel yourself.

TRUFFALDINO : Do you mean a bit of the old 'Haute Cuisine', sir?

BEATRICE : Exactly.

TRUFFALDINO : You can have the utmost confidence in me, sir.

[*Beatrice nods and turns to door bell and rings it.*]

(*To audience.*) I can order what I like ! What do I fancy? What do I fancy?

BEATRICE (*turning back*) : A moment !

TRUFFALDINO : He's gone off his food again ! Yes, sir?

BEATRICE : Take this Banker's order, will you, (*Hands it to him.*) and put it in my trunk. Now be careful with it . . . It is a letter of credit for four thousand crowns.

TRUFFALDINO : Don't worry. Everything's safe with me, sir.

BEATRICE : Then I shall leave everything to you. I won't be long.

[*Smeraldina ushers Beatrice off. Truffaldino sees her and greets her saucily. She reacts then goes out. Truffaldino is left alone.*]

TRUFFALDINO (*to Smeraldina*): Hey up! (*To audience.*) Now's my chance to impress him with my taste and discernment. You didn't think I could be gastronomical, did you? Let me tell you I've had many a master what's gourmetted themselves. The problem, though, is this Banker's Note. Still, I can always pop it in his trunk later. There's no time to lose. Food's calling! Brighella! Brighella! (*He goes out.*)

Scene 30

The same. Truffaldino calling 'Brighella' re-enters. Brighella enters.

BRIGHELLA: You called me, did you?

TRUFFALDINO: I did.

BRIGHELLA: What do you want?

TRUFFALDINO: My master is entertaining a friend for lunch. He know's I'm a bit of a connoisseur in these matters, and he's left the table arrangements to me.

BRIGHELLA: Oh, very well, then.

TRUFFALDINO: Now then. I want the best table you've got.

BRIGHELLA: I'll have you know this is a first class establishment. All my special guests eat in private rooms. I'll put your master and his guest in there. (*Pointing off.*)

TRUFFALDINO: Now what can we have to eat?

422

BRIGHELLA : For two persons—two courses—four dishes each.

TRUFFALDINO : My master asked for five or six—so we'd better make it seven or eight. (*To audience.*) Seven or eight, eh?

BRIGHELLA : Something special, perhaps?

TRUFFALDINO : Something special, naturally.

BRIGHELLA : Well, as a first course, may I recommend my *gazpacho andalus con cerezas*.

TRUFFALDINO : Oh yeth—and wath thath?

BRIGHELLA : Cold Spanish soup with cherries. Then I can offer a choice of my pasta or my fish, or my fricassee, and to finish off with, you shall have my pudden.

TRUFFALDINO : I beg your pardon?

BRIGHELLA : I said to finish off with, you shall have my pudden.

TRUFFALDINO : Say Poodeeng.

BRIGHELLA : No Pudden.

TRUFFALDINO : Say Pooo

BRIGHELLA : Pooo.

TRUFFALDINO : DINNGG.

BRIGHELLA : DINNNGG.

TRUFFALDINO : GGE.

BRIGHELLA : GGE.

TRUFFALDINO : POOODINNNGE.

BRIGHELLA : Pudden.

TRUFFALDINO : What is it, anyway?

BRIGHELLA : It's an English dish. And I'll have you know that people come from miles around, just to gaze at my pudden.

TRUFFALDINO : DO they really? What about the laying of the table?

BRIGHELLA : Oh, I leave that to the waiters.

TRUFFALDINO : Oh no, you don't. The laying of the table is the very first ingrediment. Everything

depends on it. Allow me to demonstrate the laying
of a table . . . (*Starts miming laying the table.*) Get
hold of that.
BRIGHELLA : Get hold of what?
TRUFFALDINO : The table.

[*Truffaldino and Brighella mime picking up heavy
table and moving it downstage centre. Truffaldino
then picks up imaginary table cloth and spreads
it over imaginary table.*]

Music : 'Palm Court'.

[*Truffaldino smooths down table cloth and gestures
to Brighella who drops corner of table cloth neatly
into place. Truffaldino goes to table left, and brings
back imaginary cruet and places it on table.*]

Condiments—Salt—Pepper—Mustard.

[*He holds up three fingers. So does Brighella.
Truffaldino goes to table and gets knife.*]

Knife. (*Goes back to table left and returns holding
up another knife.*) Guess what?
BRIGHELLA : Another knife.

[*Truffaldino puts second knife on table and goes
back to table left to get a fork.*]

TRUFFALDINO : Fork. (*He puts it down and goes
back to table left.*) And another.

[*He brings back another fork but drops it. Bends
down to pick it up and bangs his head on table.
Brighella picks it up and rubs it clean. Truffaldino*]

gestures to Brighella to put it on table. Brighella does so. Truffaldino then moves it slightly.]

The table is laid. Now where do we put the food?
BRIGHELLA : Ah, the food.

[*He lays out the food in a balletic fashion, Truffaldino reacting as required.*]

I puts my meat here. (*Puts it on table from above it.*) My taters here. (*Puts it at top left hand corner.*) My carrots I put here. (*He trips round left end of table holding carrots high and does ballet jump when over at left.*) And my peas . . . (*He walks into bottom right hand corner of table and hurts himself.*)
TRUFFALDINO : Yes, it does bring the water to your eyes.

[*Tape music runs out about now. The rest of the mime is done without music.*]

BRIGHELLA (*walking as though in pain*) : And my peas I put here. (*He puts them down from above table.*)
TRUFFALDINO : Meat — potatoes — carrots — peas. And what goes in the middle, please?
BRIGHELLA (*Miming it as he speaks*) : In the middle I puts—My pudden.

[*Both greet this with rapture. Then Truffaldino says—*]

TRUFFALDINO : Wrong. The meat goes in the middle.

[*They start to argue, then start to walk and bump*

425

into table, walk round it and come to the centre of the stage still arguing.]

TRUFFALDINO : There's the taters, carrots, peas, pudden, and the meat goes in the middle.

They kneel down and to demonstrate his point Truffaldino starts tearing up the banknote and putting the bits in various places on the ground.

Scene 31

The same. Beatrice and Pantelone enter and come behind them. Both have hats and sticks.

BEATRICE : What have you done to my banknote?
TRUFFALDINO (*in horror*) : Banknote?

[*Brighella gets up. Truffaldino starts picking up the bits.*]

BEATRICE : So that's the way you look after my things, is it?
TRUFFALDINO (*picking up bits*) : Don't worry, sir. I can always stick it together again.
BEATRICE : You deserve a good beating? Don't you think so, Signior Pantalone?
PANTALONE : Don't worry. I can always write you out another one.
TRUFFALDINO : It's not my fault, sir. I was only demonstrating my table arrangements.
BEATRICE (*giving Truffaldino both sticks, her hat in his hand and Pantalone's hat on his head which*

426

goes down over his eyes): You have got excuses for everything. Now then, off with you.

[*Truffaldino goes out with hats and sticks.*]

PANTALONE : I really don't understand that chap, you know. Sometimes he's as shrewd as they make them, other times, you couldn't think of a bigger fool.

BEATRICE : He acts stupid on purpose, the rogue. (*To Brighella.*) Well now, is dinner ready?

BRIGHELLA : Well, if you're going to have seven dishes for each course, it's going to take a bit of time, I'm afraid.

PANTALONE : What's all this about seven dishes? If you'll allow me, sir, we'll take pot luck—a soup and a couple of dishes—my tastes are simple.

BRIGHELLA : Very good. Is there anything particular that you fancy, sir?

PANTALONE : I'd like some meat balls if you have them. My teeth are not very good nowadays.

BRIGHELLA (*peering at Pantalone's teeth*): No they're not, sir, are they. If you'll stay here, dinner will be ready directly.

[*Brighella heads towards exit.*]

BEATRICE : Tell Truffaldino to wait on us.
BRIGHELLA : Yes, I'll tell him. (*He goes.*)

Scene 32

The same.

PANTALONE : It is most kind of you, Signior, to take me out to luncheon.

427

BEATRICE : Not at all, Signior. Think of tomorrow. Tomorrow I shall wed your daughter.

PANTALONE : Ah, I could not have given her to a more manly man—the power of your sword—your looks—and if I may say so, sir, your riches—you have it all, sir, you have it all.

[*Brighella enters. Followed by fat waiter who carries very large tray with two place settings and the check pudding cloth on it. He also has table cloth over arm. Second comes young waiter with smaller tray with bread, jug of wine, and two glasses on it. Third comes old waiter with very small tray with silver vase and one rose on it.*
They cross in line in front of Brighella and go out.]

BRIGHELLA (*as he enters*) : Come along, then. This way. Lay the table.

PANTALONE : They're very quick about their business here.

BRIGHELLA (*as old waiter crawls past him*) : Oh, they're like lightning, sir, like lightning. (*He helps old waiter on his way with a kick, and then goes out.*)

Scene 33

The same. Very slow 'Palm Court'.

PANTALONE : In my younger days I used to dine at a lovely little place along the Grand Canal, facing the Rialto. I used to eat there with my friends. What times we had. Such wines—such exquisite dishes. Oh, had you but known that company. Such hearts—sincerity—openness—truth. We talked and we talked—we thrashed it all out—we were young then. Why isn't it the same now? It should be better . . . I'm older—wiser . . . and I've got more money. Why has it all gone? Gone . . . It'll come back . . . My daughter off my hands. I'll be gone again . . . Young!

Music fades.

During this speech the three waiters have re-entered. The fat waiter and the young waiter have set the table in the centre of the stage. The old waiter goes off but can be seen setting a tray. (This tray has four dessert plates on top of which are two clean soup plates, one plate of grated cheese, one plate of croutons and also one table spoon.) The fat waiter puts table cloth on tables and places red check pudding cloth at one end and then fetches tray, the contents of which he then lays on the table. All the waiters have gone off stage by the end of Pantalone's speech.

Scene 34

The same. Truffaldino enters with enormous tureen half-full of thick green pea soup with ladle in it. He has table spoon in his pocket.

TRUFFALDINO : Soup? Would you kindly oblige me by taking your seats in the other room, sir, with your spoons at the ready. (*He puts the tureen on the table.*)

BEATRICE : Go and put the soup on the table.

TRUFFALDINO : After you, sir.

PANTALONE (*moving to exit*) : I suppose we'd better humour this strange servant of yours.

BEATRICE (*following him, then turning back to Truffaldino*) : I want less foolery and more service, understand?

[*Beatrice and Pantalone go out.*]

TRUFFALDINO : Always a privilege and always a pleasure, sir. (*Picking up the crouton and cheese plates, then the two clean soup plates, waiter fashion, on his left arm and in his left hand. To audience.*) No taste—no discernment! After all the trouble I've taken over his cold Spanish soup with cherries, what does he end up with? Pea soup and crumbs! I ask you! Look at that!

(*Picks up a ladle full of the green pea soup and lets it slop back into the tureen, then fills both soup plates half-full and comes left of table still talking to audience.*) Oh well, I suppose I'd better taste it for them. (*Takes tablespoon out of pocket.*) Always got my spoon at the ready. (*Has two tastes.*) Mmmm—lovely.

BEATRICE (*offstage*) : Truffaldino !

TRUFFALDINO : Coming, sir. On the pea soup ! (*And he goes out with all four plates.*)

[*Enter young waiter with covered dish containing 'Lasagne bolognese' with a fork sticking in it.*]

YOUNG WAITER : Where's that Truffaldino chap? I thought he wanted to serve. Oh well, I'll do it myself.

430

[*Truffaldino enters (with nothing in hands) and to right of young waiter.*]

TRUFFALDINO : What's this?

YOUNG WAITER (*lifting lid and offering dish*): Lasagne Bolognese!

TRUFFALDINO (*taking dish*): It looks like Lasagne— it smells like Lasagne—(*Taking forkful and eating*) and, by golly, it tastes like lasagne. On the lasagne!

[*Young waiter takes soup tureen from table and goes out with tureen and lasagne lid. Truffaldino sets off to serve the lasagne. Just as he gets near the door Florindo enters with hat and stick, and to left of table.*]

FLORINDO : Truffaldino!

TRUFFALDINO (*turning*): Sir?

FLORINDO : Where are you going with that dish?

TRUFFALDINO : I was just about to put it on the table, sir.

FLORINDO : Who's it for?

TRUFFALDINO : For you, sir.

FLORINDO : Why are you putting it on the table before you knew I was back in the house?

TRUFFALDINO : Er—I saw you through the window, sir.

FLORINDO : You were quick, weren't you?

TRUFFALDINO : Always my anxiety to please, sir.

FLORINDO : Haven't you made a mistake?

TRUFFALDINO : Sir?

FLORINDO : What is that curious-looking stuff? Lasagne? Isn't it?

TRUFFALDINO : Yes, sir.

FLORINDO : Yes, I thought it was. Then why are you bringing me the lasagne before the soup?

431

TRUFFALDINO : In Venice, sir, we have the soup last.

FLORINDO : Indeed.

TRUFFALDINO : It's very much the custom—very much *di rigeur*, sir.

FLORINDO : Be that as it may, I'll have my soup first. Take that lasagne back into the kitchen and bring me my soup.

[*Florindo crosses right below table heading for room where Beatrice and Pantalone are. Truffaldino goes to other side.*]

Tell me, Truffaldino, where do I have my meals. Is it in here? (*Pointing off.*)

TRUFFALDINO (*yells*) : No!

[*Florindo turns in a surprised manner.*]

(*very softly.*) I mean 'no'—you eat in here, sir. (*Pointing other way.*)

FLORINDO (*crossing below table*) : Oh, very well.

TRUFFALDINO : What would you like to order, sir?

FLORINDO : Oh, leave that to the Innkeeper. Let him provide of his best. (*To audience.*) Do you know, I've been to the Post Office and I can't find out where Beatrice is staying. Oh, well, I'd better keep up my spirits. Still, a good meal might help. Yes, that's it. Eat, and live in hope.

[*During this Truffaldino has been tiptoeing across with the dish of lasagne. Florindo turns and sees him.*]

Truffaldino! Take that lasagne back into the kitchen and bring me my soup! (*He goes out.*)

TRUFFALDINO (*to audience*) : I've got one master in here and one master in there. If I pull this off it really will be something to boast of. (*As he goes out*). On the lasagne! (*He goes with dish.*)

[*As he goes we hear Beatrice's voice offstage*: 'Thank you, Truffaldino, that looks delicious. *Old waiter enters carrying fish dish with lid and followed by the young waiter.*]

OLD WAITER : Truffaldino? Where is he?
YOUNG WAITER : He's not here. Right. I'll take it.

[*Old waiter and young waiter both tug at dish Truffaldino enters empty handed.*]

TRUFFALDINO : Hey, just a minute. What's this?
OLD WAITER (*lifting lid and handing it to young waiter*) : River trout with Bearnaise sauce.
TRUFFALDINO (*taking it*) : River trout with Bearnaise sauce!

[*Truffaldino goes above table and puts fish down. Old waiter goes out. Young waiter stands, holding lid.*]

TRUFFALDINO (*to young waiter*) : Don't just stand there. There's a gentleman waiting to get his soup down him.
YOUNG WAITER (*starting to go*) : Right. I'll serve him at once.
TRUFFALDINO : I said *lay* the table. I'll do the serving.

[*Old waiter has re-entered with small copper tray. On it are two fish knives and one fish fork.*]

YOUNG WAITER (*as he goes*) : Please yourself.

[*Old waiter comes down to left of Truffaldino with small tray. They both bend down and smell fish and straighten up again. Truffaldino lifts right arm above his head. Truffaldino takes knife from tray held by old waiter. and makes cut in fish.*
(NOTE :—*Fish has base stuck to dish. Then bone with head and tail. Then top part divided in two down line of bone.*)
Truffaldino gets squirt of juice in eye. He rubs it having put knife down he brings right hand above his head again.
Truffaldino takes second knife and makes another cut. This time juice squirts into old waiter's eye. Truffaldino mops it for him. Truffaldino brings right hand up again.
Truffaldino takes fork from tray, separates fish from bone and finishes with bone in hand. He and old waiter bow to each other and old waiter goes out with tray. Truffaldino plays fish bone like a mouth organ, and hums 'Santa Lucia'. As he does this enter fat waiter with large tray, young waiter with medium tray and old waiter with small tray plus vase and rose. (Exactly as they made their first entrance at beginning of banquet.)
They stand in line at left of table gazing in astonishment at Truffaldino.]

TRUFFALDINO : Come on, don't just stand there. Get the table laid up. There's a gentleman waiting for his soup in there.

[*The three waiters go out with their trays. Truffaldino hooks fish bone on to back of old waiter as he goes. Truffaldino picks up the fish.*]

434

TRUFFALDINO : On the river trout with the bearnaise sauce ! (*He goes.*)

[*Re-enter old waiter with small tray. And young waiter with duplicate medium tray (Empty).*]

OLD WAITER : Funny chap, that ! He seems to want to serve here, there, and everywhere.

YOUNG WAITER : What do I care so long as I get my tip. Come on, I'll race you back to the kitchen.

[*Old waiter and young waiter go out. Re-enter Truffaldino carrying one clean soup plate and one breakable (plaster of paris) plate.*]

TRUFFALDINO (*crossing*) : On the pea soup !

[*This phrase is echoed offstage by all three waiters. Truffaldino drops breakable plate and bends down saying: 'Anyone got a dustpan and brush? Look at all this mess, etc. etc.' At the same time the three waiters are calling offstage: 'Red hot', 'Red hot', 'Red hot'.*
Young waiter dumps duplicate soup tureen down. Truffaldino straightens up, picks it up and throws tureen offstage. There is a noisy crockery crash offstage. Almost at once fat waiter comes in with pea soup all over his head and apron. He comes to right of Truffaldino. Truffaldino takes empty soup plate (which he has put on floor) gets spoon out of his pocket and scrapes soup off fat waiter, into soup plate. Truffaldino 'Service with a smile'. He then goes off with soup plate, calling 'On the pea soup'. Florindo is heard offstage saying 'Thank you, Truffaldino, what delicious soup' or words to that effect. Fat waiter goes off. Young]

waiter enters with fricassee dish and lid. Fricassee dish has edible peas scattered over it. Young waiter crosses Truffaldino re-enters and crosses young waiter and turns to him.]

TRUFFALDINO : What's this?

YOUNG WAITER (*lifting lid*) : Fricassee.

TRUFFALDINO (*taking dish*) : Fricawhat?

YOUNG WAITER : Fricassee.

TRUFFALDINO (*picking up a pea*) : Ah, a pea. (*Sings final phrase of 'song of the flea'.*) Ha, ha, ha, ha,— ha, ha, ha, ha. I love a big fat pea.

[*Young waiter puts lid on the floor and applauds. enter fat waiter.*]

TRUFFALDINO (*sings A La Figaro*) : Fricassee.

[*Fat and young waiters stand in oblique line left of table and applaud. Enter old waiter to join the line.*]

TRUFFALDINO (*sings*) : Fricassee.

[*All three waiters applaud.*]

TRUFFALDINO (*sings*) : Fricassee — Fricassee — Fricassee—Fricassee.

BEATRICE (*off*) : Truffaldino !

FLORINDO : (*off*) : Truffaldino !

[*Music 'Figaro'.*]

TRUFFALDINO (*sings*) : Fricassee here (*gesturing right.*)

WAITERS (*singing*) : Fricassee there (*gesturing left.*)

[*This repeats to the music. Truffaldino gets angry and throws peas at waiters. On last phrase . . .*]

TRUFFALDINO (*sings*): What do you mean—what do you mean—What do you mean?

[*Waiters rush off in fury. On last four chords Truffaldino does knees bend, then takes fricassee dish and goes out.*]

TRUFFALDINO (*as he goes*): On the fricassee!
BEATRICE (*off*): Thank you, Truffaldino.

[*As he goes. Old waiter comes in with big dish of trick spaghetti. He has loose end tucked under his arm. Truffaldino re-enters.*]

TRUFFALDINO: What's this?
OLD WAITER: Spaghetti.

[*Music*

Truffaldino takes dish and crosses. Spaghetti starts unwinding.]

BEATRICE (*off*): Truffaldino!
TRUFFALDINO: Sir. (*And he winds spaghetti round old waiter as he crosses him.*)
FLORINDO (*off*): Truffaldino!

[*And more spaghetti is wound round old waiter. They each call offstage once more. By this time old waiter is tightly wound in spaghetti. The rest drops off the dish as Truffaldino heads off. He unwinds old waiter by spinning him round and picks up rest of spaghetti and goes out. Returns at once*

437

with spaghetti tray, bumps into old waiter, handing him tray and spins away. Goes to side and hands tray out. Enter young waiter, with lidded dish of meatballs. (Small rubber balls painted brown).]

YOUNG WAITER *(taking off lid)*: Here—take these meat balls to your master.

[Truffaldino takes three of the meat balls off the dish and starts to juggle with them. Young waiter goes out with dish and lid.]

BEATRICE *(off)*. Truffaldino.

[Truffaldino bounces a ball then takes spoon out of his pocket and goes out with meatball in spoon.]

TRUFFALDINO *(as he goes)*: On the meat balls.

*[At once fat waiter (from offstage side) puts big pudding on wheels on stage. Old waiter takes it from onstage side and staggers downstage with it. Truffaldino re-enters with pile of trick plates and one breakable plate on top. He staggers with them to old waiter, bumps into him and knocks him on to ground. Truffaldino then drops breakable plate and staggers along stage seeming about to throw plates into audience. While all eyes are on Truffaldino, old waiter hooks string that runs to offstage on to hook on pudding. Truffaldino reels round stage with plates, finally throwing them off left. There is a very loud crockery crash off. By now the old waiter has gone off.
Music fades on crash.
Truffaldino comes to pudding and looks at it.]*

TRUFFALDINO : If they think they're going to have any of that, they've got another think coming. That is for me, later.

[*He takes check cloth from table (placed there originally by fat waiter when he laid the table cloth at the beginning of banquet) and covers the pudding.*]

TRUFFALDINO : The pudding's off, and we're on the Flambee.

[*The three waiters repeat his shout 'On the Flambee' as they enter.*]

TRUFFALDINO (*sings A La Figaro*) : Flambee.
WAITERS (*having entered sing*) : Flambee.
TRUFFALDINO (*sings*) : Flambee.
WAITERS (*bringing things down to Truffaldino who is above table; fat waiter puts burner down. Young waiter puts frying pan on burner. Singing*) : Flambee.

[*Music 'Figaro'.*]

TRUFFALDINO (*singing*) : Flambee here.

[*Old waiter hands bottle to Truffaldino, who pours liquid into pan and tips dry ice in.*]

WAITERS (*singing*) : Flambee there.
TRUFFALDINO (*singing*) : Brandy here.
WAITERS (*singing*) : Brandy there,
ALL (*singing*) : mix it up—mix it up—mix it in— mix it in—mix it in. (*Continuing trend of phrase to music.*)

[*While this is going on the two liquids have com-*

bined to make foam in the frying pan—the dry ice is sending out puffs of smoke. Then Truffaldino spoons some foam from frying pan and goes out with it, meanwhile, fat waiter has picked up a paper plate with cotton wool on it and the three (fat, young, old) waiters are in a line just left of table and downstage of it, passing the plate from one to another from inside their pockets—singing 'Oh, it's hot—Oh, it's hot—Oh, it's hot repeated in time to the music. Truffaldino re-enters, crosses the waiters to left, takes the plate from old waiter and throws it with a yell into the audience. The three waiters go out. Truffaldino spoons more foam on to another paper plate and goes off with it. Fat waiter enters with enormous dish of cheese and heads across. Truffaldino re-enters, dashes across, snatches cheese with cry of 'look out!' and off with cheese, shouting 'On the cheese'. Young waiter has come in with second cheese and is heading for other exit with it when Truffaldino comes tearing back with another shout and takes cheese from young waiter and goes out with it. Fat waiter has gone off again and re-enters with huge dish of fruit heading for other side. Truffaldino dashes across stage, grabs fruit, and goes out with it, with another shout, old waiter comes in with second dish of fruit. Truffaldino re-enters. dashes across and misses the fruit. Comes back to old waiter, takes the fruit and turns it sideways, so audience can see fruit is stuck on and goes off. All waiters go, Truffaldino returns and leans on table exhausted.

Music fades.]

TRUFFALDINO (*he stands in centre of stage and shouts off to right*) : Everything all right, sir?

BEATRICE (*off*) : Thank you, Truffaldino.

TRUFFALDINO (*shouting off left*) : Everything all right, sir?

FLORINDO (*off*) : Thank you, Truffaldino, that was delicious.

TRUFFALDINO (*to audience*) : I've done it. Served two masters at the same time, and neither of them knows the other exists.

Fast curtain.

ACT TWO

Scene 1

Area before Inn.

Music.

There is soft laughter and live music coming from inside the Inn.

Music, 'Fiesta'.

Smeraldina enters. She carries a fan and has one letter to Federigo Rasponi tucked in her bosom, and a duplicate tucked up her pantalettes.

SMERALDINA : Here's a fine how d'ye, do, if you like. My young mistress wants me to go inside that Inn and deliver this letter.

[*Laughter from inn. Music is still playing softly.*]

What? Go inside a tavern? A young girl like me? Never! And here's another thing : this letter is addressed to Federigo Rasponi. Now what do you make of that? My mistress is supposed to be in love with Silvio. Right then. What's she sending this letter to Federigo for? Makes you think, doesn't it? What's her game then? Hey, one for winter, one for summer, is that it?

[*Laughter from Inn. Music still plays.*]

Anyway, I'm not going in there. Some people have to be respectable, don't they? If I shout loud enough somebody might come out . . .

442

[*Music and voices fade.*]

Ho there! Anybody there? Landlord? Waiters? Anybody?

[*Enter old waiter. Napkin under chin.*]

OLD WAITER : Were you calling me, miss?

SMERALDINA : Tell me, my good man, is Federigo Rasponi staying here?

OLD WAITER : Eh?

SMERALDINA : I said—Is Federigo Rasponi staying here, you silly old fool.

OLD WAITER : Yes, he is, miss. He's just finished eating.

SMERALDINA : Tell him I've got a letter here for him.

OLD WAITER : Why not step inside and give it to him?

SMERALDINA : What? Go inside there! I'm a good girl, I am. You tell him I'm here.

OLD WAITER : I can't disturb him now. He's with Signior Pantalone.

SMERALDINA : My Master, oh dear!

OLD WAITER : I could send his servant to you if you like.

SMERALDINA : His servant? Oooo, you mean the one with the blue eyes and the fair hair?

OLD WAITER : Yes, that's the one.

SMERALDINA : Oooo—you tell him I'm here.

OLD WAITER : All right, I will. (*Aside.*) Fancies him, does she? She won't come inside, but she'll be seen talking to a young fellow in the street. I'll never understand these modern young girls. (*He goes.*)

SMERALDINA (*to audience*) : Hey, what if my master should see me here, what shall I say? Ah, I've got it. I came looking for you, sir, bumped into this servant, and thought he might tell me where you were. That'll do.

Scene 2

The same. Truffaldino enters with napkin under his chin, obviously having just finished eating.

TRUFFALDINO : You sent for me Signiorina?

SMERALDINA : Oh yes. O, I haven't disturbed you, have I.

TRUFFALDINO : Not at all, my pleasure.

SMERALDINA : Oh, I haven't taken you away from your meal, have I?

TRUFFALDINO : Don't worry. If needs be, I can always return to it.

SMERALDINA : Oh well, I'm sorry if I've put you out.

TRUFFALDINO : Don't mention. In fact a little tranquil gazing in your eyes might help me to digest things a bit.

SMERALDINA : Oh, you flatterer!

TRUFFALDINO : What can I do for you, sweetheart?

SMERALDINA (*aside*) : Sweetheart! He doesn't waste his time, this one, does he? (*To Truffaldino.*) My young mistress would like this letter given to Federigo Rasponi.

TRUFFALDINO : Say no more. It'll be delivered. But in the meantime I've got a little message for you too.

SMERALDINA : For me?

TRUFFALDINO : Yes, do you happen to know a chap that goes by the name of Truffaldino?

SMERALDINA : Truffaldino. (*Aside.*) But that's his name, isn't it?

TRUFFALDINO : Well?

SMERALDINA : The name does seem vaguely familiar. Tell me about him.

TRUFFALDINO : Ah, I'm glad you asked that. He's a lovely looking fellow. He's lively, full of spirit, a lovely talker . . . an extremely fine master of ceremonies . . . he's elegant—he's dignified.

SMERALDINA : Ah, I don't know him.

TRUFFALDINO : What do you mean, you don't know him?

SMERALDINA : No such man exists.

TRUFFALDINO : I think you're mistaken—he not only exists but . . .

SMERALDINA : But what?

TRUFFALDINO : He's taken a bit of a fancy to you.

SMERALDINA : Taken a fancy?

TRUFFALDINO : Fallen head over heels.

SMERALDINA : Oh, don't be ridiculous.

TRUFFALDINO : Can't you take pity on him. He loves from afar.

SMERALDINA : Does he indeed?

TRUFFALDINO : Tell me, if he was to show himself to you . . .

SMERALDINA : You what?

TRUFFALDINO : I mean, if you was to see him, how would you take to him?

SMERALDINA : Well, I haven't seen him yet, have I?

TRUFFALDINO : But if you saw him?

SMERALDINA : Well, if he was to my liking, then . . .

TRUFFALDINO : Then what?

445

SMERALDINA : It could be I might give him a little encouragement.

TRUFFALDINO : A little encouragement? I'll get him.

SMERALDINA : Get him?

TRUFFALDINO : He's in here.

SMERALDINA : Who is?

TRUFFALDINO : Him what loves you. Hold on. I'll send him out. (*He goes.*)

SMERALDINA (*to audience*) : Oh dear ! It wasn't him after all. It's some stranger.

[*Music. 'Tango' with introductory chords.*
Truffaldino enters dancing. With a rose in his hand.
He does tango round Smeraldina, offering her rose and snatching it back. During this he says 'For you'. He leans over and they collapse on floor. Then dances her about the stage. She enters into the spirit of it and follows him across. Truffaldino goes off still dancing.
Music fades.]

SMERALDINA (*to audience*) : What was all that about?

TRUFFALDINO : (*re-entering without rose*) : Did you see him?

SMERALDINA : Who?

TRUFFALDINO : Him what loves you.

SMERALDINA : I only saw you.

TRUFFALDINO : Well?

SMERALDINA : You mean . . . ?

[*Truffaldino nods slowly.*]

SMERALDINA : You?

TRUFFALDINO : Me.

SMERALDINA : Why didn't you say?

446

TRUFFALDINO : I'm shy.
SMERALDINA : Shy?
TRUFFALDINO (*nods*) : Bashful.
SMERALDINA (*aside*) : Hey, he's serious, he's not fooling.
TRUFFALDINO : Well?
SMERALDINA : Well what?
TRUFFALDINO : D'you have nothing to say to me?
SMERALDINA : Yes.
TRUFFALDINO : What?
SMERALDINA : I'm bashful as well.
TRUFFALDINO : Then why don't we team up? We'd make a right couple of bashfuls.

[*He starts to sing tango music and dances her to left, she breaks away right.*]

SMERALDINA : That's enough.
TRUFFALDINO : Don't ring a bell? Strike a chord? Aren't you the least bit smit?
SMERALDINA : I'm not saying.
TRUFFALDINO : Tell me, purely as a matter of information . . . if a feller was contemplating marriage, what would a feller have to do?
SMERALDINA : Ah, now, you're asking.
TRUFFALDINO : I'm putting it to you purely hypertheroretical, you understand.
SMERALDINA : Well, seeing as how I've got no father and mother, such a fellow would have to speak to my master and mistress.
TRUFFALDINO : And if such a fellow did that, what would they say?
SMERALDINA : Well, if they thought such a fellow was going to make me happy . . . then . . .
TRUFFALDINO : Say no more. Give us the letter and when I come back we'll have a chat.

SMERALDINA : That'll be nice.

[*She feels in bosom and looks up horrified. Then turns her back on Truffaldino and feels up her skirt. Truffaldino lies on floor and tries to see up her skirt as she finds the letter. She springs away with a squeal.*]

TRUFFALDINO : Just a peep. (*He gets up.*)

[*Smeraldina hands him the letter.*]

Know what's in it then, do you?
SMERALDINA : No, but I'm very curious.
TRUFFALDINO : So am I.
SMERALDINA : You're opening it?
TRUFFALDINO : Well, there might be something in that letter that would so enrage my master, he'd give me a good thump. You don't want that, do you?
SMERALDINA : Oh, no.
TRUFFALDINO : Well, then. We read it.
SMERALDINA : How will you seal it up again?
TRUFFALDINO : Leave it to me. I've got a knack that is fantastic. (*He studies the letter.*) Oh well, here goes. Can you read?
SMERALDINA : A bit . . . can you?
TRUFFALDINO : Well yes, . . . just a bit. Here goes then.
SMERALDINA : Here goes.

[*Truffaldino opens it tearing part of the letter.*]

SMERALDINA : Go on, then, read it.
TRUFFALDINO : No, no, you read it.
SMERALDINA : You read it.

TRUFFALDINO : It's your mistress's handwriting, isn't it? You read it.

SMERALDINA : Truffaldino . . . I must confess to you . . . I can't read.

TRUFFALDINO : You can't read? Heugh! Neither can I.

SMERALDINA : You can't . . . why did you open it then?

TRUFFALDINO : Well, I've had a few lessons.

SMERALDINA : How far did you get?

TRUFFALDINO : I almost learnt the A, B, C, all the way up to D.

SMERALDINA : I learnt the alphabet once.

TRUFFALDINO : You did? Well, we've got the basic fundamentals. Let's get down to it. Comfy?

SMERALDINA : Yes.

TRUFFALDINO : This letter looks like an M.

SMERALDINA : Is it? No, I think it's an R.

TRUFFALDINO : Are you sure it's an R?

SMERALDINA : Yes, R's have got little squiggles on them.

TRUFFALDINO : I thought it was M's that had got the squiggles.

SMERALDINA : No it's the R's.

TRUFFALDINO : Oh well, M's or R's. Let get down to it.

[*He kisses her. They come up for air.*]

What's next?

SMERALDINA : Ah!

TRUFFALDINO : We've been through all that.

They kiss again.

Scene 3

The same. Beatrice and Pantalone enter.

PANTALONE : What are you doing down there?

SMERALDINA : Me, sir? Nothing, sir. I was looking for you, sir.

PANTALONE : Eh? What about?

SMERALDINA : Er . . . My mistress wants you.

BEATRICE (*to Truffaldino*) : What's that you've got?

TRUFFALDINO : Nothing, sir. It's just a piece of paper, sir.

BEATRICE : Let me see it.

TRUFFALDINO : It's of no importance whatsoever, sir.

PANTALONE : Let me see it—Smeraldina, give me that letter.

BEATRICE : I've got it. (*Taking letter from Truffaldino.*) This letter is addressed to me! Did you open it?

TRUFFALDINO : Me, sir, no, sir.

BEATRICE : This is the second time today!

PANTALONE : What is it, Signior?

BEATRICE (*to Pantalone*) : A letter from Clarice . . this rascal has opened it.

TRUFFALDINO : No, sir.

PANTALONE (*to Smeraldina*) : You helped him, did you?

SMERALDINA : No, sir. Innocent, sir.

BEATRICE (*to Truffaldino*) : So you must have opened it!

TRUFFALDINO : No, sir. Innocent, sir.

PANTALONE (*to Smeraldina*) : Then you did?

SMERALDINA : Not me.

PANTALONE : Who was delivering it then?

TRUFFALDINO ⎫
SMERALDINA ⎭ *(together)* : ⎰ She was.
⎱ He was.

TRUFFALDINO : Yes, but Smeraldina brought it to Truffaldino.

SMERALDINA : What did you say that for? You've dropped me right in it now. Well, I've done with you!

PANTALONE *(to Smeraldina)* : So you are responsible, you hussy. I've a good mind to smack your . . .

SMERALDINA : How dare you, sir. No man has ever slapped my . . .

PANTALONE : Answer me back, would you? I'll soon show you, you witch!

SMERALDINA : Have to catch me first. Come on then. Let's see you run. *(She runs off.)*

PANTALONE : Wretched girl . . . You'll see if I can run or not. I'll get you! I'll get you!

He leaves, running after Smeraldina. They chase through various openings and leave.

Scene 4

The same.

BEATRICE *(looking over the letter)* : Poor sad Clarice. Silvio's jealousy makes her desperate. Perhaps I should tell Silvio who I am.

[*Meanwhile Truffaldino tries to creep away left.*]

BEATRICE : Hey! You! Where are you going?

TRUFFALDINO : I've got a headache.

BEATRICE : Come here! Why did you open this letter?

TRUFFALDINO : *Me*? I thought it was Smeraldina, sir.

BEATRICE : Smeraldina! . . . It was you, you rogue. That's twice in one day you have opened my letters. Well, you've asked for a beating and now you're going to get it.

[*Beatrice takes the carpet beater from nail on wall, and beats Truffaldino with it. Truffaldino howls.*]

FLORINDO (*off*) : Who dares to beat my servant?

TRUFFALDINO : Ow! Ow! Ow!

BEATRICE : Silence villain! I'll teach you to open my letters. (*She strikes him again, throws the beater on the ground and leaves.*)

Scene 5

The same. Truffaldino picks up carpet beater.

TRUFFALDINO : That's how you treat me, is it? If a servant displeases, you dismiss him, you don't beat him.

[*Florindo enters in his shirt sleeves.*]

FLORINDO : What's that you say?

TRUFFALDINO : I said if a servant displeases you dismiss him, you don't . . . I mean no gentleman should beat another gentleman's servant. It's an affront.

FLORINDO : Yes, indeed, I have received an affront.
Who did it?

TRUFFALDINO : I don't know him from Adam, sir.

FLORINDO : Why did he beat you?

TRUFFALDINO : Er . . . he just felt like it, sir.

FLORINDO : And you didn't move?

TRUFFALDINO : No, sir.

FLORINDO : You did nothing to defend yourself?

TRUFFALDINO : No, sir.

FLORINDO : You exposed your master to an affront,
an insult, a dangerous situation?

TRUFFALDINO : Yes, sir.

[*Both laugh.*]

FLORINDO : I see. Truffaldino, would you mind
passing me that carpet beater?

TRUFFALDINO : A pleasure, sir. (*He does so.*)

FLORINDO : Well, you coward, you fool, you numb-
skull, since beating seems to be your delight, I
will beat you again. Come here.

[*Florindo grabs Truffaldino by the collar and beats
him with the carpet beater. Truffaldino howls.
Florindo turns his back on Truffaldino and freezes.*]

TRUFFALDINO (*to audience*): Oh, Oh, I can truly
say I'm the servant of two masters now. I've just
had my wages from both of them.

[*Florindo turns back to Truffaldino.*]

FLORINDO : You deserved that beating, my good
fellow. (*Aside.*) It has always been my practice to
have a short sleep after my meal. (*To Truffaldino.*)
When I awake we will go and find your Pasquale.

TRUFFALDINO : But, sir . . .

FLORINDO : We will go and find him together. (*He goes out with the carpet beater.*)

TRUFFALDINO : But, sir . . . Go and find Pasquale together, he said. (*To audience.*) Oh, I'm in a right mess now. Still, best face that hurdle when I come to it. Now, there was something I had to do . . . concentrate, Truff. Master Number One said to give his clothes an airing. If I do them both together it'll save a bit of time and I'll keep on the right side of both of them . . . But what with the heat and things I'll need a bit of help. Waiter! Waiter!

Music 'Fiesta'.

Scene 6

The same. Truffaldino lowers a clothes line. Young waiter and boy enter. Young waiter is chewing a chicken leg.

YOUNG WAITER : Yes? What do you want?

TRUFFALDINO : Give me a hand, will you, to put a couple of trunks out of here?

YOUNG WAITER (*to boy*): Go on then. Do as he says.

TRUFFALDINO : What about you?

YOUNG WAITER : Me? I'm sweating. (*Wipes off sweat.*)

TRUFFALDINO : Oh, all right. Come along, mate, this way.

[*Truffaldino and boy go out.*]

454

YOUNG WAITER (*to audience*): Seems a good servant, don't he? But what's he got up his sleeve, eh? In service nothing's done for love. You get your master to trust you, then swindle him for all you can.

[*Truffaldino and boy re-enter carrying Beatrice's brown trunk. They place it, inwards, under clothes line.*]

TRUFFALDINO (*as they carry it*): Careful now—over here—that's it. Down your end. Good. Now let's get the other. But we'll have to be very quiet with this one as my master's asleep in there.

[*Truffaldino and boy go out.*]

YOUNG WAITER (*to audience*): I don't know if you've noticed it, but he's got two masters. I'm going to keep an eye on him. One day he might try to rob the pair of them. I'll report him and I might make a penny or two.

[*Truffaldino and boy re-enter with Florindo's green trunk. They put this slightly upstage of the other trunk.*]

TRUFFALDINO: That's it. Careful with it. Over here. Thanks very much, mate.

[*Boy goes out. Young waiter comes to right of Truffaldino who is by Florindo's trunk, dusts it with his serving cloth and holds out his hand for a tip.*]

YOUNG WAITER: Everything all right, then?

TRUFFALDINO (*shaking his hand*): Thanks very much. I'll see you at the end of the week.

YOUNG WAITER (*as he goes*): Best of luck to you, mate. While it lasts!

(*Note*: This sequence should be done at great speed.)

[*Truffaldino starts unpacking Florindo's trunk first. He takes out a cloth covered book, looks at it, saying 'I wish I could read' and throws it on the ground between the two trunks. Then he takes out Florindo's own purple jacket. Then a rope of clothes sewn together which he throws over left end of clothes line. Then he goes to Beatrice's trunk. He takes out another rope of clothes and throws it over clothes line—just right of the other one. Then he takes out a dress.*

Music and singing fade as he brings out dress.

Truffaldino holds out dress to audience.]

TRUFFALDINO: I told you I'd have to watch myself with that one!

[*He hangs dress on clothes line (just in front of Beatrice's trunk which he has closed after taking out dress) and feels in pocket of dress.*]

TRUFFALDINO: Let's have a look in the pockets. Any sugared almonds? Nobility loves its little nibble on the quiet. (*Feeling in pocket and bringing out a small miniature.*) What's this? a portrait! What a handsome looking lad! It looks rather like my master, Florindo, in there, but it can't be him. He hasn't got a moustache in this.

FLORINDO (*off—sleepily*): Truffaldino!

TRUFFALDINO: Strike! He's woken up. If he comes out here he'll want to know whose this trunk is, and I'll be in a right mess then. Quick, Truff, get the things back.

FLORINDO (*off—louder*): Truffaldino!

TRUFFALDINO: Coming, sir. (*He starts to shove back the clothes. The miniature he shoves into the pocket [or appears to—there is a duplicate already set there] of Florindo's purple jacket and puts in his trunk with other articles.*)

Won't be a moment, sir. I've one or two things to do and I'll be with you in a flash, sir. Strewth, I've mixed them all up. (*Shoving other clothes into Beatrice's trunk.*)

FLORINDO (*yells—off*): Truffaldino! Are you coming, or do I have to come out there and beat you again?

[*Truffaldino is frantically getting remaining clothes into trunks. Last of all he picks up the diary—hesitates—and throws it into Beatrice's trunk and closes them both.*]

TRUFFALDINO: No, sir, anything but that, sir. I'm right with you, sir. (*He appears to haul up clothes line.*)

*

Scene 7

The same. Florindo enters wearing dressing gown. He looks at Truffaldino hauling rope.

FLORINDO : What on earth are you doing?

TRUFFALDINO : Never idle, sir. I' was just about to give your clothes an airing.

FLORINDO (*crossing to table, glancing at Beatrice's trunk*) : Whose trunk is that?

TRUFFALDINO : Mystery, sir. Some guest or other staying at the Inn.

FLORINDO (*taking off dressing gown and putting it on table*) : I think I'll wear my other purple coat. Give it to me, please.

TRUFFALDINO (*going to Florindo's trunk and opening it*) : One purple coat, sir, coming up. (*He helps Florindo on with it.*) Lovely cut, sir.

[*Florindo pats his pockets and feels something there. He takes out the miniature.*]

FLORINDO : What's this?

TRUFFALDINO (*breaking centre*) : That's torn it.

FLORINDO (*looking at miniature and coming to address the audience*) : Good heavens! This is my portrait! The very portrait I gave to my beloved Beatrice! Tell me, you, how did this portrait find its way into my jacket?

TRUFFALDINO (*aside*) : Oh, dear! Come on—inspiration—think! think!

FLORINDO : Do you hear me? How did this portrait find its way into my pocket?

[*Florindo backs Truffaldino into Beatrice's trunk and Truffaldino sits on it. Florindo stands left of him—menacingly.*]

FLORINDO : I can tell you in a flash, sir.

FLORINDO : Well, then, tell me.

TRUFFALDINO : Er . . . (*Aside.*) Got it! (*He swings round on trunk to face Florindo.*) The portrait's mine, sir.

FLORINDO : Yours?

TRUFFALDINO (*rising*): Yes, sir, I popped it into your trunk for safety. Do forgive me, sir.

FLORINDO : Where did you get it?

TRUFFALDINO : It was left me.

FLORINDO : What?

TRUFFALDINO : Inherited from my previous master.

FLORINDO : Inherited?

TRUFFALDINO : Yes, sir . . . inherited. The master before you, sir, I served honest and well, and when he died he left me that portrait as a token of his appreciation.

FLORINDO : Died? When did he die?

TRUFFALDINO : What's today, sir? Thursday? About a week ago today, sir.

FLORINDO : And what was the name of this master?

TRUFFALDINO : Name, sir? He didn't have a name. He was travelling incognito.

FLORINDO : Incognito? How long did you serve him?

TRUFFALDINO : Oh, about a week or ten days.

FLORINDO (*aside*): Oh heavens! I tremble at the thought that it was Beatrice. She fled in man's dress. She travelled incognito . . . Oh, if this be true!

TRUFFALDINO (*aside*): He seems to be soaking it up all right.

FLORINDO : Tell me, my man . . .

TRUFFALDINO (*aside*): Looks like he's ready for another basinful. (*To Florindo.*) Yes, sir?

FLORINDO : Tell me, my man, was he very young, your master?

TRUFFALDINO : Oh, a youth, sir.

FLORINDO (*aside*): 'Tis she, without a doubt. (*To*

Truffaldino.) Tell me, what town did he come from?

TRUFFALDINO : Town, sir? I've got it right at the tip of my tongue, sir . . .

FLORINDO : Turin, perhaps?

TRUFFALDINO : That's it. Turin. Exactly, sir.

FLORINDO : And he's dead?

TRUFFALDINO : Oh quite, quite dead.

FLORINDO : How did he die?

TRUFFALDINO : Er . . . accident, sir. He was thrown off his horse.

FLORINDO (*aside*) : Oh, reckless girl! (*To Truffaldino*.) Where buried?

TRUFFALDINO : Where buried?

FLORINDO : I must visit the grave.

TRUFFALDINO (*aside*) : There's a difficulty! (*To Florindo*.) A fellow countryman turned up with a licence and shipped the coffin back home.

FLORINDO : And this fellow countryman . . . is he the same fellow who asked you to collect the letters from the post?

TRUFFALDINO : The same man, sir?

FLORINDO : Pasquale?

TRUFFALDINO : You've hit it, sir, Pasquale, precisely!

FLORINDO (*aside*) : Then I have no hope. She is dead. My beloved Beatrice is dead. Oh, how great is my grief! It is too much to bear! (*He goes in despair*.)

Scene 8

The same.

TRUFFALDINO : What's up with him, then? Did you see the tears in his eyes? All upset. I did that. I didn't mean to upset him. I just told him that story so that I wouldn't get another beating. It's that portrait's fault. Some friend of his or other. Oh, how sad. How very sad. Oh, well, enough on my mind without worrying about his troubles. (*He gets dressing gown and puts it in Florindo's trunk.*) Get this stuff out of the way before I drop myself right in it. Hold on, Truff lad, make sure the coast is clear. (*He hears Beatrice's voice offstage, makes a dash for the clothes line*)

[*Beatrice and Pantalone enter, talking business with hats and sticks.*]

BEATRICE : I assure you, Signior Pantalone, some of the invoices you sent me . . . I have received them twice over.

PANTALONE : Duplicated eh?

BEATRICE : I'm afraid so.

PANTALONE : I shall have to look into this.

BEATRICE : Truffaldino !

TRUFFALDINO : Sir?

BEATRICE : What's my trunk doing out here?

TRUFFALDINO : You told me to give your clothes an airing? Sir?

BEATRICE : Good man. You've done it, then?

TRUFFALDINO : I was just getting round to it.

BEATRICE : You idler, what do you do with your time, for Heaven's sake?

TRUFFALDINO (*aside*) : I could tell him !

BEATRICE : Well, open my trunk and give me my . . . Whose trunk is this? (*Pointing to Florindo's trunk.*)

TRUFFALDINO : Some guest or other staying at the Inn, sir.

BEATRICE : Give me my memo book. You'll find it in there.

461

TRUFFALDINO : One memo book . . . (*He opens Beatrice's trunk.*)

[*Beatrice is standing right of Pantalone who is to the side of the table.*]

PANTALONE : I'll have words to say to those copy-clerks of mine. We can't have errors like this.

BEATRICE : Perhaps the mistake is on my side. Anyway, we shall see.

TRUFFALDINO : Here we are, sir !

BEATRICE : Thank you. (*She takes the book without looking at it too closely.*) What's this? This isn't mine.

TRUFFALDINO (*aside*) : Here we go again !

BEATRICE : These are letters I wrote to Florindo . . . His diary ! the hours of our meetings . . . our secret rendezvous . . . How is this?

PANTALONE : What is it, Signior? Anything the matter?

BEATRICE : Truffaldino, how comes this book . . . amongst my things?

TRUFFALDINO : I'll use the same rigmarole as I tried with the other fellow : it worked with him, so why not now? The plain unvarnished truth is this : the book is mine.

BEATRICE : Yours?

TRUFFALDINO : . . . I popped it in your trunk for safety. Do forgive me, sir.

BEATRICE : Yours? How can it be yours? When you gave it me, you would have recognized it.

TRUFFALDINO (*aside*) : This one's a bit more subtle. We're dealing with a brain here.

BEATRICE : Well?

TRUFFALDINO : I've only just acquired it, sir, no

time to peruse it over as one might say . . . I forgot
it was mine, almost.

BEATRICE : Where did you get it?

TRUFFALDINO : The gentleman I was serving here in
Venice suddenly decided to pay his debt to nature.

BEATRICE : What!

TRUFFALDINO : You've hit it. He croaked it! He left
me the book.

BEATRICE : How long ago was this?

TRUFFALDINO : About a week or ten days.

BEATRICE : In Venice?

TRUFFALDINO : In Venice.

BEATRICE : How comes it, then, I found you in
Verona?

TRUFFALDINO (*aside*) : What did I tell you? Brain
power! Brain power!

BEATRICE : Answer me, please.

TRUFFALDINO : I was so overcome by my poor
master's defunction, I went to Verona for a change
of air.

BEATRICE : Can it be true? My Florindo . . . no
more?

TRUFFALDINO : Ah! Perchance I heard you mention
the name Florindo?

BEATRICE : Well?

TRUFFALDINO (*hand to brow*) : Oh, how strange is
life! (*Aside.*) Best play it by ear. (*Then*). O, Fate,
what blows you deal!

BEATRICE : You mean your master . . .

TRUFFALDINO : Yes, Florindo was his name.

BEATRICE : Aretusi?

TRUFFALDINO : Aretusi . . . the same.

BEATRICE : Dead?

TRUFFALDINO : Oh, quite dead.

BEATRICE : How did he die? Where is he buried?

TRUFFALDINO : You'd like to visit the grave, no

doubt? Well, he fell in the Canal, he bobbed up three times and he hasn't been seen since.

BEATRICE : Dead? Florindo . . . dead? If dead, what is life to me? . . . I leave my home . . . my family . . . I smother my woman's heart in man's apparel.

[*Truffaldino mimes the words 'Woman's heart' to audience.*]

I face dangers . . . I hazard all . . . for what? For Florindo . . . And Florindo is no more, O, miserable Beatrice !

[*Truffaldino mimes word 'Beatrice' to audience.*]

There is but one way, then. Florindo, I shall soon be with you. (*She goes.*)

PANTALONE (*gripped with astonishment at both the speech and desperation of Beatrice*) : Truffaldino !

TRUFFALDINO : Signior !

PANTALONE : A woman.

TRUFFALDINO : A female.

PANTALONE : Strange.

TRUFFALDINO : Remarkable.

PANTALONE : I'm all confusion.

TRUFFALDINO : Snap !

PANTALONE : I must go tell my daughter. (*He leaves.*)

TRUFFALDINO : So, I'm not a servant of two masters, after all . . . It's one master; and one . . . Hey— Hey.

Music 'Tarantella'.

He goes out calling 'Waiter—Waiter'.

Scene 9

The boy and the fat waiter enter and strike one trunk.
The two serving wenches enter and strike the other.
As they do this the doctor enters down the stairs.
Music fades as the doctor speaks.

DOCTOR : Ha! How I hate and despise that dog, that rascal, that scoundrel, Pantalone! The more I think of him, the more I want to eructate, crepitate, expectorate and spew.

[*Enter Pantalone.*]

PANTALONE : Ah, my dear, esteemed Doctor . . .
DOCTOR : Ha! I wonder you have the temerity to address me!
PANTALONE : I have news for you. Do you know that . . . ?
DOCTOR (*cutting in*) : You wish to tell me this marriage has taken place. Well let me tell you this : I don't care a fig.
PANTALONE : Please let me speak!
DOCTOR : You may rot, sir! Rot!
PANTALONE : My daughter is free to marry your son.
DOCTOR : Ho! So that's it is it? Oh, much obliged, I must say. Well, my son'll not marry anyone's cast-offs! So? The fine gentleman from Turin doesn't want her any more . . . Ha-Ha!
PANTALONE : The gentleman from Turin is a . . .
DOCTOR : I don't care what he is! You saw to it your daughter was compromised by him. You left 'em alone together . . . *et hoc sufficit*.

465

PANTALONE : Not possible! Listen! The gentleman
from Turin . . .

DOCTOR : I'll not listen—not a word!

PANTALONE : The truth about the gentleman from
Turin . . .

DOCTOR : Truth? Truth? *Veritas* from you?

PANTALONE : Will you hear me speak?

DOCTOR : The Devil take you!

PANTALONE : Very well . . . to hell with you, then!

DOCTOR : You're a disgrace, sir. A dishonour to the
town. A blot upon society! O, you *homo flagitio-
sissimus*! (*He marches off.*)

Scene 10

The same.

PANTALONE : And *pons asinorum* to you! I'll bet he
didn't think I knew that one! I tried to tell him
this man from Turin was a woman and he just
wouldn't listen!

[*Enter Silvio.*]

Here comes his coxcomb of a son! More insolence.
I suppose.

SILVIO (*aside*): Oh, Pantalone! Shall I run this
sword through his breast? Will it give me peace?

PANTALONE : Signior Silvio, before you fly into a
rage, let me tell you I bring you good news.

SILVIO : What news?

466

PANTALONE : You'll listen?

SILVIO : Speak!

PANTALONE : Ah, good! Then I'll have you know, sir, the wedding of my daughter to Signior Federigo will not now take place.

SILVIO : Will not?

PANTALONE : And what's more . . . if you are still of a mind . . . you can marry my daughter.

SILVIO : Marry her?

PANTALONE : You can marry at once.

SILVIO : O, Sir! I am restored from death to life.

PANTALONE : Good! That's settled, then.

SILVIO : But, sir, how can I clasp her to my breast knowing that she is claimed by another man?

PANTALONE : Ah. That's just it! The man is not a man.

SILVIO : Not a man?

PANTALONE : Exactly—Federigo has become his sister.

SILVIO : His sister? I do not understand you, sir.

PANTALONE : Well, it's perfectly simple . . . I hope. He whom we believed to be Federigo has now revealed himself to be Beatrice, his sister.

SILVIO : Oh, I see! Dressed in man's clothing?

PANTALONE : Dressed in man's clothing.

SILVIO : Tell me, how did it happen?

PANTALONE : Let us go into the house. My daughter knows nothing as yet. With one telling of the story you will both be satisfied . . . It will hold you in amazement. So let us go in, take her by the hand and be agog together.

They go out.

Scene 11

A room at the inn.

There is a loud noise of voices offstage right and left.

Music.

Beatrice and Florindo from opposite sides both come out of their rooms, dagger in hand, in the act of committing suicide. They are restrained, Beatrice by Brighella, and Florindo by the old and young waiters from the inn. (They advance in such a way that the two lovers do not see each other.)

BRIGHELLA (*grabbing Beatrice's hand*): Stay! No!
BEATRICE: Unhand me, I say! (*She pushes Brighella away.*)
WAITER (*hanging on to Florindo*): There's no excuse, sir, for taking your own life. 'Tis against the law of heaven!
FLORINDO: Away! Let me die! (*He pushes the waiters away.*)

[*Music fades.*]

Come, blade!
BEATRICE: Come, Death! Beatrice doth welcome thee!

[*Both back to centre, determined to commit suicide. Turn, see each other, recognize each other and are transfixed in amazement. They drop their daggers.*]

468

FLORINDO : Who do I see?
BEATRICE : Florindo?
FLORINDO : *Beatrice* !

[*Music.*]

BEATRICE : You are alive?
FLORINDO : You breathe?
BEATRICE : O, Fate!
FLORINDO : Oh, my soul. Oh, my beloved . . . my Beatrice . . . My own.
BEATRICE : My Florindo . . . My own.
FLORINDO : Oh, ecstasy! Wonder and content do vie within my heart.
BEATRICE : Happiness and amazement in mine!
FLORINDO : My love!
BEATRICE : My all! (*They embrace.*)

[*Music fades.*]

BRIGHELLA (*pointing to the daggers*) : Quick! Pick the knives up before they change their minds!

Young waiter picks up Florindo's dagger, old waiter picks up Beatrice's dagger, and Brighella and the waiters go out.

Scene 12

The same.

FLORINDO : Tell me, my dearest, what brought you to such desperation?

469

BEATRICE : I tremble to think on it. I was told that you were dead.

FLORINDO : Who told you?

BEATRICE : My servant . . . And you, my dearest one . . . What drove *you* to such desperation?

FLORINDO : I, too, tremble to think on't. I was told that *you* were dead.

BEATRICE : Who told you?

FLORINDO : *My* servant.

BEATRICE : It was this diary that made me believe . . .

FLORINDO : My diary? But that was in my trunk . . . And look you, Beatrice, it was this portrait that made me conclude that . . .

BEATRICE : But this portrait was in *my* trunk.

FLORINDO : Good heavens! These rogues of servants we have . . . they are in league.

BEATRICE : Indeed they are! Well, my servant's forever telling me about your servant.

FLORINDO : And mine's forever telling me about yours. What game have they afoot? We must get to the bottom of this. I'll soon fix them! (*Calls.*) Brighella! You wait till I confront them with the truth.

[*Brighella enters.*]

BRIGHELLA : At your service, sir.

FLORINDO : Brighella! Have you seen our servants?

BRIGHELLA : No, I haven't. Would you like me to go and look for 'em, sir?

FLORINDO : Yes, I would, and when you find them, both of them, bring them to us here.

BRIGHELLA : To tell you the honest truth, I've only met one of them, sir. But I'll ask the waiters. They're bound to know the other one. I'll soon fish out the pair of them for you . . . and if I may say so, sir, with all respect, I'm mighty glad to see you've both found death to be so sweet.

BEATRICE (*shaking hands across Florindo with Brighella*) : Thank you, Brighella.

BRIGHELLA (*to Beatrice*) : Ever your servant, sir . . . (*To Florindo, shaking his hand.*) and Madam.

Brighella goes out. Florindo 'registers' being called 'madam'.

Scene 13

The same.

FLORINDO (*urgently*) : Tell me, Beatrice, quickly : Federigo, your brother . . . is he dead?

BEATRICE : Do you doubt it? He died there and then.

FLORINDO : But I was told that he was alive, and here in Venice.

BEATRICE : I followed you, pretending to be him. These are his clothes.

FLORINDO : Why, so they are! I should have guessed . . . I learned from the letter that you were disguised as a man.

BEATRICE : What letter?

FLORINDO : A letter from Maria . . . It fell into my hands. I could not but read it.

BEATRICE : So it was you who opened it! But my servant told me he'd opened it.

FLORINDO : Ah. Now my servant told me that your servant asked my servant to collect it from the post. Still, never mind. When they arrive, we must not treat them with too much severity.

471

BEATRICE : Not?

FLORINDO : No. It would be wiser to treat them with gentleness, kindness, and forbearance. That way we will learn everything.

BEATRICE : You are right.

Scene 14

The same. Voices are heard off. Brighella, old waiter, and Truffaldino. Truffaldino dashes in, sees Beatrice and Florindo, and dashes out again.

FLORINDO : Here comes one of them now.

BEATRICE : Him! To my mind he is the greater rogue of the two.

FLORINDO : He most surely is.

[Beatrice crosses in a temper.]

But calmly, now, Beatrice, calmly, calmly.

[Truffaldino, conducted by force by Brighella and old waiter, enters.]

BRIGHELLA : We've found this one, sir. As soon as we've found the other one, we'll bring him to you.

FLORINDO : Yes, I'd like to deal with both together.

BRIGHELLA *(to old waiter)* : Do you know what the other one looks like, do you?

OLD WAITER : Me? No.

BRIGHELLA : Well, go in the kitchen and find out, you silly old fool.

OLD WAITER *(as Brighella helps him on the way*

with a kick): All right, I'm going . . . I'm going—
I've gone.

Brighella and old waiter go out.

Scene 15

The same.

FLORINDO : Now my man, while we're waiting for
your friend, perhaps you'd tell us a little of how
the portrait and my diary came to be changed
around.
TRUFFALDINO *(quietly to Florindo)*: Sir, there's
something very personal and urgent, I ought to
tell you. It's a matter of honour.
FLORINDO : Honour, you say?
TRUFFALDINO : Just a word on the quiet, sir. Over
there, if you please, sir. *(Gestures to the right.)*

[*Florindo moves away. Truffaldino moves quickly
to right of Beatrice.*]

I've got something to say to that gentleman over
there that I couldn't possibly say in front of a lady.
Excuse.

[*He hurries over to Florindo. Beatrice walks left
and looks up.*]

FLORINDO : Now then . . . a matter of honour, you
say?
TRUFFALDINO : Yes, sir, my honour, as I'll explain.

473

As you probably know the servant of the lady over there is a chap called Pasquale.

FLORINDO : I should by now.

TRUFFALDINO : Well, I'd like you to know, sir, nothing's my fault. Pasquale done the lot.

FLORINDO : Pasquale?

TRUFFALDINO : Yes, it was Pasquale opened up the trunks, jumbled up the clothes, changed round the portrait and the diary. He came to me and confessed all. Pasquale, I said, you mad, heedless, reckless fool, what have you done? He fell to his knees, (*He kneels.*) he begged me, implored me to do something in case his master found out . . . and me, sir, with my tender heart (*He clasps Florindo round chest.*) what could I do? 'Stop your trembling, dry your eyes.' I said, 'as long as you're the best friend I've got, I'll cover up for you.' (*He rises.*)

FLORINDO : Cover up? Do you know that I'm not awfully sure that I follow you?

TRUFFALDINO : Let you think it was me when it was him.

FLORINDO : Oh I see. What a sensitive nature you have.

TRUFFALDINO : I was born with it, sir.

BEATRICE (*calls*) : Have you two finished discussing your secrets yet?

FLORINDO : Beatrice . . . the most remarkable thing! This fellow has been telling me all about a servant whose name . . .

TRUFFALDINO : No . . . don't tell her, sir. Don't tell her. I must save Pasquale.

FLORINDO : You show a strange affection for this Pasquale.

TRUFFALDINO : I love him like a brother, sir. Now with your permission, I'm going to tell the lady everything's my fault. She can beat me, chastise me, ill treat me as she will, but I shall save Pasquale! (*He starts backing away to join Beatrice.*)

FLORINDO : Good man.

TRUFFALDINO : Thank you, sir. (*He comes to right of Beatrice.*) I am by your side.

BEATRICE : A lot of man to manning, was there not?

TRUFFALDINO : The point is, I couldn't tell the gentleman, in front of you, what a fool he's got for a servant.

BEATRICE : Indeed?

TRUFFALDINO : Yes. A fellow called Pasquale. You see it was Pasquale opened up the trunks jumbled up the clothes, changed round the portrait and the diary . . . everything. He came to me and confessed all. 'Pasquale', I said, 'you're a mad, heedless, reckless fool, what have you done?' He fell to his knees, (*He kneels right of Beatrice.*) he begged me and implored me to do something in case his master found out, and me, sir, with my ten—(*He starts to clasp Beatrice round chest—remembers she's a woman—and breaks off and turns round and rises.*) I've just told the gentleman over there that everything's my fault.

BEATRICE : Accuse yourself of a crime you did not commit? Why?

TRUFFALDINO : For friendship. For the love I bear Pasquale.

BEATRICE : This we cannot allow. (*She starts to move towards Florindo.*)

TRUFFALDINO (*stopping her*) : Oh no, Madam, please. Don't tell him. I must save him.

BEATRICE : Who?

TRUFFALDINO : Pasquale.

BEATRICE : You and Pasquale are a fine pair of rascals.

TRUFFALDINO : But I'm innocent.

BEATRICE : Very well . . . since you insist on taking the blame, a beating you shall have.

[*Truffaldino breaks away right Florindo moves to right of Beatrice.*]

FLORINDO : No Beatrice, no. I'm sure our servants did nothing out of malice. In token of our own happiness, let us forgive them.

BEATRICE : So be it. If it is your will. You are the master now. I am but the mistress.

FLORINDO : The mistress of my heart.

BEATRICE (*playing the man*): And so, sir, have I your leave to go. Presently I must join Signior Pantalone. Will you meet me there?

FLORINDO : By all means.

[*They click heels to each other and Beatrice goes out. Florindo looks after her and laughs.*]

TRUFFALDINO (*coming to right of Florindo*): Sir?

FLORINDO : Yes, what do you want?

TRUFFALDINO : I have something to confide, sir.

FLORINDO : Really, what's that?

TRUFFALDINO : I'm in love too.

FLORINDO : You—in love?

TRUFFALDINO : With Smeraldina, the maidservant of Signior Pantalone. I was wondering if your Lordship would kindly do me a favour.

FLORINDO : And what is that?

TRUFFALDINO : I was wondering if you'd speak to Signior Pantalone for me.

FLORINDO : Well now, first we must find out whether the wench wants you.

TRUFFALDINO : Sir, she adores me. And I know

that just a word in Signior Pantalone's ear is all that's needed. Oh, please grant it me, sir.

FLORINDO : Very well, I could deny no man the joys of love. Come.

Florindo and Truffaldino go out.

Music 'Opera'.

Music fades on dialogue.

Scene 16

Room in Pantalone's house.

Exterior lights fade to blackout. Stars appear. fat waiter brings on lamp. Smeraldina brings on lamp and puts it on table. She stays on. Fat waiter goes out. Pantalone, Doctor, Clarice and Silvio come in.

PANTALONE : Clarice, dear, don't be difficult, please. Signior Silvio, here is wholly repentant. What was done was done through love. Speak to her, Silvio.

SILVIO : Clarice, forgive me. It was fear of losing you that made me mad. I love you with all my heart. Heaven wants us to be happy. Now do not reject heaven's blessing.

DOCTOR : To the prayers of my son, may I add mine.

SMERALDINA : Come on, lady mistress, what are we going to do? Men are always cruel, selfish, thoughtless. They ill treat us, they scold us, some of them might even want to murder us. Still, man

wants woman, woman wants man. You're bound
to get married some time or other. So why not screw
up your face and take your medicine, that's what
I say. (*She looks from Silvio to Clarice, makes a
gesture of frustration and turns away.*)

SILVIO : My dear, dear Clarice, can not one single
word come from those sweet lips? I know I deserve
your chastisement, but, for pity's sake chastise me
with your words, not with your silence. See, I
kneel at your feet. Show me some compassion,
please.

CLARICE (*sighs*) : Oh, cruel one.

PANTALONE : Did you hear? She spoke.

DOCTOR : A good sign. Press on lad.

SILVIO : Clarice, although you hate me for my
cruelty. See these tears a token of my love.

CLARICE : Oh Silvio, you unkind creature.

PANTALONE
DOCTOR } (*together*) : You're nearly there.

SILVIO : My dearest Clarice, have mercy.

CLARICE : Ungrateful one.

SILVIO : My darling.

CLARICE : Brute.

SILVIO : My soul.

CLARICE : You cur.

SILVIO : My life, my hope, my knees, my fairest
one.

CLARICE : Ah !

PANTALONE
DOCTOR } (*together*) : She's giving way.
SMERALDINA

SILVIO : Sweet radiant creature.

CLARICE : Ah—AH.

SILVIO : For the love of heaven forgive me.

CLARICE : I—

SILVIO : Ye—es.

CLARICE : I—
PANTALONE ⎫
DOCTOR ⎬ *(together)* : Yes—yes.
SMERALDINA ⎭
CLARICE : I—I—I—I—I forgive you.
ALL : Bravo. Doctor . . . etc. . . . .

Scene 17

The same.

[*Enter Brighella.*]

BRIGHELLA : With your kind permission, ladies and gentlemen.

PANTALONE : Ah, Brighella, I have a bone to pick with you.

BRIGHELLA : You pick a bone, sir? With your teeth?

PANTALONE (*angrily*) : What?

BRIGHELLA : No offence, sir, no offence.

PANTALONE : Now look here, Brighella, you told me a whole pack of lies this morning. You assured me that Signior Federigo was Signior Federigo.

BRIGHELLA : So I did, sir, so I did. But who wouldn't have been taken in? What with the family resemblance, and her being dressed up as a man, I made a simple mistake, that's all.

PANTALONE : A simple mistake, he says. A right rumpus you caused with your simple mistake. Oh very well, never mind, let it pass. What brings you here?

BRIGHELLA : Signora Beatrice has arrived and would like to pay her respects.

479

PANTALONE : Then by all means let her enter.
BRIGHELLA : This way, my Lady,

[*Beatrice enters from top of stairs in woman's dress, duplicate of that unpacked by Truffaldino.*]

ALL : Ah !

Scene 18

The same.

BEATRICE : Ladies and Gentlemen, I come to beg the forgiveness of you all. If this day I have caused you any pain, disturbance, or alarm, I hope all now is set to rights and that you will pardon me.

[*Beatrice curtsies and is assisted to rise by Pantalone.*]

PANTALONE : Granted, my dear. Oh, what a transformation !
CLARICE : Oh, what radiance !
SILVIO : What courage !
PANTALONE : What bravery has been shown in one so young and fair. Don't you think so, Doctor?
DOCTOR (*kissing Beatrice's hand*) : Yes, well, an excess of spirit, I'd say.
BEATRICE : But surely, Doctor, we have it on authority, love conquers all things.
DOCTOR : Ah, yes. *Amor vincit omnia.*
BEATRICE : Precisely.
DOCTOR : But you'd better watch your reputation. You'll never get over the tongue wagging, never.

SILVIO : Now, father, I beg you. People must live their own lives. Their business is their business.

BEATRICE : Thank you, Silvio.

SILVIO : Now that I'm happy, I want the whole world to be happy. (*To Clarice.*) But marriage is best. (*To all.*) Marriage for everybody. That's what I say.

SMERALDINA : Due pardon, sir, but what about me then?

SILVIO : Smeraldina, now whom are you going to marry?

SMERALDINA : The very first one that comes along.

PANTALONE : Smeraldina, you don't mean it, do you?

SMERALDINA : Oh, yes, I do, sir. I agree with Signior Silvio, marriage is best. But for a girl it's like this. She looks round her, but she can't go on being picky and choosey for ever. And if she does, more fool her. She'll end up missing the boat, she will. So there you are. If anybody comes up to one of you ladies and gentlemen and says that he wants me . . . don't hesitate. I'll have him.

PANTALONE : Ah, dear girl, you're all yearning for marriage, aren't you?

SMERALDINA : With due modesty, sir, I'm fair busting.

PANTALONE : Is there no young fellow, then, who may have approached you directly, huh?

SMERALDINA : There is one, sir, ah, but there's a whole world of difference between a bit of flirtation and a ring on that finger, isn't there, sir?

PANTALONE : How forthright you are! Still, 'tis true . . . we will have you married, have no fear.

Scene 19

The same. Truffaldino enters.

TRUFFALDINO : Greetings, respects, and heartiest salutations to one and all.

BEATRICE : Where is Signior Florindo?

TRUFFALDINO : He's outside, Ma'am, and if all's willing, he'd like to come in and pay his respects. (*He moves to Smeraldina during the following.*)

BEATRICE : Signior Pantalone, has he your leave to enter?

PANTALONE : Signior Florindo is your young gentleman, is he?

BEATRICE : We are going to be married.

PANTALONE : Oh, then, by all means, show him in! I shall receive him most heartily!

TRUFFALDINO (*aside*) : Have you decided yet?

SMERALDINA (*aside*) : What about?

TRUFFALDINO (*aside*) : Me and you, tie the knot!

SMERALDINA (*aside*) : You didn't mean it?

TRUFFALDINO (*aside*) : Course I do!

BEATRICE : Truffaldino!

TRUFFALDINO : Ma'am?

BEATRICE (*to Pantalone*) : Signior Pantalone, do please forgive this wretch of a servant I have. Truffaldino, you have been asked to show in Signior Florindo.

TRUFFALDINO : At once, Ma'am. (*He goes out.*)

[*Pantalone rings bell.*]

SMERALDINA (*excitedly she runs to Clarice*) : Lady —mistress! . . . (*To the rest.*) Pardon, everybody. (*To Clarice.*) Can I have a word?

CLARICE : What is it?
SMERALDINA : In your ear, madam?
CLARICE : Oh, very well.

[*They move to the side of the stage.*]

CLARICE (*aside*) : What is it?
SMERALDINA (*aside, excitedly*) : He's just proposed.
CLARICE (*aside*) : Proposed?
SMERALDINA (*aside, excitedly*) : The servant of Signora Beatrice. He wants to marry me.
CLARICE (*aside*) : Oh, I'm so very happy for you.
SMERALDINA (*aside*) : I wonder, would you ask his mistress to agree to it?
CLARICE (*aside*) : Certainly, I'll speak to Beatrice at the first possible moment.
SMERALDINA (*relieved, breathlessly*) : Oh, thank you, ma-am. Thank you, my lady.

Scene 20

The same.

Florindo and Truffaldino enter.

FLORINDO : Ladies and Gentlemen, allow me to present myself. My name is Florindo Artusi. (*To all.*) I am your humble servant. (*To Pantalone.*) You, sir, are the master of this house?
PANTALONE : You are most welcome, sir, I am at your command.

FLORINDO : Then permit me to dedicate my service to you.

PANTALONE : It delights me to know you, sir . . . and from my heart I am most pleased to learn of your happiness.

FLORINDO : Ah! You have learnt that Signora Beatrice agrees to be my wife?

PANTALONE : We congratulate you, sir.

FLORINDO : Then you will not refuse to honour us by being match-maker to our wedding.

PANTALONE : Ha! Make the engagement official, eh? Most surely. Very well, witness it. Doctor— witness it. Everybody!

[*All three waiters, the boy and the two serving maids enter.*]

Now then, Florindo, give her your hand.

[*Music.*]

FLORINDO : Signora Beatrice, here is my hand, and with it take my heart.

BEATRICE : Here is my hand. I promise to be your wife.

FLORINDO : And I to be your ever loving husband.

[*Music ends.*]

ALL : Bravo! 'Tis done! Huzza! etc.

SILVIO (*to Florindo*) : I congratulate you, sir.

CLARICE (*to Beatrice*) : May you be very happy.

BEATRICE : And you too, my dear.

CLARICE (*squeezing his hand*) : Well, I'll always be happy with Silvio.

PANTALONE : Oh, yes! Two engagements under my roof in the one day. Who would have thought it? All is settled; all is come to rights.

TRUFFALDINO (*to Florindo, drawing him aside*): Signior Florindo? First and foremost, many congratulations, sir.

FLORINDO : Thank you, my man.

TRUFFALDINO : You haven't forgotten your promise, sir?

FLORINDO : What promise was that?

TRUFFALDINO : Signior Pantalone—Smeraldina—and myself.

FLORINDO : Ah! I remember. I'll see to it at once ... Signior Pantalone, although it is the first time I have had the honour of knowing you, may I dare to ask you a favour?

PANTALONE : I am at your command, sir. In any way, I can, I will serve you.

FLORINDO : My servant craves as wife your maid-servant. Have you any objections to the match?

SMERALDINA (*aside*): Glory be! Another one wants me. Who the devil is it? I wonder what he's like.

PANTALONE : No objection whatsoever. I agree to it most happily. (*To Smeraldina.*) There you are. I've done what you asked for. What do you say?

SMERALDINA : Who is it?

PANTALONE : I don't know.

SMERALDINA : Ah well, first come, first served. I only hope he turns out all right.

CLARICE : A moment! Signior Florindo, you have forestalled me in something I intended to do.

FLORINDO : Oh!

CLARICE : I had been asked to give Smeraldina to the manservant to Lady Beatrice.

FLORINDO : Oh dear!

TRUFFALDINO : Here we go!

485

CLARICE : Still, you spoke first, so . . . there's no more to be said.

FLORINDO : No—no—no—no, I cannot allow it. Since you have taken this interest, dear Lady, I withdraw completely from the affair.

CLARICE : In truth, sir, you are our guest, so I cannot allow my interest to take preference over yours.

FLORINDO : Ah, you are too kind. But a guest must not take such advantages. In order that you may have absolute freedom in this matter, I absolutely forbid my servant to marry her.

CLARICE : Well, if your man is not to marry her, then neither must the other fellow. Fair is fair, don't you think?

TRUFFALDINO (*aside*): Marvellous! Isn't it? They swop compliments, and I stay wifeless.

SMERALDINA (*aside*): I'll be on the shelf, that's what!

PANTALONE : Come now, let's be sensible. The girl needs a husband. So then, which one is it to be?

FLORINDO : She'll not marry mine, sir. It would be an insult to Signora Clarice.

CLARICE : And I'll be no party in offending Signior Florindo.

TRUFFALDINO (*coming to centre*): Sir, Madam, would you allow me to settle matters. Please, Signior Florindo, did you not demand Smeraldina as wife for your servant?

FLORINDO : You've just heard me do it.

TRUFFALDINO : Signora Clarice, did you not decide Smeraldina should marry the servant of Signora Beatrice?

CLARICE : That was my intention.

TRUFFALDINO : There we are then! Smeraldina, give us your hand.

PANTALONE : What's that? Take her hand? Who the devil do you think you are to take her hand?

TRUFFALDINO : I, sir, am the servant of Signior Florindo.

ALL : What?

TRUFFALDINO : I am also the servant of Signora Beatrice.

FLORINDO : What?

TRUFFALDINO : I'm the servant of the both of you.

ALL : What?

FLORINDO : Signora Beatrice . . . where is your servant?

BEATRICE : Why, here! Truffaldino, of course.

FLORINDO : Truffaldino! No—no—no. Truffaldino is my servant.

BEATRICE : No—yours is Pasquale.

FLORINDO : Pasquale? No—no—no—no! Pasquale is . . . (*He breaks off and looks at Truffaldino.*) Oh, I see . . . what have you been up to? You rogue!

BEATRICE : Cheat!

FLORINDO : Trickster!

BEATRICE : Dodger!

FLORINDO : Rascal!

BEATRICE : Knave!

FLORINDO : Tried to serve two masters at the same time, did you?

TRUFFALDINO : I plead mitigating circumstances! There was no malice aforethought. I went into it without thinking, and it didn't last long. But at least I can boast you this, you would never have found me out if I hadn't fallen in love.

(*He holds out his hand to Smeraldina who runs to his left. To audience.*) But if you can find it in your hearts to forgive me, I promise you this. Never again, as long as I live, will I ever aspire to be—

[*He swings Smeraldina to his other side and the other two couples come down level, Silvio and Clarice at his right—Florindo and Beatrice at his left.*]

the Servant of Two Masters.

Fast curtain

PLAYS OF THE YEAR

Plays of the Year was launched in 1949. So far thirty-six volumes have appeared, chosen and edited by J. C. Trewin. It is regretted that Volumes 1, 2, 3, 4, 5, 7, 8, 10, 12, 13, and 15 are now out of print

˒ Plays marked thus are also available in single editions, cloth-bound and paper-bound.

Also available

A SWORD FOR A PRINCE and Other Plays for a Young Company, by J. C. Trewin 8s 6d.